Cervantes in the Middle

Cervantes in the Middle:
Realism and Reality
in the Spanish Novel
from *Lazarillo de Tormes* to *Niebla*

by

EDWARD H. FRIEDMAN

Juan de la Cuesta
Newark, Delaware

MANUFACTURED IN THE UNITED STATES OF AMERICA

ISBN: 1-58871-091-2

Table of Contents

Acknowledgments

I AM DEEPLY INDEBTED to the National Humanities Center for a John E. Sawyer Fellowship, with which part of this project was completed. I would like to thank Dr. Richard McCarty, Dean of the College of Arts and Science (and his predecessor, Dr. Ettore F. "Jim" Infante), and Dr. Dennis G. Hall, Associate Provost for Research and Graduate Education, at Vanderbilt University for their generous research support. My thanks also to my engaging and exemplary colleagues in the Department of Spanish and Portuguese and in the Program in Comparative Literature at Vanderbilt, and to the scholars of early modem Spanish literature who have been professional associates and friends over the years, and from whom I have learned so much. I thank Gretchen Selcke and Robert Turner for research assistance. I am especially grateful to Dr. Alan J. Burch for his careful reading of the manuscript and for his invaluable insights, and to Dr. Thomas Lathrop for his interest in this project. Finally, I thank Susan Krug Friedman for tolerating the fluctuations within my personal quixotism.

Parts of chapter 1 of this study are based on the essays "Narcissus's Echo: *La vida del buscón* and Questions of Authority," *Indiana Journal of Hispanic Literatures* 1.1 (1992): 213-60; "Insincere Flattery: Imitation and the Growth of the Novel," *Cervantes* 20.1 (2000): 99-114; and " 'El pobre servicio de mano': *Lazarillo de Tormes, Don Quixote,* and the Design of the Novel," *1605-2005:* Don Quixote *across the Centuries,* coord. John P. Gabriele (Madrid: Iberoamericana, 2005) 29-50. Part of chapter 4 will be published in the selected proceedings of the 2005 "Framing the *Quixote*" Conference at Brigham Young University.

To my students,
past and present,
for their good ideas, good work,
and goodwill.

Introduction

THE PUBLICATION OF THE two parts of *Don Quijote*, in 1605 and 1615, signifies a critical moment in the development of narrative. Cervantes builds into his text a consciousness of—and a tribute to—his literary precedents. If the general concept of intertextuality asserts that no work exists in a vacuum, but is dependent on pre-existing systems of texts, codes, poetics, and socio-cultural relationships, *Don Quijote* validates the thesis by acknowledging the past. The idealism of chivalric, sentimental, and pastoral romance is there, if demystified. The Italian novelle and the early picaresque narratives are there, to provide a model and to allow for deviation from the model. Classical and medieval literary traditions are there. The Inquisition, with its autos-da-fé, exiles, and censorship, is there, as are the Counter Reformation, early modern economics and class consciousness, gender issues, the play of oral and written traditions, and much more. Notably, theory and criticism are represented, and the dialectics of history and poetry (the Aristotelian dichotomy) supplies one of numerous unifying threads. Chivalric romance is arguably the guiding spirit of Part 1, while that role in Part 2 belongs precisely to the 1605 *Quijote*. Cervantes references the literary legacy throughout the narrative, and this is remarkable for at least two reasons. He is turning away from the texts that he recognizes, and the literary amalgam does not prevent him from writing about the real world. *Don Quijote* becomes a balancing act, on several levels, a baroque collision of extremes, a movement into and beyond literature. There is ample space for the imagination and for the re-creation of reality. If one were to seek a visual analogue, Diego Velázquez's paintings would serve: the artist and works of art juxtaposed with members of the royal family in *Las meninas*, the god Bacchus with rustic villagers in *Los borrachos*, or Mars in helmet and sheets in *Marte, el dios de la guerra*. The syntheses are daring and ultimately convincing, because the two elements in opposition need not be mutually exclusive.

The anonymous author of *Lazarillo de Tormes*, first published in 1554, invites the reader not only to consider the story, but also the conditions under which that story is told and the effectiveness of the discourse. Rhetoric is certainly at work in Lázaro's defense, as it is in an ironic alternative version based on the questionable reliability of the narrator. As Russian Formalism would say, *Lazarillo de Tormes* "lays bare the devices" of its fictionality. The story and the construction of the story are inseparable. Readers—and their intrafictional counterpart, the narratee—may note that the movement from the signifier (Lázaro's manuscript) to the signified (the messages of the text) is mediated by a judgment of the validity of his words. A necessary ingredient here is the recognition on the part of the reader that fictional autobiography is a step removed from autobiography, and that the single voice is actually double. That is, history is poetry, or poetry posing as history. Reality is portrayed by art, and the recourses of art are grafted onto this scheme. This paradigm is not lost on the later picaresque writers, including Mateo Alemán, author of *Guzmán de Alfarache* (1599, 1604), or on Cervantes, who effects a remarkable synthesis of poetry and history in *Don Quijote*. Picaresque narrative introduces the theory-as-praxis technique, and Cervantes carries it to baroque heights. He multiplies the number of narrators, and the narrator of the opening chapter lays claim to historical veracity, while the Arab historian Cide Hamete Benengeli enters the story in chapter 9. The work-in-progress is a motif of Part 1, and critical reception of the book is a motif of Part 2. The real-world referents in *Don Quijote* and the picaresque compete with the literariness of the texts. The break from idealism leads to a type of realism, but the realism is inflected by a consciousness of the creative process, which means that, from the beginning, realism is accompanied—or compromised—by metafiction.

Subject positionality is important on both ends of the creative spectrum. The interplay of satire and sympathy in early modern Spanish realism involves the reader in an intricate system of stimuli and thus of responses. The picaresque outsiders commit despicable acts, but they bare their souls. They are to be laughed at and ridiculed, but their humiliations are likely to evoke compassion, as well. Society sets the standards for conduct, but those in power can abuse the defenseless, and this discrepancy can turn the social order, along with the social outcast, into the object of satire. Cervantes arranges *Don Quijote* around the binary oppositions that would become so dear to structuralism, but his (precociously poststructuralist) trick is to elide difference. The dialectics of history and poetry allow him to shift repeatedly from the present to the past, from literature to life, from reality to appearance, and so forth. Don Quijote is an absurd figure, and madness was a legitimate laughing matter at the time, but it is difficult not to feel for him when his pursuers are often mean-spirited and morally inferior. Whenever these protagonists can be seen as victims—be it of cruel masters, jealous adversaries, or rival authors—they will have left the realm of pure satire, to tug at the hearts of readers. Even though narrative realism in the sixteenth and seventeenth centuries differs from notions of realism in the following centuries, the detachment from idealism brings quotidian reality into art. Peter Brooks refers to the fact that the authors of realism remove housetops "in order to see the private lives played out beneath them" (3). The Spanish predecessors give the reader access to the circumstances that dominate the existence of the protagonists and to their thoughts, concerns, and illusions. One may speak of the psychology of the *pícaro* (or *pícara*), of Don Quijote, and of other characters of Cervantes and of his immediate successors, including María de Zayas. These *entes de ficción* are deep, complex, and fascinatingly pre-Freudian. They reside in an identifiable world, but this world has an added dimension: the accoutrements of art.   PicaroS

The *pícaros* fabricate their stories in such a manner as to cause the reader to notice the form as well as the content, and perhaps to notice the indivisibility of the two. The first-person narrator's place in the text is an analogue of the protagonist's place in society, and the discourse is therefore central and marginal, because nominal control and real control over the narrative are two different things. That difference is the distinguishing mark of the picaresque. The discourse is ironic, duplicitous in a double sense, with a highly charged rhetorical foundation and a challenge to the reader. The picaresque accomplishes an extraordinary feat, by transforming a single point of view into multiperspectivism. It reflects society from a new angle: the underside. It satirizes the upstarts and those around them, many of whom do not behave as befits their superior social status. The narrative stance, frequently defensive, may be incriminating rather than protective. The allusion to literary precedent manifests itself most prominently in a deconstruction of the ideal, the exemplary, and the revered. The sensibility of the picaresque is, to a degree, saturnalian. It gives voice to the silenced, and it gives textual (and, by implication, social) space to the disenfranchised. It is indebted to lofty paradigms, which it refurbishes in a minor key. This lowliness produces surprisingly strong aesthetic results. The artistic design of the picaresque narratives is far more sophisticated, and the *pícaros* are more human and more vulnerable, than each would seem at first glance. The combination of realism, artistry, and parody is impressive in absolute terms, and surely so for a subgenre that appears in the mid-sixteenth century, as what we know as the novel is coming into being.

In *Don Quijote*, Cervantes expands the scope of the picaresque by intensifying point of view and self-referentiality. He fictionalizes himself, adds an alter ego and a stream of narrators of all persuasions, and has various narrative agents proclaim the text's veracity, despite evidence to the contrary. The final product does not—cannot—bask in its seamlessness. The reader witnesses the ups and downs of chivalry and of composition. The dual plot revolves around the adventures of the knight errant and the adventures in storytelling. Don Quijote is aware of the chronicle that will herald his exploits the minute he departs from home, and the narrators hardly conceal their task of gathering data, sorting through archives, and organizing the material. Reading and writing push the plot forward, and the narrative and dialogue are laced with commentaries, critiques, theoretical statements, debates on literature, and suggestions for revision. In Part 2, Don Quijote hears discussion of the chronicle and holds the false second part, by Avellaneda, in his hands. Depending on his memory, he imitates the penitence of Amadís de Gaula, compartmentalized within his own madness. He is mindful of the Muslim scholar to whom his history has been entrusted, concerned about the truthfulness of the chronicle, and furious that an unauthorized sequel has made its way into the public domain. For Cervantes, the mock heroic epic has new priorities. The 1615 *Quijote* treats personal honor and literary supremacy as if they really mattered, and, of course, they do. The narrative structure must accommodate modified directions, a revitalized protagonist, and a rethinking of the ending. The books of chivalry feature heroes with pedigrees and with noble lineages that continue in successive volumes. *Don Quijote* is more self-contained, and its continuity is internal. Part 2 grows out of Part 1, one might say, naturally and artificially. For example, the structuring device of the "disenchantment" of Dulcinea derives from the allusions to the wise enchanter throughout Part 1 and from the coming into his own of Sancho Panza in Part 2. Death conquers the knight at the end of the text, but *Don Quijote* remains abundantly active as an intertext.

Narrative realism begins as an antidote of sorts to idealism, but from its inception it is tied to a self-consciousness regarding the making of a story. Within this semiotic practice, the signified includes both the evocation of reality and the acceptance of a distance between observation and expression. The real world offers a comprehensive backdrop to the characters' actions, and the discursive performance—writing and narrating, putting together a text—is of equal importance. Lázaro de Tormes confronts a hostile society; when he writes his life, or explains "the case," he is, in a sense, writing *for* his life. Guzmán de Alfarache is not merely describing his life, but attempting to convince the readership that his professed conversion is sincere. He plays to the audience, with an effort to justify his decisions and to lament the absence of poetic justice, and with asides that threaten to overwhelm the balance of the narrative. He and Alemán, injured parties of a literary theft prior to Avellaneda, seek to redeem themselves (and to expose the thief) in the pages of the text. Quevedo's *La vida del buscón*, which reportedly circulated in manuscript before 1605, joins the narrator/protagonist's story with the author's conceptist adornments, thereby mixing the downward spiral of transgression and delinquency with the ostentation that marks baroque artistry. Cervantes situates Don Quijote in contemporary settings in order to highlight the knight's affinity for an earlier period, while at the same time he exaggerates the work-in-progress motif. The decision to coordinate the progress of the sallies with the composition of the (hi)story is genial, given that the story and the discourse find a connection in reading and writing. Don Quijote is an obsessive reader turned knight and consequently a subject of history. For his madness to be perceptible, he needs correlatives from reality against which to react. The mediating factor between idealism and realism is metafiction, the concession to literary strategies that foregrounds life and art.

The object of picaresque narrative and *Don Quijote* is not a flight of fancy or an avoidance of reality but rather an approach to the world that, among other elements, (1) gives credence and credit to the observer, (2) chooses the partial and the relative over the all-inclusive and the absolute, (3) shuns the doctrinaire and the dogmatic, (4) believes that skepticism can be advantageous, and (5) refuses to consider the real world and imaginative literature as mutually exclusive. I would submit the term *periphrastic realism* to cover these emerging forms of fiction that would come to be known as the modern novel. The early modern displays of realism could be said to delay—or, in the parlance of poststructuralism, to defer—mimesis. That is, as mediated by metafiction, the imitation of reality is, on an initial plane, indirect—and inwardly directed—but never oblivious to the real world or to the society with which the characters interact. It is not the ends of the signifying process but the means by which the writers access reality that differentiates these particular reflections. Even without the depiction of the artist in a painting, the framed object cannot pretend to hold a mirror to reality. Although the art may be representational, the medium connotes approximation, divergence, a unique set of recourses. Having taken his lead from the picaresque, Cervantes calls the reader's attention to the configuration of the narrative: the discrete elements, the ordering of events, the gaps, the contradictions, the decisions to be made, in effect, the process of preparing a manuscript, the inscription of words on paper. The individual words stand in the middle of a visible sign or an idea and its full articulation. The disruption that occurs in this mediating space is not an obstacle to realism, but a realistic answer to the changes implicit in the movement from one medium to another and a compliment to the creator within the product itself.

Don Quijote is about *the perception of reality*, which is not synonymous with *about reality*. Cervantes explores how historiography and fictional writing—history and poetry—refashion and conventionalize the raw materials of the world. As Velázquez was to do some thirty years later, he brings the historian and the poet, their surrogates and doubles, and the consumers of art into the frame. With the king and queen of Spain as his models, Velázquez positions himself near the *infanta* Margarita, one of a number of spectators. The artist achieves visually what the writer achieves in the narrative: an image of the creative continuum. The works of art on the walls and the books in Alonso Quijano's library are as much a part of reality as the princess or as the city of Barcelona in *Don Quijote*, II, for example. Culture obviously has never been separated from the real, but the printing press and increased literacy seem to have inspired Cervantes and other artists to allegorize these and similar phenomena in their works. The prologue to Part 1 opens with an author bearing a manuscript in his hands, anxious over the prospect of writing an old-style preface. The friend's suggestion puts tradition on hold, and with it questions of authority, literary and otherwise. The satirical frame of *Don Quijote* belies its depth as poetry, poetics, and, one might add, metahistoriography. Cervantes probes a universe in which theological polemics, political doctrine, social philosophy, a new science, and a New World—and their permutations—disturb the status quo and vie for dominance. Censorship was a force to be reckoned with, and artists had to learn to be cautious in their critiques. Fear of reprisal was a fact of life. This was a dilemma that had to be managed judiciously and subtly, although the chosen methods may not have appeared to be subtle at all. Periphrastic realism becomes, then, an analogue of rhetorical circumlocution, of the need to resist controversy without renouncing one's principles or corrective prescriptions.

Because Don Quijote lives in a literary dream world, based on the romances of chivalry and born of nostalgia for the Golden Age, he regularly clashes with the world from which he has escaped. He puts considerable energy into encouraging those around him to conform to his imaginary, or intertextual, world. The harsh realities of society—of the Iron Age—form part of this system of contrasts. Characters suffer in *Don Quijote*, not just the guilty or the criminal but those rendered undesirable by virtue of their class, age, religious background, or gender. Don Quijote himself is beaten, stoned, and trampled upon, but, in his chivalric zeal, he also wounds innocent bystanders. The Roque Guinart episode in Part 2 symbolizes the cruelty of the times, but in a setting that emphasizes the bandit's legendary qualities, which include the appeal of a Robin Hood. The corpses hanging from trees are a reminder of reality and of death; they inflict themselves on the fiction as do the encounters with fragments of Spanish society on the flights of fancy of the knight. The narrator of the first chapter shares details of the gentleman's routine, but cannot specify his name or that of his village. The duke and duchess, avid readers of Part 1, incorporate metafiction into metafiction in the palace and island sequences, but Cervantes is able to satirize the idle rich and to delve into human psychology, and later to place Don Quijote in a familiar urban locale. The blend of realism and metafiction in the story and in the discourse—appropriated and reworked from the picaresque—establishes a pattern for the narrative, Cervantes's and those to follow. This study centers on the creation of the paradigm, starting with *Lazarillo de Tormes*, and on three later texts whose authors seem to have emulated it and extended its parameters.

Chapter 1 looks at the development of realism in the picaresque and at the ties between the tales of antiheroes (and antiheroines) and *Don Quijote*. The demystification of idealism brings a self-consciousness of the creative process that forms part of the model. The personality and the rhetorical strategies of the narrator, as well as the communication with a narratee and a readership, initiate a type of fiction that merges realism with the production of a manuscript. The mimetic is supplemented by the artistic. Point of view is a crucial component, because it has to do with the juncture of story and storytelling, which, in turn, corresponds to subjectivity, in the double sense. The picaresque puts forth profoundly flawed and tortured subjects, but endows them with a space, at once central and marginal, when society denies them centrality of any kind. Their take on their situation, on their place in the world, and on the act of writing gives them an identity—a subjectivity—that ordinarily would have been denied them. The narrators project a merciless and confining social order, and the construction of the text isolates them, to an extent, from even the narrative center of authority. Realism reaches to the lowest rungs of the social ladder, but the literary proposition remains part of the picture. The paradox of mimesis here is that it is never free of mediation, never capable of shedding its literariness, crude realities notwithstanding. The discourse—the narration proper—conveys and encapsulates the story. The reader has the opportunity to evaluate, and to judge, the narrator/protagonist in both of those functions. The picaresque has what might be deemed a prenaturalist air, offset by a display of narrative strings being manipulated from several sources. As a genre, it rejects idealism and practices deconstruction on social institutions, on the lead character, and on its operating premises. This textual energy and irony seems to have impressed Cervantes.

Don Quijote maintains the link to realism, for the protagonist's madness can only have validity in the context of a pseudo-reality, with points of reference to the undeluded. His misperceptions must conflict with some measure of normalcy, some semblance of reality. Cervantes's decision to contest the disengagement of history from poetry, and vice versa, compels him to deal with the historical and cultural record, with historiography and the province of letters. Point of view is his means of entry into the demystifying rendition of history, where not only reliability but truth is at stake. If there is a negative exemplarity in the picaresque, and in predecessors such as the fourteenth-century *Libro de buen amor*, Cervantes achieves a hermeneutics of doubt by writing historiography into his fiction and by historicizing the trials of authorship. It is hard to read Hayden White's "The Historical Text as Literary Artifact," from *Tropics of Discourse*, without noting Cervantes's anticipation of the argument that histories are constructed along the lines of fictional narrative, through the rules of selection, emplotment, and rhetoric, and with inescapable perspectives. Whereas the picaresque demonstrates the intricacies of first-person narration (and implied authorship), *Don Quijote* increases the narratorial ensemble as flourish and conceit. The changing role—and fate—of Cide Hamete Benengeli in the two parts of the novel can attest to the means by which authors can manipulate, and find themselves manipulated by, discursive conventions. Realism aligns itself with history, and metafiction with poetry, and the two categories cross as history in the making, or the making of story and history. There is a theoretical and philosophical thrust to *Don Quijote*, painstakingly camouflaged, when Cervantes chooses, by satire, humor, and irony. The *historiador arábigo* is a deferral mechanism in more ways than one.

Lazarillo de Tormes becomes a template for *Don Quijote*, but Cervantes is a master of the dynamics of similitude and difference. He starts with the books of chivalry, but pays homage to—if not always with the greatest respect—an assortment of literary genres. He seems to find in the picaresque an intriguing streak of rebelliousness, in form as well as in content, and he adopts the model to fit his own narrative aims and ambitions. As scholars have pointed out, the reference to *Lazarillo*, via Ginés de Pasamonte in the episode of the galley slaves (1, 22), serves to confirm the presupposition of a picaresque genre. The spirit of the picaresque includes a reconception of *dispositio*, a constant summoning of the intertext, and an exponential amplification of irony. Cervantes takes the new art of writing narrative seriously, and comically, and he appears to relish the innovations in perspective and in the examination of literary history wrought by the picaresque. The economy of *Lazarillo de Tormes* is at variance with the amorphous quality of *Guzmán de Alfarache*, full of interpolations and fluctuations in orientation and control. By a stroke of fortune, Alemán had to contend with a spurious sequel, and the ramifications of the intrusion are felt in the second part of *Guzmán*. Cervantes has the chance to commiserate with his fellow writer and to observe Alemán's reaction in print. This will come to bear on his own response to Avellaneda—and, one may conjecture, on the use of ironic distance—in Part 2 of *Don Quijote*. He likewise will have been influenced by baroque language, including changes in register, as seen in Quevedo's *Buscón*, which also delves into the psychological makeup and the social negotiations of the outsider. Pablos's discourse is as elegantly textured as his story is inelegant and his lifestyle corrupt. The double voicing within the first-person narration makes point of view an agent, jointly, of dissonance and harmony, insubordination and lawfulness.

Early modern Spanish realism is a precursor to later fiction, but scarcely an ill-conceived or primitive blueprint. Realism takes hold, but with a metafictional edge. The tension between the two remains an aspect of the evolving novel, which during the height of realism tends to downplay its conventions. The move away from realism and naturalism at the end of the nineteenth century and in the first decades of the twentieth represents a return to the more conspicuous union of mimesis and metafiction. Chapters 2 through 4 concentrate on three novels in which the interplay of realism and metafiction points backward to the structure of the picaresque and *Don Quijote*, and forward to the currents of modernism and postmodernism. Benito Pérez Galdós's *El amigo Manso* (1882) and Miguel de Unamuno's *Amor y pedagogía* (1902) and *Niebla* (1914) are experimental and transitional novels, with an unmistakable debt to tradition and an almost palpable desire to break away from the literary past. Using structuralist terminology, one might submit that the deep structure of the three novels (or, in the case of Unamuno, *nivolas*) resembles that of picaresque fiction and *Don Quijote*, especially with respect to the delineation of reality. Reality is the signified, but the method is circuitous and often strikingly anti-mimetic, and thus the designation of periphrastic realism. From one vantage point, realism is the site of mediation. From another, it is *Don Quijote*, as revisionist history and revisionist literature. Cervantes's ability to draw from his forebears and to convert the struggle with the accumulated riches of culture into a cause for creation, and for celebration, keeps him—and *Don Quijote*—in the middle of intertextuality and in the mainstream. Galdós and Unamuno want to move the novel ahead, and to inscribe themselves into the pantheon of illustrious writers, but their gaze turns repeatedly to masters whose imprint cannot easily be erased.

Chapter 2 focuses on *El amigo Manso*, whose title character is on occasion compared to Don Quijote, for his noble but misplaced idealism. Máximo Manso is a loner by choice, a scholar enamored of philosophy and of the earnest and ground-breaking educational ideologies introduced into Spain. Galdós, a prolific and brilliant realist, ventures into a somewhat different territory—less that of idealistic literature than that of metafiction—in *El amigo Manso*, which follows the tenets of European realism but veers toward a self-consciousness that prefigures modernism. He relies on the quixotic archetype, a character consumed by books and by his imagination, but replaces the man of action with a thinker and social critic. Like Don Quijote, Manso is out of touch with life around him, generous of spirit but continually distracted and oblivious to things that seem evident to others. His love is more theoretical than practical, and his faith in the power of the mind and in academic solutions to life's problems leads to disappointment. Galdós borrows from Cervantes a protagonist out of step with the rhythm of society, along with a dose of metafiction. The author makes his presence known, and he calls on the reader to contemplate the writing process as well as the social and political content. He unites characterization and narration, and his guide appears to be the discursive system associated with the picaresque. Irony is the principal trope of *El amigo Manso*, which, like its picaresque antecedents, would seem to propose that the storyteller is the story.

Because Manso is subject and object, interpretation is rarely disengaged from discourse analysis. The message lies between the lines, behind an ironic code that must be perceived and broken. The metafictional frame takes the narrative beyond realism, while the text illustrates Galdós's gifts in that area. The supplement becomes an emblem of mutability, a sign (and perhaps a rite) of passage.

El amigo Manso is placed curiously between the thesis novels and later novels, such as *Fortunata y Jacinta*, linked by some critics with spirituality, and *Misericordia*, with an ending that reverts to idealism. It is the middle period, roughly the decade from 1880 to 1889, when Galdós actively reads Zola, aligns himself with French naturalism, and seeks to adjust his writing to the materialist bases of the naturalist novel. Walter T. Pattison speaks of "mitigated naturalism" in describing the compromise of naturalism and metaphysics in *La desheredada, El doctor Centeno, Tormento, La de Bringas, Lo prohibido,* and other novels of the period (*Benito Pérez Galdós* 63-87). Although *El doctor Centeno* allots considerable space to the theme of education and *Lo prohibido* employs first-person narration, *El amigo Manso* stands apart from these novels, and from the historical *episodios nacionales*, because naturalism cedes to a display of narrative virtuosity, incisive but good-humored social criticism, and a glimpse beyond the extremes of realism to a joy in subjectivity and ironic perspectivism. Society and history are fundamental to its message system, but so is literariness. *Don Quijote, Niebla,* and possibly *Lazarillo de Tormes* could be regarded as theories of the novel—theory in practice, or practical theory—whereas *El amigo Manso* would seem to have more modest pretensions. Galdós imbues a single, and singular, point of view with a capacity to resonate on several levels. Following the picaresque writers and Cervantes, he goes to the margins for inspiration, while finding the means to generate a panoramic vision. The double duty of the discourse echoes the resonant voices of the *pícaros*, and a sense of the reader, hardly *desocupado*, is made clear from the beginning. Galdós is not trying to revolutionize the novel, but to test a technique. He affixes metafiction onto realism in order to stress the collaborative effort of making fiction. That he does so when inventing a quixotic protagonist seems both clever and opportune.

Unamuno's program is more sweeping. He makes a case against

realism as he outlines his variation on the novel, the *nivola*. He immortalizes classic realism (much as Cervantes immortalizes Avellaneda in the authentic Part 2 of *Don Quijote*) by conceding its importance, as the *nivola* defies, or redefines, its conventions. Galdós helps to bring realism to Spain and to determine the path toward naturalism, as well as to modify the historical novel and to foreshadow a modernist direction. At the center of *El amigo Manso* is a well-crafted realist novel, with a minimal use of artifice, as if the reader were granted access to Máximo Manso's diary or journal. Galdós chooses to open and close with a nod to metafiction and with a wink at the reader. Unamuno, on the other hand, wants to accentuate his dissidence and his originality, yet he is not reluctant to allude to the more distant past, and specifically to Cervantes. By nature an iconoclast, Unamuno takes pride in bucking tradition and in opposing the public taste. His timing is good, for European naturalism has reached its culmination. Unamuno indicates in his first novel, *Paz en la guerra* (1895), that he understands and can adhere to the poetics of realism. Seven years later, he settles into an altogether different novelistic mode, one that will allow him to affirm his reverence for the other Don Miguel and, as a corollary, his preference for the studied free-play of metafiction.

Chapter 3 traces Unamuno's cry for independence from narrative realism in *Amor y pedagogía*. The writer does not attempt to imitate the trajectory of *Don Quijote*, but he responds to realism as Cervantes responds to idealism, by unabashedly taking his text, and his protagonist, on alternate routes. *Don Quijote* addresses the phenomenon of newness in the early modern world by striving for change. Because all that was new in theology, science, and politics was intimately tied to the past, Cervantes drafts his vision for the future through anachronism. He moves the novel forward by moving Don Quijote backward, in time and in worldview. The authorial figure pretends to be an "ancient," respectful of the boundaries of genre and decorum, when he is, in fact, a "modern," willing to resist the pull and the protocols of tradition. The new form is a chronicle, a "true history," which contains but endeavors to separate itself from poetry, from fiction. The pervasive trope is irony, and beneath the comedy there is seriousness of purpose. Cervantes is an aesthetician—a philosopher of aesthetics, one might say—for he venerates art as an epistemological vehicle as well as a channel for beauty and entertainment. Unamuno the professor is a specialist in language, an ardent admirer of classical culture, and a polemicist. He takes inordinate pride in standing "contra esto y aquello." It is clear from his writings that he wants to make an impact, a personal imprint, on the realm of letters, and he brings a rhetorical arsenal, an anti-establishment attitude, a rather large ego, and an immense talent to the effort. His subject matter per se has little in common with Cervantes's novel. Unamuno selects love and pedagogy, or parental affection and education, as the driving forces—and as the central dichotomy—of his narrative. In *Amor y pedagogía*, there is something on the order of the new science and the threat to the old world order that one finds in *Don Quijote*. The underlying assumptions are related to perception and to the force of history, but humoral theory and psychological intuition yield to Freud and to Unamuno's inquiring mind.

Narrative realism is a mimetic form. Its goal is to connect the verbal discourse with correlatives in reality, in general with the shortest distance possible between signifier and signified. Cervantes's model plays *with* and *in* this space by celebrating rather than minimizing the distance. That seems to be Unamuno's objective, as well, in the *nivola*, the very name of which announces difference. *Amor y pedagogía* is not about time and place but about concepts. Its temporal orientation, accordingly, relates less to a moment in history than to a moment in the history of ideas. Psychology is at the core of realism, but Unamuno presents anguish and personal crises in a unique way; characters are demarcated through their suffering and through a tendency toward intellectualization. There is a clash of ideas that has some points of contact with the thesis novels of Galdós, for example, but the execution differs radically. Unamuno's fictional beings enact a type of secular agony that supersedes, or essentially comprises, the plot. The *nivolas* operate in a cerebral space that shuts out the external signs of realism. Don Avito Carrascal, his son Apolodoro, and Don Fulgencio Entrambosmares are dominated by existential issues that seem paradoxically to suck the life out of life. Unamuno seems to be saying that the world is an academy, a place for reasoned debate, a scientific laboratory, but that a lingering faith imposes itself on the scenario, deepening the ideological chasms and the pain of the *agonistas*. In his effort to deviate from realism, Unamuno finds a narrative style that conforms to his approach to life and letters. He erects—or, more accurately, imagines—polemical arenas for dialogue, introspection, and trial by fire. He stands closer to Brecht than to Aristotle, but at times only slightly closer, because the narratives mix intellectualism with emotional density; the heart is, for better or worse, indelibly joined to the mind. Like Cervantes, Unamuno conducts his experiment by integrating rather than destroying the data of the past.

A center of *Amor y pedagogía* is the unfortunate Apolodoro Carrascal, pulled by maternal love on one end and paternal pedagogy on the other. His position in the text resembles that of Pablos in Quevedo's *Buscón*. A sublimely eloquent and impersonal discourse tends to mask the tormented spirit of the individual, but Pablos's mortification, although glossed over, is discernible throughout the narrative. Apolodoro, as the focus of a scientific hypothesis, seems at times to be like a rat in a maze, but he is defined equally by an inner turmoil that leads to the tragedy of his suicide. As with Pablos, although with a decidedly dissimilar tone, he is the target of the linguistic derring-do of the author, and the artistic and conceptual display can threaten to encroach upon the content and the sentimental level of the text, despite the weighty psychological issues being explored (unconsciously, perhaps, by Quevedo, and resolutely by Unamuno). A facet of Unamuno's strategy is to set up a literary battleground between the forces of humanization and dehumanization, that is, between raw emotion and disinterested science. As an analogue of Don Avito's (pseudo)scientific method and Don Fulgencio's pedantry, Unamuno's narrator laces the presentation with a satiric iciness and a sense of superiority over the characters and their motives. Nonetheless, the reader can feel the desperation of Apolodoro and may sympathize with his father's badly focused zeal, and even a bit with the henpecked scholar. The crosscurrents and the crossing of borders in *Amor y pedagogía* replicate, in a fashion, the play of satire and psychology, and of mimesis and metafiction, in *Don Quijote*. Cervantes takes satire and humanizes it, gives it not only a skeletal identity but a protagonist who refuses to remain a hollow man. By the end of the novel, he has not only fought off the Avellaneda imposter, but he has chased dreams and illusions in such a way as to make many, if not all, readers care about him as if he were real. Unamuno, always wanting to extend his signature, varies the model.

Amor y pedagogía takes science as a starting point. Don Avito believes that he can best serve his son, and himself, if he can produce a genius. This means of training, or child-rearing, requires methodological strictness and the dispassion of pure science, but there is always another side of the experiential scale, symbolized here by maternal love. Doña Marina is not a fully realized figure, but she is an emblem of expressive, demonstrative affection, an emblem of the anti-scientific urge. Apolodoro, already something less than an *hombre de carne y hueso*, cannot breathe in this stifling atmosphere, yet his reaction to the pedagogical devices gives him, through an irony that does not seem coincidental, an air of humanity and of pathos. Realism begins as a counterargument to idealism, but the early modern Spanish writers move quickly into metafiction through picaresque self-invention and quixotic deviations from—or deconstructions of—historiography. In the first years of the twentieth century, truth has new sources, which may not be history or the faith(s) of the past. There is a connection between realism and science. Narrative poetics looks to what it would like to claim as objective reality, and characterization is impacted by advances in psychology. Unamuno, the fervent defender of subjectivity, personalizes psychology as he continues to wrestle with theology and with what one might label his special demons. The father who sires a genius—or, stated in more proactive terms, oversees the training that leads to genius—himself becomes immortal, and it is not hard to perceive Unamuno's identification with the plot, the symbolism, the challenges to existing paradigms, and the soul-searching of *Amor y pedagogía*. The narrative itself takes the discursive persona(e) to heights of self-consciousness and its players to the marrow of mental distress. The prologue is Cervantine and Unamunian, terms that are distinct yet (from Unamuno's angle of vision) interdependent. Both authors move from the ridiculous to the sublime, in wavering patterns. It is hard to imagine the *nivola* without Cervantes. Arguably, the ultimate tribute comes in *Niebla*, the focal text of chapter 4.

Cervantes occupies a decisive place in the *Quijote* prologues, first as a fictitious version of himself and then as a writer wounded by a literary rival. The speaker with the greatest participation in the 1605 prologue is the visiting friend, whose subject is jointly the author and the manuscript. *Niebla* also has two prologues, in one volume. The voices belong to another friend, Víctor Goti, and in a post-prologue, to a doubly invested

Don Miguel de Unamuno. Unamuno is more obviously the subject than his predecessor. He has a character from the narrative critique him, his views, and his prejudices. The pretext of the prologue is the mysterious death of Augusto Pérez, although this seems to be almost an afterthought. The post-prologue gives Unamuno the final prefatory word on the matter, as well as a chance to assert his authority, which is never fully persuasive and which probably never intends to be. The *Amor y pedagogía* prologue ponders the fate of the book in the marketplace and the author's commercial responsibilities. Writing is a business. Cervantes alludes to the need to satisfy custom, protocol, and inquisitors of various stripes, and, in the prologue and the early chapters of Part 2, he refers to critical response and the demands of the public. The introductory materials in *Niebla* defer to Unamuno rather than deflect from him. He is a celebrity and the inventor of the *nivola*, and he wants the reader to be aware of a mystery, which he insists on resolving, however. Like Cervantes, but in his own style, he is shaking foundations, of power, thought, and fiction. He confronts realism and delves with gusto into new mergers of form and content. Realism is his guide by circumstance, by default, a guide that functions vigorously but negatively. His spiritual guide is *Don Quijote*, because he wishes, imitating Cervantes, to pursue the thesis that originality is a collaborative notion.

Cervantes's "friend" is a reader and critic, a "modern" as opposed to an "ancient" with regard to theoretical disposition. Víctor Goti, Augusto Pérez's friend, and the one whom Unamuno has entrusted to compose the prologue to *Niebla*, is a writer, more precisely a writer engaged in the art of the *nivola*, for which he offers a description and poetics. Unamuno takes Cervantes's double plot of chivalric action and literary composition, and adapts it to Augusto Pérez's quest for fulfillment, in love and life, and the making of the *nivola*. Like Don Quijote, Augusto stands apart, not only from real people but from the more real(istic) characters within the fiction. He twice becomes a guinea pig, as part of an authorial experiment and as conductor, and finally casualty, of his own scientific testing of women. The intervention of the author and of author surrogates, the interpolated stories, ironic distancing, and the ambivalent relation between philosophy and satire, among other elements, attest to Unamuno's devotion to Cervantes, a devotion that is unrestrained. The shatteringly comic dialogue between Unamuno and Augusto Pérez in chapter 31 allows the character to cite Cervantes at his creator's expense, and, of course, to reverse the creative hierarchy, for it is Unamuno who famously has spread the word that Don Quijote invented Cervantes. As in *Amor y pedagogía*, Unamuno hopes to defame realism—"derribar la máquina mal fundada destos libros realistas y naturalistas," one might suggest—but not without honoring its influence and immortalizing it in print, in the process of pulling out all the stops to immortalize himself. Perhaps the most arresting similarity between Don Quijote and Augusto Pérez is the faculty, against the odds, to traverse the space that separates the extremes of fictional identity and emotional complexity. Both writers place their fictional entities, and the narratives into which they are embedded, in the depths of literariness—literary self-consciousness—only to culminate their stories in acts of symbolic redemption.

Cervantes helps to define realism, which will be redefined and reconfigured in the centuries following the publication of *Don Quijote*. He begins, it would appear, by noting (and applauding) the attack on idealism in picaresque narrative. Because the picaresque deconstructs the exemplary autobiography of Renaissance humanism, early modern realism is linked to the construction of a given writer's life. A component of this process is the fictional autobiography, which underscores its deviation from the source, the model. The narrative enters the commerce of society, and it gets down and dirty, as it were. The margins and the outsiders who reside in the margins bring reality into the frame, but the roguish protagonists are often the narrators of their own stories, and, as such, they make the reader privy to the instruments and the stratagems of the narrative art. Cervantes seizes upon this combination of mimesis and metafiction as he structures *Don Quijote*, expanding the narrative options and the historical revisionism of the picaresque. Readers, in general, will not laugh *with* Don Quijote, because Don Quijote rarely laughs. They likely will laugh at him—at his distance from reality and realistic thought, and at his personality and deeds based on chivalric romance—but they also likely will grow to feel his wounds and, ironically, in this countergenre, to respect his idealism. The construction and the "constructedness" of the narrative occupy the mediating space of the text, the space between the author's desired message and its expression, that is, between the author's reading of reality and his writing of reality. If one were to contend that, for Cervantes, the medium is the message, the term *medium* would refer both to the metafictional dimension of the narrative and to the middle ground between the designated objects and their representation. The picaresque includes a metafictional supplement to mimesis. *Don Quijote* scrutinizes mimesis and the very concept of reproduction. By recording the investigation, Cervantes transforms metafiction into the basic aspect of the narrative.

The departure from idealism sets up a paradigm of realism that affects the course of the European novel. Eighteenth- and nineteenth-century realism tends to gloss over its conventions, although narrators and signs of difference are never absent. Daniel Defoe's *Moll Flanders* borrows from the psychological base and the ventriloquized voice of the Spanish picaresque, for example; the story is a function of the discourse, and the act of ventriloquism belongs to each category. A novel such as Laurence Sterne's *Tristram Shandy* connects to *Don Quijote* by flaunting the writing process and the creative energy transferred from the author to the reader. Here, metafiction is part and parcel of the novel, but the predominant movement is toward a realism (and, later, naturalism) that would deemphasize literary convention. Metafiction, which for some attends the birth of narrative realism, becomes latent and unwelcome, but certainly never obliterated. The metafictional impulse returns at the zenith, and thus at the waning, of classic realism and naturalism. The realist Galdós and the antirealist Unamuno contribute to this transition. *El amigo Manso, Amor y pedagogía,* and *Niebla* illustrate—and, to an extent, allegorize—the search for new directions for the novel and the recognition that the new is often a remaking of the old. Their intertext is expansive, and it includes the picaresque, but Cervantes is a primary mediator and a sine qua non of the forward movement. It is not merely characters who are quixotic. The works themselves are, to use a phrase of Elias L. Rivers in his study of Hispanic literary tradition, "quixotic scriptures," yet they are imitations that are anything but mirror images.

Given that *Don Quijote* foregrounds reading, writing, criticism, theory, and the corresponding *meta-* prefixes, it is not surprising that questions about the origins of the novel and analyses of individual narratives cover a broad range of alternatives. The critical endeavor depends on the capacity of texts to attract, enchant, and bewilder readers, and to force them to come to terms with gaps, with ambiguities, and with calculated or unwitting inconsistencies. The picaresque is born of gamesmanship that takes unexpected turns and ends by satirizing subjects as well as objects. Its language is unstable, deceptive, and symbolic. Its focus is society, but it arguably privileges discourse over story, poetry over history. Or, restated, it brings society under the mantle of literature, in a constant stream of intersections and exchanges. The *pícaros* struggle and squirm as writers just as they reside uncomfortably in a cruel environment. The points of synthesis are numerous, audacious, and exceedingly suggestive. Picaresque narrative becomes one of Cervantes's many models, one from which he extracts the meaningful junctures and the alluring incompatibility of word and world. Along with Don Quijote's three sallies, Cervantes presents the journey of the imagination, the protagonist's and his own, through a series of narrators and metaphorical authors. *Don Quijote* is about a man made mad by books, an overly voracious reader, and also, and perchance primarily, about the rendering and reception of his story. Writing is analogical, and reading is an exercise in perception. Cervantes did not need poststructuralism to inform him that the most significant position is that between signifier and signified, where language and thought mediate and are mediated by each other. He places *Don Quijote* (and Don Quijote) in the middle of creation and interpretation, and in the middle of art and the culture in which it is produced.

For Galdós and Unamuno, *Don Quijote* is a narrative primer, self-referential and keyed to reality in strange and wondrous ways. In *El amigo Manso*, Galdós gives realism a metafictional frame that permits him to tell a more comprehensive story and that redirects the discourse. Máximo Manso is a Quijote figure whose narration is reminiscent of the discursive patterns, and the irony, of the picaresque. Society and politics come under the novelistic umbrella, but the form and content of art seem to take precedence. Unamuno, an admirer and critic of Galdós, enters new narrative territory with the *nivola*, a personalized approach to the novel whose theoretical bases, and bases of reality, distance themselves from the Spanish and European realists. Unamuno finds in *Don Quijote* a decisive break from the past and an acceptance of idiosyncrasies. Cervantes encodes his narrative with remnants of his forebears, and the sense of nostalgia extends to the mythic Golden Age, to the institution of chivalry, and, paradoxically but somehow fittingly, to the deconstructed idealist texts. Cervantes is the guiding spirit of Unamuno, who never takes his mind off of *Don Quijote*, narrative realism, and his own persona, public and private. More than a structuring principle, *Don Quijote* is re-romanticized, and thereby made his own, by Unamuno. *Amor y pedagogía* lays the groundwork for the *nivola*, while *Niebla* adds a sense of free play to the equation. In *Don Quijote*, the intellectual meets the popular. In the *nivolas*, the intellectual rebounds within itself, but with entertaining and inspiring results. Modernism and postmodernism profit from these literary exploits. Augusto Pérez (along with Don Avito, Apolodoro Carrascal, and others) can be said to invent Unamuno, just as Don Quijote invents Cervantes and Unamuno keeps him alive. Unamuno helped to celebrate the three-hundredth anniversary of *Don Quijote*, and he helps to celebrate the four-hundredth. Like the romances of chivalry, with their never-ending adventures, the narrative process marches along, with the Cervantine paradigm in force. Don Quijote is its standard bearer, and periphrastic realism is one of its legacies.

The Picaresque, *Don Quijote,* and the Design of the Novel

Suplico a Vuestra Merced reciba el pobre servicio de mano de quien lo hiciera más rico, si su poder y deseo se confirmaran.

CRITICS HAVE LONG DISCUSSED the relation of *Don Quijote* to picaresque narrative. In an essay published decades ago, Carlos Blanco Aguinaga posits what he determines to be a radical contrast in point of view, and, in a major comparative study of narrative, Walter Reed addresses "the Quixotic *versus* the picaresque," and the list goes on.[1] At a time in which the Hispanic world, and, it seems, the world at large, is celebrating the four-hundredth anniversary of the publication of Part 1 of Miguel de Cervantes's master work, the theme—now classic in itself—of "the first modern novel" continues to challenge us. There will be no answer to that question here. What is crucial to this discussion is the fact that in 1605 the novel was in the process of self-formation. Cervantes recognizes the value of tapping the literary past as he creates anew, and that is perhaps his greatest gift as a writer. He is not so much an exponent of what Harold Bloom would term "the anxiety of influence"—an anguished and combative attitude toward tradition—as a refurbisher with a magical touch, one who surpasses the intertext. Cervantes is so conscious of—and so self-conscious about—the literary past that one has to stand at a distance to note that *Don Quijote* is about breaking away from, rather than honoring or satirizing, its predecessors. The random and haphazard feel of *Don Quijote,* surely a work of the imagination in flux, hides a systematic

---

[1] A topic of inquiry has also been the presence of picaresque elements in the works of Cervantes. For a summary, see Durán ("Picaresque").

plan on the part of Cervantes to move in new narrative directions. The same is true of the author of *Lazarillo de Tormes* and other writers of the picaresque.

There is some value, one could argue, to the zero-degree definition of the novel as a narrative fiction of a certain length, in which case the emphasis would be on the texts rather than the critics—or the critics' direct contact with concrete texts rather than with abstract concepts—in a contemplation of the qualities of what has come to be called the novel, or the modern novel. The richness of *Don Quijote* is both a help and a hindrance in this respect. It is easy, because there is so much there; it is difficult, because there is almost too much there, almost too much to compartmentalize or frame. What stands at the exact center of *Don Quijote*, and thus would be the first point to bear in mind? Although *Don Quijote*, in a way analogous to Velázquez's *Las meninas*, seems to want to defy—or program us to shift—centers, its central object, and objective, is the creation of the work of art itself. More specifically, the writer occupies center stage, from the prologue onward. But in that prologue the fictionalized Cervantes cedes the word to his "friend," an alter ego who discusses the writing of the prologue and, significantly, the author's intentions, the "purpose" of the book. He is the first reader, and he is the dominant speaker in the prologue. In chapter 1 of Part 1, the principal reader (yet one of many) enters the picture: the *hidalgo* who transforms himself into Don Quijote. His reading of the romances of chivalry has dried up his mind and filled him with the desire to re-create knight errantry. Reading promotes chivalry, which becomes cause and effect. Don Quijote's modus operandi and his reactions are based on literary points of reference. And we as readers are invited to see parallels between Don Quijote and other readers within the text *and* ourselves. At the same time, we must recall that the first character in the narrative is the writer, and Cervantes presents, in the text proper, a narrator in search of archival data and informants that will help him delve into and, it would be hoped, complete the "true history" of Don Quijote.

Don Quijote places great emphasis on the act of composition of the chronicle that logs the adventures of an animated reader. Reading and writing comprise what could be labeled a dialectics or a plan of complementarity, depending on whether one wishes to see a manifestation of the competitive side of the baroque or its longing for plenitude. Alongside the account of Don Quijote's search for chivalric adventure is a parallel search for information about his exploits, which yields the manuscript of the Arab historian Cide Hamete Benengeli. Cervantes uses the occasion of the discovery of the manuscript—itself inspired by the narrator's announcement that he has run out of material at the end of Part 1, chapter 8—to treat the burdens placed on the historian and on the writer in general. The fact that story and history, encapsulated in the Spanish *historia,* are fused, or confused, juxtaposes observation, research, and the imagination. Cervantes, then, uses both the deeds of the knight errant and the compositional process to create suspense, tinged on each level with satire and irony. One learns to expect the unexpected with regard to story and discourse. The reader will likely want to observe how Don Quijote fares in the plot continuum—the encounters on the road—and how the narrator will accumulate material and present the Arabic manuscript, as mediated (and deferred) by the process of translation and editing. The major constant within the story line per se is, of course, the presence of Don Quijote, who in Part 1 not only faces a series of trials but invents, or fabricates, a chivalric frame for the characters, situations, and chance meetings on his path toward glory as a righter of wrongs, as a defender of the weak, and as a loyal subject of Dulcinea del Toboso. The log of a story in the making complements and becomes vital to the story in its own right. By converting the craft of historiography into a mystery—and into an open space—Cervantes creates the ideal balance between the reader and the writer, and, fittingly, between arms and letters.

The combination of ingenious plotting and literary self-consciousness, which constitutes a coupling of process and product, sustains the narration of Don Quijote's story. The text manages to detach readers from the main character as a figure of ridicule and satire—in Unamunian terms, as a pure *ente de ficción*—and, at the same time, to put them in the position of empathizing with the knight errant as a man who suffers defeats, who bleeds, and who endures pain. *Don Quijote* exhibits a dual movement, intensified by re-creations at either extreme. Characters fall into chivalric alternate realities and often pretend to accept Don Quijote's status as knight. They progressively engage in their own chivalric ploys, most notably in the case of Sansón Carrasco and the duke and duchess in Part 2. In general, they enter into Don Quijote's metadramas in Part 1 and script metadramas of their own in Part 2; thus, they fulfill roles as actors and metadramatists. A character such as the Caballero del Bosque or the Caballero de la Blanca Luna is a reflection of a reflection, with Don Quijote as the mediating factor. By the same token, Cervantes's narratorial figures have counterparts in the numerous storytellers within the text, as well as in the interpolated tales. If one were to argue that *Don Quijote* is plot-driven, it would be because reading and writing, and critique, were considered basic catalysts of the narrative action. If Shakespeare, in *Hamlet*, makes indecision the basis of dramatic conflict, Cervantes, in *Don Quijote*, activates and makes public the solitary enterprises of the reader and the writer; that is, they become the foundation for narrative activity as opposed to contemplative exercises. The opening phrase of Part 1, "Desocupado lector," is decisive because it highlights the reader and because the adjective proves to be consummately ironic.

The predominant triad in *Don Quijote* adds criticism to reading and writing. As early as Part 1, chapter 2, the knight, having just set out on his initial sally, imagines the chronicle that will be written about his excursion and hopes that he will have the good fortune to merit an honest, accurate, and well-intended chronicler. Cervantes anticipates the "everyone's a critic" motif by offering a number of commentators within the 1605 narrative (including, but hardly limited to, the priest Pero Pérez, the innkeeper Juan Palomeque, Don Fernando, the canon from Toledo, and Don Quijote himself). The criticism and the critics grow exponentially in Part 2, which starts with Sancho's description of what the villagers are saying about Don Quijote, and Sansón Carrasco's excursus on the publication of and reaction to the chronicle of the knight's undertakings, as history and as a literary work. Part 2 is a narrative of supplements. The writer's supplement, in addition to other writers, is the critic. The reader's supplement is the performance artist, who emulates the protagonist by formulating elaborate schemes to take charge of the action. Not only are there characters who usurp Don Quijote's dramatic space, but emblematic figures, such as Basilio in the episode of Camacho's wedding, who help to construct a paradigm for the special breed of metadramatists that populates Part 2. Toward the beginning of each part—in the scrutiny of

Alonso Quijano's library and in the intervention of Sansón Carrasco, with his report on reader response—criticism plays a major role in the narrative trajectory. In the 1615 *Quijote,* Part 1 replaces the romances of chivalry as the chief intertext, and the scrutiny of other books becomes the scrutiny of *the* book and its continuation. Returning to Unamuno, one easily can see the attention that Cervantes places on the narrative in formation, *haciéndose,* in the double sense of the elaboration of the *Quijote* and the elaboration of the "new" genre of the novel.[2]

The plot development and the self-reflexivity of *Don Quijote* receive a bolt from the blue in the form of the unauthorized sequel to the novel by the pseudonymous Alonso Fernández de Avellaneda. Avellaneda certainly meant to disrupt the transition from Part 1 to Part 2, and, more importantly, to avenge the attack by the priest and the canon from Toledo on the "comedia nueva" of Lope de Vega (1, 48) by mounting a counterattack against Cervantes and his literary property. The intrusion forces Cervantes to reconfigure and reconceptualize the closing sections of the second part, the culminating chapters written after the appearance of the Avellaneda tome in 1614. That is why Don Quijote and Sancho Panza do not travel to Zaragoza to participate in the jousting tournaments, presumably why they consider a move into the pastoral zone (and mode), and why the knight errant must die in the end. Equally significantly, the "false sequel" has a strong impact on the "true history," and now Cervantes and his editorial cohorts can align themselves with—rather than distance themselves from—the Arab historian. The dichotomies that help to define the narrative course, and discourse, find an analogue in the duplicity of the ending, simultaneously a professional and personal exigency and a moment of dis-illusionment (*desengaño*) followed by a Christian death. Avellaneda motivates, or provokes, Cervantes into adding a dimension to his narrative endeavor. As it moves forward and the first part is integrated into the second, the novel becomes increasingly self-conscious. With the spurious continuation spurring him on, Cervantes himself becomes more self-conscious, more self-defensive, and,

---

[2] One may find commentaries on the state of the novel throughout Unamuno's writings, in prologues, dialogues, and other manifestations of theory in practice.

serendipitously, more resourceful. The false history joins with the true history in overpowering the "old" chivalric romances in favor of narrative, generic, and metafictional shifts.

Because of its classic status and its anticipation of the theoretical questions that currently preoccupy us, we have to be reminded from time to time of the humor in *Don Quijote*, which some critics see as fundamentally a "funny book."[3] The best way to do that, of course, is to refer directly to the text. The humor is situational, linguistic, and literary, based primarily on the anachronistic return to the domain of chivalric romance and on the knight's madness (a source of humor that is, for most of us, anachronistic, even when it is a by-product of the reading experience). It is a humor derived from incongruity in a variety of spheres. A good portion of Cervantes's achievement rests on his ability to place the densest of epistemological and theoretical issues within a context of humor. Although Don Quijote defers to the past—to his cherished Golden Age—*Don Quijote*, its universality notwithstanding, operates in the present of early seventeenth-century Spain. The society and the social conflicts of the day figure in the narrative, and, like other matters, they are treated seriously and comically, in a manner that goes well beyond traditional satire. If Lope's "new art of writing plays" focuses on tragicomedy, Cervantes's narrative blends the ridiculous with the sublime, slapstick with philosophy, politics, literary theory, and the problems of an unstable society. Much of the humor of *Don Quijote* involves Sancho Panza, squire and companion, who can be silly and clever, and who evokes oral culture, the Old Christian sensibility, the hierarchical order, the rural economy, and the pragmatics of daily life. Even more than Don Quijote, who tends toward the monomaniacal, Sancho grows in the narrative, moving from peasant farmer not only to governor but to a commanding presence, in control of the enchanted Dulcinea plot that comprises the center of Part 2. He is multifaceted, inscrutable, and deceptively simple, able to adapt to the surprises that

---

[3] The classic essay is P. E. Russell's. See also Anthony Close for broader surveys of the question. *The Romantic Approach* explores the move away from comic interpretation, while *Cervantes and the Comic Mind* focuses specifically on comedy.

come his way and capable of ingenious thinking. Humor in *Don Quijote* is a testament to the writer's recognition that the reader needs to be entertained and that under the umbrella of humor, as it were, can fit a broad spectrum of amusements and ideas.

In an oft-cited passage from chapter 22 of Part 1, the galley slave Ginés de Pasamonte boasts that his autobiography, a work-in-progress, "[e]s tan bueno... que mal año para *Lazarillo de Tormes* y para todos cuantos de aquel género se han escrito o escribieren" (Cervantes 165). Cervantes recognizes *Lazarillo de Tormes* and the generic associations with what would come to be known as the picaresque novel, including Mateo Alemán's *Guzmán de Alfarache,* published in two parts, in 1599 and 1604. He can differentiate between the realistic tendencies of the picaresque, along with *Celestina* and the Italian *novelle,* for example, and the idealistic strains of chivalric, sentimental, and pastoral romance. His own works, notably the *Novelas ejemplares,* interrogate the tensions between literary realism and idealism.[4] Whereas *Lazarillo de Tormes* boldly eschews its idealist intertext, *Don Quijote* plants its realism in the territory of idealism, in a nostalgia for the Golden Age. The picaresque author is less nuanced in his treatment of Renaissance humanism and, for that matter, in his parody of the spiritual confession. Although frequently character-ized—and dismissed—as episodic, there is an art and a craft to the structural design of *Lazarillo de Tormes.* The narrative has a richness and an intricacy that belie its misleading simplicity. Scholars have acknowl-edged the internal unity for seventy-five years or more,[5] and they have tried to explicate this relatively short text for a considerably longer period of time. My thesis here is that *Lazarillo de Tormes* and the picaresque genre provide Cervantes with a type of template for *Don Quijote,* especially from the narratological perspective. Essential to this correspondence is the interplay of reading, writing, and criticism.

Lázaro de Tormes—as prologuist, narrator, child, adult, and social

---

[4] Among numerous examples on this topic, see Ruth El Saffar's *Novel to Romance.* El Saffar uses realism and idealism as criteria by which to date the order of composition of the novellas.

[5] The seminal commentary in this regard may be an article by Courtney Tarr, published in *PMLA* in 1927.

misfit—is an intriguing subject and object. It is hard to pin down his motives, his feelings, his memory, his intelligence, and his circumstances, and, in many respects, the same applies to his creator. An underlying theme of *Lazarillo de Tormes* is control. A corollary would be the illusion of control. Lázaro is the professed author of the narrative. He would seem to have within his grasp the advantages, including poetic license, that the power of rhetoric and the power of selection and arrangement (*dispositio*) afford him. He can manipulate his curriculum vitae and his past, which is to say that he can manipulate the truth. He can search for ways of presenting himself in the best possible light; that is, he can fashion a protagonist that is superior to its model. The stumbling block is a major one, however. Fictional autobiography is distinct from historical autobiography, because the author and narrator are not one and the same. The autobiographer acts, while the fictional autobiographer is acted upon. One can make a case for the subtleties of multiperspectivism in autobiography, but the dialectics of point of view is a given in fiction. As Lázaro tells his story, he shapes that story to fit his needs, or conspicuously does the opposite. In either case, he offers a defense and underscores its mechanisms, so that readers may find themselves alternating between absorbing the story and weighing the evidence, and perhaps identifying rhetorical, conceptual, socio-historical, and narrative deep structures. There is always more to the text than meets the eye, and there are, appropriately, many blind spots. A key component of any inquiry, I would submit, will be the positioning of Lázaro in relation to an implied author.[6]

In chapter 19 of Part 1 of *Don Quijote*, the knight comes across a group of mourners (*encamisados*) carrying torches, and, believing that they are up to no good, he attacks and breaks the leg of one of the men, a licentiate who has begun taking holy orders. Sancho Panza informs the victim, "Si acaso quisieren saber esos señores quién ha sido el valeroso que tales los

---

[6] The term *implied author* derives from Wayne Booth's *The Rhetoric of Fiction*. It refers to the signs of the author's presence—as an abstraction felt rather than seen or heard—in a text. Seymour Chatman, Gérard Genette, Shlomith Rimmon-Kenan, and Susan Sniader Lanser are among those who have dealt with the topic. My analysis of picaresque discourse in *The Antiheroine's Voice* depends heavily on this concept.

puso, diráles vuestra merced que es el famoso don Quijote de la Mancha, que por otro nombre se llama el CABALLERO DE LA TRISTE FIGURA" (Cervantes, *Don Quijote,* ed. Lathrop 137). When Don Quijote asks his squire how he arrived at that epithet, Sancho replies that the sad countenance, fatigue, and missing teeth of his master have prompted the designation. Don Quijote refutes this explanation in favor of the following: "No es eso,… sino que el sabio a cuyo cargo debe de estar el escribir la historia de mis hazañas, le habrá parecido que será bien que yo tome algún nombre apelativo, como lo tomaban todos los caballeros pasados" (137). Cervantes deconstructs direct discourse, first by mediating Sancho's original Spanish through the Arab historian and the Morisco translator and then through the narrator/editor, and finally by having the protagonist attribute his comrade's speech to another, to an author. There is a strikingly beautiful absurdity to the statement, a concession to the maker of the text. Despite the corps of narrators and storytellers in *Don Quijote,* Cervantes accentuates the writer poised beyond the pages of the text, who happens to be himself. The author of *Lazarillo de Tormes* hides behind anonymity and behind the first-person narration, but his input on the message systems of the text should not be ignored. Lázaro is responsible for a particular kind of rhetoric, or rhetorical strategy, and, arguably, the author exposes the seams in the narrative fabric, the markers of control from without. Ironically, the anonymous writer inscribes his authorial function into the text proper, a text that is as much a revelation of the process of inscription as a self-defense.

Lazarillo de Tormes satirizes society at large, and among its targets are not only social customs and institutions but also literary idealism and idealistic ways of thinking. Cultural and literary intertexts merge; life and art are never mutually exclusive. Lázaro is a social creature turned writer, apparently by command. We may sense a double-edged sword, as his explanation on demand becomes an opportunity to forge a place for himself in the scheme of things. He is accustomed to existing in the margins, and, even though he must adopt a defensive posture, this may be his single moment to shine. The private communication with the elusive Vuestra Merced is, for all intents and purposes, nullified by the allusion in the opening of the prologue to a book in the marketplace, by a "voice" that is not distinguished from the voice of Lázaro in the second half of the prologue. The prologue invites us to read the manuscript in two ways: as special access to a private document intended for a single reader (narratee) and as a satirical narrative with multiple and competing objects. The economy of the presentation and the gaps in the story, or history, demand the complicity of the reader in the interpretive process. One has to judge Lázaro's accuracy and sincerity, and to consider the implied author's stance vis-à-vis Lázaro and his masters. The very fact that Lázaro is narrator and protagonist of the account is innovative and audacious, for he wavers from the exemplary at every turn. He is ill-born, disenfranchised, badly educated, tricky, haughty, and, it would seem, deluded. He is the antithesis of heroic; in short, he is antiheroic. And, as would follow, his commentary concentrates on the lowly and the marginal, on the dregs of humanity and the underside of society. He deviates at once from high-minded ideals and from high-minded literary precedents, both of which are demystified in the text.

Idealism serves as a catalyst for the elaboration of Lázaro de Tormes's narrative. He corrupts the image of the exemplary autobiography, and of the exemplary individual, celebrated by humanism. His name suggests the biblical Lazarus, but he is reborn ironically in a manuscript purported to be his own. His is a secular confession—*confesar* and its variants occur throughout the text—that contrasts with Saint Augustine's spiritual confession and with those modeled after it. Augustine's *Confessions* portray a progression or evolution toward goodness, while Lázaro's journey is not only entirely of this world but dubiously successful, although the narrator would like to convey his life in Toledo as a social triumph. The centering of Lázaro yields brilliant results. We are able to see him as a writer and as a rhetorician, as a child and as a mature man, as a social critic and as the butt of criticism, and as a victim suddenly in charge of the narrative agenda. Having been treated with scorn (and worse), as writer and lead player he has the occasion to refashion history. But, alas, only to a point, since there is another writer—a real person—from whose imagination Lázaro is spawned. The dynamics of *Lazarillo de Tormes* revolves around the author-narrator relationship. The author has discursive power over his creation, which means that he has the *authority* to take hold of the narrative—and the narrative reins—in order to render ironic and ludicrous, respectively, Lázaro's words and social pretensions. Whether consciously or unconsciously (illogicality intended), Lázaro's extratexual progenitor has the wisdom, or the instincts, to attach a psyche onto his character, to make the *pícaro* think, feel, remember, forget, aim to please, and so forth, and to have him start his narrative at the beginning, so that the reader may observe and meditate on the advancement of the plot and on the psychological development of the protagonist. The storytelling complements and competes with the story. Consequently, metafiction enters a story that calls itself a personal history.

Lázaro de Tormes is a character with a soul, in spite of his demonstrably humble origins, and with a unique voice, which takes a variety of forms. He begins by addressing an audience and then Vuestra Merced. The adult narrator recreates the speech of his youthful counterpart, including his input in dialogue and his thoughts, offered as asides. Some of the discourse—and the point of view—seems to fall between the two stages. Lázaro knows folklore, the Bible, the clergy, and human nature. He learns self-protection from his earliest masters, and that knowledge makes its way into the narrative, patently if not flawlessly. The social backdrop and the literary backdrop coalesce as the narrative projects the *pícaro* in a number of lights. What manuals of literature routinely cited as loosely connected episodes united by the presence of the protagonist and a series of masters have been shown to be extraordinarily inventive parts of a unified whole. Lazarillo becomes Lázaro. The honoring of a request for an explanation becomes a calculated and sound defense. Patterns of language and imagery link the *tratados*, most prominently 1 and 7. The search for survival intensifies and then turns into a hunger for respectability. The errant mother has a surrogate in the errant wife. The squire's obsession with honor in the third chapter becomes Lázaro's obsession at the end of the sixth and throughout the seventh. The destruction of idealism that seems to motivate the author comes into focus in all the episodes, which may be variations on the theme of disillusionment. At least one critical essay urges the reader to assess *Lazarillo de Tormes* in a straightforward manner, without forcing irony onto the narrative.[7] This may be an impossible task, because the text resounds in irony from the first words to the last. It is a complicated and cumulative irony because the author is performing a literary juggling act that condemns and sustains the status quo and that foregrounds a social outcast as it puts him in his place.

The prologue to *Lazarillo de Tormes* is as striking and momentous as the *Quijote* prologues. The writer, using the topos of humility, or false modesty, appeals to readers, asking them to look for the value that every work must possess. Quoting Cicero, he makes the point that writers seek fame through their art, and that critical approval can bring them honor. In the first paragraph, we feel the tension that mounts as the narrative continues. The anonymous author hides behind his creation, so that the question of honor becomes paradoxical. A reflection on the search for praise and the reference to "esta nonada, que en este grosero estilo escribo" (*Lazarillo* 4)[8] provide a transition to Lázaro's case, in the broad sense of the term. Immediately prior to that allusion, Lázaro inserts the phrase "confesando yo no ser más santo que mis vecinos," which, it could be said, initiates the rhetorical charge of the narrative. Lázaro will endeavor to demonstrate his peculiar theory of relativity, his precocious lesson in social determinism. He starts at the bottom, so his climb upward, while not necessarily impressive in absolute terms, must be taken into consideration. He is a product of his environment, and he must rely on his "neighbors" as examples to guide him. He does not live in a vacuum, but, rather, as structuralism would have it, he is a function within the social system of the period, bound to conduct himself within established parameters. Judgment of his behavior therefore must bear in mind the limited options that he enjoys. Before he attends to the "case," he sets up a frame through which to view his explanation and to adjudicate his behavior. The prologue ends with the reminder that those who are born noble are granted benefits in life, while those of lesser inheritance must fight for subsistence. The distinction should never be

---

[7] See Archer for an anti-ironic reading, and Friedman, "Fortunes of Irony," for a commentary on that reading.

[8] All quotations from *Lazarillo de Tormes* will refer to the Fiore edition, and page numbers will be indicated in parentheses.

overlooked.

Rhetoric and reverence mix in the prologue. Vuestra Merced takes it upon himself to request an explanation, and Lázaro feels compelled to respond. The unidentified Vuestra Merced is yet another master, albeit figurative, of Lázaro, who reacts with deference to the mandate, but who starts to justify his actions, as well. The narrative is autobiographical, while not an autobiography in the strictest sense. The pretext for the narrative is not the life story but the case, which Lázaro contends can only be comprehended through the supplement of selected information from his life story. To compensate for the lack of privilege, Lázaro will accentuate the recourses available to those of his lot: "fuerza y maña" (4). What is remarkable about the prologue is its concise summary of class consciousness. Lázaro cannot level the playing field, but he can empha-size the discrepancies that reign in early modern Spanish society, and he can base his argument on the theme of inequality. He does not have to choose between reason and emotion for his presentation, because he can maneuver from both fronts; he can plead for sympathy as he rationalizes his angle of vision. The need to safeguard his interests may make Lázaro uncomfortable, but from the artistic perspective the response gives him a forum, and a centrality, that society denies him. The discursive space is symbolic—a sign of difference and of modified authority—and ironic, precisely because the authority is rendered problematic by what amounts to a voice-over. Lázaro's every utterance has an echo that is circumstantial and semantic. What he says and the way in which he says it bespeak subversion of two kinds, ultimately attributable to the implied author, who permits the narrator to contradict and incriminate himself, and who marks the traps into which Lázaro falls as he articulates his case.

The literary romance stresses bravery, nobility, and elegance. Heroic knights errant, dashing and curiously urbane shepherds (whose diction is more neoplatonic than rustic, and whose sheep never smell or intrude upon the action), and the writers of eloquent amatory epistles point upward, and the spiritual confession aims even higher. Lineage is a vital factor in the romances of chivalry, in which heroes of noble blood succeed each other. That is why the undistinguished backgrounds and misfor-tunes of Lázaro's parents—introduced in the first section of chapter 1—help to separate the text from its lofty precedents. Lazarillo has nothing, *is* nothing. Unlike the illustrious knights, he has no land to call his own, merely a river where he was born as if by accident. When his mother entrusts him to the blind man, he becomes an orphan, his curriculum vitae a *tabula rasa*. Having been robbed of his most modest history, he resides in the depths of solitude, so that, in the narrative, he reinvents himself a second time. In that narrative, he seems to want to elucidate the case and to engage and entertain his audience, whether of one or of many. Although the length of the chapters varies, the narration has a rhythm and a unifying principle. Stated succinctly, Lázaro sets forth his case. He shows that whatever he has accomplished in life has been due primarily to his internal fortitude and to the survival skills that he has picked up from his masters.[9] He needs to be the protagonist of his saga, but his fellow men and women—his neighbors—must remain in the picture, as his moral equals. Hunger and abuse are his first challenges, and in the climactic third chapter, in which he serves the honor-obsessed squire, the abuse lessens (or ceases to be caused by malice) while the hunger is intensified. As Lazarillo grows older, he has sufficient food but little guidance, and the pardoner of the fifth chapter teaches him about subterfuge and deception. The seventh chapter is, to my mind, the most important, for we see the product of a process that we have followed, and we reach a synthesis of sorts, discursive and psychological, of the adult character and narrator.

The imagery of *Lazarillo de Tormes* discredits the reading of the narrative as disjointed episodes or folkloric anecdotes. The first and last *tratados* feature frames, repetitions, and reenactments that cannot be attributed to chance. Lazarillo loses his father and is abandoned by his mother. He gains a father-figure, and ironic savior, in the person of the Archpriest of San Salvador, and his wife, as the mistress of the archpriest, becomes an ambiguous love object and substitute mother. He regains a family, in a strongly qualified way. Wine figures prominently in Lazarillo's tutelage under the blind man, is notable by its absence in the squire's gloomy household (and replaced by water here and in the sixth chapter), and returns at the end with Lázaro's official position as *pregonero*

---

[9] Harry Sieber studies the linguistic lessons taught by the masters in *Language and Society*.

de vinos. To me, the most significant motifs in the narrative are speech, sight, and hearing, and their antitheses, silence, blindness, and deafness. Throughout the narration, Lazarillo/Lázaro speaks when it would behoove him to remain silent. As a child, he tells the officers of justice of his "stepfather" Zaide's thefts, for example, and he likely raises the reader's suspicions in chapter 4, when in the service of the meandering Mercedarian friar he refers to the "otras cosillas que no digo" (54). Announcing silence is not equivalent to remaining silent, and in the final chapter Lázaro's inclusion of his warning to his fellow citizens not to spread rumors or to instigate a scandal apropos of his wife, along with other details that I will not mention, produce the same effect. Lázaro continually forsakes minimal coverage of an event in his life when *less* truly would have been more, as far as his defensive stance and self-interest are concerned. How does the fact that his wife has given birth three times before their marriage aid his argument? Lázaro goes so far as to say that he does not deny the gossip, only that he wishes to silence it. His tendency toward loquaciousness may strike the reader as a sign of the implied author at work.

On the symbolic level, the decision to make Lazarillo's first master a blind man is paramount to the story. The innocent child is, of course, the one who is blind to his surroundings and to the cynicism and evils of the world. While the blind man's lessons may be valuable, his pedagogical methods are far from perfect. His "cruel to be kind" approach encourages Lazarillo to lie, cheat, and steal, in part in order to survive. As he gains insight—a charged concept—he seeks means of escape by exploiting the blindness of his master. This leads to his service to the miserly cleric of chapter 2, who is even more miserly and more watchful. Hunger intensifies to the point at which Lazarillo devoutly prays for the death of others, so that he can be fed at their wakes. A second master promotes his delinquency and his expertise at trickery. When Lazarillo gives himself away by sleeping with a whistling key in his mouth, we have an objective correlative of the tendency to verbalize too much, to make too much noise, so to speak. When the boy, in turn, finds a kindly master in the squire, he must beg for food for two. The squire introduces the theme of honor, in this instance, honor as obsession. As an impoverished nobleman, he cannot depend on manual labor to make ends meet, and he must rely on his servant for his daily bread. Lazarillo flees from his first master, is dismissed by the second, and is left alone to face the creditors of the squire, who runs off on his own. Even the kindly soul—who would be generous to the boy if he had the wherewithal—disappoints, teaching Lazarillo yet another negative lesson in trust. The lacunae in the fourth *tratado* intimate that the friar may be errant in more ways than one, and the observant protagonist of the fifth *tratado* learns how to mislead with words, to confuse truth and falsehood, reality and appearance. The protagonist's physical absence in the pardoner episode allows the reader to move, credibly and gracefully, from the child to the young man in the following chapter (see Willis). Lázaro is no longer fighting for his life, but attempts to rise above his station, giving up his job as a water seller after he can afford to purchase second-hand clothes that, not coincidentally, resemble the squire's attire.

Lázaro's education is complete by chapter 7, at which juncture he is living and working in Toledo. The play of speech and silence—and the subjugation of the latter to the former—is brought to the fore when he announces that he has attained the position of town crier. The mystery of *el caso* seems to relate to the gossip mongering among the townspeople regarding an affair between Lázaro's wife and the archpriest. Lázaro does not really explain anything, but instead discusses the roots of the scandal. One may note without acute inspection that his statements contain no denial, but draw attention to the archpriest's advice not to overreact and to his personal campaign to silence the rumors. Those who want to remain his friends should respect his privacy and should keep quiet. He reproaches them for making the rumored affair public, as opposed to spreading lies. Lázaro is caught in a discursive trap, since he has committed himself to supplying information when that information cannot favor his position. Throughout the text, his is a calculated discourse, with severe miscalculations. Self-defense comes close to self-incrimination when he depicts himself as a complacent cuckold, willing to let the archpriest have a dalliance with his wife in exchange for social legitimacy. That is why appearances—with an accompanying silence on his neighbors' part and blindness on his—are imperative. Lázaro claims to have conquered the odds, as he notes that he was prospering and at the height of all good fortune at the time represented in the final *tratado,* though his ending and his story in general may pose more questions than they answer.

The first struggle for the young Lazarillo is survival itself. His masters willingly or unwillingly come close to starving him. He breaks rules in order to continue to exist, and he achieves a degree of sharpness as he battles parsimony and penury. In his period of greatest hunger, he is introduced by the squire to the conventions of the honor code, and, at the time, his master's attitude strikes him as overly zealous, even fanatical. And yet later his purchase of a new wardrobe seems too emblematic (and too metonymical) to be disregarded. Figuratively stepping into his former master's clothing, he evokes the *pundonor* that he had previously derided. The conclusion of chapter 6 is, in my opinion, the clue to breaking the ambiguity of the concluding chapter. Lázaro integrates himself into society. He has a job, a set of responsibilities, a group of associates, a mentor, and a wife. The starving orphan has tolerated hardship after hardship and now can take pleasure in his rise and in creature comforts. His very marginality—his distance from inner circles, from centrality, from acceptance in any real sense—ironically frees him from the values of those who reject him and from their fixation on honor.[10] That reading is commendably logical, satirical, and amusing, but I think that it may be superseded by a reading based on Lázaro's words themselves, words that display his anguish over the fact that people are talking about his wife, her reputation, and her work at the archpriest's house, all of which affect his mental state. As he concludes the narration, Lázaro does not seem to be winking slyly at Vuestra Merced (or at the readership at large). On the contrary, he seems to be suffering as one who cares about honor, about society's perception of him, about the *qué dirán.* After all that he has gone through, it would seem that abundant food on the table, a legitimate job, an influential ally, and an air of domesticity would suffice, but—and here could lie the ultimate irony—they may not be enough. Once Lázaro buys into the honor scheme, he is locked into a way of thinking that places honor above life itself. He may have lifted himself from the margins, and he may, in fact, be more like his neighbors, warts and all.

---

[10] This argument is made by Frank P. Casa in "In Defense." See Friedman, "Coming to Terms," for an opposing argument.

As a child facing starvation, Lázaro could make little space for morality. A sense of probity seems to appear elliptically in the fourth chapter, but it is overshadowed by the intricate hoax of the pardoner and his accomplice in the fifth. The admirable work ethic of the sixth chapter is, in the end, turned on its side, overshadowed by the purchase of the clothes and a rather comical feeling of superiority. When Lázaro boasts of his ascendancy in society in the last chapter, following the account of his time in the lower depths, our inclination may be to accept his vision (and his version) of a success story. If we look at where he was and where he is now, there is no question that he has improved his lot. The facts would seem to speak for themselves. Yet it is Lázaro himself—Lázaro the narrator—who diverts us from his own tale of conquest by insisting on his marital dilemma. To his disadvantage, he employs mimesis, or direct discourse—by quoting himself as he admonishes his neighbors—rather than diegesis, or indirect discourse, whereby he would have more rhetorical control over the representation. Lázaro appears to show, on a decidedly minor scale, that success does not guarantee happiness. He has so much more than he had in the past, but honor seems to have replaced appetite as the mediating element of his existence, his lifestyle. The focus shifts from the stomach to the mind, and the *pícaro* incongruously falls prey to an early modern Spanish variation of middle-class morality, as his own words would seem to attest.

The voices of *Lazarillo de Tormes* include an author who presents his book to the literary public, an adult narrator-protagonist who presents his case to Vuestra Merced and who summons the past, a child who participates in dialogue and who offers asides, and an intermediary presence who seems to dangle between the past and the time of narration. The request to explain the case places Lázaro in a precarious position. He must defend himself in writing when he would benefit from silence. When he recounts his story, one can see a number of examples in which he has amplified his problems by speaking too much, and this refers, as well, to the narrative performance itself. The interpretation of the concluding section will be influenced by what Lázaro reveals about the situation and about his feelings. It is to be celebrated, perhaps, that the text acknowledges that someone of Lázaro's stature has feelings, even if the phenomenon is not rendered with unequivocal sympathy. Returning to the question of the object of the satire, it is possible to posit that both Lázaro and his society—his masters and his neighbors—are critiqued, in different ways. *Lazarillo de Tormes* does not impugn the Church but its agents who do not comply with their holy mission. Those who should be devoting their efforts to sacred matters often stumble and become immersed in the mundane. They use religion as a tool for self-advancement or earthly rewards. They fit easily into the social panorama, where ethics are subordinated to materialism and greed. There is a sardonic earnestness to Lázaro's statement that he is as holy as his fellow citizens and, later (in the seventh chapter), that his wife is as good as any woman in Toledo. Lázaro is a less-than-stellar man in an atmosphere of deceitfulness. As narrator, he can take society to task, but he also inserts himself into the picture of corruption. The narrative does not advocate social mobility, which means, paradoxically, that Lázaro must stay on his original plane as he moves upward.

The author of *Lazarillo de Tormes* defies tradition by taking conventional recourses and turning them inside out. Idealism and exemplarity are recalled, but fall by the wayside. Nobility of birth and noble demeanor mark idealism in the secular sphere, and thoughts of eternity and paths of righteousness mark spiritual aspirations. Lazarillo is born beyond—or, more correctly, under—these boundary lines. His fate is largely determined as he comes out of the womb. His parents are disreputable, he must live in poverty, and his prospects are negligible. His father serves a jail term and dies, as a prisoner-soldier, fighting for his nation. His mother's attempt to align herself with the good people (*arrimarse a los buenos*) of Salamanca yields disastrous results. His various masters can instruct him about life, but they cannot redirect the course already traced out for him. When Lázaro, as his mother before him, settles in Toledo in search of the influence of the good people, he finds himself tested in new ways. He attempts to gloss over the hardships that confront him and describes himself as having been enlightened by God ("quiso Dios alumbrarme y ponerme en camino y manera provechosa," 63). He outlines what could be called a deep structure of success: employment, guidance, marriage, a home. What he shows, however, is the ungainly aspect of each element. His complacency seems forced, because his document proves otherwise. The domestic turmoil reduces gratification.

His wife may be deceiving him with his employer, people are talking, and the archpriest advises him to keep his eyes and ears closed. The predicament shadows—and threatens to shatter—his comfort level. In theory, he has what he has sought in life, but dishonor, which, like honor, never seemed to be within his reach, could be his undoing. Immediately before he alludes to his prosperity at the end of the narrative, Lázaro hardly appears to be happy or satisfied with his lot. He seems to want to convince his narratee that his story must be appreciated in context, and, be it wittingly or unwittingly, he supplies that context. He wants to excuse behavior about which he is ambivalent and about which he may not really have excused himself.

My reading of the narrative requires stepping beyond Lázaro's intervention to focus on the figure who opens the text, the speaker who refers to his book and its audience and then casually cedes to the title character and Vuestra Merced. He is not the implied author, who by definition is an abstraction, but, as a reminder of a historical author and a real readership, he is our link to the implied author. He *authorizes* an ironic reading, and, whether intentionally or not, he orients the reader toward a search for dualities, for reciprocal plays and ploys. As narrator and protagonist, Lázaro is a schemer. He records how he has learned trickery, in word and deed, and he illustrates this knowledge in the makeup of his response. He is not always forthcoming, but at times he exceeds the demands of the narrative, even when trying to explain himself in full. As his story gives instances of the protagonist talking too much, the narrator talks too much and undermines some of his theses. We see him fighting to conceal or reconfigure data, and we can infer that this is because the signs are there, intercalated by someone geared to direct the reading.[11] Recognition of the unity of *Lazarillo de Tormes* reveals a pattern that suggests co-authorship, since Lázaro's commentary is infused with indicators of literary technique—conscious patterns and circularity, for example—and irony made accessible to the reader. There is a ventriloquizing effect that relates, ironically, of course, to the issue

---

[11] In "The Critic as Witness for the Prosecution," George A. Shipley offers a comprehensive analysis of Lázaro's rhetorical strategies, which include "expedient renaming" and "recontextualization" (184 ff.).

of control. Society's control of the individual is replicated in the discourse, in which the narrator's voice is never free from co-optation by a discursive other. Narrative ventriloquism becomes an analogue of censorship, power structures, and instruments of power. Lázaro comes to us diluted, in a manner of speaking, but with enough force to move the reader and to counter ironic distance with empathy.

Lazarillo de Tormes is, simply put, a sophisticated narrative. The doublings of the protagonist—child/adult, narrator/character, victim/self-fashioner, distanced/sympathetic, marginalized/assimilated, creator of the discourse/a virtual puppet, etc.—make the text first and foremost about perspective, about how the individual views the world and how the world views the individual. An author's perception of the world naturally will take into account the mode of representation. The author of *Lazarillo de Tormes* chooses to bring idealism, literary and socio-cultural, into the picture, as he moves toward realism. The decision to oppose idealistic tendencies is brought to bear on style, discourse, content, and characterization. The framework of duality covers the ethos of the age. The antihero can replace the hero, but anarchy—that is, in this instance, a freedom of movement or changing of protocol—cannot replace the hierarchical order and the authority of the regulatory institutions. Lázaro is entitled to literary space, but it is a compromised space, and thus his voice is a compromised, or composite, voice. The new and daring centering of the antihero is unsettled by a decentering. The satire strikes out at narrative idealism, at social mores, and at the protagonist, the alleged writer of the explanation, and it becomes a social and a literary statement. Lázaro can test the boundaries, but he cannot exceed them. The same is true, more or less, for his creator, who can allow his fictional character to transgress, up to a point. Lázaro seems to strain to give his defense a happy ending—an ending that validates his having taken the slings and arrows that fortune has thrown at him and having persevered. This is his victory and his excuse. And his particular spin on the enigmatic case. The play of overdetermination and underdetermination in the text may become a source of frustration, and of joy, for its readers.

One of the most lauded innovations of *Lazarillo de Tormes* is its emphasis on the development of the protagonist, on the cause-and-effect relationship between experience and maturation. We see more than a progression of incidents; we see Lazarillo growing up, and we are privy to his point of view at distinct moments of his life. We can gauge his progress, or lack thereof, his veracity, and his sincerity. It could be noted that there are several stages—not prescribed, not certified—of shock and recognition in the narrative. The first might be Lázaro's status in society and in the text, his lowliness and destruction of the heroic myth. Neither as a storyteller nor as a protagonist does he conform to the prototype of idealism. Next might be the content per se, a battle of wits in an ugly world, a world inhabited more by sinners than saints, and without a noticeable faith in the goodness of humanity. Then, perhaps, would be the layering of ironies, together with the competition for—and illusions of—control. A consequence of the ironies imposed by the situation and by the implied author is a more active involvement on the part of the reader, who presumably will react intellectually and emotionally to the narrative, and work to fill in gaps. If that happens, the anonymous writer will have foregrounded the person and the vita of a novel type of protagonist, summoned from the undesirable regions of society. The outsider may not be new to literature, but he is new to the center.[12] The *pícaro* is a figure to look down on, but the text emphasizes that this person and those like him count, that they are part of the social amalgam, and that—to quote a well-known line from twentieth-century American drama—attention must be paid. The changes in literary form reflect, and contribute to, changes in society.

What could Cervantes have gleaned from the structure and ideology of *Lazarillo de Tormes*? The picaresque narrative treats the production of the text. It is concerned with the composition and reception of a book. In conjunction with the declared pretext—Vuestra Merced's request—an author summons his audience. The rhetoric of *Lazarillo de Tormes* is especially complex because it is directed toward an internal figure of authority and to an external readership, both alluded to in the prologue. On the first front, a figural master-servant relation drives the narrative,

---

[12] One may cite the eponymous protagonists of *Celestina* (1499, 1502) and Francisco Delicado's *La lozana andaluza* (1528) as earlier examples. Celestina shares the stage and the title with Calisto and Melibea, and Lozana with the figure of the *auctor*.

which will be largely about the *pícaro*'s service to many masters as a factor in his development and in his tribulations in the seventh *tratado*. The reader can get a sense of Lázaro's rhetorical strategies through his presentation of data and through ironic clues left by an implied author. This is the principal dialectics of discourse, but dichotomies and oppositions are prevalent throughout the text. The narrator's individualized voice vies with a voice-over, but each has discursive weight and strength. The reader is left to decipher the vocal registers—from the child to the adult to the participants in the dialogue to the audible silence of the implied author—and their significance. If *Lazarillo de Tormes* deconstructs an idealistic intertext, it likewise forces an examination, or reexamination, of the social record and social practice. The parody of humanism seems mocking at times and good-natured at others, just as the antihero may provoke our contempt at times and command our sympathy at others. Society might dehumanize or objectify Lázaro and his ilk, but the text does otherwise, even when its satire is most biting, because the protagonist shares the stage—and the critique—with his society. The vision is panoramic and mutable, modified in the course of the narration and as generations, social thought, and the politics of individualism change.

The author of *Lazarillo de Tormes* conveys a precocious social determinism and a pre-Freudian intuition. The image of the parents remains throughout the text—in the masters as father figures, in the disjointed family portrait at the end, and in the desperate quest for respectability—as the orphan meets society head-on. The first surrogate father, Zaide, ironically prefigures the negative exemplarity of the "fathers" to come, and the first official master, the blind man, introduces the blindness/(in)sight motif that the text will sustain throughout. Alternating the immediacy of experience with the distance of time, Lázaro treats the reality of hunger and poverty with pathos and humor. For me, Lazarillo's tenure with the cleric in the second *tratado* demonstrates most effectively the narrator's ability to cast the indisputably tragic incidents of Lazarillo's life with a storyteller's wit and an eye on suspense. The events in this chapter are arguably the most distressing in the narrative, but also, as recited after the passage of many years, among the funniest. The tragicomic episode would seem to take Lázaro away from his self-defense (and Vuestra Merced) to a consciousness of a broader audience, whom he aims to amuse at his own expense. On another level, by expanding the scope of the narrative act, Lázaro ceases to be merely a victim. He attempts to outsmart the niggardly cleric by transforming himself, figuratively speaking, into a mouse and a snake. If eventually he is caught and punished, he has made himself the center of attention, in the narrative past and in the present of the narration. Even in the third *tratado*, where the focus is on the squire and his obsession with honor—a theme that will reverberate in what follows—Lázaro keeps himself in the frame through the intensifying pangs of hunger and, discursively, through his role in the dialogue and through his asides. The plays on absence in the fourth and fifth *tratados* may push the reader to seek out Lázaro and to justify the chapters as part of the explanation of the case. Above all, perhaps, the author discerns the link between social determinism and subjectivity. He does not so much anticipate the debates on heredity versus environment as capture the intersection of the two in early modern Spain.

   Lazarillo de Tormes turns satire into something far more profound. It takes fiction and social commentary in fresh directions, balancing the literary past with contemporary culture and testifying to changes in each. The prologue serves as a microcosm or analogue of the basic issues of the narrative: textual dualities as symbols of interpretive options and multiple perspectives, the rigidity of hierarchical systems, the power and limits of rhetoric, the openness of the literary object, and so forth. The single narrator is similarly doubled, or tripled, through an assortment of voices. This opens the way, in the narrative proper, for a dual path that places the story, or versions of the story, against the construction of the narrative, Lazarillo against Lázaro, and the individual against society. The notion of a fictional autobiography—or, in this case, a defense in autobiographical form—invites transgression of norms as it reports on transgressive behavior. Historical autobiographers can choose and manipulate facts to their advantage; they also can rely on selective memories and what euphemistically may be described as supplements to the truth. Generally, they will program the text (and reprogram their *modus vivendi*) in order to embellish their lives and accomplishments. The fictional autobiographer, voiced by another, realizes the supplement in two ways: directly and indirectly, the latter by an external creator whose agenda or game plan will most assuredly be different. When Lázaro communicates his story, the reader is privy not only to that document, which operates on several temporal planes, but to the process of composition and an ironic refashioning by the implied author. The two voices of the prologue suggest two categories of reader—the narratee and the implied reader—which parallel and encroach on the real reader.

To summarize: *Don Quijote* starts with the reader—never idle—who becomes a principal player. Cervantes privileges and fictionalizes the reader in a variety of ways, not the least of which is by making his protagonist the most engaged of readers and by populating Part 2 with readers of Part 1. The author is intimately vested in the reader, and the illumination of one within the text usually implies the illumination of the other. The "friend" in the first prologue makes clear the author's intention, but the text seems to have a mind—or, at any rate, a stratagem—of its own. The interconnection of process and product in *Don Quijote* leads, in macrostructural terms, to a double plot built around Don Quijote's adventures and the chronicling of those adventures, complemented by critique (another sign of reader response). The chronicler and other narrative subjects introduce the story-history dichotomy and, by extension, questions of truth, perception, perspective, and authority. Such topics as relativity, flexibility, subjectivity, multiperspectivism, and scrutiny and subversion of the mechanisms of control thereby insert themselves into the text. The obsession with the "true history" also calls to mind the interrelation of art and life that Cervantes seems to underscore on every possible occasion, and, as a corollary, one might add verisimilitude and approaches to the expression of reality. Don Quijote and Sancho Panza grow over the course of the narrative, influence each other, and are influenced by experience. Madness in *Don Quijote* is a condition of art and life, a book-induced ailment and a mental problem, equivalent to the characterization of the knight errant as a wholly fictional entity and as a confused being worthy of the reader's sympathy. That is why the reader's laughter probably will be qualified, because the beatings and the bruises suffered by Don Quijote likely will not fill us with glee, although the humor of the novel is constant and rich. There are always other readings, other dimensions, and alternative propositions to pursue. And, finally, Cervantes may be seen as a cultural alchemist, who reworks the literary past to create something uniquely ingenious and uniquely modern. As *Don Quijote* looks at society, it does so through the lens of literature.

Meditating on the *Quijote* with an eye on the picaresque, one may note the validity of the following statements based on those made in the preceding paragraph: (1) *Lazarillo de Tormes* starts with the reader. (2) The prologue of *Lazarillo de Tormes* announces its purpose, but the text does not fully adhere to its purported goal. (3) A key component of *Lazarillo de Tormes* is the author-reader dialectic, manifested in various strata within the narrative. (4) *Lazarillo de Tormes* accentuates process and product, the act of self-fashioning and the defense or explanation itself. We see Lázaro at the service of his masters and at work as a writer, so that the fiction acquires a metafictional component. (5) The structure of *Lazarillo de Tormes* depends heavily on the use of doubling on many levels. (6) The narrative scheme of *Lazarillo de Tormes* fosters a consideration of multiple points of view. (7) In *Lazarillo de Tormes*, fiction is presented as truth, but not totally convincingly. (8) *Lazarillo de Tormes* examines questions of authority from a number of angles. Subversion forms part of the examination. (9) As Lázaro complies with Vuestra Merced's request, his writing—his art—becomes a function of his life. (10) *Lazarillo de Tormes* can be classified as incipient realism, but it might be further designated as realism with a twist. (11) Lázaro de Tormes is the sum of the incidents and characters with whom he has come into contact. He develops as the narrative moves forward and as he tells his story. His narrative is a supplement to his life. (12) *Lazarillo de Tormes* is a literary experiment with origins in social satire and in the deconstruction of idealistic forms and formulas, but the result far supersedes satire and parody. It vacillates between the broad and the subtle. Acknowledging the familiar, *Lazarillo* offers a radically different paradigm for narrative; energized by the intertext, it comes to occupy the other side of intertextuality, a model for future novelistic creation.[13]

---

[13] One could, of course, make a list of differentiating elements based on the intricate structure of *Don Quijote*. These might include, among others, (1) madness; (2) the move from a single, multifaceted story to variations on the theme of storytelling; (3) genre-identity problems; (4) a dialectics involving a

The underrated *La lozana andaluza* may be the closest precedent to *Lazarillo de Tormes.* Its dialogue centers on the author figure and the *pícara,* a woman with a discernible voice and a fascinating—and flagrantly low—story to tell. *Lazarillo* places the *auctor* behind the scenes and puts the *pícaro* in the spotlight, and his story has a beginning, a middle, and an end. He and his account are products, and in both instances we have followed a process that leads to a conclusion, enlightening if not definitive. Much of *Lazarillo* has to do with irony, and it is ironic that the revelation of Lázaro's psyche may be clearer than the explanation of "the case." This little book from the mid-sixteenth century maps a course for Cervantes and his successors. The text is a performance that unites the author, the narrator-protagonist, and the reader. Both the manuscript and the narrating subject are presented as works in progress, capable of being read from more than one perspective. The satire of literary genres and conventions becomes the starting point for revolutionary changes in narrative structure and ideology. Realism and self-referentiality coexist on the page. It seems credible to assume that Cervantes, an astute reader if ever there was one, saw something—shall we say?—quixotic in *Lazarillo de Tormes* and incorporated it into his master plan.

The year 2004 commemorated the four-hundred-fiftieth anniversary of the appearance of *Lazarillo de Tormes,* published fifty-one years before *Don Quijote* and cited by Cervantes as having a generic identity all its own. At the time that Cervantes was composing *Don Quijote,* Mateo Alemán's dense and perplexing *Guzmán de Alfarache* was enjoying great success and, despite notable differences in style, length, and focus, helping to cement the picaresque genre. Like Cervantes, Alemán had to suffer the indignity of a false sequel, and this surely had an effect on the development of the 1615 *Quijote.*[14] These were defining moments in the lives and in the art of the two authors—important to a great extent because they blurred the distinction between life and art. Curiously, and

---

linear plot *and* a conscious and unconscious play of continuity and discontinuity (intensified by the Avellaneda sequel); (5) radical shifts in direction; (6) a dependence on metafictional conventions; and (7) an explicit display of the dichotomies theory/praxis and criticism/metacriticism.

[14] On Alemán, Cervantes, and the false sequels, see Friedman, "*Guzmán.*"

most engagingly, the well-known appearance of a false second part of *Don Quijote*—wedged between Cervantes's two parts—was preceded by an analogous intrusion into Alemán's *Guzmán de Alfarache*. The implications of this double set of "parallel lives" are worth exploring.

Alemán's *Guzmán de Alfarache* is divided into two parts, published in 1599 and 1604. Part 1 was an immediate bestseller, more successful, in fact, than *Don Quijote* would be a few years later. A spurious continuation by Mateo Luján de Sayavedra appeared in 1602, and, despite its dubious quality, rode the wave of success, selling more copies than Alemán's sequel (see Whinnom and Ife). Cervantes published Part 1 of *Don Quijote* in 1605. As Cervantes was completing Part 2, Alonso Fernández de Avellaneda (a pseudonymic code that has yet to be broken) entered the literary market with his second part. As one can imagine, the "legitimate" authors were none to pleased with this turn of events, this usurpation of authorial space. The ways in which Alemán and Cervantes respond to the "false" sequels affect not only the "authentic" continuations but also, I would submit, the development of the Western novel. As in the case of the texts themselves, the metaliterary meets the real; narrative plots enter the world, and vice versa. Life imitates art as art imitates life. The particular trajectories of *Guzmán de Alfarache* and *Don Quijote* move the novel forward. Paradoxically, what had to be the source of tremendous exasperation for Cervantes is the best thing that could have happened to the novel in a key moment of transition. One could describe the situation as a play in three acts and an epilogue: the establishment of the picaresque genre, the adventure of *Guzmán de Alfarache* and its sequel, the adventure of *Don Quijote* and its sequel, and the future course of the novel, as influenced by these phenomena. The figurative play affects the "big picture" of the novel, namely, the shift from satire to the novel and the shift from the novel to the metanovel, which combines narrative and critique.

The picaresque, with *Lazarillo de Tormes* as its prototype, undoes exemplarity by inverting the contextual scheme. Like the "mona vestida de seda" or the sow's ear posing as a silk purse, the *pícaros* stand as emblems of substantive lack, of disenfranchisement, of ridicule. Their social negotiations and their discourse invite us to laugh at them, but they also make us aware of the process of self-fashioning, aware of the questioning of authority, and—most unexpectedly, perhaps—aware of the soul beneath the defensive posture. What begins as satire ends as something else. The *pícaro* is the victim of the reigning hierarchies, but society itself fares little better. On one level, the upstart is put in his, or her, place. On another, the cracks in the social foundation—hypocrisy, dishonesty, immorality, and so forth—are exposed. Lázaro, the secular casuist, claims to have climbed from the lower depths to a position, if barely, within mainstream society. A dialectics of discourse informs picaresque narrative. Antisocial conduct cannot be rewarded, according to the protocols of this time and place, but the subversion of the discourse is itself subverted by the centrality allotted to the *pícaro*, by the criticism aimed at a corrupt society, and by full-fledged picaresque subjects, complex and rounded characters, who manage to move beyond the literary ventriloquists who invent them. The rogues fight a battle for subjectivity, which they lose in one sense but not in another. The world defeats them, while the texts grant them an ironic legitimacy.

Obviously, it takes a minimum of two texts to comprise a genre, or subgenre. *Lazarillo de Tormes* and *Guzmán de Alfarache*, published forty-five years apart (exactly fifty, if one counts the second part of *Guzmán*), feature pseudo-autobiographical narration by mature men who recount their lives; each has sought upward mobility in a rigidly hierarchical and inflexible society. Their illusion of control on the social plane is mirrored by their illusion of control on the narrative plane. Their arguments, intended as defensive, are often incriminatory. *Guzmán de Alfarache* is about ten times the length of *Lazarillo de Tormes*. Guzmán's narrative alternates between episodes of transgression and so-called moralizing digressions, so that the reader must judge whether the sermons have been inserted in order to counterbalance the low humor or whether the low humor has been inserted to make the sermons more palatable, that is, whether entertainment is at the service of edification or the reverse. (Alemán seems to anticipate the polemics of interpretation by composing two prologues, the first to the vulgar public and the second to the discreet reader.) The brevity of *Lazarillo de Tormes* brings a type of elliptical complexity to the text. *Guzmán de Alfarache* operates in the opposite fashion. The narrative is overdetermined; it presents opinions on all manner of things, and the anonymous author of *Lazarillo* is replaced by

Mateo Alemán, who seems to have some difficulty differentiating his bitterness and anger from his character's.

The anonymity of *Lazarillo de Tormes* places the narrator against an abstract author and an indeterminate biographical context. The same cannot be said of Mateo Alemán, or of Francisco de Quevedo, in the case of *La vida del buscón*. Alemán and Quevedo, each in his own way, become rivals of their narrator/protagonists, by putting words into their mouths and by writing misfortune into their destinies. Quevedo is a nobleman who has no use and no sympathy for the wayward Pablos, except as an object of scorn and as a vehicle for baroque linguistic flourishes, but Pablos is a rich creation nonetheless, with a psyche primed for analysis. Critics have noted that, despite the obstacles set before him, Pablos liberates himself from Quevedo. The relation between Guzmán and Alemán is quite different. The middle-class Alemán, like Pablos, is of Jewish stock, so the author's distancing of himself from his character is especially striking. Guzmán's probable father is presented, ostensibly by Guzmán, in derogatory, and anti-Semitic, terms. A substantial portion of the narrative deals with the protagonist's quest to find his paternal relatives in Italy, a dubious venture with less than satisfactory results. On the one hand, Alemán seems to want the reader to join him in mocking the protagonist. On the other, he allows the narrator to break the rules of decorum by "sermonizing" on topics that would appear to go beyond the scope of his story. The discourse of *Guzmán de Alfarache* extends the dialectics of discourse to include the subject positionings of the author as well as those of the narrator. Not only can we perceive Alemán pulling Guzmán's strings, but we can recognize that the amorphous structure of the text provides a welcome—and, it must be emphasized, deflective—forum from which to complain of personal indignities. The air of push and pull, of protesting too much, produces the double, or dialogical, discourse highlighted by Mikhail Bakhtin in his studies of narrative. The picaresque may begin as satire for its own sake, but even in its initial manifestations the form progresses into deeper, more ambitious, and more ambiguous areas.

The movement from satire to the novel is enacted in the prologue to Part 1 of *Don Quijote*. As Daniel Eisenberg and other critics have argued, the prologue "clearly states" the objective of the book: "to destroy the base machinery of the romances of chivalry." This is correct, and the statement underscores the satirical nature—as well as the Counter Reformational thrust—of the text. What the approach fails to consider, however, is the context—and the staging—of the commentary. The prologue dramatizes the challenges to authority by the new print culture. The players are a fictionalized Cervantes and the friend who enters to advise him on the writing of a prologue. The resulting meta-prologue flaunts its divergence from precedents, its newness. The tripling of the author—the historical Cervantes, the prologuist, and the alter ego—bespeaks an increased distance, or deferral, between event and expression, between raw material and historiography, between absolute and relative truth, and, intriguingly, between literary idealism and literary realism. Another allegory takes place early in the narrative, when Don Quijote returns home after his first sally. His niece, his housekeeper, the village priest, and the barber scrutinize his library and burn those books deemed offensive. The inquisitional imagery is unmistakable. The interlude is important also because Don Quijote chooses a squire—a servant and a dialogue partner—to accompany him on future sallies. Commentators have suggested that Cervantes had planned to write a short novel—a *novela ejemplar*—that satirized the romances of chivalry but that he realized the potential for amplification. The return home furnishes the knight errant and the author a time for retooling, for moving beyond the original expectations.

Cervantes acknowledges the self-fashioning of picaresque narrative while expanding the field of reference. He appears to defer control to a team of narrators and surrogate authors, and to alternate storytelling with metacommentary on the process of composition. The "something else" beyond satire is marked by variations on the themes of perspectivism, perception, and the limits of writing. The vision is realistic, but not in the sense of eighteenth- and nineteenth-century literary realism, because Cervantes "lays bare the devices of art" and because he values the place of literature as a visible presence within the world.[15] Truth, history, madness, social identity, the interplay of past and present, acts of framing,

---

[15] Robert ter Horst, in *The Fortunes of the Novel*, reads Cervantes and the picaresque in the context of European realism.

modes of writing, and the consequences of reading are among the topics that he highlights, always in unique ways. The picaresque underscores the shaping of the self and circumstances of the protagonists—and the reshaping of their stories to conform to the narrators' agendas. Cervantes takes this template and converts it into baroque art. This is Stage One of our scenario: the transit from satire to the novel and the emerging metanovel. Stage Two, motivated by several instances of malicious mischief, accentuates the reciprocity of life and art.

If *Lazarillo de Tormes* foregrounds the fictional defense, *Guzmán de Alfarache* finds its ruling temper in the dichotomy legitimacy-illegitimacy. "Bad blood" determines society's treatment of Guzmán, who nevertheless pursues his kinsmen in Italy. He suffers unbearable humiliation in Genoa, whence he makes a hasty departure; he is embittered yet powerless before his fate. Legitimacy eludes him at all levels, and it could be said that picaresque narrative illustrates how those in the margins attempt to compensate for the missing pedigree and how institutional mechanisms thwart deviations from class protocol. *Don Quijote*, in turn, is a masterful exercise in double plotting, a combination of narrative adventures and adventures in narration. The knight worries equally about righting wrongs and slaying giants and about how chroniclers will record his exploits. He is concerned that his brave deeds may be bastardized when they make their way into print. In chapter 9, the narrator—whose story has reached an impasse—discovers a manuscript in a marketplace in Toledo. When translated from the Arabic, the manuscript by the historian Cide Hamete Benengeli proves to continue the tale at exactly the point, in mid-battle, where the narrator had left off. That the staunch Spanish Christian Cervantes, who fought the infidels on the European battlefield and who suffered through five years of captivity in Algiers, should choose to place the "true history" of Don Quijote in the hands of an Arab historian, of a race known—among its enemies—as liars, cannot go unnoticed. The distance between unadulterated truth and truth deferred scarcely could be more evident, nor could the distance between the historical author and the fictional historian. Through Cide Hamete Benengeli, Cervantes adds a brilliant touch—one of thousands—to *Don Quijote*. Precociously and, if you will, pre-poststructurally, he supplies a glaring mediating space between signifier and signified, wherein he calls attention to the processing of data by the reader, the spectator, the writer, the historian, and the individual citizen. Reality is not just "out there," but formulated by the beholder and subject to deformation.

The means by which Mateo Alemán distances himself from Guzmán de Alfarache and by which Cervantes distances himself from Cide Hamete Benengeli contribute to the irony and to the metaliterary (and socio-historical) depth of the texts. On numerous occasions, Alemán would seem to cross the line that represents detachment by blending his voice and his frustrations with Guzmán's, but the professed Old Christian author above all wants to separate himself from the conspicuously New Christian character. Analogously, Cervantes's invention of the Arab chronicler widens the gap between an absolute, idealized—and unrealizable—form of historiography and the fabrication that underlies every act of interpretation. Don Quijote is also a significant Other, a purely literary object, an object of ridicule, the antithesis of flesh-and-blood humanity. One could suppose that the distancing devices would be, if anything, more pronounced in Part 2 of each text, but that is not the case. The "false sequels" affect the "real" authors and their own continuations. Cervantes is able to study and to learn from Alemán's response. Their novels take a detour, but the novel advances.

In 1602, there appeared in Valencia a *Segunda parte de la vida del pícaro Guzmán de Alfarache* by Mateo Luján de Sayavedra. The narrative continues Guzmán's story in Rome and Naples, and then back to Spain, to Alcalá de Henares, Madrid, and Valencia. The protagonist undergoes further mortification, disastrous love intrigues, and time in jail, and finally he is sentenced to the galleys. Guzmán ends with an allusion to his escape from the galleys and with the promise of a third part. The text contains digressions, intercalated tales, and considerable padding, most notably perhaps in a long proof that the Spanish kings and queens descended from the Goths. The Luján sequel can by no means be considered a magnum opus, but it serves as a catalyst for the crowning achievement of Mateo Alemán. There is speculation that Luján may have stolen part of Alemán's manuscript. What is certain is that he entered a private and sacrosanct space within the realm of art. His intervention not only enrages Alemán but distracts him from the crafting of his own second part. When the "real" second part is published in 1604, its debt to the false sequel is unconcealed. Alemán's personal response may be filled with venom, but his artistic response is ingenious, calculated, and effectively—and hyperbolically—vindictive. His second part includes an allegory of the literary theft—the robbery of Guzmán's baggage—along with the killing off of a Guzmán imitator (named Sayavedra) and the exposure of the pseudonymous author, Juan Martí (see McGrady 113-29, Ridley, and Kartchner on the rendering of the theft). Guzmán avenges the mistreatment by his Genoese relatives through an elaborate deception, and the intensity of his anger—and, one could surmise, his creator's—is palpable. The element of injustice, present in Part 1, arguably becomes the dominant motif of Part 2. Alemán reinscribes Guzmán's victimization with an empathy that is missing from Part 1. In fact, he misreads Part 1—while accusing Luján/Martí of doing so—by stating that the usurper did not understand that he was endeavoring to portray a "perfect man," as opposed to a scoundrel. Even so, the competition between Guzmán and Sayavedra has no spiritual dimension and little moral impetus. The victor is the craftier, the fitter, the more picaresque, so to speak.

Alemán's *Guzmán* concludes with the protagonist's religious conversion. He is persecuted as a prisoner in the galleys, but he informs his captain of a planned mutiny and is granted a pardon. Guzmán promises a third part, which never appears. In the end, God and his fellow men have come to the *pícaro*'s aid. He is redeemed, but he is not really good—not even noticeably better—and there is reason to be skeptical of his conversion. Since the third part does not materialize, there is no testing of the conversion within the story. The discourse, in contrast, is post-conversional, yet points more to rancor and to narrative unreliability than to a changed man. The spurious sequel forces Alemán to modify the story and its subject, and, in a sense, to defend what he previously has condemned. *Lazarillo de Tormes* projects an ironic and illusory success story, in which—despite the defensive posture—an implied author seems to want to alienate the reader from the narrator/protagonist. Alemán's attitude is a bit more mystifying. His brand of ventriloquism produces a barrier between narrator and author, yet constantly challenges the separation through extended commentaries and critiques that take Guzmán out of character. The intrusion of Juan Martí into the equation creates a bond between Alemán and Guzmán that further threatens internal consistency. Guzmán writes an autobiographical narrative in which he strays from the path of righteousness until the unannounced, unconfirmed conversion. The open form of the text allows Alemán the opportunity to leave his character dangling in the margins and to articulate his own opinions—however antisocial, however anti-establishment—by way of the social outcast. Although they have been termed "moralizing digressions," the commentaries and interpolated stories of *Guzmán de Alfarache* cover a wide range of materials, some of them not remotely moralizing and some not easily reconciled within the narrative structure. The *Guzmán* is Alemán's only fictional narrative, and the text becomes a forum that is personal, socio-political, and—thanks to Martí—metaliterary. I would like to try to answer two questions: What made *Guzmán de Alfarache* enormously popular in its time, and what is the significance of the *Guzmán* in the history of the novel?

It seems logical to surmise that a major factor in the success of Alemán's narrative is its entertainment value. The lower-class subject as the object of humor will have had its appeal, in an atmosphere that has been compared to carnival or to saturnalian inversion, to the world turned upside-down. Misadventures and antisocial behavior can amuse the reader or listener, who also will take note of the order restored at the end (here, through the conversion). Alemán follows a tradition of negative exemplarity, which includes *Libro de buen amor*, written in the first half of the fourteenth-century, whose didacticism stems from examples to avoid rather than to heed. The satire leads into a "life," which then is transformed into a "double life" that merges the protagonist with the author, as metaphor and microcosm. Both are isolated individuals, in conflict with an all-powerful social system, whose correlative in the literary realm is the writer faced with the instruments of censorship. Like the author of *Lazarillo de Tormes*, Alemán subtly manipulates the reader, who can be repulsed by and who can identify with the narrator/protagonist. Because in 1599 there is no standard form for the novel, the author can design the work in the way that he sees fit, bearing in mind the classical concept of unity but free to interpret unity in a "modern" sense. The source of unity in the *Guzmán* perhaps could be reduced to the psyche: a composite psyche that professes to find in the spiritual domain—through conversion—an inner peace that earthly justice cannot proffer. By the same token, access to the inner self, or selves, relates not only to psychological realism but also to the random order of thought in the interior monologue. The field of associations in *Guzmán de Alfarache* is impressively broad and impressively disjointed, driven by a metonymical force, the force of contiguity, which has been associated with the novel.

The ability of *Guzmán* to please its readership has to do with transgression—in word and deed—diverting but never sanctioned. The Luján/Martí sequel pushes the historical Alemán into the foray. Justice, vengeance, and the struggles of the individual reach higher levels in the "true" second part, where the author's love-hate relationship with his character—his own identification and repulsion—grows. Guzmán's conversion opens the floodgates of ambiguity and provides a center geared for deconstruction—as do, correspondingly, the focus on the *infanta* Margarita in Velázquez's *Meninas* and the illumination of Alonso Quijano in Part 2 of Cervantes's *Don Quijote*. The more we sense the presence of Alemán in his narrative, the more metafictional *Guzmán de Alfarache* becomes—and, paradoxically, the more metahistorical. The inner workings of the novel are not divorced from history but are interdependent with events in the real world. *Guzmán de Alfarache* is suggestive, unpredictable, meaty, and deceptively open. In a sense, Alemán does not cope well with the invasive sequel, but the aggressive defense of his intellectual property energizes and frames the narrative. Cervantes can learn, positively and negatively, from his example.

Alonso Fernández de Avellaneda's continuation of *Don Quijote* may have been inspired by Cervantes's criticism of the theater of Lope de Vega in Chapter 48. Whatever his motives, Avellaneda wounds Cervantes with the timing of the sequel and with an *ad hominem* attack on his age, on his physical condition, and on his arrogance, among other factors. The tone and the mode of attack are anything but reverent. Avellaneda takes to heart a reference, in the last chapter of Part 1, to the participation of Don Quijote and Sancho Panza in jousting tournaments in Zaragoza, and much of the "false" second part takes place in that city. One could mention, briefly, that the Avellaneda sequel is less metafictional than its predecessor, that its Don Quijote is less complex, that its Sancho is less resourceful and less sensitive, particularly with respect to a new female character named Bárbara, and that its rhetorical scheme lacks the spark of the original. Don Quijote ends up in a mental asylum in Toledo. In contrast with Cide Hamete Benengeli, Avellaneda's Arab historian, Alisolán, is content to remain on the sidelines, in the margins of discourse.

Cervantes defends himself in the prologue to the 1615 *Quijote,* which concludes with a promise to leave Don Quijote dead and buried, in order to ward off further imitations. It is generally believed that Cervantes had written about two-thirds of the second part when the "false" sequel was published and that he did not make extensive revisions in these chapters. Crucial features of Part 2 would, then, already have been in place before the appearance of Avellaneda's book: the incorporation of a critique of Part 2, the response to critical commentary, the inclusion of characters who have read Part 1 and thus know the knight's modus operandi, an increasingly shrewd Sancho Panza, and the implicit rivalry between the "real" Don Quijote and his counterpart on the written page. The "other" second part does, however, disrupt the narrative flow, but in serendipitous ways. Cervantes's tongue-in-cheek "true history" is now *the* true history, or at least the true story (one and the same in Spanish, "la verdadera historia"), which makes Cide Hamete Benengeli the true historian and ally of the author. Don Quijote has the chance to visit a printing establishment and to leaf through the Avellaneda sequel. Cervantes undoes his own foreshadowing by rerouting Don Quijote and Sancho away from Zaragoza, but they do meet Don Álvaro Tarfe—an invention of Avellaneda—who certifies before a notary that the man who stands before him is the authentic Don Quijote. There are signs that Cervantes may have envisioned a third part, in which the knight and the squire remove themselves from the world of chivalry in order to enter the world of the pastoral, but the Avellaneda text animates him to seek closure. The moment of truth, or the dis-illusionment, of Alonso Quijano is spiritually sound but somewhat inconsistent with what has preceded it. At one end of Part 2 we have a statement regarding literary exigency—the need to guard against imitation—and at the other a rejection of fantasy in favor of the divine. In the middle lie the real world and the "real" books, poised to divert and baffle us, and most assuredly to reconfigure themselves before our eyes.

From the opening of the text—the prologue to Part 1, presumably written last, and Chapter 1, presumably written first—Cervantes offers new insights into the dialectics of reality and fiction and of history and poetry. The acquisition of Sancho Panza as a partner in dialogue functions as an analogue of the continuous dialogue with the literary and theoretical past. Cervantes anticipates Hayden White's ground-breaking essay, "The Historical Text as Literary Artifact," by setting forth "the literary text as historical artifact." The fundamental dialectical play in *Don Quijote* may be the writer's use of perspective and the reader's skills at perception. While Avellaneda's sequel shakes up an already volatile mixture of elements, Cervantes's response to the intrusion is more "natural" than Alemán's. Unlike Alemán, in the position of having to defend a *pícaro*, Cervantes does not have to invert his premises to speak of Don Quijote's superiority over his rival. He expresses his personal disappointment only in the prologue, and wisely plots the defense in Part 2 around Don Quijote rather than Cide Hamete. Although he makes the Arab historian more prominent in Part 2 (see Mancing 182-209, esp. 196-97), Cervantes can speak through Don Quijote, and Don Quijote can speak on behalf of the "legitimate" author. All of Part 2 deals with the reciprocity of world and text, and with the interchangeability of macrocosm and microcosm. Avellaneda spurs Cervantes to heighten the interrogation of the potential of the written word and its ties with questions of authority. The intertextual conflict—the desire to supersede precedent, which now encompasses chivalric romance, other genres, Part 1, and the "false" Part 2—is synonymous with the creative impulse.

The spurious sequels to *Guzmán de Alfarache* and *Don Quijote* lead to a redirection of the "genuine" continuations. A search for closure results in problematic happy endings: revenge and conversion in the *Guzmán* and an awakening from madness and a spiritual release in *Don Quijote*. Along with a series of hardships, failed marriages, punishment for crimes of various sorts, the ill-fated reunion of Guzmán with his mother, and the time in the galleys, Alemán inserts the allegory of the robbery, the revelation of the identity of the author, and the breakdown of Sayavedra, who leaps from a ship to his death crying, "I am the ghost of Guzmán de Alfarache." Alemán exorcises a number of demons, but the process comes across as heavy-handed. Not only does the conversion raise doubts, but the voice and point of view of Guzmán, especially in the commentaries, are hard to differentiate from Alemán's. Still, *Guzmán de Alfarache* remains a novel of character, a harbinger of—and a guide to—psychological realism. Self-reflection and internalization in the picaresque are unstable yet basic steps toward the nuanced character studies that distinguish eighteenth- and nineteenth-century narratives. The later writers will refine the transference of the personal to the Other, and will move more comfortably from the author's space to the narrator's.

Cervantes approaches character, and most other aspects of narrative, through textuality, a synthesis of the structure of experience and literary design. His extreme self-consciousness, matched by Laurence Sterne in *Tristram Shandy,* substitutes metafiction for strict idealism and realism, and serves as a paradigm for the self-referentiality of modernism and postmodernism. *Don Quijote* capitalizes on the recourses of literature to go ever deeper into, and farther beyond, the text. Cervantes's determination to come to terms with the Avellaneda sequel enhances the interplay of themes in *Don Quijote,* among them truth, history, the imagination, and forms of representation. The publication of Part 1 places Don Quijote at the mercy of his historical self, the hero of a book, who robs him of his active nature and robs him, as well, of a reading public unfamiliar with his record. The readers within Part 2 take over the directorial duties that once were within the purview of the knight errant. Thanks to the spurious Don Quijote, the "real" knight can defend himself with renewed vigor. The intersection of life and art has a seamless quality in Part 2, as exemplified in the sequence of episodes in Barcelona, where Don Quijote enters society, peruses the Avellaneda continuation, and encounters a Spanish-Muslim former neighbor whose tribulations are the stuff of history and of romance.

The much-cited phrase, "the anxiety of influence," refers to the confrontation between the individual writer and the forebears who must be surpassed, and suppressed. Creation is emancipation from the shackles of tradition. In their first volumes, Alemán and Cervantes initiate a war against the intertext, but Luján/Martí and Avellaneda give them new animus, new ammunition, and new targets. When Sayavedra jumps overboard in *Guzmán de Alfarache* and when Don Álvaro Tarfe legally denounces the imposter in *Don Quijote,* the anxiety is reified. The novel as a genre exhibits a special kind of self-awareness, often manifested as reaction, rejoinder, or rebuttal. As the novel develops, it becomes its own principal intertext, its own catalyst. *Guzmán de Alfarache* and *Don Quijote* prefigure these scenarios-to-come by facing their adversaries in print, in fiction. We of quixotic disposition revel in the precocity of the early modern Spanish writers, who are able to get to the heart of their characters and of theoretical matters. The notorious imitations may not be the sincerest form of flattery, but these thorns in the side of Alemán and Cervantes are boons to the narrative process. The muses and the antimuses work in tandem, the first to provide inspiration and the second, it might be said, perspiration. From the anxiety of influence and the anguish of literary larceny comes the novel, armed to do battle with tradition and with itself.

In *Guzmán de Alfarache*, Alemán draws from *Lazarillo de Tormes* the first-person narration of the mature outsider, with special emphasis on causal relations. The adult protagonists are products of their experiences, which, in turn, depend on genetics and social practice. Within *Guzmán* there lies a linear structure reminiscent of *Lazarillo*. This includes a rocky and tumultuous journey through life with a problematic rise at the end of the story (prosperity for Lázaro and a conversion for Guzmán). The plot and the character development, complemented by a clever and cleverly ironic discourse, form the essence of *Lazarillo de Tormes*. The same holds for *Guzmán de Alfarache*, except that the stability and the comprehensiveness of the earlier plot are notably missing. For better or worse, Alemán's narrative exemplifies baroque excess. Its verbosity is based less on ornateness than on a combination of opinions, judgments, complaints, anecdotes, parables, and additional rhetorical and emotional meanderings, some relevant to the story line, others not. One could attribute to Alemán an early experiment in stream of consciousness, but Guzmán's discourse regularly confuses narrator/protagonist and author, and, while the text has running themes (such as the search for family, success, revenge, and salvation), the text lacks the succinctness, the consistency, and ultimately the unity of *Lazarillo de Tormes*. The same irony from beyond the text—the result of a dastardly act of infringement that disrupts the writing process but leads to a beneficial refocusing in *Don Quijote*—causes Alemán to sharpen his concentration. He continues to blend himself into the character, but their new alliance creates a paradoxical merger. Alemán bands with Guzmán against the "false" Guzmán (and the "false" *Guzmán*), thus undoing the discursive apparatus of the 1599 novel, altering his objectives, stated and unstated, and substituting subjectivity for satire and self-defense for self-hatred. *Lazarillo de Tormes* gives Alemán the plan for a linear argument, while reliance on the traditional miscellany and the testing of narrative techniques not only allow him flexibility, but justify the shifting rhythms and amorphousness of *Guzmán*. Martí's continuation forces a change in the scheme and, arguably, a change in Cervantes's scheme in Part 2 of *Don Quijote*.

The publication of the two parts of *Don Quijote* stands between the publication of *Guzmán de Alfarache* and *La vida del buscón*, although it is possible that Quevedo's narrative, first published in 1626, circulated in manuscript as early as 1603. Although every new work within a genre represents the rewriting of a model, some authors are more radical, and more competitive, than others in offsetting imitation with deviation. Cervantes exploits and, for some, extinguishes chivalric romance. Quevedo adds a baroque sensibility to the picaresque formula, most obviously through language but also through a surprising outlet: the psyche of the *pícaro*. The exaggerated discourse delivers a profound and touching story, almost despite itself. Like Cervantes, Quevedo starts with a set of conventions, which he adjusts for his own purposes and in his own style; this style seems to aim at besting a rival rather than emulating a predecessor. The ideological play of the early picaresque narratives and of *Don Quijote* is clearly present in the *Buscón*, where artistry and message systems function dialectically. The baroque highs on the discursive level work against the baseness of the protagonist and the negative depiction of society. Quevedo has the opportunity to flaunt his conceptist gifts, yet plot is more than a pretext for a display of wit. Cervantes uses metafiction to explore art as process and as an analogue of the act of perception. Don Quijote is a literary construct that can nonetheless elicit empathy from readers. Quevedo the writer makes his presence known throughout the *Buscón*. Pablos becomes, for many reasons, a despicable and unsympathetic character, but his struggle for identity occupies the pages of the text, and his actions become understandable, if not admirable. He is detached from Quevedo in a way that Guzmán is not detached from Alemán, and the separation enriches the psychological scheme. As is fitting, Quevedo is a unique puppeteer. The unexpected pathos of his novel may not transcend the linguistic artifice of the narrative, but the *Buscón* helps to push the incipient novel toward psychological realism.

The anonymous author of *Lazarillo de Tormes* gives the narrator/protagonist a textual authority that few, if any, characters of his rank had enjoyed. The novelty of this narrative act mediates Lázaro's words from the beginning, and not in a favorable manner. The author addresses literary conventions through ironic transformations. The object of the changes and of the humor they elicit is not just the intertext but also the narrator himself, who cannot view the proceedings from the comfortable distance of his creator. In the overturning of protocol and of idealism, he becomes the carnivalesque figure, the scapegoat of change. His authority, like his success, is an illusion. Alemán, for his part, tries to dissociate himself from the New Christian outsider Guzmán and from the false sequel to his novel.[16] The unanticipated rivalry with Martí makes him turn his support to Guzmán, but this leads merely to a different type of intervention, a new usurpation of the narrator's space. The intrusion does not have the fortuitous blend with the original that Cervantes effects in *Don Quijote*, where deferred authority is a given. As Alemán fights Martí, he seems to lose track of Guzmán's conversion or at least to place the conversion in competition with delinquency. In the *Buscón*, Quevedo intensifies the modification of the intertext, which now includes the

---

[16] Carroll B. Johnson offers a reading of "authority and the subject" in *Guzmán de Alfarache*: "Guzmán's discourse posits a struggle for authority, for control of the discourse, between the writing I and an inscribed reader. This struggle for discursive hegemony is in turn a struggle for an identity, *pícaro* or *atalaya*, narrator or sermonizer, entertainer or teacher, servant or master. This struggle in turn determines the form of the discourse itself, which is devoted in part to dramatizing the conflict and in part is the result of the inscribed reader's exercise of authority over the writing. But as we have had ample opportunity to witness, the demand to which the writing I responds, and which determines the shape of the discourse, comes from within itself. The inscribed reader-critic has no objective existence. He/she/it is a projection of Guzmán's own insecurities, of his own inability to be the person he thinks he wants to be, what he wants his life to mean, because he thinks he knows who he really is, what his life really means" (179). Anne J. Cruz discusses "rhetoric and the role of the reader in the picaresque," with a focus on *Guzmán* (106-15).

picaresque, and he puts a greater distance between the author and the character. His treatment of Pablos's pretensions to gentility is not mediated by shared origins. The devices that he employs to keep Pablos in his place reflect Quevedo's own place in the social order. Self-deception, humiliation, repeated failure, falls from grace, and disastrously timed chance events—constants in Pablos's "life"—stem from his lowly status. Quevedo is above him in every way, intent upon converting his ambition to irony. Unwilling to see the *pícaro* as a victim, he allows Pablos to engage in crime as a diversion and to give the antisocial behavior sacrilegious overtones. In a supremely ironic touch, he ends by converting Pablos into the moralizer of his own story and the one who leads the reader to believe that the untold continuation will bring more of the same. Discourse in the *Buscón*—and, specifically, the baroque tenor of the narrator's voice—is Quevedo's strongest weapon in the battle for narrative authority.

As *Lazarillo de Tormes* deflates tradition, the primary agent of that deflation—Lázaro himself—finds it difficult to mix artistry and deconstruction, self-defense and self-praise. When Guzmán gets off the subject—his life and times—Alemán's presence and, hence, his authority become more apparent, even if the unity of the narrative is threatened. Quevedo endows his persona non grata with an impressive lexicon and with considerable linguistic skills. Pablos has dreams of becoming a gentleman, and he has metatheatrical skills that permit him to invade mainstream society. Each potential success is a near miss, that is, a defeat. Quevedo seems to loom at every corner in order to hinder Pablos's plans. Bad fortune becomes almost predictable, and its representative in the text is Don Diego Coronel, Pablos's former master and nemesis. The structure of the *Buscón* relies on an implied reader who will condemn the prospect of upward mobility. There is only negligible middle ground here, and Quevedo makes his argument stronger by underscoring the absurdity of Pablos's aspirations. The *pícaro* does not want a modicum of success; he wants to be an aristocrat, and he will go higher and fall harder. Not only is Pablos, as narrator, the bearer of his own bad tidings and a subject turned object, but his identity within the text is fraught with irony. His voice hardly seems to correspond to the person whose life is recounted. He has a great deal of practical experience and some formal education, but he is not trained to soar the heights of language and thought. The complex, elegant style of his discourse shifts reader's attention to the author. The distancing mechanisms of the *Buscón* place the marginalized Pablos in the margins of a discourse that he offers as his own.

In order to revise precedent, the author of *Lazarillo de Tormes* rejects idealized storytelling in favor of an ironic new mode. As a result, the narrator loses the glow of idealism that surrounds the models. He is exposed to the elements of satire and social pressure. This early form of realism may come as a rude awakening to the reader, who, like Lazarillo in the episode of the stone bull or on encountering the squire, is not on the lookout for irony. In society and in the text, Lázaro stands apart, conspicuously and ironically proclaiming one thing and revealing another. Pablos is at the mercy of a hostile environment, a chain of catastrophes, and a voice several decibels above him. The wordplay of the first chapters of the *Buscón* separates the narrator from the discourse. Pablos describes himself in such a way that form and content are in disharmony. This is not like a beautiful portrait of a deformed subject, but like a masterwork created by a novice. The reader is inclined to search for the artist, whether within or beyond the frame. The first-person narration is a fictional autobiography, in effect, an oxymoron. Pablos is not only a divided self, but he is detached from the creation of discourse. The reader may be less disposed to appreciate the narrator's rhetorical virtuosity than to notice the incongruity of speaker and enunciation. The discrepancy points to another fundamental question posed by the text. Baroque art in Spain is elitist, catering to a chosen few. Literature, following the example of society, excludes those whose learning and birth do not qualify them for participation. In this sense, Pablos should not be reading conceptist literature, much less writing it. Quevedo, however, may discover a means of resolving the problem through well-wrought strategies of exclusion.

Pablos has no need to justify his existence, as does Lázaro when faced with Vuestra Merced's request. Nor does he lead the reader to a turning point in his life, as does the (self-proclaimed) reformed Guzmán. The idea of narration for its own sake relieves Pablos of the burden of compliance or forced unity. Having nothing in particular to defend and no prescriptive formal mandate, Pablos seems free to determine the direction of his narrative. He would appear to have control over the events to be incorporated into this story and over the means by which he will emplot himself and others. The narratee is unspecified, little more than pure convention. And yet from the moment that Pablos begins to speak, or to write, he comes across as an overachiever, a narrator whose discourse is, in general, unsupported by his story. Not only does he exhibit exceptional ingenuity and verbal acumen, but when the witticisms are decoded, he—along with his family and other poor souls—is most likely to be the butt of the humor. Quevedo, outspoken in his disregard for the lower echelons of society, borrows, from the subgenre that has come to be known as the picaresque, a disenfranchised member of society to relay the story in the first person. The writer of *Lazarillo de Tormes* and Mateo Alemán present two models for an ironic exchange of authority. Quevedo seems to recognize the dialectical base of the earlier texts and the possibilities for extending the gap between author and narrator.

In a consideration of the *Buscón*, it is necessary to remember that there is a character in the novel. Edwin Williamson signals several occasions in which Pablos "wriggles out of Quevedo's coercive grasp and seizes a fragile fictional life which follows the logical direction of his own ambition rather than the vicious circularity of his creator's manipulations" (59; see also Friedman, "Trials of Discourse"). The comment recalls Lionel Abel's treatment, in *Metatheatre*, of self-conscious characters who reach levels unimagined by their creators. The dialectics of voice do not drown out the narrator/protagonist of the *Buscón*. He has a soul, despite Quevedo's wit. The author makes him speak against himself, but the reader is able to share his perspective. Most striking, perhaps, is the beautifully realized psychological portrait of the young Pablos. The intricate and playful prose of the opening chapter demonstrates how quickly and how sharply Quevedo enters the discursive space, with grotesque descriptions of Pablos's father and mother, the revelation of the boy's noble intentions, and the paradoxical thanks to God for parents so zealous of his well-being. Quevedo sends the reader the message early on that this is a narrator who cannot be trusted and a character who should not be taken seriously. Nevertheless, there is something pro-foundly moving about Pablos's mortification on discovering (from the horse's mouth) that his tormentors are telling the truth when they call his mother a prostitute and a witch, or on being mocked and beaten when he arrives (with the protected Don Diego) at the university of Alcalá de Henares, or on reading of the ignominious death of his father, to cite but three of many examples. Recounting the moments of extreme embarrassment, Pablos notes that he hides his feelings. As a narrator, he does the same. Words are a cover-up, a dissimulation. They are the tools of Quevedo's trade, but they also serve Pablos. In this sense, the discourse does reflect the story.

Seymour Chatman emphasizes the distinction between voice and point of view in fiction (see *Story and Discourse* 51-58). Simply stated, the narrating voice may present information from the perspective of another. Chatman's examples show how the narrator can integrate an external point of view into the narrator's voice, often quite subtly and often, it would seem, for structural rather than for manipulative purposes. Narrative exigencies aside, it is clear that some writers will pretend to operate, for whatever ends, under the premise that there is no difference between voice and perspective. When narrators successfully blur the distinction, they can gain greater control of reader response, especially when they are able to create the illusion of objectivity. Lennard J. Davis argues that "[t]he novel is a form which depends on mimesis—the imitation of reality through realist techniques—and because of that fact, novels depend on their ability to make readers feel as if they are witnessing not art but life" (25). *Don Quijote* and the early modern picaresque narrative, while reacting to literary idealism, deal with mimesis far differently than does the so-called novel of realism. A common thread of the Spanish texts may be a conception of mimesis (or a refashioning of mimesis) that would encourage the writer to remind readers, first, that they, in fact, are witnessing art, and, secondly, that this art imitates life through its own conventions and recourses. The rigors of storytelling are elements of the story, and the play of voices becomes an analogue of the image-processing that leads to perception.

When Davis states that "[n]ovels do not depict life, they depict life as it is represented by ideology" (24), he acknowledges the crucial factor of mediation, as an organizing principle, as a foundation for semiosis, and as a source of authority. Ideology in the baroque period is, of course, a formal and conceptual construct that regulates the production of art and that is, in turn, regulated by a number of agencies, including Church and State. Ornamentation carried to extremes has political as well as artistic dimensions. Baroque excess is not gratuitous but a part of the ideological systems at work. The competitive nature of baroque art, with its obscurity and hierarchies, its violent oppositions and daring combinations, its poetic liberties and enforced conservatism, challenges any sense of complacency with the past. A consequence of the new aesthetics on narrative is to reorient the reading process toward the mediator of story and discourse, the author, and toward that most significant Other, the narrator. *Don Quijote* is about gathering the facts, about reporting events, about making history. The author reduplicates himself many times over in order to investigate the inexhaustible teleology of the quest for truth. The inward movement of the text is Cervantes's way of projecting outward, and the novel's strange but true history aids him in this pursuit. The picaresque accentuates the novelty of both sides of the undertaking: the restructuring of literary goals and the restructuring of marginal lives. Collaboratively or contentiously, narrative writes its own story.

Arnold Weinstein believes that, through the wordplay of baroque language, Quevedo delights in linguistic creation per se and, at the same time, that "Pablos *learns* the style that Quevedo lends to him, [and] that Pablos, as a character, needs and enjoys the verbal resources with which he is endowed" (37). For Weinstein, even the most deprived *pícaro* can find gratification in thought and language, and "[i]f we ascribe the wit entirely to Quevedo, we impoverish the novel and reduce the character to a vehicle" (37-38). The idea of words filling the empty spaces of Pablos's life is a sound one, but what the critic does not relay to us is precisely how the transference takes play, in sum, how Quevedo teaches Pablos his style. Rejecting the view that Quevedo's wit is somehow "grafted onto" Pablos, James Iffland uses Freud's *Jokes and Their Relation to the Unconscious* to suggest that self-directed humor—the type of humor often seen to be the marker of the author's intrusion into the narrator's realm—is consistent with the *pícaro's* character. The act of writing allows Pablos the opportunity to release his aggressions and to win "favorable attention from the society from which he is thoroughly estranged, conceivably even from the class which has soundly rejected him. And as part of this effort, Pablos—much like a buffoon—is willing to describe incidents in which he himself looks foolish or base" (241). Iffland sees the comic structure as related to what he calls "an underlying strategy of revenge" (241n49): "Pablos is not ingenuous enough to believe that satire, notably that written by a person of such little moral weight as he, is sufficiently effective to change society. The most he can hope for is to lure the readers into feeling disdain toward that which he himself despises" (233).

Pablos indeed has a narrative identity, but the separation of his personal contribution—his unique qualities, his selfhood—from the wit and counterdiscourse of Quevedo is problematical, tantamount to the separation of the dancer from the dance. The critical images of Pablos learning ingenuity from Quevedo or writing the book as an antidote to repressed emotion may tend to ignore the discursive competition implicit in the *Buscón*. *Lazarillo de Tormes* and *Guzmán de Alfarache* bring the lower-class character to the traditionally noble domain of autobiography. The circumstances of narration give them an authority that the world has denied them, but the content of their lives bursts the bubble of respectability offered through generic association. They are in good company, but they cannot sustain their place in polite literary society. They are as good as doomed from the beginning by an implied author who seems to be cognizant of the force of juxtaposition. Similitude rapidly turns to difference, and the reader may be more aware of the inversion than of the imitation of paradigms. The *Buscón* exaggerates the difference between text and intertext, as Quevedo competes with idealistic fiction and with the earlier picaresque. To erase the implied author from the narrative scheme—and to suppose that an "absent" author is preferable to double-voiced discourse—may be to overlook the depth of the analogue and the full significance of mediation in the novel.

George Mariscal observes that the *Buscón* is among the writings that Quevedo sought to withhold from the public during his lifetime (101). Seeking to gain a reputation for his more elegant, more devout, and more classically oriented texts, he renounced the novel, refusing to recognize it as his own. This may lead one to see the *Buscón* as Pablos's story, but Quevedo has left his imprint on the narrative, as well as on the satirical and burlesque works that he seems intent on disclaiming. From *Lazarillo de Tormes* onward (or from the time of Francisco Delicado's less than delicate dialogue, *La lozana andaluza*), the picaresque tradition offers an interplay of discursive control and restraint. Delicado's Lozana, for example, has a well-defined voice in the text—a text that, after all, bears her name and relates her ups and downs—but another key participant in the dialogue is the authorial figure himself, and he, of course, directs all phases of the narrative. *Lazarillo* and *Guzmán* recreate the dialogic structure within the narratives, but with a radical shift to the first person and the expectation of a single, limited perspective. It is the sublime disruption of the solitary viewpoint, among other factors, that links the picaresque texts. The autobiographical frame allows for the opening of narrative options. One person and one story project a retrospective vision and a writing subject as graft, temporal progressions and disjunctions, recollected experience, tales of overdetermined delinquency and underdetermined success. Most importantly, the autobiographer is not the author. *La lozana andaluza* prepares the way for the feminine variations of the picaresque, in which male authors attempt to create female voices for their protagonists (*La pícara Justina, Teresa de Manzanares*) or resort to third-person narration (*La hija de Celestina, La garduña de Sevilla*). The obvious space between the inventor of discourse and the protagonist in these narratives serves as a guide to the strategies of mediation.

Probably the most richly textured of the variations, Francisco López de Úbeda's *La pícara Justina* (1605) is heavy in psychological and moral insights, despite its plot twists and burlesque tone. Justina has learned life's lessons the hard way, and she shares her adventures and her fortunes with the reader. She realizes that sin has left its scars, physical and emotional, for crimes cannot go unavenged by the powers above her. It is not just the retribution that places the narrator at the wrong end of her exempla but also the decidedly masculine tenor of her commentary. *La pícara Justina* renders feminine psychology as filtered through the author, that is to say, through male authority. Narratives such as *La pícara Justina* and Alonso de Castillo Solórzano's *Teresa de Manzanares* (1632) help to demonstrate, ironically perhaps, the distinction between voice and point of view, a distinction that here proceeds along gender lines.[17] The

---

[17] My study *The Antiheroine's Voice* focuses on the creation of female voices in picaresque and other fictions. For female variations of the picaresque in early

authors get their way by sacrificing moral ground to the narrators, whose "feminine" vision could barely adhere more to the masculine party line; women, in essence, keep themselves in their place. Pablos's self-condemnatory moral commentary at the end of the *Buscón* similarly is inflected by institutionalized thought and, more notably, by a point of view that does not necessarily conform to the protagonist's expressed attitude and habits.

Baroque literature is always, in one way or another, a statement about language, about language intensified and made hyperbolic. In many cases, linguistic decoding is at the core of the reading process, but the text is always about something else. Language mastered, refamiliarized, will tell a story. The *Buscón* brings conceptist discourse to picaresque narrative. It is a critical commonplace to view *Don Quijote* as a work that grew in creative potential as Cervantes was writing it, that what could have been another exemplary novel became an intertextual melting pot and, paradoxically, a true original. By the same token, Quevedo may have started with a more modest proposal: to incorporate his particular style of difficulty and ingenuity into the picaresque. Whereas *Don Quijote* expands dialogue and perspective after the first sally, the *Buscón* declines in conceptist intensity after the opening of Book 1, chapter 4, yet the discourse continues to reveal a psyche behind the verbal display. Quevedo is, of course, not only present in the wordplay but in the undermining of Pablos's ambitions. Determinism in its theological context finds an analogue in the literary determinism of the author, who sets his protagonist (or, more properly, antagonist) against insuperable odds, from beginning to end.

Heredity could not be less favorable to Pablos. Witticisms may serve as a type of euphemism—a legacy from his father, the "shearer of cheeks and tailor of beards"[18]—but they cannot hide public disgrace. The mother also has great notoriety. Her many Christian names bespeak overcompen-

---

modern Spain, see ch. 3. See also Harvey, whose analyses center on English Renaissance texts.

[18] "... que el era tundidor de mejillas y sastre de barbas" (95). Quotations from *La vida del buscón* will refer to the Ynduráin edition, and page numbers will be indicated in parentheses.

sation, another of Pablos's legacies. She is known to be a prostitute and an enchantress, and all the poets of Spain, among others, it would seem, "hacían cosas sobre ella" (97). The thief and the bewitching lady want their son to follow their own trades, but, in spite of the hostile environment and the guilt by association, Pablos is set on becoming a gentleman and on "learning virtue." The rejection of his family sets a pattern for his life. He finds other homes and other families, but there is little that is inviting about the new situations. "Father" Cabra nearly starves him, Don Diego and the students in Alcalá force him to fend for himself, and his success at the university is extracurricular (in the field of delinquent behavior). Taking French leave of his uncle the executioner, he joins the brotherhood of Don Toribio and his makeshift gentlemen, a collaboration that lands him in prison, where he acquires two substitute families: his fellow prisoners and the jailer's brood. In order to win favor, Pablos inscribes himself into the family history of the jailer's wife, a slovenly New Christian with two ugly and whorish daughters. His improvised identities give him temporary families—the residents of the boarding house, the troupe of actors, the nuns, and the band of rogues in Sevilla—and he almost marries into Don Diego Coronel's family, but no relationship is stable, no home permanent, no success lasting. The reader does not need the promised (but never published) sequel to understand that the remainder of Pablos's life, including his adventures in the New World, will bring little change, because the narrator himself announces that he has changed places but not habits.

In Cabra's school and on the road to Alcalá, Pablos and Don Diego are equals. They reside outside of society, outside of the hierarchy. In their primary schooling in Segovia and at the university, Don Diego's social status provides him with a second family, people who will protect him. Pablos is alone, unable to defend himself against those who would treat him as they would his mother or an antichrist. He leaves Don Diego's employ by proclaiming that he is "another person" ("ya soy otro," 165). He is no longer the rich boy's servant, but the reader may be struck instead by the circularity of his experience. When he returns to Segovia to collect his inheritance, his drawn and quartered father "meets" him on the road; his mother is absent, having been apprehended by the Inquisition. His search for alternate families is fruitless, and his desire to detach himself from the past fails as if by clockwork. The culminating gesture is the reappearance of Don Diego (just as the scheme to marry Doña Ana is coming to fruition), punctuated by a symbolic fall from a horse which may remind readers of his disastrous tenure as the boy-king. The unhappy reunion with Don Diego is, one could argue, more than chance. Followed by Pablos's voicing of his failure, it is an unequivocal sign of authorial control.

What stands out in Pablos's story of his life is the element of shame. No amount of verbal camouflage can hide the revelation that the rumors about his mother are true or that his father is a criminal, executed by his uncle the hangman. The events of the first day in Alcalá go well beyond schoolboy pranks. Pablos is ostracized in the most humiliating way possible. He knows from the time with Cabra and from the mishaps on the road that Don Diego is no more equipped to live independently than he. He is awakened, once again, and certainly not for the last time, to the fact that how he is treated by his fellow man is a function of a predetermined identity. He can continue to be a servant and to suffer the indignities of his rank, or he can accept his place in the social order and strive for the only identity possible, a negative identity. As he moves farther and farther into delinquency, he becomes a self-consciously protean character, with a new name to fit each role. For a time, he believes that money can buy anything, and he entraps the naïve Doña Ana. Don Diego crushes the plot aimed at matrimony by identifying Pablos, thus exposing the false status and the insincere words of the opportunist. When Pablos returns to his home, he finds that his so-called friends have robbed him. When he persists in pursuing Doña Ana, Don Diego invents a stratagem of revenge which leaves Pablos, literally and figuratively, no exit. He is wounded, penniless, without friends, with no marriage prospects, unable to stay in Madrid or to go away. The episode has cost him his dignity, such as it is, and he uses the same terms here as in the opening chapters to express his discomfort. Traumatized by the turn of events, he conceals his humiliation and his rage.

The narrator of the *Buscón* stands between the protagonist and the author. When Pablos strays from what could be considered a reasonable field of linguistic competence, his creator enters the picture. The extent of the intervention depends on the "reading" that one would give of the overt intrusion into the autobiographical frame and, specifically, into the discourse. When Pablos sounds like Quevedo, the mediating presence seems evident. When misfortunes accumulate in "chainlike" fashion, with adverse destiny a constant (echoing what Pedro Salinas, in another context, calls "seguro azar," or certain chance), it is likely that the reader will see Quevedo in the story, as well. When the humor is perhaps excessively self-reflexive and the selected anecdotes seem to have little purpose other than to emphasize Pablos's failures, the reader may choose to hear a voice-over. There is no pretext to the *Buscón* other than the narration of a life, so the writer has the option of including what he judges to be the most significant events. Pablos differs vastly from Guzmán with respect to moralizing commentary. In the opening note to the reader of the *Buscón,* Quevedo asks his public to take advantage of the sermons, but, presumably recognizing that the text contains no sermons, he proceeds to focus on his work as a book of entertainment. He makes the point that a story of roguish life is enhanced by clever writing—writing with gusto—and he remarks that readers find this type of composition more to their liking than weightier materials. The ending is necessary to reorient one's way of thinking. We sense that Pablos has yet to attempt a reformation, and there is no indication that he intends to do so. Pablos's narrative is not so much about his life as process as about the factors that combine to determine—to control—his life. Whether part of Quevedo's design or a reflection of the times, the *Buscón* is about the confusion of subject and object.

Quevedo uses the opening section of the novel to establish his own discursive identity within the text. He is the master of wit and the manipulator of Pablos's presentation of his life. For Quevedo's audience, a major feature of the early chapters probably would have been the foregrounding of the absurd juxtaposition of the *pícaro's* background and his goals. The fact that the description of his parents' less than illustrious callings comes from Pablos himself may have elicited more laughter or scorn than sympathy. The notion that one could hope to become a gentleman under these circumstances or that he could somehow deny his blood overlooks the rigidity of the class system of the period. It suggests—incorrectly, illegitimately—that the child is a blank slate, that justice is absolute, and that individual merit can bring success. Rather than a victim, Pablos may appear to be a ridiculous dreamer, out of touch with social reality. And, as if to cement his fate, Quevedo makes sure that Pablos does not try to—and does not have the chance to—get to the top through lofty accomplishments but through crimes and deception. Nonetheless, it may be the question of justice that allows Pablos to escape his fate, if only in a relative sense.

Lazarillo de Tormes and *Guzmán de Alfarache* show the progression of the protagonist from a starving child to a family man with gainful employment, in one case, and from a juvenile delinquent to a repentant sinner, in the other. The irony of the texts notwithstanding, each narrator proposes to demonstrate how an individual can aid in forging his destiny. Lázaro attributes his rise to hard work and to social contacts. Guzmán prospers from an act of contrition, linked in the text to the carefully timed reporting of a planned mutiny on the galley. There is a mixture of spirituality and secularity in both stories. Lázaro's mentor is the archpriest, whom gossipmongers claim is far more than the employer of his wife. Guzmán, in turn, gains his freedom by informing on those who have treated him badly. His motives may be questionable, as may the conversion itself. Narrating his story, Pablos offers no pretense of advancement. He comes close to success, but his schemes and his falsehoods cannot displace the person behind the ruse. With every defeat comes some kind of revelation, most often the exposure of the suppressed identity. It seems that what Pablos learns from his failures is not that he must consider a different path but that he must try harder to deceive. His sole contact with the religious community comes in the form of his courtship of a nun, whom he serves and then robs. To add insult to injury, the narrator leaves it to the "pious reader" to determine whether the jilted sister would have lamented the loss of her coins more than the loss of her gentleman caller. It is appropriate that the story ends in Sevilla, known for its active underworld, with Pablos housed in a church in order to escape the law. There is no remorse, no rationalization of success, no illumination, no moral transformation, not even a bit of optimism for the future. Pablos closes the book on his life without the prospect, and without the hope, of change.

The crusade against Pablos may make the reader turn away from the protagonist as an uncaring, unfeeling, misguided person, critical of those around him but rarely self-critical and, it must be noted, a threat to the policies of the State. As he becomes increasingly contemptuous of social protocol, his crimes become increasingly serious in nature. He does not seem to be interested in substantive matters—in improving his personal worth or his value to society—but in maintaining his deceptions long enough to reap the desired rewards. To be a gentleman, for Pablos, is to be taken for a gentleman rather than to adhere to gentlemanly ideals. He does not necessarily want to be a better person but to enjoy the luxuries of life without earning them, without deserving them. His hoaxes are mean-spirited and cruel, often aimed at women. On reaching the end of the story, the reader would be hard put to find a single redeeming feature in the *pícaro,* who has long since lost his innocence and feeling of helplessness. The reader may bear little concern for Pablos's welfare in the untold portion of the story, where the protagonist must face the challenge of a new world. He has made unwise choices and has hurt those around him. We can surmise that he will continue to use poor judgment, to exploit others, and to remain, as he calls himself, an "obstinate sinner."

The intensity of Quevedo's language and of his opposition to the protagonist threatens to move Pablos into the margins of his own discourse. The author replicates the social hierarchy in the narrative structure. If the text is unsympathetic toward Pablos, the credit must go to the implied author, who inverts the force of what are purported to be the narrator's own words. Stated in another way, the implied author obscures Pablos's words, by coating them with baroque conceits, and by accentuating the differences between established codes and illusions of grandeur. There is irony in the elevated discourse born of metaphysical subtleties and in the social fantasies of the lowly narrator/protagonist. Both his thoughts and their articulation suggest alterity, otherness, interpolation. Quevedo succeeds in detaching Pablos from what is exclusively his own: his life, his life story. So great is the distance that the reader may forget at times that Pablos is the (nominal) creator of the unflattering portrait. Nonetheless, and, again, ironically, the ferocity of the attack from within serves to redeem the *pícaro,* casting him as victim and supporting the contention that he has no viable options. There is the question of whether he is naturally evil or pushed into evil by a society that prejudges him. Similarly, one may ask if the uncomplimentary autobiography is edited, altered, or rewritten (within the fictional premises) in order to stack the odds against him, to make his story less his own.

By using first-person narration, Quevedo makes Pablos the commentator and the contaminated. The *pícaro* cannot escape his disgraceful heritage. When he laughs at his parents through the power of language, he is no less their son. When he attempts to laugh with society at them, he only confirms his marginal status, his inability to integrate himself into the community. Every adventure is a stumbling block, every scheme a misfire. It is not difficult to sense the presence of Quevedo behind the discourse and behind the emplotment. The surprise is that Pablos does not allow himself to be obliterated. He perseveres in the text as he does in society, with extreme tenacity and with a voice, however weak, of his own. The *Buscón* does not present a forward movement in moral terms, but from a psychological perspective we see how the events of Pablos's childhood determine—as clearly as his blood—his attitudes and his course of action. The pattern of Pablos's life (and of his autobiography) is apparent through a process of mortification and dissimulation. Time after time, he is humiliated and, to combat feelings of inferiority, he overcompensates, with little success. After major blows to his sense of self, he can do nothing but hide his shame and his anger. It is this shame that explains the wish to reject his family ties and this anger that pushes him to victimize others. He can be held accountable for his actions, but it would be hard to argue that life presents him with attractive alternatives. Even as a dutiful servant, he suffers unprovoked abuse. With no one to protect him, he must follow Don Diego's advice to stand on his own. Delinquency may be the only means to preserve his ego—to make a name for himself—but following his glory days as a thief and trickster in Alcalá, he resumes his former identity on his return to Segovia. Shortly thereafter, his rejection of family leads to a string of pseudonyms, symbolic erasures of the ego.

Pablos refers in the opening chapter to "una vieja que me crió" (98). He is treated as an orphan while his parents are alive, but if they do not care for him directly, they remain the principal mediators of his status in society. They do not seem disturbed by their scandalous images, so he cannot defend them against their detractors. They force him into silence, for no words can suffice to express or to offset his embarrassment. Circumstances deny him mother love and an outlet for his emotions, and Quevedo denies him unimpeded access to the mother tongue. Wordplay, conceit, euphemism, and allusion take the place of direct discourse. Pablos speaks periphrastically, thus calling attention to the language itself. Chapter 3, which tells of his stay at Cabra's school, is as rich in verbal artifice as it is empty of nutrients. The starving Pablos competes for reader attention with a cornucopia of words and with tests of decoding. He wastes away toward nothingness, but hyperboles give him substance, sustenance. During the rites of passage in Alcalá, he can use only words and gestures to distract the enemy. At one point, he pretends to have a seizure. He tries to hide the evidence of his fear, without success. And, in perhaps the most telling event of this sequence, he shouts to a Moorish convert about to spit on him, "que no soy *Ecce-Homo*" (144), a spontaneous reaction that hardly would seem the response of an Old Christian. Pablos learns from the initiation that it is easier to be on guard than to alter one's identity. He becomes a leader among the delinquents, with whom he lives "todos los de la casa como hermanos" (148). This is probably the closest that he comes to being himself, and his choice is between notoriety and nonentity. In the future, he will take refuge in anonymity, as during his time as an actor, or in invented roles on the stage of life. He fashions identities in the hope of a merciful fate, but the specter of the past never ceases to haunt him, as the return of Don Diego Coronel makes clear. He is bound to his roots and thereby condemned to suffer for offenses beyond his control. Ultimately, it is the dearth of recourses that determines his identity in the narrative.

Pablos's impotence as storyteller and as protagonist serves to underscore the power of the subtext. The studied discourse and the consistencies of chance treat him, within the text, as society treats those of his kind. He is an outcast, a casualty of class consciousness. He is the victim of irony, the abused and overly eager son in search of a family. At the end of his story, we find him in Toledo, courting a nun, calling the abbess "ma'am," the vicar "father," and the sacristan "brother," and afterwards in Sevilla, with a new brother (Matorral) and sister, or mistress, in crime (La Grajal). He is pursued by officers of the law, as his parents had been pursued, and the escape motif remains in force. His life has come full circle, which is to say that it has gone nowhere. His actions are worthy of contempt, but the deferred discourse and the recast story reveal why Pablos is motivated to lash out at society. His bravado is a last resort, his way of coping with a hostile world. He is forced to decide in favor of limited freedom (continued service to a master) or the fabrication of his own reality (the roguish metaplots). Dutiful service would be the scrupulous choice, but with this option there would be no narrative. The story needs a rebel, and a dupe, and Pablos complies. It is to Quevedo's credit that he is able to dislodge the narrator from the linguistic and ideological center of the text—through negative characterization and borrowed discourse—while pretending to cede authority to him. Pablos recounts his story without a clear structural design, and he describes his life to a vaguely defined narratee. Quevedo's designs are more easily discernible. He converts the linear plot into a circle of failures, and he is not reluctant to deploy chance over cause and effect. He refuses to permit Pablos to flee from his humble origins and the sins of his parents, even though he himself abhors all that is ignoble and impure. He converts Pablos's speech into a style that resembles his own and makes the *pícaro* the purported source and, directly or by association, the object of the humor. He advocates the status quo through the first-person narration and social history of the outsider. The manipulation of control and the encoding of irony are so successful that authority in the text is incontrovertible: it belongs to Quevedo, the implied author who will not tolerate the likes of Pablos in the real world or in fiction. *Lazarillo de Tormes* and *Guzmán de Alfarache* give Quevedo a model for marginal narrative. Perhaps sensing a competitive relation intimated but not fully elaborated in the earlier texts, he deconstructs the narrator's authority from within. He turns a dubious success story into a dark and retrogressive journey, with no change for the better and no final repentance. Knowing that the format gives the narrator the responsibility for ordering events and words, he can stand at a distance to observe the art object that would deny direct intervention to—that would distance—its subject. Pablos survives, in the text as in society, by accepting his marginality and by enduring as an antisocial being, despised but not erased.

Authority in early modern Spanish literature takes a number of forms. In some cases, the status of the artist and the validity of the work of art need to be clarified, or solidified. In others, the writers seem to feel compelled to compete with, and to best, their predecessors. At times, the competition is benign, a natural part of the process of creation, while at others an imaginative present seems to imply a belittling of the cultural past. The gaining of authority can mean the subversion of previous centers of authority. In picaresque narrative, authors confront a tradition based on idealism and artificial elegance of style. They are influenced by Renaissance humanism, but their views on life and language, and their own ideals, are different. They are willing to break the balance of nature and of words through antithesis, distortion, elitist diction, and elitist principles. In the picaresque, as in *Don Quijote*, narrative perspective reaches new heights. Cervantes approaches the issue dialogically, by using the accumulation of historical data (and of narrating personae) to broaden the portrait of the knight errant. In the picaresque, the relation between the implied author and the narrator is more often dialectical, a response to the spirit of competition. The creators of the *pícaras* may be the most obvious examples of a double system of discourse, exemplified by male inflection of female voices, but Quevedo is, arguably, the author who shows the greatest hostility toward his protagonist. Cervantes and the writers of picaresque narrative comment on authority through acknowledgment and revision of the intertext and through strategies of mediation. As the authors define their own roles within the texts, they demonstrate a transfer—and a radical questioning—of authority in the novel. As their power increases, they may undermine the concept of absolute control.

In a series of essays, Tamar Yacobi discusses the impact of reliability and mediation on narrative analysis. Her starting point is the reader's interest in resolving "textual tensions" or contradictions, both internal and external ("Fictional Reliability" 113). Guided by the work of Meir Sternberg, Yacobi introduces five "reconciling and integrating measures," which she terms genetic, generic, existential, functional, and perspectival. The genetic principle covers "the causal factors that produced the text without coming to form part of it... and above all the situation and tendencies of the historical producer, including the environmental as well as psychological pressures that operated on him" (Yacobi, "Fictional Reliability" 114). Tobias Smollett's partiality for his native land can serve to explain why in *Humphry Clinker* "a short and uneventful vacation in Scotland is enough to transform a middle-aged hypochondriac and misanthrope into a robust lover of mankind" ("Fictional Reliability" 114). Analogously, the creation of "a ridiculously improbable fictive world" in chapters 1 through 10 of *Joseph Andrews*, followed by psychologically motivated conduct from chapter 11 onward, relates to Henry Fielding's need to come to terms with Samuel Richardson's *Pamela* and his own sense of realism ("Fictional Reliability" 114). Yacobi sees Fielding as under the influence of his satirical *Shamela* as he begins to write *Joseph Andrews*. Only after ten chapters does he "manage to free himself from parodistic tendentiousness and reference" ("Fictional Reliability" 115). Inconsistency of method in the text has to do with the process of composition and the processing mechanisms of the author. The generic principle, in turn, "dictates or makes possible certain rules of referential stylization, the employment of which usually results in a set of divergences from what is generally accepted as the principles governing actual reality" ("Fictional Reliability" 115). The direction of the text may respond to the conventions of the genre or medium rather than to pure logic. The structure of drama, for example, addresses the demands of the theater, often at the expense of the laws of probability. In a similar vein, the internal logic of satire may promote discontinuity rather than coherence. In contrast, the existential principle finds coherence in an external referent, in the accommodation of tension within the text through correlation with structures in the real world. The chaos and anomalies of the literary text may be justified by the phrase "Such is the or this world" (Yacobi, "Narrative Structure" 336). The functional principle allows discordance in the text to serve "thematic and normative ends" ("Fictional Reliability" 117). Lack of harmony has a purpose. Yacobi uses the example of Günter Grass, who subjects readers to a series of incongruities, both for shock value and in order to effect a reconsideration of values in the real world.

The fifth principle deals with perspective, specifically with the relation between narrators and the information that they convey, so that "the coherent organization of the narrative is made possible once the reader recognizes the characters' interference with the facts of their significance" ("Fictional Reliability" 117). In some narratives, the identification of the perspectival factor leads the reader to correct or discount the interference and to comprehend what really happened. Yacobi argues, using a Spanish example, that when we recognize the narrator's self-interest and modify our reading accordingly, we realize that "Lazarillo de Tormes's wife is, despite his rationalizing statements, the priest's mistress" ("Fictional Reliability" 118). She notes that in other texts, especially in modern narrative, "the refracted object is so hopelessly distorted as to become irretrievable, thus moving the center of focus to the observer" ("Fictional Reliability" 118-19). The first four principles have in common a means of resolution through agents or agencies other than the narrator, whose reliability may not be brought into question. When, however, "the reader infers an unreliable narrator (or any other fallible observer) who unconsciously reveals his eccentricities and distortions[,] this information forms part of the intentionality underlying the overall act of communication. To construct an hypothesis as to the unreliability of the narrator is then necessarily to assume the existence of an implied (and, by definition, reliable) author who manipulates his creature for his own purposes" ("Fictional Reliability" 123). The fifth principle engages us, then, to seek coherence through an ironic reading of unreliability. When we discover the extent and the forms of manipulation, we can arrive at the other side of irony.

Yacobi's genetic principle offers a way of incorporating the conditions of writing and the ideologies of the writer and of the period into textual analysis. What we know about Mateo Alemán and Francisco de Quevedo and about baroque Spain can be related to the direction and to the messages of *Guzmán de Alfarache* and *La vida del buscón*. The biographies of the New Christian fearful of his status in society and of the Old Christian scornful of opportunists help to elucidate the "lives" of the *pícaros*. *Guzmán* shows the impact of the false sequel on Alemán, and the allegorical treatment of the theft gains coherence in light of the reader's knowledge of the extratextual factors. The relevancy of Pablos's encounter with the fencing master in the first chapter of Book 2 of the *Buscón* is more apparent if one understands that the episode is directed at Luis Pacheco de Narváez, author of the *Libro de las Grandezas de la espada* alluded to in the text, with whom Quevedo had an ongoing dispute (see Quevedo, ed. Lázaro Carreter, annotated by Alcina Franch 271n206). Similarly, what is known of attitudes toward the underclass in seventeenth-century Spain can affect how one analyzes the trials and tribulations of the protagonists. It is interesting to consider, in the genetic context, how the study of *Lazarillo de Tormes* is affected by ideological but not by biographical evidence. The reader cannot shape Lázaro's text, that is, cannot elaborate its inconsistencies, on the basis of a historical author. This absence points to the advantages, and to the disadvantages, of presence (see Friedman, "'Cómo se hace un autor'").

The foregrounding of an undesirable citizen marks picaresque narrative. The generic principle could suggest that readers not belabor the circumstances of narration in picaresque fiction. Given the liberties of generic convention, the reader does not have to know how Lázaro can allude to the classics or how Pablos can handle the intricacies of conceptist art. Causality may function generically, as well, bound to a picaresque mode of poetic justice as opposed to a purely rational or chance ordering of events. We may tend to see these problems as signs of unreliability rather than as generic devices that could make a case for reliability, but the generic principle nonetheless gives us the option of attributing the course of events—action and discourse—to the conventions of representation.

There is an easily discernible interplay among the genetic, generic, and functional principles in picaresque narrative. (The existential principle, for its part, allows us to see consistency in inconsistency, or to view the instability of signifiers as reflecting the semiotics of the universe.) The Cabra episode of the *Buscón* may be associated with the author's desire to display his baroque artistry (genetic), with the motif of hunger (generic), and with the narrator's appeal for reader sympathy (functional), among other options. Pablos's inability to deny his blood relates to Quevedo's, and to his society's, intolerant stance (genetic) and to the *pícaro*'s struggle for upward mobility (generic), and each failure in this regard offers a variation on the theme of social determinism (functional). And so on. With respect to the picaresque, the first four principles gear us toward the fifth, based on the complexities of perspective. Yacobi argues that "to read or interpret fiction is exactly to define the mediation-gap, to cross it by inferring the author's frame from the inset(s), so as to put them into some perspectival relation: anywhere between total accord (i.e., [the] mediator's reliability) and the sharpest discord (i.e., unreliability). Clearly, everything depends on this reconstruction and placing of viewpoints" ("Narrative Structure" 336). Reliability is often linked to control, "[s]o the more artful the speaker shows himself in the handling of discourse and addressee, the less grounds (or incentive) we have for inferring an authority of superior artfulness and coherence that exploits and exposes him for its own ends" ("Narrative Structure" 336). We tend to respect a narrator with good judgment, vision, and art, just as we lose faith in an inept, artless narrator. The first achieves a degree of independence from the authorial figure, while the second builds a case for the opposing side. The closer the two perspectives, the stronger the building of shared goals, and, by contrast, the greater the distance between perspectives, the more divergent the message systems. The reader must gauge distance and must differentiate the self-conscious articulation from artful manipulation. Yacobi emphasizes the role of the critical act in questions of unreliability; a decision "is always an interpretive, hypothetical move. As such it always has competitors that suggest a reading of the data along lines that need not involve, much less target and determine, point of view" ("Package Deals" 224).

Yacobi's essays on mediation provide a useful frame for picaresque narrative, which in various manifestations seems always to be a battle of voices. While Lázaro de Tormes explains a case, his text breaks from tradition and allows us to observe that imitation out of context produces a new story, a new discourse, and a new type of protagonist. Lázaro's lack of art—his incriminating disclosures, his ironic repetitions and image patterns—reveal the art of the author. Yacobi's genetic principle may clarify the conflictive plot elements of *Guzmán de Alfarache.* Alemán vacillates between ridiculing his protagonist and defending him, between directing the reader toward the conversion and settling the matter of the false sequel. The five categories encompass Alemán's personal business inserted into the text (genetic); the picaresque model and other literary forms, including the sermon (generic); selective justice (existential); the interpolated novellas (functional); and questions of discursive control (perspectival). One could make a case here for the overtaking of the perspectival principle by the genetic, but Guzmán's voice remains problematic, due in part to the mixed messages of the voice-over. The example is significant because it illustrates what appears to be a loose end in Yacobi's commentary: a faith in the reliability of the (implied) author. The perspectival principle would seem to demand nearly perfect craftsmanship, not on the part of the narrator, whose duty it is to deviate (egregiously or minimally) from the path of coherence, but on the part of the implied author, whose job it is to bridge the mediation gap. The postulation of a cohesive macrostructure that will subsume the studied incongruities of the text proper may ignore the poststructuralist (and earlier) distrust of closure. *Guzmán de Alfarache* sets forth two different discourses, but the implied author's text is not necessarily more articulate, more unified, or more reliable than the narrator's. In his note to the reader in Part 2, Alemán could be accused of misreading his own, or Guzmán's, Part 1. Interference is not synonymous with reliability.

The *Buscón* produces the type of mediation gap that is at the heart of Yacobi's perspectival principle. The text is encoded in such a way that the reader can see (1) that Pablos's attempt to describe emotional situations from a detached position does not succeed, because he does not remain silent on the issue of hiding his shame; (2) that his unrealistic goals make him look as foolish in his role as narrator as they do in society; (3) that the background of the narrator does not substantiate the sophistication of the discourse; (4) that certain of his qualifying statements (regarding his evil inclinations or Don Diego's pious temperament, for example) seem forced or out of character; (5) that he consistently is the victim of chance events; and (6) that he is a bit too disposed to moralize at the end. If these are markers of Pablos's unreliability, they may lead the reader to the ironic portrait that Quevedo wishes to present. The implied author is unyielding in his resistance to social change or upward mobility. He is an enemy of the lower classes, of tainted blood, and of egalitarian social politics. He is an advocate of witticisms, extended conceits, and endless categories of wordplay. He has a strong sense of humor, and his comedy is black. He is, when all is said and done, reliable, with qualification. He is reliable to the extent to which we can visualize him pulling the strings of his creation. And he is reliable to the extent to which we can comprehend his ideology, without having to accept his views. In her search for coherence — for something on the order of the sense of an ending — Yacobi may overlook the effects of time on ideology and, it may be noted, the ripeness for deconstruction of the implied author.

The perspectival principle, which stems from an unequal struggle of narrator and implied author, can be used to demonstrate differences between the picaresque and *Don Quijote*. Cervantes as implied author does not develop an alternate structure with the aim of bringing together the disparate and contradictory narrative voices within the text. Rather, he emphasizes multiple or partial viewpoints, the difficulties of perception, and the impossibility of completeness. He offers shreds of stories, shredded stories. In Yacobi's classification, he favors the existential and the functional principles over the perspectival. When Michel Foucault notes in the essay "What Is an Author?" that the author ("author-function") represents but one of many discourses in a given text, he is echoing Cervantes, who refuses to compete with his narrators for control, who shares authority, who on this level prefers dialogue to dialectics. Quevedo, on the other hand, will not voluntarily relinquish control. Yet, by choosing the first-person narrative of his predecessors in the picaresque mode, he proves how willing and how eager he is to make a battle of it.

Much of the authority of the *Buscón* derives from the author's feelings of social superiority and, one reasonably might conjecture, of moral superiority over the narrator/protagonist. Quevedo controls elements of plot and language, and he endows his character with bad blood and absurd ambitions. He conspires to make Pablos look and sound ridiculous. He seems to expect the reader to separate the seeds of wit (his own) from the chaff (the *pícaro's*). Pablos, by nature and by lot an underdog, becomes the victim of an author who places him in a position of authority, as determined by genre, only to undermine his actions and his words, as determined by the social structure. On one end of the plot(ting) are Pablos's self-destructive tendencies and on the other a creator in charge of his destiny. The magnitude of the inequity becomes, perhaps, the character's saving grace. His power, such as it is, comes from his role as victim. Readers may notice the analogue of social marginalization, and they may process it in a number of ways, not all of which would be flattering to Quevedo. Juan Martí and Alonso Fernández de Avellaneda live today, not by virtue of their gifts as writers, but because they are preserved in the master works of Alemán and Cervantes, who by no means would have wished to immortalize them. The solitary Pablos — with no mother to nurture him and no father to teach him to distinguish good from evil, with a cruel stepfather who denies him success and who grants him no voice of his own — enjoys the same classic status. The *Buscón* finally is about the loss of authority, and Pablos is the hero and teller of that story.

Meir Sternberg notes, as recently as 2001, that "[f]or all its growing sophistication on matters of detail, narrative theory is still in its infancy because the disciplinary foundations have yet to be laid" (115). Stalwarts such as Seymour Chatman, Susan S. Lanser, Brian McHale, Peter Rabinowitz, James Phelan, Marie-Laure Ryan, Gerald Prince, and others, continue to discuss such issues as narrative reliability, implied authorship, and the relation of story and discourse.[19] Dan Shen and Greta Olson are among those who have surveyed the issues and offered critiques and their own approaches. Concentrating on the models of Wayne Booth and Ansgar Nünning, Olson distinguishes between the fallibility and the untrustworthiness of narrators. She asserts that readers attribute these qualities to narrators as they would to individuals in other contexts: "Depending on their perceived deficiencies, narrators elicit different responses and require varying reading strategies. When narrators are untrustworthy, their accounts have to be altered in order to make sense of their discrepancies. Fallible narrators by contrast make individual mistakes or leave open informational gaps that need to be filled in" (104). Olson concludes that "[u]ntrustworthy narrators meet with our skepticism about their characters, whereas fallible narrators are more likely to be excused for their failure to deliver on the informational goods" (104-05). *Don Quijote* and early modern Spanish picaresque narrative offer remarkable variations on the rhetoric of unreliability, which is intimately linked to variations on the theme of self-conscious-

---

[19] Each of these scholars is represented in the special issue of *Narrative* (2001) on contemporary narratology, ed. Emma Kafalenos. Essays by Meir Sternberg, Tamar Yacobi, Dan Shen, and others are included in the number. See Genette esp. 135-54, O'Neill, Cohn esp. 18-37 and 109-31, and Currie esp. 19-32 and 62-70. For narratology as related to *Don Quijote*, see also Parr, *Anatomy* 3-67 and *Related Subjects* 52-96.

ness. Cervantes and the picaresque writers invite reader participation and arbitration. Although the demands that they place on the reader differ (and that is the point, of course), these texts display the intricacies of narration and the vital distinctions between trustworthiness and fallibility, as outlined by Olson, and, early in the history of the novel, they position realism against metafiction.

In "Defense and Challenge," Shen builds upon the "deconstructive attempt" to subvert story and discourse "as an absolute binary in which we have to choose one term as privileged"; this would signal a reversal of "the allegedly-existing privilege (story over discourse)" (222). She finds in the commentaries of Jonathan Culler and Patrick O'Neill, for example, the basis for an argument that espouses the interdependence and inseparability of story and discourse. In the mid-sixteenth century, the anonymous author of *Lazarillo de Tormes* puts essentially the same argument into practice (as had, for that matter, Juan Ruiz in the *Libro de buen amor,* with a sort of primitive—and not in a derogatory sense—ingenuity). Lázaro tells a very different story from the narrators of sentimental, pastoral, and chivalric romance. The baseness of the plot and characters represents an extraordinary divergence from the conventions of idealistic fiction, but it is the first-person narration by the protagonist that truly defines the novelty of the undertaking. Lázaro assumes a defensive posture from the beginning, and "the case" would suggest that he has something to hide. The opening passages of the text proper place the narrator in the lowest social class; his father is a criminal and his mother the mistress of a man with Muslim blood. His reliability is tested from the start, and the incidents in the account depict him as a victim, but also as a person who has learned how to deceive through word and deed. At the end of the narrative, he is a product of the experiences that he has undergone, many of which are mentioned in his explanation of the case. From the beginning, he is a product of linguistic experience, and deception is a part of the picture on both planes. The narrative situation is controlled by irony: by the elevation of the rogue to the position of narrator/protagonist, by the inversion of idealism and social prominence, and by the reverberating impact of the discourse and of the satire.

One could say that, as a narrator, Lázaro is untrustworthy and fallible, with the first category as predominant. He is not as committed to telling the truth as to protecting his interests. In certain respects, his story might lead the reader to believe that Lázaro is more skilled at subterfuge than his discourse conveys; that is, he is fallible. It is this fallibility—this failure to preserve his innocence and sense of victimization—that takes us into the realm of the implied author, the ultimate ironist. By differentiating the two forms of unreliability, Olson distinguishes an apparently intentional plan to mislead the reader from a mishandling of the facts through error, incomplete knowledge, or ignorance. While endeavoring to persuade Vuestra Merced of his rise in society against all odds, Lázaro discloses data that hurt rather than help his cause, as if his discourse were mediated by another, and that is the case, if not "el caso." There is a social component to the literary devices. The *pícaro*'s success would be a defeat for the reigning hierarchies and for social determinism. The system can withstand the challenge of the outcast, as long as the dénouement puts him in his place. He can control the direction of his explanation, but only to a degree. The internal usurpation of authority—a magnificent reworking of autobiography and exemplarity—establishes a paradigm for the picaresque. Not only is there a discursive analogue of social norms, but the single voice of the narrator is doubled, or tripled. *Lazarillo de Tormes* combines an emerging realism and a new type of narration that makes the discourse—the narrative art and the narrative act—a fundamental element of the story. The move away from idealism incorporates a type of social realism and a concern for the composition of the text; in essence, the life story is complemented by a discourse with a story of its own. The correspondence between the plot events and Lázaro's organization of the material is irrefutable. Because his language is ironic, story and discourse are constantly altered, and neither is fully his. The social backdrop directs the plot and promotes the ironic rendering of the narration, but irony works, as well, to tease and to displace the centers of power.

Deviation also becomes a matrix of *Guzmán de Alfarache*. Guzmán's transformation depends on his life of delinquency (and worse), for his narration demonstrates the profundity of the offenses. Even though he may consider himself more sinned against than sinning, the record shows that he succumbs to temptation and self-pity. He strives to disavow his heritage and hopes to establish new roots in Italy, but meager triumphs lead to sound defeats and, on numerous occasions, to public humiliation. He is mistreated, beaten, entrapped, robbed, and ridiculed, and his spirit is crushed. His pessimism is understandable, but the incongruities remain. The digressions not only stray from the main plot but from the themes evoked by the events, and there seems to be, at best, only a small trace of remorse in the commentaries, despite their post-conversional status. Readers may sense that the digressions provide a sounding board for Mateo Alemán, whose most viable, least threatening forum may be the fictional text. There is another kind of deviation, probably inadvertent. The author puts the plot aside in order to vent his anger through Guzmán's particular oratory, in the form of double-voiced soliloquies. The reader may find Alemán to be pulling away from his creation and, conversely, to be using him as a mouthpiece. Guzmán is introspective, but he fails to profit from experience. He does not get better as he goes along. The same is true of his discourse. During the time that he writes his autobiography—after the conversion, in the period in which he reflects on past and present—his attitude does not become more exemplary, more compassionate, more sensitive, or wiser, but remains sardonic and disenchanted.

By appending the elements of the false continuation into the plot—into Guzmán's life—Alemán uses the protagonist as an agent of vengeance. He does not confine his critique of Martí to the commentaries, but writes his frustration into the text as a metafictional subplot. As he approaches the final stages of Guzmán's trajectory, Alemán removes his protagonist from center stage so that he can attend to personal business. The moral victory may be pyrrhic, in that the retribution distracts the author (and the reader) from Guzmán shortly before the supposed conversion. Alemán, then, has a special stake in Guzmán's narrative. Concocting a nightmarish heritage, he pushes his creation in all the wrong directions, and he allows Guzmán to stumble, to fall, to repeat his mistakes, to pursue impossible dreams. Failure is a shared responsibility: determined by Alemán, courted by Guzmán, and demanded by society. The author gives the narrator a discursive space in which to express his anger and to campaign for reader sympathy. The doubly digressive pitch of the commentaries may attest to the voice-over of Alemán, who, out of dissatisfaction with his lot, finds it hard to contain his own resentments. The apocryphal second part does not lend itself to the structure of *Guzmán de Alfarache* as the other false continuation does to *Don Quijote*. The allegory of the robbery in Book 2 of the 1604 *Guzmán* is an engrossing exercise in literary exorcism, but the success of Guzmán, in competition with Sayavedra, produces conflicting results. When Cervantes has Don Quijote hold the Avellaneda sequel in his hands and Don Álvaro Tarfe certify that the "real" Don Quijote is superior to the impostor, he expands the world/text and truth/fiction dichotomies, among others. Nothing is lost but the real Cervantes's peace of mind. Alemán wins the argument, but he sets Guzmán (and *Guzmán*) on an errant course. He seizes control of the struggle for identity, yet the narrative is not about Guzmán's strengths (if criminal ingenuity is a strength) but about his weaknesses. Settling the score becomes a distraction, an ironic digression, and an ironic display of authority.

Guzmán de Alfarache shares with Lázaro de Tormes, and with Pablos, a genealogy that makes him undesirable as a fellow citizen. Groomed in the margins, he cannot be trusted, and neither can his words. He is, at first, like Lázaro, guilty of incriminating himself. He becomes untrustworthy because his creator forces him to place himself and his family in ridicule. His "fallibility" as a narrator comes initially from Alemán's ventriloquism for satirical effect; he spouts insults at his lineage when society operates in a deterministic mode. His failures often seem more comic than pathetic, although the commentaries include strong shifts of tone as well as content. Guzmán's conversion falls prey to untrustworthiness and fallibility, in that the sincerity and the reporting seem deficient. When Alemán orients himself toward revenge, the narrative escapes both labels through the inconsistency of the narrative stance. The implied author who leads Guzmán into denouncing his bloodlines and producing laughs at his own expense switches direction in Part 2, where the motive (and motif) is a show of faith in his invention, through the identification and condemnation of the author of the false sequel, and the paradoxical defense of Guzmán's birthright. Like Alemán, Guzmán is angrier and more disillusioned by circumstances, for he, too, is the injured party in a theft. There is a mock-heroic air to Don Álvaro Tarfe's declaration of the legitimacy and the superiority of (Cervantes's and Cide Hamete Benengeli's) Don Quijote. Cervantes moves away from the satire, but his refashioning of the plot in Part 2 affects the position of the Arab historian more than that of the knight. As a figure of poetry and history, Don Quijote is subject to the variables of representation, as he himself recognizes.

In addition to animating Don Quijote and forcing him into action—after other characters have intruded upon his metatheatrical space—the Avellaneda sequel pushes Cervantes to bring the knight's (and the *hidalgo's*) life to an end. Reminiscent of Golden Age drama, the closing is ambiguous, a sign of conservatism or an ironic gesture toward conservatism to please the censors, an essential aspect of the ideology of the text or an addendum meant to contrast with the primary messages, in short, an author's strategy of revenge or a veritable *desengaño* replete with a Christian death. The ambiguity of the ending reiterates the vagueness of the first chapter and the relativity of truth and perspective that Cervantes stresses throughout the narrative. Improbability and lack of verisimilitude are not defects in *Don Quijote* but part of its emphasis on the mutability of the interpretive act, and on the distance between event and expression. Alterity makes Cide Hamete untrustworthy, while historicity makes him and all other narrators in *Don Quijote* fallible. Unreliable narration is a metonym for the impact and the variability of perception. The narrative scheme of *Don Quijote* validates the conceptual scheme, in which storytelling is as unsure a venture as life itself. The realistic approach in this case is disorder, and the chaotic, perplexing text is a reflection of the way of the world. There is more than one version of Don Quijote's story and of other stories in the novel. That is not only because narrators are untrustworthy and fallible—and many are—but because one's grasp of reality is always partial and potentially conflictive. The picaresque model contains a protagonist who changes over time and a voice that accommodates itself to the temporal shifts. There is a presupposition of truth as an option in the picaresque, and, certainly in general terms, a presupposition that, due to his background and motives, the narrator will be untruthful. Social and literary practice are always in the frame and are at the service of an implied author. *Guzmán de Alfarache* quickly breaks the mold, by wavering from its organizing principles. Dealing with Avellaneda, Cervantes remains "true" to his project as he seeks revenge.

Despite its brevity, *Lazarillo de Tormes* examines human psychology in depth. The construction of Lázaro's narrative becomes a form of characterization, but the personality is a composite of revelation, reading between the lines, and "reading into," or alternate construction of, the implied author. Alemán adds many more words and greater depth, but his voice is compromised by a poorly concealed duality, in which the author inserts himself as a type of co-protagonist. As the narrative develops and the writer faces an external challenge, the implied author of *Guzmán de Alfarache* comes close to being an explicit presence, a voice unto itself. This threatens to draw attention away from Guzmán's story and discourse, and to put Alemán, somewhat awkwardly, in the center of his picaresque tale. The case of the *Buscón* may seem to be parallel, but there are major differences. Quevedo determines Pablos's fate from the beginning, and he places the *pícaro* in harm's way from childhood. He inserts himself into the narrative unabashedly, as a baroque stylist, but, after the intense wordplay of the early chapters, the language sounds more feasibly as if it emanated from Pablos. Just as Cervantes seems to have begun with the idea of parodying the romances of chivalry in an exemplary novella and then realized the more comprehensive options, Quevedo may have envisioned a conceptist take on the picaresque, only to extend his plan in order to delve more profoundly into Pablos's mind, perhaps in spite of his wish for distance. His language identifies his presence without subtlety, but his recession of sorts contrasts with Alemán's ever more obvious presence in *Guzmán de Alfarache*. Lionel Abel refers to Hamlet as "one of the first characters to be free of his author's contrivances" (58). Pablos is another, and so, of course, is Don Quijote, although the freedom seems to come *despite* the author in the first case and with his approval in the second.

The picaresque brings narrative to the lower classes, to the poverty and hardships of the underprivileged. Its realism involves a break from higher orders, notable personages, and the conventions of idealism and autobiography. Quevedo's exaggeration of the lower depths could be said to anticipate naturalism, although the starkness of the depiction acquires a uniquely baroque cast when presented in conjunction with deliberate verbal excesses. As with *Don Quijote*, the blend of realism and literary self-referentiality points the picaresque in two directions, which is also a foreshadowing of things to come. In a range of permutations, realism and metafiction combine resources, and recourses, in sixteenth- and seventeenth-century Spanish picaresque texts and in *Don Quijote*. These narratives establish the directions and paradigms of narrative realism, which will allot a space, however minimal, for conveying a sense of process and an awareness of the narrator's mediating role. The picaresque decenters nobility of blood and conduct while examining society from the margins. The grittiness of the subject matter is offset by the consciousness of the creative act. Rhetoric and artistry engage with the crudeness and ostracism of the outsider's life. The defiance of precedents can be seen on all levels, from the protagonist's transgressions to the writer's retreat from idealism and deflation of custom. *Don Quijote* follows the lead of the picaresque, especially with regard to questions of perspective, truth, and composition. Cervantes's strokes are, arguably, even broader, in the sense that he brings tradition and rivalry more prominently into the picture, expands the treatment of poetry's ties with history, and divides the construction of the narrative among a large group of figures. From the start, literary realism recognizes its commitment to life and to art.

In the century between the publication of *La lozana andaluza* and *La vida del buscón*, narrative takes a new shape. There is a move away from idealism, but the novel in progress represents the external world of social institutions, politics, and history, along with the internal world of artistic production. The narrator is a source of authority and a means by which authority is called into question, negotiated, mocked, revoked, and compartmentalized. The single voice and single perspective of the picaresque are illusions, and reliability becomes a symbol of the complexity of perception. Not only is the *pícaro* the narrator and protagonist, but time separates the child and the adult, thus giving a diachronic force to the narrative. Fictional autobiography introduces a second writer into the frame, along with an ironic recasting of discourse and, by extension, ideology. Story and storytelling work reciprocally; each is a function of the other, and the ambiguities of the text capture and amplify the ambiguities of existence. The picaresque deals with real-world experience as recreated by the imagination and by the recourses of art, and, in this context, it follows that the literary artifact would reflect both images of reality and the imprint of the artist. Cervantes takes this model to even higher levels. He is concerned with history, notably with the mediating ground between history and poetry, and with historiography as it relates to the dialectics of observation and expression. He brings these preoccupations to bear on the author's task, which becomes a fundamental aspect of the allegories of reading and writing in *Don Quijote*. Inspired by the picaresque to work beyond (and below) idealism, Cervantes places a supremely idealistic protagonist in the real world, while providing the knight with the trappings of chivalry and the narrative with a consciousness of the creative process. The crossing of realism and metafiction, present as the novel comes into being, will remain at the heart of things.

The Metafictional Imperative: Realism and the Case of *El amigo Manso*

"...juro y perjuro que no existo..."

IN *REALIST VISION*, PETER Brooks offers a general description of realism as "a kind of literature and art committed to a form of play that uses carefully wrought and detailed toys, ones that attempt as much as possible to reproduce the look and feel of the real thing. And this kind of fiction becomes in the course of the nineteenth century the standard mode of the novels we continue to think of as great, as classics" (3, 5). He notes that "even today we tend to think of it as the norm from which other modes—magical realism, science fiction, fantasy, metafiction—are variants or deviants" (5). When one considers sixteenth- and seventeenth-century Spanish narratives as early forms (or, for some, precedents) of realism, it becomes apparent that what Brooks labels as deviation is, to an extent at least, built into the design. The picaresque breaks from the idealism of sentimental, pastoral, and chivalric romance with a discourse that self-consciously treats the process of creating a narrative, and that calls on the reader to reflect on questions of reliability. *Don Quijote* takes on the books of chivalry (and other genres) even more aggressively. Cervantes's venture into realism is, from its inception, mixed with metafiction, thereby diverging, paradoxically, from the model of realism as that model is being established. A similar pattern emerges centuries later, but with radical differences in timing and effect. Benito Pérez Galdós's *El amigo Manso* (1882) belongs to what might be called the beginning of a transitional period between realism and modernism. The novel, which is somewhat unique within the author's canon, calls to mind

107

the Cervantine crossing of art and life.

The novels of Galdós hardly could be more impressive in range or depth. These include the early thesis novels, multivolume series of historical novels, and the so-called "contemporary" novels, which cover realism, naturalism, and more. In the various narrative registers, Galdós blends history and poetry in admirable permutations. He combines political history with social custom, and with the conflictive and rapidly changing ideologies of the nineteenth and early twentieth centuries.[1] One of the stable elements of Galdós's novels, most strikingly the *novelas contemporáneas*, is the author's relationship with his audience. For him, realism seems to mean not only a representation of society, and of social practice, but also a reaching out to—and the pursuit of a comfort level with—the reading public. Some writers in the realist tradition appear to want to hide from, or to hide behind, the inevitable conventions that separate literature from pure observation, from life. Galdós acknowledges that life provides the raw material, but that one of his tasks as a writer is to find a form of expression in which to convey a given story within a vivid social panorama and with a determined perspective. Both story and discourse are crucial, and equally important. Needless to say, Galdós is an exceptionally perceptive reader of the big picture and of the minutiae of existence. He has a strong sense of history and of what Miguel de Unamuno terms *intrahistoria*, a type of life-force beyond history, a quotidian reality that is arguably more penetrating and more durable than the catastrophic events that historiography accentuates. Unamuno's concern with the essence of the people, *el pueblo*, is found in Galdós as he describes and engages society and its dramatis personae, the national character and characters of Spain. No less significant than panoramas and plots is the creation of narrative voices, through dialogue and through narrators that have familiarity with the subject matter, style, allure, wit, and, quite regularly, a bent toward irony.[2]

---

[1] Gustavo Correa cites as a fundamental aspect of Galdós's narrative discourse "el de la transmutación de la realidad en material estético. Si la novela es reproducción, no por eso deja de ser también imagen, lo cual significa reconstrucción simbólica de la realidad. Además, tal manera de reproducción, o más bien, de simbolización, debe ser hecha en forma bella, y, en cuanto tal, dar lugar a la fruición del sentimiento estético" (*Realidad* 20).

[2] William H. Shoemaker, who notes idealist tendencies in *El amigo Manso*,

Galdós consistently merges omniscience with the point of view of a witness. The narrator comes across as an onlooker or secondary character, but the scenario does not necessarily contain the space for another character. The narrator fades into the background, but addresses the foreground, at times almost imperceptibly and at other times rather conspicuously. *Tristana* (1892), for example, depicts a disturbing and incongruous love story, and a sharp glimpse of social hierarchies, the education of women, and shifts in values at the end of the century. Galdós concentrates on the present, but he counts on one of the most prominent myths of Spanish literary history, that of Don Juan Tenorio, to frame his characterization of Don Lope Garrido, a protagonist (or antagonist) of *Tristana*. Age is catching up with the seducer of women, but he manages one final conquest. The narrator is absent from the story, but to a degree he makes the discourse a story in itself. The tired Don Juan is symbolic on a number of levels, a demystification of the glories of the past and a reminder that titles of nobility have difficulty competing with the marketplace and the technologies of a society more motivated by money than by blood. The class system in flux has an impact on the lives and fortunes of women, in part because the industrial revolution and the rise of the middle class point to a lack of change in the academic and career opportunities for this often silent majority. Through his narrator, Galdós addresses the transgressions and economic hard times of Don Lope and the precarious situation of the orphaned Tristana. In the first case, he creates a complex structure of irony to expose and critique, with exquisite subtlety, the decrepit Don Juan. In the second, he gives Tristana a voice, notably in letters that she writes to Horacio, the man whom she trusts to help her flee from convention, but who shows himself to be surprisingly conventional. Her progressive stance and her solitude serve the ideological base of the novel, as symbolism turns in on itself.

The language of *Tristana* is highly stylized. Galdós focuses on social reality, but he draws the reader's attention to the evocation of Don Juan (and thus of the literary intertext) and to a certain linguistic heaviness reminiscent of the baroque. The narrator does not merely reveal facts, but takes pride in deploying a figurative idiom that is allusive, eloquent, and

---

uses the term "ironical realism" in his analysis of the novel, which he sees as often humorous and sometimes sharply satirical (2: 177).

clever. The novel would seem to demand identification and deciphering of the irony. Don Lope is outmoded, the vestige of an earlier world view that is, in turn, the vestige of its predecessors. His feelings of pride and entitlement not only presuppose ideals of other eras, but they are unmatched, or unsubstantiated, by his actions; his is a limited conscience, egotistically directed inward. Don Lope is out of touch with the ways in which society is redefining itself, but he cannot ignore the changes, especially as they affect him financially. The young and inexperienced Tristana seems at first an unlikely sign of disjunction, but she anticipates a new society that (ironically) goes beyond the scope of the novel. In *Tristana*, Galdós both emulates and diverges from the thesis novels by repackaging his messages. His style here is indirect and his literary artifact is more ornately crafted than the works of the first period, and the thematic center can be vague and mutable. Galdós's choice of ambivalence demonstrates greater sophistication on the part of the artist and greater faith in the reader to distinguish the underlying meaning of the text. *Tristana* becomes a study in social history, economics, gender politics, and discourse. Point of view is intricately imparted and deceptive, because the narrator would cast Don Lope in a more favorable light than the circumstances warrant. It is not hard to differentiate the old from the new, or the victim from the victimizer, but the discourse appears initially to associate Don Lope with tradition in a positive way. The reversal comes, and in all likelihood quickly, when the reader grasps the ironic scheme of things. Galdós trusts his readers by trusting in himself as an encoder of irony.

Ambiguity, irony, and self-conscious artistry separate Galdós's "contemporary novels" from the thesis novels. The author's personality is integrated into the narrative discourse in a manner that unites history (the past and a recorded present) and poetry. Although the method of intervention of the narrators may vary substantially, they are marked by an air of familiarity, emanating from a voice that may be calming, authoritative, likeable, satirical, or a combination of these qualities. Despite a move toward naturalism, there is no illusion of scientific objectivity in the narration of events or in the characterization. The narrator is a mediating presence, a signifying practice, and, as such, a means of access to form and ideology. In *Gender and Nation in the Spanish Modernist Novel*, Roberta Johnson notes that "[b]y the time Don Juan arrives at the modernist turn of the century, he comes laden with a confusing variety of national meanings. Don Juan... lent himself to a wide array of political and philosophical ideals; for some he continued to serve as an emblem of national energy, whereas for others he was a decadent degenerate who reflected Spain's contemporary diminished state" (111). Although *Tristana* does not fit within Johnson's purview, the commentary captures the spirit of the novel, which vacillates between a kind of begrudging affection—and even a dose of nostalgia—for the aging roué and a condemnation of his attitude and an implicit cult of degeneracy. For me, the most brilliant touch of *Tristana* is the wearing down of the title figure, by Don Lope, society, and nature. Her illness and the amputation of her leg make her undesirable, and Don Lope is able to rescue her through a marriage that ostensibly can make them both respectable. Galdós returns to the "triumph-of-evil" motif of the thesis novels, but refinement and nuanced discourse attest to the author's growing maturity and dependence on the reader. The analysis of the faded aristocracy and of the dearth of options for women operates on a multifaceted creative level, which allows Galdós to demystify the past, social and cultural, as he examines the present.

If *Tristana* is inflected by Don Juan, it is Don Quijote against whom *El amigo Manso* is cast. Johnson emphasizes the knight's idealization of women: "His experiences with women ranged from the controlling, manipulative housekeeper and niece to the protofeminist and vocally independent Marcela. His tactic in the face of such baffling female diversity was to transform the women he met in his travels into characters from chivalric or pastoral romances through sheer force of his powerful imagination" (70). She adds that "Don Quixote's idealism often surfaces in the male-authored narratives of the modernist era as a refuge from modern social change" (70). There is no question that some aspects of Máximo Manso derive from Don Quijote, updated and placed in a setting that has nothing to do with the original. Manso is a dreamer, a reader, an idealist. He views life—and justifies his conduct—through the lens of philosophy. Events transpire around him, and he participates in those events, but he is detached from the pragmatic drives that habitually rule those with whom he is aligned. The ties with *Don Quijote* supersede idealism, however. *El amigo Manso* has much in common with Galdós's other novels of the period, but the first-person narration lends itself to a particular scrutiny from the angle of reliability. This factor, along with the self-fashioning of the narrator/protagonist, may have ironic consequences, in the manner of the picaresque. Galdós produces and stands aloof from his protagonist and the narrative voice that portrays and delicately betrays Máximo Manso. The comprehensive structure of *El amigo Manso*—the fusion of characterization, approaches to reality, metafiction, and discourse—suggests that Galdós seeks a variation on Cervantine themes.

Every novelistic endeavor is a challenge, a dialectical struggle between tradition and innovation, a search for uniqueness within a recognized set of conventions. A challenge that Galdós faces in the composition of *El amigo Manso* is the need to adapt the poetics of realism to his delineation of a quixotic narrator/protagonist. He sets a subdued love story, and a clash between politics and philosophy, in his own time and place, but he superimposes discursive strategies that simultaneously anticipate modernism and summon the early modern texts of Cervantes and the writers of the picaresque. *El amigo Manso* is an experimental narrative, notably with regard to perspective. The reader enters the main character's mind, but with an awareness of a group of filters that pass through and reorient the discourse. As in *Tristana*, and as in the picaresque and *Don Quijote*, the discourse becomes a story in itself, and an analogue of the principal theses of the novel. The myth of Don Juan is, of course, antithetical to that of Don Quijote. Male vigor and excellence in the sport of seduction notwithstanding (and not necessarily to his credit), Don Juan has few redeeming qualities. He can be damned for his sins and for his failure to repent, as in *El burlador de Sevilla*, or saved by love, as in *Don Juan Tenorio*, but he is a scourge to social protocol. Women suffer cruel punishment at his hands. Don Lope Garrido depends on his position of authority as guardian of Tristana, together with her youth and innocence, to entice, overpower, and, in society's eyes, corrupt her. It is not the beginning or the end of her story, but the middle section, that contains the ideological center, the point at which Tristana accepts her status and dares to dream of social change, with a strong and sensitive man by her side. The men whom she trusts as protector and savior let her down, but her disillusionment is eloquent; her sentiments and her voice remain on the record. The sacrament of matrimony at the conclusion of *Tristana* becomes a marker of disharmony. Discursive irony corresponds to the irony of the dénouement.

It may be Máximo Manso's blind idealism that best connects him to Don Quijote. Manso is a reader, but he is not mad or reckless, nor does he wish to push an alternate reality on others. He is sedate and introspective, a scholar and a thinker. His society is blatantly politicized, brimming over with institutions and on the brink of transformation. There is a complacency to Manso's existence until a tutee and his brother's family, who arrive from Cuba, disrupt his routine, and love comes slowly but surely into his life. As with picaresque and other first-person fictional narratives, character development in *El amigo Manso* stems from internal characterization and selection, thereby setting up the possibility, or probability, of an ironic relation between the narrator and the author. Manso's self-portrait and its movement over time will be of special interest, as will the play of dichotomies. During the course of the narrative, the contemplative man enters the realm of men of action, the confirmed bachelor into the realm of amorous attachments, and the teacher into life's classroom. Manso typically has stood in the margins of politics, but now he must take steps forward, against his instincts and inclinations. He epitomizes a category of alterity that might be called the outsider-from-within, not so much an outcast as a singular and isolated soul, and, through the narrator, Galdós can juxtapose this alienation with other forms of alterity, including the family members (and their staff) from Cuba, and those who must yield to social hierarchies and denied opportunities. Critique and judgment will come from Manso himself and from the dialogue. Galdós's decision to use a first-person narrator influences the scope, and the frame, of *El amigo Manso*. The perspective of this brand of social realism is partial, shaded, even if the intentions are honorable. The technique is clearly valid, yet there is a datum which readers of realism, and Galdós's novels, may not expect: Manso initiates his narrative by proclaiming that he does not exist. He is a figure "sin carne ni hueso" (143).[3] The statement is not in a preface, but in the first words of the first chapter.

The brief opening chapter veers dramatically from the norms of realism. Máximo Manso is adamant about defending his nonentity. He is a falsification born of one of those slackers who have existed from time immemorial and who adopt the title of artist: "Quimera soy, sueño de sueño y sombra de sombra, sospecha de una posibilidad" (144). Manso

---

[3] All references to *El amigo Manso* will refer to the edition by Francisco Caudet, and page numbers will be indicated in parentheses.

speaks of a self-contained world where something on the order of life goes on until the character is summoned forth by "a friend" — the author of some thirty tomes — who asks for his collaboration. Through a devilish enchantment, "poco después salí de una llamarada roja, convertido en carne mortal. El dolor me dijo que yo era un hombre" (146). Galdós begins in the metafictional domain, with a character who, though not human, has a modicum of autonomy. Approached by the author, Manso agrees to participate in the venture; that is, he agrees, paradoxically, to make himself approximate humanity, to subject himself to pain, and to collaborate in the "detenido crimen novelesco sobre el gran asunto de la educación" (145). By having Manso narrate the story in the first-person, Galdós is giving him cognizance of the deep structure of the narrative. With this responsibility comes a measure of authority that can be sustained or lost as the narration progresses. The dehumanizing of Manso casts an aura of unreality on the proceedings. What might have been an issue of point of view becomes a questioning of how art serves reality. It is as if Galdós were threatening to compromise the project, and its realistic potential, from the outset. Manso's comments playfully divert the reader's attention to the construction of the narrative and to the role of the author. Why would Galdós the realist have chosen to frame the novel in metafiction and to give his narrator/protagonist an existence that defies the laws of logic?

Máximo Manso is thirty-five years old when the narration begins. Having been attracted to "speculative labors" since childhood, he has studied philosophy assiduously, but he looks for practical application of the theories that engage him and for the means to share his knowledge with the students in his charge. He describes himself as sturdy, modest, and unaffected, wearer of a stovepipe hat and a cape, a devotee of the chickpea. A native of Asturias, he grew up as the son of the town druggist. When he was fifteen years old, his father died. His brother José María, seven years older, left for Havana in search of a pot of gold, and his mother moved with Máximo to Madrid, where he was absorbed in his training and in giving private classes. Manso praises his mother for her total dedication to him. He attributes to her his rigid principles, his work habits, and his sobriety. Thanks to her thrift, they were able to live "en decorosa indigencia" (157), with no distractions from the outside world on his academic duties. The mother had died immediately after her son was awarded a chair, as if her maternal duties had been fulfilled.

Manso had been dependent on her, and he says that it took some time for him to adjust to life on his own. He lived in a series of boarding houses, finally settling into a home of his own, where he is served by a faithful housekeeper. He is able to read, to prepare lessons, and to write essays for publication in periodicals within an agreeable monotony that is afforded professional academics. Little occurs to deprive him of the peace to reflect and to further his mental divagations.

There is a moment in *La vida del buscón* in which Pablos is faced with resigning himself to his inferior status, and to work as a servant, or to rebel by fighting by hook or crook to find a position in society. He chooses to become a delinquent and a con artist rather than a nonentity, and to break rules rather than to fall into oblivion. He may have a choice in the matter, but Quevedo does not. The narrative can continue only if Pablos becomes an insurgent in a class warfare that may be more about self-promotion than social ethics. Novels cannot stand still. They advance through a series of turning points. Cervantes cannot have Alonso Quijano quietly reading in his study and minding his own business. Galdós cannot have Máximo Manso spend his remaining years contentedly living on his own and giving classes to receptive students. His life must be shaken up. In this case, he does not go in search of change, but change gradually comes to him. Galdós lays out the threads of the story and then, slowly and expertly, begins to weave them together. The introduction of Doña Javiera will lead to Manso's tutelage of her son Manuel, the introduction of Doña Cándida will lead to Manso's attraction to her niece Irene, and the exposition of his early life will lead to the return of José María and his family from Cuba. The novel is richly textured, and its focus is not only on the action but on the glimpses of society and human nature in every episode. Galdós explores, and interrelates, education, class consciousness, and love in its multiple manifestations, as part of a character study of a kindly, meditative, and insulated man who becomes awakened—rudely, on occasion—to the world around him. Manso remarks at the end of the second chapter that he has had to become accustomed to the noises of the busy marketplace that can be heard from his window. The detail signals that he will not be able to block off human contact beyond the classroom, that the sounds and the emotions of life will intrude upon his schedule. Otherwise, there would be no story.

In the first paragraph of chapter 3, Manso advises readers "que por nada del mundo pasen por alto este capítulo" (158), not because of

possible intrigue with a female neighbor, but because this will be a link
to what follows. Doña Javiera is a well-to-do widow, the owner of a
butcher shop, down-to-earth, direct, and respectful of the intellectual
leanings and saintly habits of her friend. She is concerned about her son,
a twenty-year-old playboy in the making, with an aversion to schooling.
She asks Manso to become Manolo's teacher and guide, and he agrees.
On meeting the handsome and charming Manuel Peña, Manso takes on
the task with zeal: "Mi complacencia era igual a la del escultor que recibe
un perfecto trozo de mármol más fino para labrar una estatua. Desde el
primer día conocí que inspiraba a mi discípulo no sólo respeto sino
simpatía; feliz circunstancia, pues no es verdadero maestro el que no se
hace querer de sus alumnos" (167). Manso starts his charge with classic
Spanish poets and contemporary poets. Manolo proves to be a gifted
student, articulate but not good at writing. He is especially drawn to *Don
Quijote*: "Al comenzar nuestras conferencias me confesó ingenuamente
que el *Quijote* le aburría; pero cuando dimos en él, después de bien
estudiados los poetas, hallaba tal encanto en su lectura, que algunas veces
le corrían lágrimas de tanto reír; otras se compadecía del héroe con tanta
vehemencia, que casi lloraba de pena y lástima. Decíame que... le venían
ideas de imitarle, saliendo por ahí con un plato en la cabeza" (168). It is
worth noting that Manolo's reading of *Don Quijote* joins the ludicrous
with the serious, and that Manso's opinion of the young man grows by
virtue of his response to the novel: "Era que, por privilegio de su noble
alma, había penetrado el profundo sentido del libro en que con más
perfección están expresadas las grandezas y las debilidades del corazón
humano" (168-69). The association with Manolo will put into motion a
chain of events that will bring out the quixotic nature of Máximo Manso
and of *El amigo Manso*.

Next to the exuberant but plebeian Doña Javiera stands Doña
Cándida de García Grande, a widow of another stripe altogether. Doña
Cándida is an inveterate spendthrift, used to having money but now in
desperate straits. Her pocketbook does not tally with her extravagant
tastes, but she is proud, shameless, and aggressive in her quest for funds.
Because she was a friend of Manso's mother, she appears frequently for
loans, and he grudgingly accedes, mentally cursing her and himself. At
one point, Doña Cándida begins to send her niece Irene, aged twelve
when she first appears in the narrative, with notes to request money and
with promises of prompt paybacks that never materialize. Unlike her aunt

(by marriage), Irene produces in Manso the highest regard, and he refers to "[l]a compasión que esta criatura me inspiraba" (181). He sees her as sweet, precocious, and serious about her studies, and he is concerned that she complete her education. She obviously has been neglected by her aunt, and Manso buys her boots and books. Irene's visits become more intermittent, due in part to her revulsion at the chore of begging for money. Manso is pleased to learn that she has taken the initiative to enroll in the Escuela Normal de Maestras, where she has excelled. At the end of chapter 6, Manso informs the reader that he has brought his story up to about 1877, the year in which he made the move to his current residence, and he adds that it was at this time that he met Doña Javiera and took over the education of Manolo. He alludes to having sacrificed chronological order for logical order, as is his wont: "El tiempo como reloj que es, tiene sus arbitrariedades; la lógica, por no tenerlas, es la llave del saber y el relojero del tiempo" (184). Galdós, through his narrator, sets up what will become a love triangle, in the style of Leandro Fernando de Moratín's *El sí de las niñas* and other versions of "el viejo y la niña." As in all the novels of Galdós, the details and the shadings of characterization are as decisive as the action itself.

Manso stresses Manolo's skills as an orator, but regrets his pupil's disdain for philosophy. He wonders if Manolo will use his talents wisely or if he will become a showy but empty speaker, but there is no doubt that the young man has a personal magnetism. Doña Javiera is immensely grateful for the guidance that Manso has given her son. Manso comments that Manolo, now twenty-three, has taken to assuming the mannerisms and dressing in the style of those in bullfighting circles, and he has begun to court the daughter of an impresario of the *corrida*. Doña Javiera is not upset, because the family is wealthy and thereby well regarded in society. Manso digresses a bit on the fact that social democracy has rooted itself into the national sensibility and that humble origins are no longer an obstacle to success or respectability. Emulating the United States of America, Spain "va siendo un país escéptico y utilitario, donde el espíritu fundente y nivelador domina sobre todo"; history (meaning tradition) cedes to "[l]as improvisaciones de fortuna y posición.… [L]a libertad de pensamiento toma un vuelo extraordinario, y las energías fatales de la época, riqueza y talento, extienden su inmenso imperio" (189). Nonetheless, he submits, remnants of the old order still may hinder the up-and-coming, despite their discretion and noble disposition. That is why his classmates at the university call Manuel Peña "el hijo de la carnicera." In these musings, Manso's argument seems rather muddled, as if he resented social leveling yet valued sound moral fiber above all. He appears to think less of Doña Javiera for sanctioning the courtship because she is won over by the social prestige and financial clout of the nouveaux riches, but he hardly condones the fact that Manolo's colleagues would hold him in less esteem because of the family business. Society is in transition, and change seems to fascinate and bewilder him, because he is caught between utopian notions and a past that he has been taught to venerate. Galdós permits him to share his thoughts in a free-flowing, and ironically dialogic, manner.

Manolo's entry into society takes him away from his protector. Manso, his duties having come to a close and finding himself without a constant companion, speaks of his loneliness. He places the date as the spring of 1880. Doña Javiera plans to sell her business and to "legitimize" her relationship with Ponce, an over-the-hill baritone of the musical theater with whom she has kept company. Doña Cándida comes more often to Manso's house, as pompous and mendacious as ever. Galdós places them in a scene together in order to accentuate their distinct traits. At this moment, Irene reenters the story. She is nineteen years old, and Manso sees her by chance as he passes by the market, "su estatura airosa, su vestido humilde, pero aseadísimo, revelando en todo la virtud del arreglo, que, sin duda, no le había enseñado su tía. Claramente se mostraba en ella el noble tipo de pobreza llevada con valentía y hasta con cariño" (193). The stage has been set for the love story that will transpire over the coming years. Manso indicates a break and a new direction with the title and first sentence of chapter 8, "¡Ay mísero de mí! ¡Ay infelice!," an echo of Segismundo's first words in *La vida es sueño*.[4] The tragic cry is a reaction to a turn in his life, his fall from a "paradise of tranquility," from "placeres, descansos y tareas a discreta medida" into turmoil and disorder (193-94). The culprit is José María, who has brought his family to Madrid after having spent twenty years in Cuba. The commotion will disturb Máximo Manso's agenda and will push the narrative plan in new directions. The plotlines will cross, as the love story expands and

---

[4] See the Caudet edition of *El amigo Manso* 193n60. Caudet alludes to Gustavo Correa's study of the influence of Calderón on Galdós.

intensifies.

The hyperbolic rhetoric that announces the arrival of José María's family is telling. This is not an earth-shattering event by most standards, but for the structured lifestyle of Máximo Manso it is catastrophic. Their move and settling into a home force him to relate to more than his students and a handful of intimates; it forces him into the world. José María brings his wife Manuela, her mother Doña Jesusa, a sister, three young children, and two servants. Their domestic customs are torture for Máximo, who cannot abide chaos. He describes a scene in which the adults are gathered, his brother and the women smoking, with talk of politics, "hasta que llegada la hora de la abolición de mi esclavitud, me despedía y me retiraba, enojado de tan miserable vida y suspirando por mi perdida libertad. Volvía mis tristes ojos a la Historia, y no le perdonaba, no, a Cristóbal Colón que hubiera descubierto el Nuevo Mundo" (200). José María has come to Spain with political pretensions. He has concrete ideas and programs to implement. Máximo cautions him against the confusion of a hypothetical nation with insubstantial reality. Only deep thinking and rigorous observation can save the State: "Mostréme indiferente en las formas de gobierno, y añadí que la política era y sería siempre para mí un cuerpo de doctrina, un sabio y metódico conjunto de principios científicos y de reglas de arte, un organismo, en fin, y que por tanto quedaban excluidos de mi sistema las contingencias personales, los subjetivismos perniciosos, los modos escurridizos, las corruptelas de hecho y de lenguaje, las habilidades y agudezas que constituyen entre nosotros todo el arte de gobernar" (202). José María, who himself finds the British manner of doing politics stimulating, sees his brother as an impractical, "metaphysical" dreamer, amusing but not to be taken seriously despite his destructive tendencies, given that they are only in his mind. Meanwhile, adjustment has not been easy, and things are out of control in the household. José María urges Máximo to help find a governess. The choice is Irene. She is installed in the new position, and this brings Doña Cándida into the family circle, where she is received enthusiastically by the women.

José María is eager to acquire celebrity status and thus anxious to surround himself with important people. As would follow, he becomes host to noteworthy figures and to hangers-on, which gives Máximo an excuse to satirize the guests of his brother's salon. José María takes a special liking to Manuel Peña, "mi amado discípulo,... mi hijo espiritual,... que fue bien recibido, no obstante su humilde procedencia" (208). Informally supervising the work of Irene as schoolmistress, Máximo is delighted to be in the company of such a young lady, "cuya belleza, talento y seriedad me agradaban en extremo" (215). As he discusses the start of Manuel's political career, Manso offers (notably in chapters 13 and 14) descriptions of Irene. Aware of her natural beauty and kindness, Máximo observes that "la imaginación tenía en ella lugar secundario. Su claro juicio sabía descartar las cosas triviales y de relumbrón, y no se pagaba de fantasmagorías como la mayor parte de las hembras" (216). Galdós is willing to let his narrator make judgments, on people and situations, that may become ironic. Máximo believes that he knows Irene (and, by implication, women) well, and his faith in his power of discernment may be unfounded. One can sense the author's understated mingling of elements, as the principals in the love story are now present under one roof. The staid and dispassionate protagonist may not be in full command of his emotions. The nearness of Irene has put him "como fuera de mí y haciéndome como diferente a mí mismo, en términos que noté un brioso movimiento en mi voluntad... [e] impulsos semejantes a los que en otro orden resultan de la plétora sanguínea" (217).

Máximo applauds the sensible and moderate views of Irene, who favors neither the integration of women into the professional world (the province of men) nor the abject ignorance in which the majority of Spanish women live. He deems her outlook on politics, religion, and social conditions—and even on bullfighting, the theater, and Doña Cándida—to be impeccably accurate, that is, in accord with his own. Irene appears to be a soulmate, but she is capable of making him feel discomfort: "La misma belleza y gracia de Irene, lejos de espolearme, ponía como un sello en mi boca, y en todo mi espíritu no sé qué misteriosas ligaduras" (221). As if to confirm that Máximo is tongue-tied, the reader can notice that the word *love*, much less the word *desire*, is never enunciated. The meditative soul finds itself in an unfamiliar place, and, perhaps not coincidentally, much of chapter 14 takes place in the theater. Events and sentiments conspire to create a disequilibrium in the heart and mind of Máximo Manso, the stable man par excellence. He adores Irene, cherishes her prudence, and yet elaborates her physical flaws and lapses in taste, while questioning the concept of an aesthetic ideal. One evening he discovers her reading late into the night and guesses that she may be engrossed in one of his essays, when it turns out that she is pouring over letters from Manuel. He comes to relish being in his brother's home (six minutes and 560 steps from his own), noting that the world conditions us, and not vice versa. He is joyfully connected to her, as if their two natures had collided. In the meantime, Manuel Peña has broken off from his girlfriend and presumably is playing the field. He and Máximo discuss feminine psychology, with the teacher advocating patience and optimism. In a conversation at a pastry shop in the wee hours of the morning, they stare at two Flamenco dancers whom Manso compares to the women perched outside the inn where Don Quijote is armed a knight.

Manuel confides in his mentor that he is restless and bored, that he is desperate for action; he is reading the works of Machiavelli, which he finds astonishing. Máximo cautions him to study general principles, and Manuel replies that philosophy nauseates him, that metaphysics is impenetrable, and that he prefers the concrete to the abstract. Manso says that he needs to illuminate his charge, but not at this precise moment. Manuel confesses that his current mood is such that every response is intense, that dislike becomes hatred, and that the person he most despises is José María. Exasperated by Máximo's attempts to defend his brother, he cries out, "Usted no vive en el mundo, maestro" (259). Máximo has taught Manuel how to think, and how to think for himself. The younger man will not be content to philosophize. He wants to be involved in the business of society, but he has learned idealism, and the pretense and falseness of José María repel him. As in other episodes in the narrative, the scene at the *buñolería* plays off of previous scenes and foreshadows what is to come, in this instance the political speeches of teacher and student, and, more immediately, a growing disenchantment on the protagonist's part with respect to his brother. Máximo begins chapter 21 with a tongue-in-cheek paean to the chickpea, which he misses from his diet, due to the exquisite dinners at José María's house. He fears that the admission will make him appear to be common, "pero pongo mi deber de historiador por delante de todo y así se apreciará por esta franqueza la sinceridad de las demás partes de mi narración" (261). The tone is light, but the narrator makes an effort to assure his reliability as a "historian." He then returns to the family conflict. Evidence supports his suspicion that José María, in addition to having been tainted by his latest associations, is cheating on his wife, and in a brazen fashion. Worst of all, Manuela believes that he is pursuing Irene, who, although above reproach, has now asked to be relieved of her duties. The scorned wife is willing to forgive her errant husband if he reforms. The narrator states that "yo, Máximo Manso, el hombre recto, el hombre sin tacha, el pensamiento de la familia, el filósofo, el sabio era llamado a arreglarlo todo, haciendo ver a José la fealdad y atroces consecuencias de su conducta inicua" (264-65).

Maintaining the reflexive tenor, Máximo speaks of the events before him, and the reader, as the *protasis*, or exposition, of a drama that is unfolding. He worries about the well-being of Manuela and Irene, and wonders if Doña Cándida is involved in some way. Although he realizes that his fear is not rational, his confidence in Irene is slightly weakened, because he perceives that something is upsetting her. She senses his uneasiness and, berating his inquisitorial line of attack, she refuses to consult with him about the problem. His reaction is paradoxical: "Su resentimiento me pareció bellísimo, y diome tanto placer, que no pude ocultarle cuánto me agradaba aquel noble tesón suyo" (269). He pledges his earnest friendship, and they declare a truce, but she is not ready to reveal any secrets. He spends the night thinking about her, asserting that the less perfect Irene seems in his eyes—the less she conforms to the ideals of womanhood—the more he loves her. When he returns to his brother's house the following day, a startling piece of news awaits him. Manuel Peña and the Marqués de Casa-Bojío had exchanged words, and the matter had been settled by a duel. Manuela gives Máximo the news that Manuel has killed the Marqués, but it turns out that the wounded man, grazed by the sword, spilled only a few drops of blood. The episode is ironically symbolic and proleptic.

Máximo consents to deliver a speech at a prestigious charity event. He chooses the topic of Christian charity and approaches the enterprise with gusto. His most pressing thoughts, however, are on Irene, and he vows to be more aggressive in his suit: "... me cansaba del papel de observador que yo mismo me había impuesto" (278). Philosophy has governed his life, and now it is time to let actions speak louder than words: "¡Ay de aquel que en esto de mujeres imite al botánico que estudia una flor! ¡Necio!" (278). It seems that Doña Cándida has come into some money—a fact that strikes Máximo as odd—and she is moving to another flat. Seeking Irene near the new residence, he runs into Manuel Peña. He reports that the next day he followed Irene onto the street, where she came to a doorway that opened to reveal his brother, and then he informs the reader that this had been a dream. Wedged among thoughts, dreams, and uncertain realities, Máximo must deliver his oration in a large auditorium with a capacity crowd. The speech, which his brother describes, not favorably, as "truly philosophical," produces polite encomiums and little excitement. The speaker who captivates the audience is Manuel Peña. Máximo says that he rarely has witnessed a more brilliant display of eloquence, and the public evidently agrees. Such is the outpouring of affection, that Máximo is unable to catch up with his pupil in order to congratulate him. His night is filled with anguish and insomnia. The next day he teaches half-heartedly and rushes to his brother's house, to discover that José María is locked in his study with Doña Cándida. When she appears, she advises Manuela that she will have to take her niece back to her new place. Irene will only tell Máximo, somewhat coyly, that she has plans. José María departs with her in his carriage, to the consternation of his wife, who says that she has been misled, calling Irene a hypocrite. This wounds Máximo to the core. José María is clearly up to no good, but his specific meanderings remain a mystery. Máximo does know that his brother, whose political success seems guaranteed, is not to be trusted.

Máximo Manso—he of the life of contemplation and tranquility—enters the world of domestic and sentimental folly. He receives a letter from Irene entreating him to see her immediately, just as Manuela begs him to find her a wet nurse, as hers has walked out. "¡Ay!" he observes, "la familia confiaba principalmente en mí, en mi rara bondad y en mi corazón humanitario" (322). His heart is with Irene, while he must proceed in the search for a wet nurse. He is helped by his friend, Dr. Augusto Miquis (who appears in *La deheredada* and *Tristana*), a physician with a sense of humor that is not to Máximo's taste at the moment. Miquis has a young woman named Regustiana in mind, with only one stumbling block: she is accompanied by her boisterous family. The doctor cannot refrain from mentioning—maliciously, from the philosopher's perspective—that he lives in the same building into which Doña Cándida and a young lady have moved, and that he has seen José María there every day. Máximo accepts Regustiana, escorts her and her family to their new residence, and rushes to Doña Cándida's house. The interfering lady will not give her niece the chance to talk alone with Máximo. Irene slips him a note saying that he has arrived late and that she needs him badly; he should take his leave, informing Doña Cándida that he will return in a week, but he should come back at three o'clock. On his way out, Doña

Cándida informs him that there had been burglars in the house the previous night and that the intruders had frightened the women but did not steal anything. When he returns in the afternoon, he is alone with Irene, who reveals that her aunt is keeping her there as a prisoner to sell her to José María, who has set Doña Cándida up in the flat. Máximo interrogates Irene about the wisdom of her decision to leave his brother's home, where she had better defenses against the enemy than in her aunt's house. Irene bursts into tears and says that she is unworthy of his protection. He confronts Doña Cándida on her return, and she acts offended. She claims that Irene had a suitor in Manuela's house and offers to show proof. As he utters his refusal, the doorbell rings. It is his brother.

Máximo's dialogues with Irene and Doña Cándida show his crisis of thought and feeling. His emotions are heartfelt, but he struggles between his roles as father figure and admirer, and he can never eliminate the philosopher's sensibility. He suggests to the distraught Irene, "Veamos la cuestión; examinémosla fríamente," which he instantly concedes is a "tontería" (335). The conversations set up the crucial dialogue between the brothers in chapter 36. José María's strategy is to reverse the roles by demanding to know why Máximo is there. He makes excuses for his absence from home and, aiming to ignore the issue at hand, praises his brother for locating the wet nurse. Máximo calls his brother on his lies, and censures him for plotting with Doña Cándida to take advantage of a decent young woman and for neglecting his marital responsibilities. José María insists that the charges are unfounded and argues that he deserves credit for coming to the aid of two helpless women. He also suggests there is more going on with Irene than meets the eye: "Yo no comprendo el interés ridículo que te tomas por la pobrecita Irene, que de seguro se reirá de ti bajo aquella capita de bondad..., porque, eso sí, otra que tenga mejores modos y que sepa esconder tan bien sus picardías" (347). Máximo rigorously counters his brother's alibis and accusations. He threatens to cause a public scandal by publicizing the indiscretions, and throws José María out of the house. José María affirms that no woman will ever find Máximo appealing, and he adds further barbs: "tú, con esos aires caballerescos," "el verdadero perseguidor de la honra de las doncellas puras" (347), "tu papel de deshacedor de agravios," "el señor de la protección caballeresca" (348), and so forth, all with a quixotic flavor. He reports that Doña Cándida has found a packet of letters in her niece's possession and "[v]eremos si con rociadas de moral ahuyentas al enemiguito" (348). Máximo sees himself as the victor and believes that the fear of exposure will deter his brother. He has proven himself to be a solid debater, calling his tactics "sublime," but he has not listened to everything that José María has revealed.

Máximo has little patience with the insincere and obsequious Doña Cándida, who tells him that Irene has been so unnerved by the experience that she has fallen ill. He peeks in on her and is disturbed by her demeanor. He writes a note to Dr. Miquis and leaves to eat dinner, with the intention of returning later in the day. On the way out, he runs into Manuel Peña, who says that he is going to see the doctor. Máximo does not believe the excuse, and the real source of the problem dawns on him: "¡Tú eres, tú, pollo maldito, orador gomoso, niño bonito de todos los demonios; tú eres, tú, el ladrón de mi esperanza...!" (355). He takes his anger out in writing, with an apostrophe to "news, background information, and details." When confronted, Manuel confesses, and "[c]uando... me dijo: «Está loca por mí», yo apreté tan fuertemente el pasamanos de hierro, que me pareció sentirlo ceder, como blanda cera, entre mis dedos" (357). Manuel seeks his mentor's counsel, and Máximo must conceal his anger and hurt. Manuel was the "burglar" in the night, having gone to the house with a revolver to protect Irene from José María, who fortunately did not make an appearance. At home and in pain, Máximo discloses to the reader, that, in spite of all his troubles, he is able to eat a hearty meal, while sharing also that he has only morbid thoughts, including the composition of his obituary. He wakes up the next morning unexpectedly refreshed, and keen on imparting to his students selected pearls of wisdom, including the following: "Existe perfecta unión entre la sociedad y la Filosofía. El filósofo actúa constantemente en la sociedad, y la Metafísica es el aire moral que respiran los espíritus sin conocerlo, como los pulmones respiran el atmosférico" (364). He submits, as well, that "[e]ll hombre de pensamiento descubre la verdad, pero quien goza de ella y utiliza sus celestiales dones es el hombre de acción, el hombre de mundo..." (364), which hints, it would seem, of a shift of perspective.

Máximo titles chapter 40 "Mentira, mentira," "porque ahora trae mi narración unas cosas tan estupendas, que no las va a creer nadie" (365). The fictional narrator treats the theme of versimilitude, concluding that truth is sometimes stranger than fiction. He gives the examples of his robust appetite and professorial eloquence at a moment in which he was under duress. Then there is the visit of Doña Javiera, who makes known that she has cut off ties with Ponce — who has shown himself to be vulgar and a wastrel — in recognition of Manuel's social and political aspirations. Máximo notices that his friend is modulating her speech and that she is dressing more conservatively. She has already sold her business and bought a building in the fashionable Retiro area, and, in gratitude for all he has done for her son, she invites him to take a flat there for his current rent. One more strange event occurs: he finds José María and Manuela together at home, seeming to get along ("partiendo un piñón"). Máximo notes in José María a sweetness that he had not detected before. The wet nurse was behaving, and so was her family. Manuela says that her husband has never been so obliging and that he is even speaking of a trip to Paris. But the biggest revelation is saved for last, one that will be hard for the reader to swallow: Doña Cándida extracts more money from Máximo, through what he calls an ambush. When he visits her home, he forces her to let him be alone with Irene. He asks for an account of her relationship with Manuel, and she obliges, in detail. He expounds on the nature of the attraction, also in detail, to which Irene replies, "Sabe usted... más que Dios" (374), and, in fact, it seems as though he were eliciting a confession. She may not love him, but she and Manuel revere him: "Usted no tiene precio... Es la persona mejor del mundo" (376). He accepts the praise, but is aware that the savvy young woman needs him as an ally to facilitate her marriage.

Irene explains to Máximo that she is miserable living with her aunt and affirms that she will get out soon, either married or dead. She says that she accepted the position as governess only as a means of escape. She confides that she hid from him her aversion to books of all kinds. Máximo is caught completely off guard, but he pretends that this jolt to his sensibility and to his ego comes as no shock. The reader is privy to his pretense and pride at work, and to his real feelings. He plays the philosopher (and amateur psychiatrist) by rationalizing and pontificating in response to Irene's revelations, while he sees his faith in his intellectual mission diminish. He says to himself, "¡Y yo que creía!...¡Y para esto, santo Dios, nos sirve el estudio! Para equivocarnos respecto a todo lo que es individual y del corazón" (382). He lectures to Irene with no sign of timidity, however, "envalentonándome mucho y empleando ese acento, esa seguridad que siempre tengo cuando generalizo" (382). Máximo shares a less than pleasurable meal with Irene and her aunt, and he leaves with a strong sense of disillusionment. He deduces, "He aquí una huérfana desamparada que se abre camino, y su pasión esconde un genio de práctico de primer orden" (387), and "¡Oh! ¡cuánto más valía ser lo que fue Manuel, ser hombre, ser Adán, que lo que yo había sido, el ángel armado con la espada del método defendiendo la puerta del paraíso de la razón!... Pero ya era tarde" (388). He is disenchanted with Irene and with himself. His world is out of kilter.

Doña Javiera, enraged by her son's interest in the impecunious schoolmistress, begs for Máximo's assistance. The narrator describes an awkward scene at dinner and laments his fate; bad things seem to befall him while he is seated at someone else's table, even though the players and the quality of the food are not similar here to the meal in Doña Cándida's dining room. Máximo agrees to try to handle the situation. In a discussion with Manuel, he puts his protégé through the ringer, but ends by supporting the marriage option, stating that if he does not marry Irene, they will no longer be friends. The grateful groom fears the wrath of his mother, but his teacher commits himself to pacifying her. Doña Javiera is hard to convince, and she accuses Máximo of betraying her. Nonetheless, Máximo is convincing. He reminds the solicitous mother of her own roots. He mentions that Irene is his charge, the daughter of a distinguished gentleman who did great service to his father. She is worthy of a good match, and he will see to it that she is treated well. Doña Javiera uses the occasion to note that "aquí tenemos al caballero quijotesco" (397). "Did they wed?," asks the title of chapter 46. Of course, they did, the narrator answers, and he gives himself full credit for answering the needs of "Conciencia y Naturaleza." He believes that Manuel was unsure of his wishes at the time of their fateful dialogue and that he needed an extra push, something for which Irene always will be indebted to him. Doña Javiera sets up her luxurious new home and enlists Máximo's aid in the process. She finally succumbs to his arguments on the matrimonial front: "Para no oírle más, Mansito..., que se casen... Lo que usted no consiga de mí... Tiene usted la sombra de Dios para proteger niñas..." (403). He considers the change of heart an act of poetic justice, or, as he calls it, a manifestation of the "ley de compensaciones" (403).

One morning shortly thereafter, Máximo is called to his brother's house. Manuela is upset because he has not visited in three days. It seems that José María—who is on his way to acquiring the title of marquis—is away for much of the time. When Máximo tells him and Manuela of the engagement, she crosses herself and he is visibly shaken, although he says that he already has heard the news. Máximo himself, hardly enthused about the nuptials, admits that the event gives him little pleasure. He speaks of Doña Cándida, who has had second thoughts about Manuel's bloodlines but even more about her not being allowed to live with the couple. She will become a permanent fixture at José María's house, in order to receive sympathy from Manuela and her mother. Máximo reluctantly accepts an invitation from Manuel to see Irene. It is sad for him to acknowledge that she views him as a friend or brother, even as he calls attention to her flaws and superficiality. Worse, "[u]n gran escozor sentía yo en mí desde el famoso descubrimiento; sospechaba y temía que Irene, dotada indudablemente de mucha perspicacia, conociese el apasionamiento y desvarío que tuve por ella en secreto, con lo cual y con mi desaire, recibido en la sombra, debía estar yo a sus ojos en la situación más ridícula del mundo" (408). When Manuel recommends that he get married, Máximo tries to mask his embarrassment by proclaiming himself the eternal bachelor: "La rutina del celibato acaba por crear un estado permanente de indiferencia hacia todo lo que no sea los goces calmosos de la amistad.... [E]l celibato ha servido en todos los siglos para demostrar la excelencia del espíritu" (409). Does he think the verbal camouflage worked? By no means.

By "coincidence," both Máximo and José María are indisposed on the day of the wedding and cannot attend. Máximo is now set up in his new residence, tended by Doña Javiera. Gossipmongers spread rumors of a liaison, but both parties laugh it off, and she is prepared to defend him to the end. He cites the apothegm "La sabiduría es la sal de los hombres" to describe the temperament and loyalty of his friend, who strives for a growing familiarity. Manuel and Irene return from their honeymoon. She looks radiant, and her mother-in-law suspects that she may be pregnant. Máximo pays tribute to Irene for treating him with the utmost respect. As tasteful, tactful, and infinitely tempting as she may be, he cannot refrain from reporting that she strays ever more from the ideal: "Sentencia final: era como todas. Los tiempos, la raza, el ambiente no se desmentían en ella. Como si lo viera... desde que se casó no había vuelto a coger un libro" (413). He trades jibes with Doña Javiera about Irene, but both know that she is living up to her wifely duties with distinction. Manuel becomes a member of parliament and thus, according to his somewhat jaded former mentor, a willing hypocrite or one who will soon be dead of asphyxiation. "¡Que vivan, que gocen! Yo me voy," Máximo titles the fiftieth and final chapter. Struck by grief and depression, he feels prematurely old. It pains him to see Irene, whom he calls, on more than one occasion, his teacher rather than his disciple, and he curtails his social interaction. His condition worsens, and one day, in the company of the steadfast Doña Javiera, "ella aterrada, yo sereno, me morí como un pájaro," and "[e]l mismo perverso amigo que me había llevado al mundo sacóme de él" (416). Like many storytellers, Máximo Manso conveys what happens with the principal characters. First, they began to forget him—Doña Javiera last of all—and that, he says, is as it should be. Manuel attains estimable success, but the lessons of his master are barely discernible in his labors as a man of action. His reference to Irene is especially vague, but she too seems relatively untouched by her time with him or by idealism in general. Without particular merits—which is not such a handicap when a meritocracy is lacking—José María continues to climb the ladder of success. Máximo uses the term *plantón* in addressing earthly existence, "la antesala del nuestro [vivir]," and he concludes by comparing his observation of family, friends, "y demás desgraciadas figurillas con el mismo desdén con que el hombre maduro ve los juguetes que le entretuvieron cuando era niño" (419).

Galdós ends the novel with an ironic concession toward realism and with a double play on the fictionality of Máximo Manso, who bids adieu via his relation to the author with whom he is complicit and from the vantage point of a heaven, whence he can look down on those he has left behind, there are dreams within dreams, and he has access to God. There is a metafictional frame in *El amigo Manso*, beginning with the creative non-existence of the narrator/protagonist and ending with his disappearance from the world and his celestial ascent. Galdós takes literally the concept of a fictional construct. Máximo Manso breaks the illusion of reality before that illusion comes into play, and he fades away in front of the reader, up to a point, since he lingers in eternity. Like Don Quijote, he seems to die two deaths, one to satisfy a literary exigency and the other to intimate immortality. It could be argued that, in death, Don Quijote becomes Alonso Quijano, but the Christian death is subordinated to the (literary) chivalric life, which is what the narrative is about. Don Quijote lives in a universe that approximates the real world but that makes room for art. Máximo Manso interprets the reality around him, but undoes realism as he functions within it. His birth seems to stem from the ink jar, to which he returns, yet his soul and his voice reappear from above. Each character is subject to the whims—and, one might add, the strings—of the author.

El amigo Manso alludes several times to *Don Quijote*, and the title character has his head in the clouds for much of the novel. The business of society eludes him despite the security and the intellectual buoyancy that philosophy gives him. Education is to Máximo Manso what chivalry is to Don Quijote: the foundation of human interaction, goodness, and achievement. It is an emblem of superiority, but in a positive sense, because the disenfranchised can profit from learning. Some would see Manuel Peña's rise in society as an offshoot of his family's money, acquired through the butcher shop but viable, and marketable, in the current economy and reordering of the class system. Manso likely would attribute the move forward to his acquired knowledge. The success owes something to each factor, but it is evident that Manuel seeks practical applications of the lessons that he has learned from Manso. As a man of action, he goes beyond his teacher, beyond theory.[5] He is the new model, as it were. Manso is the anachronism. Irene the teacher, and Manso's unofficial student, takes advantage of opportunities and of her natural resources to find a place for herself in society. Unlike Tristana, her goal is not independent womanhood but a well-chosen marriage and prominence, power by association, and creature comforts. Even Manso, who misses much of the irony that surrounds him, understands that her motives are deceptive. She is the antithesis of bookish and, alas, far from his ideal. She is no Dulcinea, but neither is she the peasant Aldonza Lorenzo, entrenched in the margins. Society has found a protected middle ground for the orphaned and destitute female through what precisely would have been anathema to early modern Spain: the goal of upward mobility, the rupture of the reigning hierarchies. Manso leaves the newlyweds poised to conquer any barriers that remain in their way, a feat that would have been unimaginable a generation or two earlier. They have absorbed some of his wisdom, but they have acquired an apprecia-

---

[5] Cf. Livingstone, "Interior Duplication": "As the embodiment of the purely methodic,... [Manso] is no match for Manuel Peña, the man of real vitality, possessed of that life which despotically refuses to submit to logical systems" (400).

tion of the laws of causality that he fails to comprehend.[6]

Máximo Manso has a literary life because his routine is broken. Manuel, Irene, José María, Manuela, and the supporting players break the monotony of his reading, teaching, and deliberately unassuming existence. Máximo does not imagine adventures; for him, erudition is an adventure unto itself. He wants to inspire people, but realizes that he will not reach all those within his hearing (or writing). He is deeply involved in the proliferation of ideas, which seem to concern him more than their consequences, until he is drawn, rather against his will, into the center of things. The first-person narrative gives Galdós a forum from which to present the progression of Manso's thinking. He humbly, or not so humbly, sees himself as the exemplar of the thinking man, the knowledgeable and knowing *magister*. He will take his charge Manuel Peña to the heights by transforming him into a well-read and prudent gentleman, *un hombre serio*. He will install Irene into his brother's home, where she will educate his older children and he will oversee her education. It takes him considerable time to surmise that he has been unaware of much that is happening within his domain, and over which he feels that he exerts control. He views himself as a guardian, of sorts, of morality, but those whom he oversees commit indiscretions galore. His false sense of security is a base of irony and eventually a tool of self-discovery. Manso becomes disillusioned at the end, because his faith in education—in theories and in the people to whom they are directed—let him down. In some ways, Manuel's success is his failure, and Irene's success is an affront to his idealism. He thought that he was imparting a moral conscience along with abstractions, and he was wrong. Yet society rewards them, anyway. They are the future. He is absent, and his legacy is minimal.

The treatment of the quest motif in *El amigo Manso* is expertly calculated. Manso's aim is to educate, to spread ideas, and to teach to

---

[6] In his structuralist study of the novel, John Rutherford maintains that "[t]he creation of an enigma is facilitated in *El amigo Manso* by the use of a protagonist-narrator whose view of events is severely impaired. What is hidden from Manso is also hidden from the reader, though the latter sometimes suspects certain facts before Manso does, as the implied author makes indirect comments behind his back, as it were. As the novel advances, a succession of questions presents itself to the reader; and as the questions accumulate so the enigma, built around the figure of Irene, grows and dominates the novel" (200).

think and to act ethically. The reader sees his program—his lesson plans—with Manuel, and the readings include *Don Quijote*. Although he would prefer to be in the classroom or locked in his study, Manso sallies forth into the world, as if by command. Others need his services. Doña Javiera wants him to rescue her son, Doña Cándida to save her from penury, José María to help him get settled in Madrid, Manuela to keep her baby alive, Irene to shield her from her aunt and his brother, etc. They turn the studious introvert into, if not a man of action, a man who is out in the world. The speech at the charity event becomes a microcosm of the locus of Máximo Manso in society. He deliberates extensively on the form and content of his oration, but the assembled crowd finds him less than stirring. In contrast, the audience is enthralled with Manuel's speech, even though it is recognized by the critics as more rousing than deep or inspiring. The grandiloquent but empty rhetoric carries more weight than learned discourse because the triumphant speaker is youthful, charismatic, and expressive. The people are looking rather than listening, placing style over substance. Manso is almost pure substance, the remnant of a scholarly ideal, a social relic. He is willing to inconvenience himself for his family and for his surrogate families, as the episode with the wet nurse illustrates. While resisting the forced activities, he does not shy away from the real-world challenges or from confrontations in which he must take the morally upright position. Manso's delusions have little to do with Don Quijote's madness, but they are built on his faith in justice and on a sense of decency. One could say that it is not life that deceives him, but his fellow men and women. His major social flaw is that he trusts his knowledge base to guide him and to aid him in guiding others, and his adversaries have the pragmatic edge.

Don Quijote's moment of *desengaño* comes late and *ex machina*. His obsession with chivalry ends with a rejection of books and conventions, but the reader knows from the prologue to Part 2 that the conclusion may have more to do with literary polemics than with medical conditions. The "natural" death of Don Quijote, replete with the trappings of Christianity, is arguably overshadowed by Cervantes's wish to preclude further continuations of the knight's (hi)story. The 1605 prologue sets a tone and a metafictional standard for the narrative as a whole. Combined with the last thing written—the 1615 prologue—the dialogue with the friend replaces mimesis with self-consciousness. The creative process becomes a focus and a topic in itself. Galdós employs a similar frame, with the summoning of both the author and the character. He substitutes an ink jar for Cide Hamete Benengeli's pen, but he replicates the disappearance of the protagonist into literary history and into a spiritual sanctuary. Near the end of the last chapter of *El amigo Manso*, it is Galdós who figuratively vanishes and an omniscient Manso who reports to the reader from heaven. This otherworldliness produces a sharp contrast with the political satire that occupies a sizeable portion of the narrative, which targets the rhetoric and the alliances—each superficial and subject to radical shifts—of leaders and followers. Society stands at the center of *El amigo Manso*, but that center is bordered, and often compromised by, the act of composition and by the recourses of art. *Don Quijote*, cited in the novel and associated with the protagonist, is a primary intertext.[7] So, I would submit, despite the upstanding eponymous character, is the picaresque.

The picaresque mode relies heavily on the positioning of the narra-tor/protagonist. The *pícaro* stands at a distance from youth and from the moment of experience. He is fashioning a plot at the same time that he is engaged in the performance of self-fashioning. The story may not be

---

[7] Francisco Ayala accentuates the flexibility of Galdós "frente a las teorías literarias, que en ningún momento adoptará con seguridad dogmática. Pues, aun cuando alguna vez tomara, como es sabido que lo hizo, apuntes del natural para luego llevarlos al lienzo donde pinta la realidad, no por ello deja de componer ésta con los elementos de la fantasía poética incorporados a la mente colectiva. Y al efectuar esta combinación sigue lecciones del modelo que nunca cesaría de estudiar durante su vida de novelista: Cervantes" (97). Ayala also considers the works of Alemán and Quevedo as intertexts for Galdós. Joaquín Casalduero writes, "El autor naturalista no podía aprender nada de la Edad Media ni del Barroco, pero sí de Cervantes" (83; on naturalism, see esp. 79-100). Rubén Benítez's *Cervantes en Galdós* is a general study of the topic. Benítez calls *El amigo Manso* an attempt on Galdós's part to imitate the formal structure of *Don Quijote*, as it relates to self-consciousness and the autonomous character; see 66-67. Raquel Asún notes, "Están los procedimientos de Calderón, los de Quevedo, los de Larra y, claro está,... no podía faltar Cervantes.... Los ejemplos son muy abundantes: sufrir alucinaciones como las de Don Quijote, transfigurar la realidad y acomodarla a su imaginación, sentirse viviendo en otro personaje. Hasta es posible que al amparo de las referencias cervantinas se le escape este contenido tono amargo, como cuando nos dice que le llaman 'caballero andante' y el lector descubre qué poco heroico es aguantar esas tardes, tantas congojas, tanta vulgaridad" (55), Diane Urey looks at Cervantine resonances in her consideration of ironic narration; see esp. 64-77 and, for *El amigo Manso*, 70-75.

a purely autobiographical fiction, but instead organized around another principle (the explanation of a case or the validation of a professed conversion, for example). There is, however, a movement through time and space, and at the dénouement the character is an amalgam of the cumulative incidents that have befallen him, or her, mediated by the narrative plan and by the author. The magnificent reciprocity of the living of a life and the making of a narrative helps to define the picaresque, as does the ricocheting effect of the satire, whose target is alternately the social misfit who dares to seek something higher and who presupposes that there would be interest in a marginal life, and a society in which appearances carry more weight than reality. Point of view has a complexity that is psychologically and artistically innovative. The child interacts with—and conceivably vies with—the adult, the narrator with the protagonist, the individual with society, the story with the discourse, and voice with perspective. The consciousness of the process of construction can point to the pretexts of the narrator and of the author, and therefore to a relationship that may be competitive or adversarial. The encoding and consequent decoding of the narrative becomes a reflection of the inevitable need to make sense of the outward signs of reality. The semiotics of the text imitates the interpretive or analytical strategies of everyday life. Using the devices of literature, the picaresque displays reality in two ways, and with a double angle of vision in each case: by evoking social reality (from the center and from the margins) and by illuminating the fabrication of story and discourse (by means of the interplay of voice and voice-over). The writers of the picaresque seem to recognize not only that there is a parallelism between perceiving verbal and nonverbal signs, but that the discourse can be as important as the story, that the discourse can *become* the story. This revelation, in turn, becomes an operating premise for Cervantes in *Don Quijote*, and the repercussions can be felt in *El amigo Manso*.

"Yo no existo" is an anti-realist creed, to be sure. Spain's premier exponent of narrative realism announces in the first words of *El amigo Manso* that he is striving for a new form, or a new frame, in which to depict life in the capital in the second half of the nineteenth century. The narrators of his "contemporary novels" are reader-friendly, with personalities of their own and with the inclination not to intrude excessively upon the action. There is a studied balance between the point of view and the plot. In a novel such as *Tristana*, the faceless narrator—a non-participant in the events depicted — is essential to the intersection of story and discourse as the purveyor of irony. The identification of ironic narration is, to my mind, the key to the message systems of *Tristana*, which may seem to strive for a fair-minded assessment of the machinations and motives of the lead characters, when, in fact, one is clearly the protagonist and the other the antagonist. Galdós takes the formula of his thesis novels to a higher level of art, and this move should have an impact on the reader. *El amigo Manso* could be described as an updated, and deflated, quixotic story clothed in a discourse borrowed from the picaresque. The thoughtful and loquacious Máximo Manso guides the reader through his story, which wavers between fiction and history. With the opening revelation of the secret of his existence, as it were, he destroys the illusion of reality before he can create such an illusion. From *Lazarillo de Tormes* (or from *La lozana andaluza*), the authors of picaresque narrative have united crude reality with artistic design, linguistic invention, and an unapologetic show of the tools of fiction. The conditions of narration inform the message systems of the text. History becomes poetry in more ways than one. In *El amigo Manso*, Galdós experiments with perspective, and the results are poetic, and, perhaps unexpectedly, akin to the picaresque.[8]

Manso begins by denying his existence and his metonymical value; he is not a person or a fictional version of a real entity. The philosopher, invoking God, defies those of his ilk to find an atom of reality in him, yet he intimates that there is a type of autonomy, and independent social structure, among fictional beings. It takes an author to force — diaboli-

---

[8] James H. Hoddie relates *El amigo Manso* to the picaresque tradition, as follows: "Máximo's is a story of shame, a confession that hurts and would like to avoid its own truth. In this sense it is similar to a *pícaro's* revealing his lack of being (honor) while simultaneously making claim to the kind of being that typifies heroes and respectable persons. The effect is to reveal that the *pícaro* does not share in the world of 'existence' any more than does Máximo in that of other men, who lead the kind of life he feels ridiculous for not sharing, a life that may be termed the male version of the bourgeois romance of success, love, marriage, and living happily afterwards. In Manso's case, painful timidity and intellectual astuteness combine to make the book itself appear the artifact of a unique mind in a vulgar situation, one that is, nevertheless, generalized enough to be understood intuitively, despite its half-truths and half-lies, as an attempt to put the best face on despondency of soul" (71).

cally—a fictional creature from his domain so that he may assume human guise, paradoxically in conformity with a literary agenda. Galdós calls attention to his intercession as writer and to the constructedness of the narrative, and then moves into a more conventionally realistic pattern. He gives Manso a back story and takes pains to show the protagonist's first encounters with Irene, when she was only a child, but the narrator emphasizes that much of what happens in the account, which he classifies as "este verdadero relato" (146), occurs in less than a year. There is a contrast between the character without ties to the real world and the man in history, with a history. *Huérfano de padre*, he comes, like Lazarillo, to the city with his mother, but the maternal figure here is self-sacrificing and obliging in every way. An antecedent of Doña Soledad in *Niebla*, she attends to practical matters so that her son can tackle the mysteries of the mind. Her care is both commendable and an obstacle to his self-sufficiency. Manso has the luxury of thinking rather than doing, and, although he is well meaning and devoted to teaching, his anti-pragmatic attitude borders on snobbishness. He is no recluse, though, and he is proud of his physical attributes and his good grooming, to the extent that he can brag that he could be mistaken for a court officer or an attorney. He believes that the exercise of pedagogy permits him to practice what he preaches. The series of events, controlled primarily by others or by fate, brings him more emphatically into the social whirl, where he finds himself somewhat conflicted, at once stirred from complacency and out of his comfort zone.

Máximo Manso is, above all, methodical. He has a set routine, through which he makes an effort to avoid disagreeable breaches of habit. Doña Javiera's request that he mentor her son is an extension of his scholarly undertaking, and, of magnanimous spirit, he believes that he can add a dash of culture to their humble background. Doña Cándida irks him terribly, but he humors her out of respect for his mother. It is the violent contrast with her aunt that first draws him to Irene, who, of all the characters, most successfully transports him from thought to feeling. The return of José María tips the scales to the side of practicality. He and his family demand nearly full-time attention from Máximo, and their needs—and José María's ambitions—bring Irene and Manuel into the plot. This decisive moment allows Galdós to examine questions of authority in life and in literature. The narrator/protagonist is disinclined to take on the burden of the large and rowdy family, but he is more concerned about his loss of time and peace than about his ability to handle the trials and tribulations of household management. This is where the gap between theory and praxis stands out, and where irony comes most perceptibly into play. Manso's version of history functions on at least two levels: his story and the story revealed between the lines. As in *Lazarillo de Tormes*, there is some confusion in the narrative based on the temporal movements from past and present. Manso certainly knows where the story is heading, and generally—but not always—he recalls events from the moment of experience. Within the exposition, he intends to highlight his deep-seated sense of morality and his dedication to the study of philosophy, noting that this self-appraisal has inspired laughter from his acquaintances. It is not so much his benign boasting as his claim to practicality that may seem overstated: "Constantemente me congratulo de este mi carácter templado, de la condición subalterna de mi imaginación, de mi espíritu observador y práctico, que me permite tomar las cosas como son realmente, no equivocarme jamás respecto a su verdadero tamaño, medida y peso, y tener siempre bien tirantes las riendas de mí mismo" (156). He is a master of sobriety and so immersed in logic that "me propuse conseguir que mi razón fuese dueña y señora absoluta de mis actos,... y... me admiro de que no le sigan y observen los hombres todos" (156). One might think of the pride that goes before a fall, but Manso's sin is born of innocence, not guile.

Manso wants the reader to know that he has been selective about the details of the narrative. That the presentation will have a logical plan is not surprising. The narrator traces his contact with the principals of the story and his entry into an environment that tests his social, or real-world, skills by taking him out of his element. The culminating point is the marriage of Irene to Manuel Peña, the traditional ending of comedy, but here leading to Manso's death. The man who sings the praises of celibacy—and who sings his own praises—is caught in the snares of love. The contrast between the ideal Irene and the real woman, who is even more provocative, recalls Dulcinea and an altered Aldonza, and augurs the idealized and flesh-and-blood Eugenia Domingo del Arco of *Niebla*. The starting point of this story is significant because it deals with the friendship, or platonic bonds, between Manso and Doña Javiera. The first time that she appears in the narrative is when he has been working on the preface to a colleague's translation of Hegel's *Aesthetics*. The thoughts on beauty have his head spinning, and her visit provides a welcome respite:

"La miré y sentí que se me despejaba la cabeza, que volvía a reinar el orden en ella, como cuando entra el maestro en la sala de una escuela donde los chiquillos están de huelga y broma. Mi vecina era la autoridad estética, y mis ideas, dirélo de una vez, la pillería aprisionada que, en ausencia de la realidad, se entrega a desordenados juegos y cabriolas" (161). She seems unusually beautiful to him that day, and he states, at the end of a list of her physical attributes: "¡Bendito sea Hegel!" (161). She is a bit plumper than the ideal, perhaps, but in his mind that merely makes her more inviting. As she stands in relief against his shelves of books, "hallaba yo tan gracioso el contraste, que al punto se me ocurrió añadir a mis comentarios uno sobre la *Ironía en las Bellas Artes*" (162), a comment not without its own irony. The first-person narration is particularly effective because it joins discourse with character; that is, it becomes an instrument of the characterization of a man enthralled with words and ideas. The dialogue amplifies this approach, by picturing him through the eyes of another. In the same scene, for example, Doña Javiera reveals much about them both when she exclaims that he is unique among men, and since she met him, "se me entró usted por el ojo derecho, se me metió en el cuerpo y se me aposentó en el corazón… Pues no parece sino que le hago a usted el amor; y no es eso, señor de Manso. No lo digo porque usted no lo merezca, ¡Virgen!, pues aunque tiene usted cara de cura, y no es ofensa, no señor… Pero vamos al caso… Se ha quedado usted un poco pálido; se ha quedado usted más serio que un plato de habas" (162). When she explains her plan to find Manolo a teacher who combines superior wisdom with kindness and generosity—himself—he observes, "Quedéme asombrado de ver cómo una mujer sin lecturas había comprendido tan admirablemente el gran problema de la educación" (164).[9]

The young Peña is by no means a difficult charge. He is polite, engrossed in the materials that Manso gives him to study, and content with the companionship of one who opens new doors for him. He is more of an extrovert than his mentor, and he has a talent for public speaking. The reader becomes acquainted with Irene through another woman, the

---

[9] In his edition of the novel, Caudet sees an extra irony in Doña Javiera's words: "Motivo tenía para el asombro porque doña Javiera hablaba como un pedagogo de la más pura raigambre krausista" (164n31).

meddling and insincere Doña Cándida. Orphaned and dependent on an indigent party, Irene somehow rises above the conditions of her living arrangements and the influence of her aunt. She is, on her own and to Manso's elation, a firm believer in education. He knows that she is smart, but in time he will learn exactly how smart. The narrator juggles the stories of the two older women with the progress of the younger characters. The plot takes a critical turn when the family arrives from Cuba. Irene becomes governess of the children, which gives her proximity to her admirers. Manolo's penchant for oratory links him to affairs of state, as do José María's political objectives, and Galdós, through Manso, is able to introduce polemical issues of the day, and to portray and satirize an unstable and apprehensive society. Chapter 9 bears the title "Mi hermano quiere consagrarse al país," for example. As Máximo Manso views culture and politics from an ironic distance, he detects the reason for Manuela's many friendships and his brother's personal victories within a short time span: "Las relaciones de la familia aumentaban de día en día, cosa sumamente natural, habiendo en la casa olor de dinero" (202). He is the critic at large, quick to chastise social parasites and even a dreadful poet, while agreeing that some of the new associates will aid his brother's cause, corrupt though they may be.

Irene works in José María's house, but she stands separate from the hustle and bustle of the family and from the political intrigues that make their way into the salon. Máximo sees her as supremely attractive and supremely correct. He confesses that "con seguridad me agradaba... y aun me encantaba un poquillo, para decirlo de una vez," but he finally is won over by "su conciencia pura y la rectitud de sus principios morales" (215). For him, her appeal lies in her respectability, and he signals "una naturaleza superior compuesta de maravillosos equilibrios" which he connects to the archetypal woman of northern Europe, "nacida y criada lejos de nuestro enervante clima y de este dañino ambiente moral" (215-16). The narrative format gives the reader a portrait of Irene based primarily on Máximo's impressions. This is love as expressed by a professor of aesthetics, and housed in the heart but centered in the head; the perfect woman is the woman of reason. The affection is not so much of the world as a respite from the world in which the protagonist has been thrust. He feels that righteousness brings them together, "como si la naturaleza de ella hubiera sido inoculada milagrosamente en la mía" (240), failing to see that they are a mismatch, not only by age but by temperament. Galdós—astutely, it would seem—keeps the reader in the dark about Irene for much of the novel. The parallel stories of Irene and Manuel hint of a connection, and the detail of Irene's late-night reading material (letters from Manuel that Máximo guesses may be essays of his) is one of many illuminating touches. Irene proves herself, in some ways, to be the antithesis of Máximo Manso, for she is first and foremost a pragmatist. In *Niebla*, Eugenia is a piano teacher who dislikes music, and Irene is a motivated student and teacher who has no real fondness for books. She does not abuse Máximo as Eugenia abuses Augusto Pérez, but she misleads a man already disposed to equate reverence with love. As he moves toward the end of the narration, Máximo records his disenchantment with Irene, whom he dislodges from the pedestal of ideal conduct, without hiding his continued attraction to her. What may upset him more than her pursuit of Manuel and of social status is his belief that she is aware of his feelings, that she is mocking him, albeit internally.

Máximo Manso's prowess as a social and political critic makes his awkward love story increasingly ironic. His wit as an observer of the follies of others puts him at the summit of intelligence and sophistication, but it ends by trapping him in his own cleverness. Those who live in a material world must learn to play its games. José María knows this. So does Manuel, even though his teacher has attuned him to the sublime.[10] And so does Irene, who proves to be reasonable in ways that Máximo has not imagined. The picaresque is marked by a mirror-effect satire, with the *pícaro* as subject and object. The view from the outside introduces a new perspective on society and its foibles, while hardly pushing for the rights of citizens in the margins. As a prototype, Lázaro de Tormes satirizes the

---

[10] Hazel Gold notes, "Although Manolo is most frequently compared to a block of unchiseled marble, it is clear that his is a generous and intelligent temperament that only awaits the hand of a master sculptor to awaken and reveal his responsiveness to the principles of aesthetics. This Manso accomplishes not by using textbook reproductions of famous art works but instead by bringing him to study the paintings themselves in situ.... The trips to the [Prado] museum become an important training exercise for Manolo, for although he had spent many an idle hour there, only now can he truly see. It is a lesson well learned, for the student soon outstrips his teacher in this quality of acuity of sight, developing a pragmatics of vision that will guarantee his success in society" (131).

hypocrisy that informs social transactions, but he also sets himself up to ridicule. The very genre in which he is encoded is an aberration, a breaking of protocol and propriety. The anonymous author generates a reciprocal motion that encompasses, and interrelates, story and discourse. A feature of the narratives of Lázaro and his successors is a multi-tiered process of revelation, through which the speakers say more—and reveal more—than they may intend, or than may be advisable. They try to remedy flaws through misleading testimonies and less-than-factual accounts, but their attempts at deception show through in the discourse, as they do in the plots proper. The question of discursive time is fundamental to the picaresque, because the gaps between experience and expression, along with the intricacies of perspective, demonstrate that every datum must be contextualized and, as a corollary for some, that every datum is suspect. The narrative scheme of *El amigo Manso* might be called a thinking man's version of the picaresque. Manso unwittingly parodies himself as he parodies society. He is unassuming, yet proud of his mental gifts, and, as would benefit any occasion for satire, he adopts a tone of superiority. As a wordsmith who evokes Quevedo in the *Buscón*, Galdós gives his creation a forum from which, poetically, to denounce objectionable individuals and society at large, without allowing the narrator/protagonist to escape censure.[11]

Manuel Peña grows tired of philosophy, and Irene grows tired of books, but at the end of the narrative they seem to be destined for success, while Máximo is not only dead but representative of a long-departed idealism. Manuel scoffs at his mentor: "[U]sted permanece en la grandiosa Babia del pensamiento, donde todo es ontológico, donde el hombre es un ser incorpóreo, sin sangre ni nervios, más hijo de la idea que de la Historia y de la Naturaleza; un ser que no tiene edad, ni patria, ni padres ni novia" (259). He speaks of Manso as if he were inanimate, not of flesh and blood, not comprehending how valid the statement is. Manuel fits ideologically between the brothers Manso. Galdós uses the

---

[11] A bust of Quevedo is one of four in Manso's study. The others are of Demosthenes, Marcus Aurelius, and Julián Romea (1816-1868), a famous actor known for his oratorical style. J. M. Price discusses the figures, which Doña Javiera calls "padrotes," in "The Five *Padrotes* in Pérez Galdós' *El amigo Manso*." The essay looks at the symbolic value of the choices. The fifth *padrote*, for Price, is Manso himself.

characters and situations of *El amigo Manso* to symbolize Spain at the crossroads of tradition, myth, and a modern economics and politics. Statesmen of many stripes fight to shape the nation, but there is discord on all fronts. In chronicling this history, as fiction, Galdós accentuates the difficult task of governing, together with human error, greed, and guile. His cynicism is visited upon the title character, but so are his generosity and love for his country. Manso is a quixotic figure for another age of great changes. He is a man of wisdom without the social impulses or the toughness that would qualify him as a leader of the battles of the time. Interestingly, however, he represents the side of philosophy in a growing political discourse that would determine Spain's fate.

In *Crossfire*, her study of the philosophical novel in Spain during the first third of the twentieth century, Roberta Johnson notes that the political atmosphere did not produce what she calls "a genuine modernization of Spanish intellectual life" until around the 1860s, when the country "experienced the peculiar anomaly of the arrival of the German rationalist tradition (in the guise of Krausism) only a decade or so before the appearance (thanks to the 1868 liberal revolution) of the several manifestations of materialism and positivism represented by socialism, anarchism, Marxism and evolutionary theory" (2).[12] If on the surface there would seem to be meeting points between these distinct orientations, namely, "a very pragmatic side with specific aims of reforming modern society in a utopian mode," they could not reach a synthesis, and "the thorough assimilation of rationalism's various phases from Descartes to Kant and Hegel that prepared the rest of Europe for a truly philosophical debate on the merits of the social theories had not taken place in Spain."

---

[12] Denah Lida's "Sobre el 'krausismo' de Galdós" offers an introduction to a topic that has special relevance for a reading of *El amigo Manso*, which the essay treats on 15ff. For Lida, Manso has ideas that are compatible with the doctrines of Krause, and she notes that "Galdós sonríe benévolo ante el idealista que aspira a ser el máxmio hombre de razón, ese Quijote manso que crea la imagen de su Dulcinea moderna: intelectual, nada católica, 'nórdica', y se encuentra con una Aldonza Lorenzo a quien–¡gran ironía!—quiere más que a la otra" (20). Sherman H. Eoff emphasizes the influence of the well-known *krausista* Julián Sanz del Río on Galdós during the early years of his residence in Madrid. Eoff sees a "readjustment" in Manso as love enters the picture and relates this to Galdós's developing thought; see 130-36. See also Shoemaker 2: 176-77 and Gómez Martínez, along with López Morillas's general study of Krausism.

The clash leads to a span of about twenty years that turn out "several generations of frustrated would-be philosophers" (Johnson, *Crossfire* 2-3). *El amigo Manso* is a product of this period. Galdós captures the uncertainty of the time and invents a would-be philosopher with familial ties to the political arena. Deep thinkers have posed problems for artists—Hamlet comes to mind, of course—because their activity is by nature more mental than physical. The decision to have Manso narrate the story resolves this difficulty, for the narrator can find energy in words. It may be noted parenthetically that Manuel Peña, who has read *Don Quijote,* may have ignored or forgotten some of its lessons.

José María's indiscretions give Máximo, the self-proclaimed flawless man, a task to perform in defense of virtuous womanhood. Unaccustomed as he is to chivalric feats, Máximo rushes on one particular day to save the life of a baby and to protect a maiden against the man or men who would rob her of her honor. He curses himself as he rushes forth to the seek the wet nurse and to arrive in time to rescue Irene, with an apostrophe to his "humanitarian heart": "Eras un adminículo de universal aplicación, maquinilla puesta al servicio de los demás; eras, más propiamente, un fiel sacerdote de lo que llamamos el *otroísmo,* religión harto desusada. Si dabas flores, te faltaba tiempo para ponerlas en el vaso de la generosidad, abierto a todo el mundo; si echabas espinas, te las metías en el bolsillo del egoísmo, y te pinchabas solo" (322). Galdós makes his protagonist an unwilling hero, more the literary descendant of Mariano José de Larra than of Amadís de Gaula.[13] Despite his alleged skepticism, he complies with the wishes of his sister-in-law, which means that he must delay the liberation of Irene, his less than transparent beloved. The idealized woman is an enigma. The real woman threatens to diminish the mental image, in a double sense. Máximo is disheartened

---

[13] In *Humor in Galdós*, Michael Nimetz looks at the influence of Larra's "El castellano viejo" on Galdós, and he mentions that "[f]arcical meals are described in *El amigo Manso, La de Bringas* and *Lo prohibido*" (44). Nimetz classifies the episode in *El amigo Manso* as "a comic gem, wherein the narrator, a prim, meditative bachelor, is obliged to sustain himself amid a disruptive family of Cubans. The satiric picture of criollo languor and petulance in this scene and throughout the book is broad but always gentle" (45-46). He notes that Robert Russell observes a connection between Manso and "El castellano viejo" in his essay on Galdós's novel.

that Irene has imperfections, but her defects seem to bring out a hidden physicality in him. When Manuela doubts the governess's motives, the statement wounds him, "como recio martillazo sobre el yunque, y hacía vibrar mi ser todo" (314). The aesthetician is conflicted by the disparity between the ideal and the real, and by unfamiliar feelings, but, like a knight errant, he tends to familial obligations and serves his love object. His principal foes are José María and Doña Cándida, and, unbeknownst to him, his rival is Manuel, which makes the younger man's oratorical triumph especially ironic. The philosopher has no illusions about his brother, but, to an extent, he has idealized Manuel as much as Irene. Like a middle-class, sedentary Oedipus, Máximo solves a mystery to his own detriment. The truth brings him a pyrrhic victory and ends by writing him out of the picture.

Manso calls himself a historian, and he worries about his credibility before readers when he conveys news that may seem out of the ordinary. He is a historian with wit and a virtuosity with words, and with a keen point of view. As in the picaresque, he writes with a knowledge of the future but, more often than not, he places the reader in the moment of experience. Galdós makes sure that all the main characters offer their "readings" of Manso's lifestyle, modus operandi, and worship of abstract thought, and "he" (understood as the author or the narrator, or both) validates, in his judgments and observations, at least some aspects of the commentaries. Note, for example, a thought shared by Manso in chapter 42, subsequent to his moment of disillusionment, concerning his opinion of Irene: "Consistía mi nuevo mal en que al representármela despojada de aquellas perfecciones con que la vistió mi pensamiento, me interesaba mucho más, la quería más, en una palabra, llegando a sentir por ella ferviente idolatría. ¡Contradicción extraña! Perfecta, la quise a la moda petrarquista, con fríos alientos sentimentales que habrían sido capaces de hacerme escribir sonetos. Imperfecta, la adoraba con nuevo y atropellado afecto, más fuerte que yo y que todas mis filosofías" (387-88). Galdós, following the bidirectional satirical model of the picaresque, depicts Manso as an incisive critic of society and politics, while interrogating his anti-pragmatic tendencies and subjecting him to the critique of others. Máximo Manso can teach, but could an individual like him run the government? Is such a person trapped in theory, or could his decency and training be put to the service of the State? The questions are not answered, because Manso lacks political ambition and because, once he fails in love, he flees the world, figuratively and literally.

Máximo Manso accommodates those who most let him down. He helps to further his brother's political future, and he even finds a way to send away the intrusive family of the wet nurse. He handles the objections of Doña Javiera and Doña Cándida to the marriage of Manuel and Irene; the mother does not want her son to marry a penniless orphan, and the aunt has reservations about the lineage of her niece's suitor. Máximo never ceases to be a mentor and never ceases to resist misused authority. The wedding is held, but he does not witness the vows. He fades away, with all good wishes for the newlyweds, and discovers that he can have an eternal perspective, be that a blessing or a curse, on his loved ones. He does not philosophize from above, and his voice sounds the same from higher ground as from below. He remains worried about Spain, a nation that at any moment will fall into the hands of inept and unethical politicians on the order of… José María Manso. The movement is complete. Máximo starts out as idyllically detached from the maelstrom of society. Doña Javiera and Doña Cándida, through a son and a ward, force him into contact with the outside, and the arrival of José María and his family intensifies this contact. The narrator/protagonist is an adept critic of the social and political climate, but he does not deal in facile remedies. Morality is his operative idea, but, idealist though he may be, he knows enough about the way of the world to think pessimistically about solutions to social ills and about the implementation of new programs by the politicians of the day. Manuel Peña and those like him may be the hope for the times to come, and they may bear the imprint of their idealistic, if impractical, teachers.

El amigo Manso borrows from the picaresque a doubling of characters, narrative actors, and time, each of which has a puzzling but crucial middle ground, a mediating space. There is a constant rebounding, an interplay and opposition of elements that result in a paradigm applicable to story and to discourse. On one level—that of the *pícaros* themselves, notably Lázaro de Tormes and Guzmán de Alfarache—the protagonist attains almost heroic dimensions as the lead in what purports to be, in relative terms, a success story. (Pablos de Segovia seems to have few redeeming features, even by his own calculation.) On another level, in contrast, the outsiders are the dregs of society, marginalized from the advantages of respectability, and rightly so. What makes the *pícaro* as an object of scorn a source of irony, among other things, is the first-person point of view. The *pícaros* are placed in the margins of discourse when the discourse is presumably their own. Authors make their presence known through the ironic inversions of defense mechanisms. All the rhetorical manipulations of autobiography are present in the picaresque, but they are augmented by an external authorial intervention, an exploitation of the (in name only) single point of view. Galdós constructs a variation on this model in *El amigo Manso*, which depends heavily on the ironic distinction between Máximo Manso's self-image—which certainly is tinted with an irony that the narrator recognizes—and the image projected by both the story and the discourse. As in the picaresque narratives, society and the outsider become objects of satire. Manso is hardly a rogue or parasite, but he belongs to a class of intellectuals who critique the status quo, with an air of superiority, without direct involvement in the business of the State. They know what is wrong with society, but instead of practical solutions they become lost in abstract notions, lost in words. The *pícaros'* discourse tells their story, in more ways than one. So, too, does Manso's.

The idealism of Máximo Manso links him to Don Quijote, as several characters mention. Galdós plays with chivalry, honor, the quest, service to ladies (including damsels in distress), and social alienation in the portrayal of the narrator/protagonist. Like Don Quijote's anachronistic speech, in imitation of chivalric romance, Manso's flowery and hyperbolic language sets him apart from his cohorts. Galdós ingeniously matches similitude with difference. His quixotic figure would prefer to remain a semi-recluse, in isolation with his books and with his students. He does not take the initiative; the world calls him out of seclusion, and he is hesitant to respond. For him, Irene is the feminine ideal and an alluring woman, and he has difficulty relating to the latter. As in the case of the distracted knight, Manso misreads signs that are obvious to others. He is out of touch with reality, but is somehow hopeful that others will see the light (of reason). He believes that intelligence and education separate not only man from beast, but the notable human beings from the masses. He is not immune from the sexism of his age—as shown by his praise of Irene for trying to improve herself while accepting the (inferior) condition of women—but his heart is in the right place. Although he is by no means mad, like Don Quijote he has a tendency to trust too much in absolute values and to jump too quickly into the attack mode, if abstractly. He is defeated by his own protégé, a younger man who understands that the rules of society's games are flexible, subject to modification, and not always fair, and that style often can replace substance. Manuel Peña realizes that he has money without rank. Irene cannot give him wealth, nor does she need to, but she can supply him with prestige, with the aristocratic past that he is missing. Each is practical in ways that Manso is not, and they seem bound for glory in the here and now. He, conversely, withdraws with little fanfare into oblivion.

The picaresque reflects a certain kind of realism, with stark reality at its base, while foregrounding the process of composition and thus the literariness of the procedure. The story events treat harsh and distasteful topics, but the reader has a consciousness of the narrator's drafting of the material. Reality fuses with rhetoric in diverse ways, and the *pícaro,* as narrator and protagonist, brings together social norms and social ostracism, defense and incrimination, and a story about marginalization and a story about the crafting of a manuscript. The idiolect of the narrator constitutes the unifying thread between the life experiences and the written record. Lázaro, Guzmán, Pablos, and their counterparts have distinctive voices and points of view. Their actions—the plot—must be seen as central, but their nature and their personalities may be the sine qua non of picaresque narrative. For all their unsavory qualities, the narrator/protagonists are lost souls, long-suffering and ridiculed. The reader comes to know them through direct discourse. They merit at least a small dose of sympathy for the humiliation that they have undergone, but they deserve special attention for their uniqueness as individuals, which comes across through the personal flavor of their language. The narrator shares with the reader a consciousness of the work in progress. The obvious hand of the author in the creation of the narrator's idiolect—which, from the start, belies the notion of singular vision—hints of ventriloquism and adds to the complexity of all aspects of the narrative. *Don Quijote* builds on the allusions to the writing process and to the role of the reader, but the first-person picaresque narratives allow for a brand of irony that Galdós replicates in *El amigo Manso.* Galdós judges Manso as Manso opines on all manner of themes and people, and the reader has the opportunity to put the messages, appropriately, into perspective. Creation and analysis, including identification of rhetorical strategies, inscribe themselves into the conventions of realism.

In a famous reversal of styles, Galdós introduces a type of idealism, and fantasy, into the ending of *Misericordia* (1897), which begins in the style of naturalism. Even the most sordid scenes, nonetheless, are conveyed by a poetic narrator appreciative of human goodness. It is, from the beginning, naturalism with a twist, and much has to do with the Galdosian narrator. In *El amigo Manso*, written within the corpus of realism,[14] the narrator is neither omniscient nor a secondary character or witness. He is the principal character and guide to the events described, alternately aware of and oblivious to the ironies of the narrative. Added to this format, which can be compared to picaresque discourse, is a frame that could be designated as literarily existential. Someone in the authorial seat conceives Máximo

---

[14] John W. Kronik ("La reseña") looks at Clarín's review of *El amigo Manso*. He writes, "Es importante subrayar que Clarín evaluara de manera positiva esta novela que los críticos durante muchos años despreciaron o pasaron por alto o entendieron mal. Más notable aún es el hecho de que Clarín expresara su apreciación y comprensión de *El amigo Manso* en el momento de su publicación. Como mérito principal alabó su pintura fiel de la realidad madrileña: 'una imitación correcta, exacta del mundo.' Esto es precisamente lo que Clarín denomina como la dimensión realista de esta obra. Los que conocen a Clarín como crítico literario no se sorprenderán ante lo que hoy nos parece una noción poco exacta del naturalismo al estilo de Zola. Aunque estaba mejor informado que casi todos sus contemporáneos de las corrientes francesas y de los escritos de Zola, Clarín no distinguía de modo bien claro entre naturalismo y realismo, entendiendo por naturalismo el amplio terreno del realismo. En esto se parecía a otros coetáneos como Emilia Pardo Bazán y el propio Galdós" (64). In "Galdós, Clarín y *El amigo Manso*," Juan J. del Rey Poveda mentions that Clarín dedicated three críticos artículos to the novel: "En ellos Leopoldo Alas distingue varias características de este libro, a saber: su carácter autobiográfico, el hecho de ser 'un pedazo de la vida de Madrid', ser 'una novela de observación psicológica', su 'humorismo triste y dulce' y haber conseguido un estilo 'propio para el género'. Y dentro del estilo, Clarín subraya que 'El diálogo, sobre todo, merece entusiástica alabanza'" (1). Rey Poveda analyzes the eleven dialogues between Manso and Doña Javiera, and he concludes that the dialogues "ponen de manifiesto su modo de hablar (él, culto; ella, popular pero evolucionando al culto, por necesidades de ascenso social), su pertenencia a un momento histórico concreto—la Restauración—y los temas que les preocupan. Además, el diálogo es un excelente instrumento lingüístico en la pintura de la realidad y en la búsqueda de la verdad, objetivos de los escritores realistas decimonónicos" (7). For the texts of the three reviews, see Alas 97-110. Kronik's essay includes the first of these texts, from *El Día*, 19 June 1882. In the introduction to *Galdós, novelista*, Adolfo Sotelo Vázquez discusses Galdós's naturalism, starting from the premise that "[p]ara Clarín, el equivalente español de Balzac es Galdós" (Alas xvii). On naturalism in Galdós with reference to *El amigo Manso*, see also Blanquat esp. 332-35.

Manso, gives him a biography, and sets him out into the world at the age of thirty-five. Some years later, during which he becomes involved in the lives of Manuel, Irene, and his brother's family, he becomes ill and dies, likely of disappointment and heartbreak. He returns to his maker, twice. He seems to evaporate into the ink jar from which he originates, yet he speaks (or writes) to the reader from heaven, with new-found narratorial gifts, including omniscience and mental contact with those on earth. It is strange as an epilogue, standard in the realist novel, because of the first-person narrative. Máximo Manso's story is compelling, even though he is by no means a man of action. His idealism and his distracted air bear quixotic traces, and his discourse, with temporal ploys and irony superimposed on irony, resembles the picaresque. Society, economics, education, gender issues, and, surely, politics enter the story, but it is Manso's entry into mainstream society and the intricate narration of his paradoxical activism that sustain and individualize the novel. Galdós gets into his protagonist's head, in a manner of speaking, and perspective becomes the crux of the narrative.

Miguel de Unamuno, in *Amor y pedagogía* and *Niebla*, also turns to the man of abstractions over the man of action. Thought and language obviously contribute to the movement from an event-based plot to a concept-based story line. There are clear contacts between the deep structure of *El amigo Manso* and that of *Niebla*. In each, a contemplative persona is stirred into participating in social negotiations, with a rival and an unattainable woman at the center. In contests of the mental versus the physical, the former consistently wins out; the "real" Irene and Eugenia cannot compete with their idealized others. Defeat in love leads to the demise of Máximo Manso and Augusto Pérez, and, although milder in Galdós's presentation, there is a correlation between overeating and death. (And Manso's words from above augur the funeral oration for Augusto Pérez delivered by the dog Orfeo.)[15] While Unamuno

---

[15] In "Unamuno and the Aesthetic of the Novel," published in 1941, Leon Livingstone notes that the "conscious relationship between author and character" in Unamuno may have "a possible forerunner... in Galdós' Máximo Manso, for whom, in his correspondence, Unamuno confesses much admiration, for he, too, is aware that he is the creation of his author" (447). Livingstone elaborates on the connection, with a focus on parallels between Máximo Manso and Augusto Pérez, in "Interior Duplication": "The clue to both characters is

their growth from rationalism to humanity. Manso progresses, as does Augusto, from the nonreality of generic reason, the status of abstract philosophic idea, to that of individual reality, achieved through suffering and doubt" (400). He goes on to say that "[t]he antirationalism of *El amigo Manso* and *Niebla* provides the key to the sudden renewal of the concept of interior duplication and of its literary appearance on the European scene" (400). In "*Niebla* and the Variety of Religious Experience," Thomas R. Franz argues that Galdós, in *El amigo Manso*, "had taken the (for him, dangerous) idealism and indomitable routine of Kant and had stuck them in the Madrid of his own times. ... The existential questioning of the tragic-comic bachelor Augusto and the self-referential quality of Unamuno's *Niebla* have their distant seeds in Galdós's handling of the distracted idealism of the frustrated Máximo Manso." (108). Franz extends the comparison in "*El amigo Manso, Niebla,* and *Oblomov*," in which he adds an 1859 novel by the Russian writer Ivan Goncharov to the equation. In both essays, he alludes to Ricardo Gullón's consideration of Unamuno's indebtedness to Galdós in "*El amigo Manso*, nivola galdosiana." Franz reduces to ten elements the points in common elaborated by Gullón: "(1) the parodic stances toward the Krausist idealism of the protagonists; (2) the quixotic quest to 'be,' even in failure and in full knowledge of the fact that one is doomed to exist only within the unsatisfying proofs authorized by literature; (3) the two texts' Dostoevskian view that life is more complicated than the narrator's unreliable vision; (4) the anti-idealist, bourgeois motivations of their heroines, Irene and Eugenia; (5) the existentially 'inauthentic' but sexually viable nature of the rivals, Manuel Peña and Mauricio Blanco Clará; (6) the quest of the protagonists to step outside the enclosure imposed by their texts; (7) the novels' conscious parallels between the relationship of the protagonist with his author, on the one hand, and that of the human creature and his God, on the other; (8) a similar use of author/character dialogues; (9) the employment of love and its reversals as a catalyst to existential 'authenticity'; and (10) a common use of analepsis to reveal the reasons for the 'literariness' of the protagonists' behaviour" ("*El amigo Manso*" 64). See Gullón, *Galdós, novelista moderno* esp. 69-76, and Ayala 137-43. See also Berkowitz, "Unamuno's Relations with Galdós." Berkowitz's investigation traces correspondence between the two writers about their art and politics. Unamuno's attitude is, at first, "characterized by extreme sincerity, affability, respect—even admiration—and self-revelation" (322), but things become more negative, for political as well as aesthetic reasons. Berkowitz notes that immediately after Galdós's death in 1920, Unamuno delivered a rather negative assessment of the intellectual and social content of his works (v. esp. 331 ff.). The essay ends with a letter from Unamuno in response to a request from Berkowitz that he readdress the question of Galdós's contributions. Berkowitz says that the letter, "which is in a very real sense Unamuno's last word on the subject, reveals no change of mind or heart on his part" (337); Unamuno writes, for example, "Los personajes emphasizes his break from realism, Galdós blends realism with elements that would defy the protocols of realist poetics. He places these counterpoints at the beginning and at the end of the narrative, seemingly in order to emphasize the intervention of the author and the implications of the defiantly fictional frame. In a variation of the pull of history and poetry in *Don Quijote*, Galdós surrounds historical reality not only with fictional characters and situations but with devices that bespeak their distance from the real. He makes the discourse an analogue of the story by having Manso, the out-of-touch idealist who does not fit—and who does not want to fit—into society, narrate from an unrealistic, and impossible, vantage point. It may not be easy to identify a plan behind the unconventional and irrational frame of *El amigo Manso*, but one has to presuppose that there was a purpose to accentuating the fictionality of the protagonist. Galdós brings the act of writing and the input of the reader into the equation. He starts with a premise that lends itself to realistic representation: the commentary by an admittedly biased narrator on incidents in his life, along with his reflections and opinions. He does not propose to tell the whole truth, but to celebrate the value of partial views. Máximo Manso exists on the fringes of active society, relishing his time for scholarly pursuits. His eloquence and his attitude make him a worthy foil and a gripping narrator, and the story itself—a love triangle set in a period of transition—unites social custom with politics. Yet Manso is but a figment of the author's imagination, and more.

Working within narrative realism, in what could be considered his middle period, Galdós chooses in *El amigo Manso* to hone in on characterization through discourse and on the fictional identity of the narrator/protagonist. Unlike the majority of picaresque narrators, Manso has no pretext to tell his story other than the wishes, and the whims, of the author who has beckoned him, and his non-existence means that he needs no justification to write. He is, in fact, a free spirit. Cervantes manages to evoke reader sympathy for Don Quijote, who is several degrees removed from reality, and Galdós achieves a similar result. The opening should distance the reader from the protagonist—as should the pompousness, however genial, of the discourse—but there is an indisputable sadness

---

de los dramas y novelas hablan demasiado para decir muy poco" (337), and "Me parece que Galdós hoy cansa a los lectores españoles" (338).

to the shattered illusions of Máximo Manso. It is as if Galdós were aiming to flaunt the fiction and then to suspend disbelief until the end. There is a prescience of modernism in the design of the novel, because mediation is an essential feature of the narrative. Manso interprets reality, but he makes no effort to mask his preferences, prejudices, and frailties. He acknowledges that he is a function of a nebulous authorial figure, whom the reader will readily associate with Galdós. The final words from heaven leave the reader with a taste of something beyond reality and beyond fiction. The comprehensive mixture is strong and suggestive. What the text imparts to the reader may be the voice of the vulnerable, sensitive, and misguided Manso, aware of his manufactured life yet moving—affecting and changing—on various planes.

In *El amigo Manso*, Galdós creates an inspired focal position, and a brilliant focalizer. When Máximo Manso is removed from his world of books and classrooms, he is placed into the commerce of quotidian reality, with identifiable social types. As in his other novels, Galdós here makes the ordinary extraordinary. A generalized vision yields an array of remarkable characters. Doña Javiera is low on culture, but aggressive about upward mobility. She follows a wise course in picking Manso to tutor her son, and she knows that Manuel will have a model of integrity as well as a teacher. As she grows more prosperous, her goals rise, but she cannot shake her background. The woman who owned a butcher shop feeds Manso sumptuously and decorates her new home with little subtlety. The next generation will be far smoother around the edges, thanks to her. Doña Cándida represents the other end of the social spectrum. She is high on culture, or at least of patrician bloodlines, but her cash flow is problematic, and she must resort to begging for money. Pride forces her to hide the truth, so she spins yarns that no one believes. She may be cagey enough to survive, and even to improve her lot, but her subclass—the poor aristocracy, still hounded by the stigma of manual labor—will remain a fact of life in Spanish society. As Doña Cándida's ward, the orphaned Irene has few recourses. She recognizes that education may provide her salvation, and, through her position as governess, love finds its way into her life. The relationship between Irene and Manuel is mutually beneficial from a social standpoint. She has the bloodlines, and he is a man of means. He is about to enter the political domain, at a time in which one who is talented, assertive, and considered to have leadership potential can be successful by virtue of these gifts; the nouveau riche is no longer a social, or political, pariah. Needless to say, Irene does not share her aunt's misgivings about the match with Manuel. José María Manso brings to the novel the figure of the *indiano*, the Spaniard who has made his fortune in the New World and who returns to his homeland to reap new rewards. He and his family are conspicuous consumers, and he seems to have learned how to look out for his interests by hook or by crook. He stands in contrast to his humble and impeccably scrupulous brother.

Throughout his narration, Máximo Manso engages the reader. He directs his commentaries to an audience, and he shows off his rhetorical prowess, through poetic language that features hyperbolic and overly dramatic asides, such as the references to his adoration of the chickpea. Manso describes himself in physical terms, speaks at some length about his background, his studies in Madrid, the devotion of his mother, and his immersion into the realm of philosophy, but it is the form of his narrative and the contact with the reader that most successfully, and endearingly, delineate his character. As with all people, Manso's public persona is not the same as his private self. The combination of narration, dialogue, and personal thoughts covers the range of events and personalities, offering a glimpse of society and of the protagonist. Galdós seems committed to both areas. He invites the reader to weigh the clues provided by Manso, some inadvertently, in order to understand, and perhaps to judge, his character. Because the view of society comes from the narrator/protagonist, the critique is affected by the reader's estimation of Manso's reliability.[16] Following the picaresque writers and Cervantes in *Don Quijote*, Galdós develops an ironic discourse that informs the story, as well, and he blurs the distinction between history and fiction. He disturbs the conventions of realism by having the narrator insist on his fictional status and by addressing the readership after his death. The author orients the reader in two directions, not necessarily to confuse the analytical process but to enrich its scope.

Garrett Stewart states in *Dear Reader: The Conscripted Audience in Nineteenth-Century British Fiction*, "Classic realist fiction requires for effect

---

[16] A considerable portion of Kay Engler's chapter on "The Unreliable Narrator" is devoted to *El amigo Manso*. Engler proposes that the narrator seems reliable until the reader recognizes the irony within the narrative. See 137-60.

a double *realization*: our activated sense, first of the rendered social and physical world of the narrative and then, second and simultaneously, of that world as focused upon and filtered through the credible interior representation of characters' mental lives. As dual coordinates of realism, objectivity and subjectivity meet at right angles: one the horizontal principle of plot and shifting scene, the other the vertical axis of interiority and depth" (19). In *El amigo Manso*, Galdós presents a physical and ideological landscape—an evocation of social and political transformations in Spain—while communicating information through Máximo Manso. Direct discourse is, arguably, most fitting for realism, for it permits the novelist to convey the thoughts of the narrator engaged in the act of writing. It melds the two axes outlined by Stewart, and it makes it logical for the narrator to be addressing the reader. This is, in essence, the inner structure of *El amigo Manso*, the first-person account of the title character's life, from his meeting of Irene and Manuel (through Doña Cándida and Doña Javiera, respectively) to their marriage, with the intervening and interconnected account of the return to Spain of José María. The content is feasible and based on what might be termed the reality of Spanish society. The figurative language and the dramatic accents of the narrative are equally feasible, given the education and the eccentricities of the narrator/protagonist. Having found a model that serves the principles of realism, a realism that he had cultivated, though not slavishly, Galdós selects an antirealist frame for *El amigo Manso*. He asks the reader to jump in and out of the fiction.

Robert Russell sees *La desheredada* (1880-1881) as initiating a new phase of literary activity for Galdós. In "*El amigo Manso*: Galdós with a Mirror," he describes the 1882 novel as an experiment in point of view, but one that must be differentiated from the first-person narration as employed in the first series of the *episodios nacionales*.[17] Galdós moves from

---

[17] Linda M. Willem notes that in the second series of the *episodios nacionales*, Galdós uses "individual protagonist narrators for three of its novels: Juan Bragas de Pipaón in *Memorias de un cortesano de 1813* and *La segunda casaca*, and Genara de Baroana in *Los cien mil hijos de San Luis*. But in each case, the omniscient narrator of the second series intrudes on these personal accounts to provide information beyond the scope of the limited protagonist narrators" (149). In addressing the narrator of *El amigo Manso*, Willem states, "Although he speaks to the reader with the 'yo' form of address, he is not subject to the limitations of

recounted history to literary self-referentiality. The opening allusion to the author gives Manso a dual role as an actor and as a writer who is learning and exercising his craft. In the creative position, he is a shadow of Galdós. Thus, the theme of education announced in the first chapter has relevance for the narrative as a whole. In "*El amigo Manso* and the Game of Fictive Autonomy," John W. Kronik emphasizes that "*El amigo Manso* won little esteem from its contemporaries: a novel without plot or action, they called it.... Unamuno pretended not to have understood it" (71). In the essay, Kronik argues that "[t]he autonomous character metaphorically raises the question of the split that exists between man as a social being with social dependency on others and man as endowed with the power to form and determine himself" (72), and he sees the first and last chapters as shaping the narrative. When he notes that "[t]he creator's control over his creation... —whether that creation is a pupil, an ideal, or a fictional character—is tenuous" (80), he links Galdós to Manso and to the abstract guides of art, society, and nature. Kronik concludes that, while "the realistic novel does its best to hide its identity as a novel,... Galdós in *El amigo Manso* creates an illusionist art that signals the coming break with illusionism" (90).[18] This is why the first-

---

first-person narration. He is able to enter the minds of his characters at will, and his privileged knowledge surpasses even that of the author" (150). The statement is misleading, since this omniscience in Máximo Manso occurs only in the frame. Willem discusses *El amigo Manso* and *Lo prohibido* in a chapter entitled "Fictional Autobiographies" (147-78). She treats, among other topics, irony and strategies for imparting information.

[18] The essay is reprinted from *Anales Galdosianos* and the Spanish passages translated into English in Labanyi 157-80. Arnold Peñuel sees the relationship between Galdós and Manso as a collaboration cemented in the first chapter. Gustavo Correa maintains that "Máximo Manso participa... de una manera de ser que es contingente y pasajera, mientras se halla viviendo con otros seres semejantes a él en el contexto de una vida real que es, ya en sí, una ilusión de realidad. Por otra parte, Manso existe como producto específico de la mente creadora del artista y, en calidad de tal, entra a formar parte de una manera *absoluta* de existencia, que es característica de los entes de ficción" (*Realidad* 107). Harriet Turner examines the character-author dichotomy (and competition) in "The Control of Confusion and Clarity in *El amigo Manso*." For me, the type of author-character rivalry that one finds in *Niebla* is missing here. Galdós cedes the floor to his narrator/protagonist, but not without making his presence known. The compatibility between the two illuminates the adversarial force of Unamu-

person narration has a central bearing on the realism of *El amigo Manso*. Rather than inventing an unidentified narrator with skills in observation and rhetoric, Galdós lets Máximo Manso speak for himself. The act of writing under these circumstances is natural and logical. Manso the narrator has as obvious and relevant a place in the scheme of things as Manso the protagonist. The metafictional frame is Galdós's sign of a break, but in chapters 2 through 49 the author shows that he has mastered realism while anticipating a shift in direction. He relies on the picaresque paradigm and on fictional autobiographies, journals, and diaries to set a standard of verisimilitude, tempered by a discursive ventriloquism. He then shatters the realism by having the narrator veer from the coherence, and from the logic, of the narrative situation into the realm of the imaginary. The recontextualization of story and discourse gives the novel a double vision. It is a convincing tale told by an individual with a past and with roots in the present, and a work of fiction that takes the reader beyond realism to the writer and to the higher ground of omniscience.[19] Versed in the cultural past, Galdós the realist is looking ahead.

The starting point for Russell and Kronik, among others, is an allegorical pairing at the intratextual level, with Galdós and Manso as artists at work. Looking outside the text, Walter T. Pattison notes, in a 1967 essay, the parallelism that exists between the lives of Galdós and Máximo Manso: "[W]e know that a decided change came into Galdós' existence in the period of 1879-80, characterized principally by the abandonment of his usual routine of steady, methodical production. One of the causes...was the presence of his brother Ignacio in Santander [where Galdós wrote the last book in the second series of *episodios nacionales*]. Ignacio was eight years older than Benito. He was an army officer who had gone to Cuba in 1864 and had married a Cuban girl... in 1873. The couple had two children by 1879.... Another daughter... was born in Santander in September of 1880 and Don Benito was her

---

no's novel. Francisco Javier Higuero expands upon the narrator-character dichotomy to analyze a range of oppositions in the novel.

[19] Eamonn Rodgers submits that "[l]os capítulos finales de *El amigo Manso* sugieren, pues, que las realidades esenciales están más allá del alcance de nuestra visión terrestre" ("Realismo" 442). Comparing this novel with earlier ones, he notes an increased subtlety on the levels of message production (moral purpose) and narration.

godfather" ("El amigo" 136). Pattison also mentions Galdós's love for Juanita Lund, an attractive and intellectual woman some fourteen years his junior. In 1879, Galdós received word of her engagement: "He was by then by his count 35, the same age as Máximo Manso. We have the word of Dr. Gregorio Marañón that Juanita remained the great love of Galdós' life, the woman whom he admired from afar and regretted having lost" ("El amigo" 139). Pattison notes that Irene is described four times as a "mujer del norte," and he observes that Juanita Lund's father was Norwegian ("El amigo" 139). The critic adds that during this time Galdós dedicated himself to studying Zola's technique.[20]

G. A. Davies argues that in *La desheredada*, influenced by French naturalism, Galdós extends his vision of society and that he further develops the social perspective in *El amigo Manso*: "Manso lives in a palpable Madrid as opposed to an airy-fairy Orbajosa; the society he describes is essentially infinite. Galdós presents us with an imagined world which merges at its farthest edges into the infinity of the real world" (17). Davies finds in *El amigo Manso* the didactic aims that inform the thesis novels, but the ambiguities of the presentation show a greater sophistication of style. The distinction is exemplified in the treatment of León Roch and Máximo Manso as *krausistas* and, not coincidentally, friends.[21] *La familia de León Roch* depicts Krausism as well intended but oblivious to certain practicalities. *El amigo Manso* concentrates on the movement as it relates to education. Manso's pedagogy consistently links instruction to morality; goodness must stand beside aesthetics. As with

---

[20] In his Twayne book on Galdós, Pattison makes the following entry in the chronology for the year 1880: "He spends the winter of 1879-1880 and the following summer in Santander with his brother Ignacio and his family. He publishes nothing; reads Zola" (10).

[21] José F. Montesinos writes, "Sospecho que Galdós fue a esta novela no desde el personaje, sino desde la concepción de ciertas circunstancias en que ha de hallarse inmerso, y como éstas no difieren mucho—aunque sí en cosas de gran importancia—de las de León Roch, no atreveríamos a decir que don Benito tuvo la feliz idea de rehacer en otro personaje la historia lamentable de [Roch], sacándola tal vez de ciertas angosturas anecdóticas que la menoscababan en vez de darle mayor fuerza, obteniendo, por la invención de un héroe mucho más verosímil—y mucho más humano—la coherencia y el sentido que *La famila...* no tenía" (2: 31). Montesinos considers the Krausist theme and a number of socio-poltical aspects of the novel (see 2: 28-60).

Francisco Giner de los Ríos and his disciples, the teacher and the pupil should be comrades in a shared enterprise, as Manso's friendship with Manuel Peña demonstrates.[22] Irene, for her part, as a "Northern woman," becomes "the embodiment of the rational, cultured woman, free from the handicaps and mean ambitions of the ordinary Spanish female," but "Manso's infatuation with her is really an infatuation with an ideal, since Irene, in spite of her education, remains a woman in whom instinct predominates over the educational veneer" (Davies 23). By the same token, his idealistic view of Manuel, along with Manuel's perceived defects of character, comes to be modified when the former student proves that he is more interested in politics than ethics. As Debra A. Castillo states, "Manso's authority as a teacher, his power over his creations, is undermined at every turn—even more than he may suspect" (49).

For Davies, the depth of characterization and the nuanced thematic scope of the novel separate it from the earlier works. Pattison stresses that the turning away, in Spain, from idealism (Kant, Hegel, and Krause) toward a "positivism of the Comptian variety" occurred around 1875, and adds that "by 1880 the newest trend was the evolutionary positivism of Herbert Spencer, based on the theories of Charles Darwin. The emphasis was now on science and natural laws, and of course this new philosophy was in accord with the scientific approach to reality of Zola and his followers" ("El amigo Manso" 144). The switch "from idealism to a new realism… is reflected in Manso's changing beliefs and… also parallels Galdós' change from the 'abstract' to a modified naturalism" (Pattison, "El amigo Manso" 144). Pattison's most important thesis is that Manso and Galdós try to effect a synthesis between the two currents: "Spencer was focusing his attention on the tangible and declared that God and

---

[22] Berkowitz notes that the critical and public reception to *La desheredada,* Galdós's attempt to write in the style of naturalism, was negative. Although the writer was fascinated with the concept of his new novel, on the conflict of ideas and reality, the elaboration of *El amigo Manso* was difficult for him. According to Berkowitz, Galdós's discouragement was of short duration, in part because he had received from Giner de los Ríos, to whom he had sent *La desheredada,* the most enthusiastic praise: "[H]e ventured to predict that all Galdós' former triumphs would be overshadowed by this one" (*Galdós, Spanish Liberal Crusader* 157-58).

metaphysics were in the realm of the unknowable. The earlier idealist [Krause] felt that reality was only the last stage of a series of forces and laws which had God as their point of origin" ("El amigo Manso" 148). Reconciliation comes when the discrete event is seen as bound to a higher law and that the universal must be sought in the particular. The narrative space becomes a forum for the testing of ideas and for the playing against each other of controversial and complicated issues, political, philosophical, and literary. It is the complexity of the structure—with ideological and artistic centers in grey areas—that helps to define the orientation of *El amigo Manso*.[23] Signaling the birth of Máximo Manso "close to the fountain of Spanish nationalism," Peter A. Bly notes that the narrator/protagonist is rendered "at the beginning as some materialized Spirit of Spanish History and then appears at times in his earthly form as a philosopher of history" (25, 32). Manso's methodological shortcomings, his refusal to contribute to practical politics, and his gradual submission to the laws of sexual love combine to negate his positive potential, and thus "[h]is return to Limbo is an admission of this inadequacy" (Bly 33). Although he would like to designate himself as such, Manso is not writing as a historian, but events that relate to history are part of his story, and the same is true of Galdós.

Nancy A. Newton sees Manso's self-doubt and suffering as producing a transformation visible not only to the reader but to the narrator/protagonist himself. Originally skeptical, he ends by believing in his own existence. As both story and discourse verify, "Manso the 'contemplativo' becomes Manso the 'comprometido.' The objective narrator becomes the involved participant" (Newton, "*El amigo Manso*" 122). The fictional frame has a rationale: "Manso moves from pure abstraction... to a philosophical-artistic posture of contemplation and observation, and on to a position from which he can recognize and evaluate spontaneous, illogical human involvement, though years of analysis of every motion and emotion impede his own participation. He

---

[23] Carlos Blanco Aguinaga brings out the interplay of idealism and positivism in *El amigo Manso*. He notes the varied usage of forms of *positivismo* and *positivista* in the text. For example, he cites Manso's description of Manuel Peña in chapter 7—"le seducían las cuestiones palpitantes y positivas"—which relates not only to positivism but to Emilia Pardo Bazán's treatise on naturalism and her effort to insert Catholicism into the program. See Blanco Aguinaga, *La historia* 19-48, esp. 43-48.

reaches the point of seeing the promised land..., but, being denied entrance, slips unobtrusively, unhappily back into 'reporter-artist' territory" (Newton, "*El amigo Manso*" 123-24).[24]

Currie K. Thompson casts Manso's development in these terms: *El amigo Manso* "focuses on the process through which its protagonist gains knowledge (his gradual realization of his standing with Irene) and the impact this knowledge has on him. It is, like Hegel's *Phenomenology of Spirit*, an exploration of the relationship between knowing and being. It invites its readers to a consideration of the engendering of knowledge—that is, of how knowledge is engendered or comes to be, how it engenders or shapes us, and the relationship that has sometimes been assumed between knowing and gender" (43-44). Manso associates the feminine with sexual attraction and imperfection, which Thompson calls "a pattern of belief that has dominated western thought from Plato through Jung—and that is reflected in Hegel" (45). The protagonist later regrets having been, as he puts it, the angel who guards the door of the paradise of reason rather than the man who (like Manuel Peña) would enjoy the desired woman. Thompson concludes that Manso's yearning "for the progress of linear time [is] mocked by a cyclic recurrence," a return to the starting place, but that Manso finds consolation in the experience, which can show the adaptability, as opposed to the repetition or rejection, of history (58). James H. Hoddie, for his part, finds that Hegel's *Aesthetics*, alluded to early in the novel, "provides numerous insights into those aspects of the elaboration of Máximo's novel meant to prove his non-existence" (62).

Catherine Jagoe analyzes the matter of engendering with regard to the depiction of Manso: "Manso's apprehensions about Irene and women's education stem from his unsatisfactorily gendered nature. Timid, bookish, asexual, he lacks masculine decisiveness and initiative, as his name itself implies (*manso* means docile, tame). He indeed becomes an increasingly androgynous figure, assuming a feminine role of concern

---

[24] For an earlier and different reading, see Eoff: "Manso ascends..., but through his contact with the earth, he not only has fulfilled his [Christ-like] mission; he has broadened his conception of philosophy, and in fact has saved himself from sterile passivity by acquiring (... like Nazarín) enthusiasm for the role of beneficent master. This is the practical, realistic idea that interests Galdós most..." (136).

with child care and matchmaking" (101). He fails to notice that Irene is just an ordinary woman and that the "mujer-mujer" Doña Javiera would be a solid match for him. The problem of gender stereotypes aside, Galdós's celibate philosopher-teacher, it seems to me, would be hard to classify as effeminate or androgynous. He is a recognizable type: the overly studious, concept-obsessed loner, ill-at-ease with women but also in social situations in general. He is absorbed in books, in his classes, in his mentoring role. He interacts with men and women with a degree of confidence, as so-called confirmed bachelors are wont to do. Jagoe's analysis of *El amigo Manso* is heightened by references to educational reform in Spain at the time of the publication of the novel. She reads matters of women's education as presented with ambivalence in the novel,[25] and she identifies the profound coincidence that "in the very year that [José Luis] Albareda's educational reforms raised in an unprecedented way the issue of women's right to secondary and higher education in her own right and not just as a future mother or wife, Galdós should create a narrative featuring a woman given all the educational opportunities of the time, who confesses that her career bores her and turns thankfully back to wifedom and motherhood" (102; see 95-102). The conservative and the progressive positions mesh here as in other parts of the novel. Irene is represented, in the course of the narrative and according to changes in perspective, as the defenseless, educated, independent, ideal, savvy, and conventional woman. Manso builds the story so that the reader sees his growing affection for her, but he also, and perhaps unknowingly, builds a case that would make her alliance with Manuel Peña a logical and suitable one.

John H. Sinnigen, in *Sexo y política: Lecturas galdosianas*, analyzes *El amigo Manso* from the dual focus of his title. He looks at the division of the narrative into the private sphere of women and the public sphere of men, and at the presence of Máximo Manso in three family circles: those of Doña Javiera and Manuel, Doña Cándida and Irene, and José María and his coterie. The *indiano* brings the colonies into the picture, and with them the European patriarchal values versus the "natural" (and perceived

---

[25] John H. Sinnigen echoes this statement when he titles a section of his analysis of *El amigo Manso* "Entre la mujer independiente y el ángel del hogar" (83-86); see 78-88.

as inferior) culture of the New World, "de modo que en *El amigo Manso* se pone de relieve el proyecto de incorporar en el tejido nacional el capital primitivo acumulado mediante guerras y matrimonios en ultramar" (Sinnigen 81).[26] José María's reacclimation to Spain and his adaptation to the political scene allow Galdós to condemn a number of strains in the national ideology of the moment. As in the case of a text such as Cervantes's *El celoso extremeño*, the figure of the *indiano* creates an automatic set of correspondences and contrasts between Spain and another way of life, another—an other—ethnicity. Manuela, her mother, and their staff bring an air of exoticism, and of difference, into a social structure built on bloodlines and now on economics. These characters are hardly noble savages, but they operate according to norms that may suggest, to Spaniards, an alternative sensibility to the civilized urban life of Madrid. They have moved a great distance, and they are the proverbial fish out of water, with an innate goodness and an eagerness to please in the new surroundings. Máximo Manso views them from a distance, with tenderness but with an almost casual disparagement of their lack of sophistication, as if he believed, at least subconsciously, in the *civilización-barbarie* dichotomy. Again, Manso's commentary on the proceedings reveals as much or more about him as about the newly arrived Cubans.

Irony is central and variable in *El amigo Manso*, or perhaps central because of its variability. H. L. Boudreau's penetrating study of the

---

[26] Sinnigen alludes to Manso's modest quantities of economic and cultural capital that comprise the material bases of what Blanco Aguinaga calls his "mediocridad" [*La historia* 21], "emblema de la actitud desdeñosa del autor ante los valores de la Restauración" (Sinnigen 79). For a commentary on Galdós's political stance, including his contributions to periodicals, see Rodgers, "Galdós ¿escritor disolvente?" Rodgers notes that Galdós "[a]cogió con poco entusiasmo la Restauración, y se reservó siempre el derecho de criticar la corrupción moral y financiera" (273), but adds: "En vista de los adelantos conseguidos desde 1876 en lo que se refería a la libertad personal y de expresión (y Galdós estaba muy consciente de ser uno de los principales beneficiarios de ésta última), el novelista era muy reacio a cualquier acción que minara las bases del orden vigente. Aunque nunca cejó en su oposición al caciquismo, reconocía, con todo, que era algo demasiado arraigado en la cultura política española como para ser extirpado rápidamente" (274-75). On the author's political views, see Berkowitz's extensive *Pérez Galdós*. See also del Río, "Notas sobre el tema de América en Galdós."

symbolism of names in Galdós, and specifically in *El amigo Manso*, shows the crafted quality of the discourse. Logically, the essay begins with an analysis of *manso* and its variations. *Manso* can mean benign, soft, tranquil, or, Boudreau submits, "one who is taken advantage of or used by others" (64). He considers the semiotic-semantic theme to be a unifying factor in the narrative: "Every significant character reflects Galdós's preoccupation with *mansedumbre*, making the work a fabric of dependency/independence, use/abuse, doing for and being done unto.... The work in its entirety is a study of the influence of the individual on his milieu and of it upon him" (66-67). Synthesizing two strains in the critical corpus, Boudreau argues that the imagery, real and implicit, joins novelistic technique (the autonomous character) with ideology (Krausist principles of education): "The two are in fact—for all their inherent interest as unique phenomena—both aspects of the elaboration of the motif of *mansedumbre*: action vs. thought, influencing vs. being influenced" (68). The narrative, like most of Galdós's novels, is pessimistic in orientation. Manso seems convinced "that the man of thought could remain, could permanently change the world. Galdós knows better, as does Manso— from time to time.... Perhaps the ultimate ambiguity of the work—whether intended or not—is after all in that word *manso*, from the Latin *manere*: *permanecer*" (Boudreau 69).[27] Boudreau posits, in the first paragraph of his essay, that the love triangle in *El amigo Manso* anticipates the Augusto/Eugenia/Mauricio triangle in *Niebla*, and his ending anticipates Unamuno's emphasis on immortality. Galdós could have made his protagonist evaporate, but he is reborn in the text and in the higher plane of the final chapter. The author may have sensed, like Unamuno does so resoundingly, that his character's fate and his own are interconnected and that creation is a two-way path.

Michael Nimetz refers to Galdós's special take on Sophoclean or

---

[27] Eugenio García Gascón proposes that "[l]a caracterización de Manso como Jesús, de tono paródico, se va revelando al lector poco a poco. El lector descubre, conforme avanza la novela, que la figura de Máximo Manso como 'maestro' de su 'discípulo' Manolito Peña tiene mucho que ver con las enseñanzas evangélicas" (202). This leads the critic to conclude that the novel operates on two levels: existence and non-existence, earth and heaven, with narrative voices to correspond to each level. Others present the idea in a more secular fashion. See, for example, Willem 163.

dramatic irony, as, for example, in Manuel Peña's declaration that his teacher does not live in the (or this) world: "What Peña does not realize is how apt it is in the context of Manso's 'Yo no existo.' Another reminder, likewise expressed by Sophoclean irony, is the pejorative 'metafísico' which José María Manso flings at his brother" (98). Diane Urey categorizes *El amigo Manso* as "ostensibly the story of an educator's education," which simultaneously "educates the reader in reading the novel, literature and life. Just as Manso learns that there is no single perspective on life, so we learn that there is no single novelistic meaning" (72). The novel becomes a subversion rather than an affirmation of realism, perspective, and objectivity. Máximo Manso not only does not start with the self-knowledge for which he gives himself credit, but his confidence in the power of reason grows faster than his ability to ascertain the truth. At no time in his "life" does he grasp the full implications of what is going on around him, an irony in need of an ironic reading. Gerald Gillespie contends that "no discussion of Galdós' mature realism is... complete without reference to the impact of Cervantine wisdom upon it. The question of truth and illusion has been standard in the European novel since *Don Quixote*, which became the revered model for English 'humor' and German 'romantic irony'. Cervantes' haunting suggestion that, in addition to the opposites reason and unreason,... a paradoxical 'reason of unreason' also undermined any neat distinction between reality and fiction — perhaps in spite of his own intention of separating them" (11).[28] Stephen Gilman writes that "Friedrich Schlegel explains Romantic irony... as corresponding to the awareness of the artist, who, like a miniature God, smiles both at his own capabilities and his own limitations" (*Galdós* 81-82). Gilman distinguishes between Galdós and his creation Manso — one of "his two ostensible 'krausista' protagonists," the other being León Roch — saying that the fictional characters "lack the gift — or curse — of irony, the very irony with which their author delivers them at birth. These are didactic lives deeply immersed in their own sincerity as against the

---

[28] Gillespie sees the interplay of reality and fiction in Cervantes — in the character, the reader, the author, and the world — as binding together "a complex realism" (13). Gillespie goes on to say that "Galdós' reworking of Cervantine themes raises questions about man's reality and freedom long before Unamuno" (18), and he compares the novel to Thomas Mann's *Tonio Kröger*. The essay is reprinted, with the Spanish translated to English, in Labanyi 77-102.

writer of novels, who stands apart, views from a distance, and in the very same words simultaneously praises and blames, admires and ridicules" (*Galdós* 81). For Gilman, Cervantes's stance as "stepfather" of Don Quijote can be applied to Galdós, even though his relation to Manso may be affectionate.

Marsha S. Collins unites several key elements in "*El humorismo,* Romantic Irony, and the Carnivalesque World of Galdós's *El amigo Manso.*" Following Raquel Asún, she notes the influence of Francisco Giner de los Ríos's "¿Qué es lo cómico?" on the novel. Guided by Jean Paul Richter, Giner argues that "the comic arises from a disproportionate relationship or a disjunction between motivation and action, effort and result, what should happen and what actually does happen. The fictional character involved in these disjointed events remains ignorant or blissfully unaware of the mismatch, while readers watch with amusement as they project their own superior knowledge and perspective onto the same occurrences" (summarized in Collins 608). Collins believes that Galdós extends the concept by injecting Romantic irony onto the scheme. She alludes to the fact that when the author arrived in Madrid in 1862 to begin his university studies, there was an ongoing debate between neoclassical and Romantic approaches to *Don Quijote,* fueled by the essays of Nicolás Díaz de Benjumea, which linked Cervantes to Romantic irony, and later by Benjumea's edition of the *Quijote,* published at about the same time as *El amigo Manso,* when naturalism had become a factor in literary debates.[29] The novel reflects the polemical mood of the times. For Collins, "[i]n his profound ambiguity, Manso epitomizes the trickster, who counts Prometheus and Hermes among his antecedents in Western mythology [and who] reigns supreme in the temporary upside-down kingdom of carnival. He generally ends his days as the victim in a ritual sacrifice that purges, revitalizes, and restores the natural order. Although the rational Manso seems an unlikely choice for the role of the Lord of Misrule, he unleashes the novel's apparently chaotic mass of characters, things, and events when he makes his pact with the fictional author" (620-

---

[29] Collins stresses that the "crossfire of radically opposed aesthetic positions supported by German Idealism, on the one hand, and materialism, on the other, coincides with the appearance of Galdós's *novelas contemporáneas*" ("*Humorismo*" 610). For an analysis of Benjumea's reading of *Don Quijote,* see Close esp. 100-13.

21). Referring to Romantic irony, and particularly to Schlegel's notion of "transcendental buffoonery," Collins concludes that Galdós "has created a novel of transcendent wisdom and artistry that wears the deceptive mask of a mere trifle, of an insignificant, entertaining farce" (621). Thus, "[w]ith *El amigo Manso*, Galdós reclaims realism as part of Spain's rich literary legacy, restoring its authentic spirit of warmth and humanity through an infusion of Cervantine Romantic irony" (Collins 625). The dialectics of the *serio buffo*, practiced by Cervantes and mentioned by Schlegel, clearly finds its way to Unamuno.

In the section on *El amigo Manso* in his *Galdós Beyond Realism*, Timothy McGovern points out that magic comes into play in the first chapter of the novel. As a result, the novel "creates a world in which a type of domino effect is at work. A character may magically pass through a world interface, and when this occurs, the entire other world must re-arrange its structure in order to maintain a sense of logic and rationality.... Th[e] text continually underscores Manso's estrangement from the world which he has invaded..., and this invader erroneously believes that he enjoys epistemic privilege, which is ironic since he is writing the story" (58). Additionally, "[t]he death scene of the book again opens an interface between various fictional worlds when Manso addresses the invisible and silent author and demands that he be taken out of the realist world and separated from his realist body" (62). Galdós engages his readership in a survey of realism and finally in a rejection of realism as a depiction of the natural course of events. Hazel Gold summarizes the phenomenon perfectly when she indicates that "[f]iction written under the aegis of realism confronts a daunting and ultimately self-defeating task. It is charged with constructing a description, distinguished by its precision and thoroughness, of the hidden inner mechanisms that animate and explain those movements of the social community as a whole and of its individual members that are accessible to superficial observation" (11). Stated a bit differently, mimesis can never be a flawless imitation; seamlessness is itself a fantasy, an unrealizable ideal. Reality is, as they say, out there, and the individual eye selects its object, its site of focus, that is, the perspective or vantage point from which vision occurs. Galdós surrounds realism with metacommentary, itself a sign of deviation. He is conscious of the writing process, of the reader, and of the acts of encoding and decoding a text.

Not unlike the picaresque and *Don Quijote, El amigo Manso* has its base in realism. The early modern narratives distance themselves from the idealism of romance. The creators of picaresque fiction regress from the heroic and the preeminent in a supremely obtrusive manner. Exemplarity is present only by denial. The *pícaros* operate in a recognizable reality, and from the lower rungs of the social ladder and, accordingly, from the discursive margins. Cervantes creates a realistic center from which the romance-obsessed knight Don Quijote diverges; it is, of course, a shifting, unstable center, tinged by literary precedent, by literariness. Don Quijote inserts poetry into history, because he unconsciously confuses the two. Cervantes inserts history into poetry, because he consciously confuses the two. The strangeness, or otherness, of the narratives stems from their repositioning of the ideal, which comes into the text as satire, as loss, or as outmoded convention. The changes in style and tone—the freshness of the compositional method and the textual ideology—herald the new, the novel. Picaresque narrative is informed by social reality, but it is as much about textuality, the fabrication of the product and discursive (and interpretive) strategies, as about class, poverty, and the overstepping of boundaries. Similarly, Don Quijote forces his madness onto a society based on the Spain of Cervantes's time, but the social significance and the political resonances share the stage with the chronicling of the adventures, the access to information, the reliability of the narrators, and the reception of the books, the story and the history. From its inception, literary realism is accompanied by metafiction, by a sense of the fashioning of a product. The picaresque starts with autobiography, and *Don Quijote* with the historical chronicle, but the protocols of self-representation and historiography are compromised from the outset by the devices of art. Galdós, in structuring *El amigo Manso*, pays homage to this poetics of realism and metafiction. And he does so most emphatically in the first words of the novel.

The early modern break from idealism is always mindful of precedent. The picaresque intertext includes—as the new formula deconstructs—the biographies and autobiographies of eminent people, the spiritual confession, and the noble lineage that is fundamental to chivalric romance. Idealism, as manifested in the institution of chivalry and on the pages of chivalric romance, is at the core of *Don Quijote*, in which the protagonist optimistically, and blindly, expects the "real world" to conform to the high standards of knightly conduct. Máximo Manso is an idealist whose vision, from the practical side of things, is impaired. His tutorial duties and the arrival of his brother throw him into the real world and into the political arena. Studiousness and intellectual snobbery have previously protected him, to a large degree, from direct contact with the business of society. Manuel, Irene, and the family of José María bring him out of academic isolation and force him to confront what might be termed real problems in real time. The incongruity of the high-minded pedagogue in the rough-and-tumble Madrid of the end of the nineteenth century, where citizens are more concerned with taking care of themselves than with defending others, evokes the chivalric enterprise of Don Quijote. Manso takes charge of the plebeian (non-aristocratic) youth, the orphan in distress, and the outsiders at risk of being scorned, who, while accepting his help, find ways to look out for themselves. Replicating the ending of *Don Quijote*, Manso becomes disillusioned and dies. He says that he is not interested in being remembered, but his inscription in a book will allow him to live on, like other immortal literary characters and like their authors. If *Don Quijote* provides a conceptual model, later writers need to find a substitute for chivalry in other forms of idealism, such as education, or science, or spirituality.

One of Cervantes's major gifts to literature is his ability to forge a seriocomic dialectics of the absolute and the relative. The bases of perception link life with art; understanding the external world and deciphering verbal and other signs are essentially a single task. Idealists tend to depend too heavily on the absolute, pragmatists on the relative. Galdós picks up on this lesson and adds his own temperament, opinions, and literary imagination to the mix. It is a brilliant stroke on the author's part that his blind idealist has a sense of irony and a sense of humor, not to mention a self-consciously declamatory style. Irony in *El amigo Manso* is masterfully enacted. Manso seems aware that his situation is a bit ludicrous. He knows that he is a loner by choice, a man of ideas, and he is being pulled into the world of domesticity. His first assignment, the tutoring of Manuel Peña, is academic in nature, and the idea of the extended classroom is perfectly in line with the desiderata of the education reformists. Manso is also committed to the welfare and education of Irene, and her story also falls within the pedagogical frame. His educational principles and his nerves are put to the test with the duties connected to his brother's family. Not only are the women and their attendants in a "new world," albeit the Old World, but the unscrupulous José María represents the worst of both worlds. Máximo, caught up in chores, also must stand guard over the women and children, in a comic variation on the theme of honor. The tone is comic not because honor can be compromised, but because Máximo Manso is simply not a fighting man, as compared with Manuel, who, in fact, becomes involved in a duel. The reader observes Manso from an ironic distance as he does the same, not realizing the full impact of his misjudgments but not unaware of his estrangement from the affairs of a society that thrives on aggressiveness (and aggression). The narrator's rhetoric verifies that he knows that he is out of his element—which seems to please more than to disturb him—but, although he clearly derides himself for his ineffectualness, he just as clearly misses the ironic repercussions of many of his observations and interactions.[30] This is Galdós's take on the dialectics of discourse as story.

As in the picaresque and *Don Quijote*, there is in *El amigo Manso* a crucial nexus between the protagonist and society, between the outsider and the mainstream. The *pícaro* is ostracized by virtue of birth and class, that is, by the social determinism of early modern Spain. Old Christians, the aristocracy, and an inflexible hierarchy stand in the center. So, in literary terms, do the lives of illustrious citizens, of past and present, together with humanism, spiritual evolution, and a morality that conforms to social politics. Don Quijote's madness pushes him off-center, where his anachronistic ideals and abnormal conduct become signs of difference. Manso is not so much lost in contemplation as displaced in the social whirl, or, one might say, lost in translation. He attempts to transfer his teaching methodology to the world at large, and the world—which functions on an opposing plan—fails to comply. His resistance to the bases of authority is countered by a progressive, troubling, and ironic attraction to the public domain. This attraction is encapsulated in the shift

---

[30] In the chapter on "The Restoration and the Established Order" in *History and Fiction in Galdós's Narratives*, Geoffrey Ribbans speaks of "outward conformity and inner subversion" (203). He notes that *El amigo Manso*, set in the early Restoration period, contains "Máximo's Olympian philosophical pronouncements.... Manso... describe[s] at great length, in... abstract terms, the transformation of society currently taking place, but he fails to see what is going on under his own nose. José María, for his part, eager to become a marquis, pushes the urge towards the reconciliation of opposites to an absurd degree" (203).

of Irene from ideal woman to love object. As Manso discovers, and enumerates, her imperfections, he recognizes an instability in his emotions and world view that comes across, for him and presumably for the reader, as both positive and negative. He straddles the line between the man of action and the intellectual hermit, and this dilemma—this existential anguish—propels him (ironically, of course) into the realm of the living. His former habits had made him immune to hurt and despair. Love, jealousy, and involvement in the lives of others transforms him into a different person, or at least a different persona. Manso's entry into society, like the *pícaro*'s search for upward mobility and Don Quijote's decision to venture forth as a knight, gives him a story line, and a plot, that subservience to a master, the staid routine of an *hidalgo*, and the choice of books over social contact, respectively, would not have offered. The opening sentence of *El amigo Manso* establishes a dual direction that mirrors those of the picaresque and *Don Quijote*.

Oversimplified, the model here consists of the narrator's account and the author's implicit rewriting, each of which includes the axes of story and discourse. The *pícaro*, from Lázaro de Tormes onward, is more committed to making a case (literally, in *Lazarillo*) than to telling the undiluted truth, while the author finds ways to undermine these pretensions. The discursive struggle affects the story and reflects the battle of the unwelcome individual against the institutions of society. Cervantes modifies the formula to feature competing narrative voices and points of view. The narrator of Part 1, chapter 1, insists on the absolute truth of his narrative, while the information that he provides is a testament to relativity. The surrogate authors manage, paradoxically, to overshadow the writer and to place him in the limelight, as the creator of the text and of the confusion; his absence is a marker of his presence. Cervantes, arguably more than any author prior to 1605, brings the act of composition into the argument of the narrative. He converts his narrators into characters, some overwhelmingly fictional and others part of an embedded "real" world. At least one is a professed sage, a historian with rather dubious credentials. The chronicle moves from an imagined record to a published book, from a mental object to a consumer—and critical—object. When acknowledged as contained within the narrative frame, the two *Quijote* prologues append to the dramatis personae the cunningly scripted fictional Cervantes and the historical figure insulted by Avellaneda. Fiction and history merge in the picaresque, and their points of distinction diminish even further in *Don Quijote*. As literature becomes more about life, it becomes more about art. Stated in a more nuanced fashion, as literature reflects life with a consciousness of perspective, it lends itself to an examination of structure, of construction. Its realism depends on the extremes: the world reduced to—and reproduced in—art, and art as a space of contention between the expression and perception, between the signifier and the signified. In *El amigo Manso* and elsewhere, Galdós reconciles this dialectics with the poetics of realism.

In *Theories of Literary Realism*, Darío Villanueva classifies as *genetic realism* a form "based on [the] principle of transparent correspondence between the literary text and external phenomena" (15). He adds, "Naturalism is nothing but genetic realism, for it assumes the existence of a univocal reality which precedes the text and which is scanned by the author's perceiving consciousness in all its hidden aspects through minute and efficient observation. Its result should be a faithful reproduction of this reality, owing to the transparency or thinness of the literary medium (language) and to the artist's 'sincerity'" (15). In turning to *conscious realism*, Villanueva notes that, "despite a continuous mimetic literary tradition originating in Plato and Aristotle, there have always been views, such as Hegel's, that consider the attempts artificially to remake, through aesthetic means, what already exists in the external world as a useless and superfluous exercise doomed to failure," and he comments that even the practitioners of genetic realism often stressed the autonomy of the literary work and granted "a purely creative status to the reality presented in it" (37). One might say that early modern Spanish writers anticipate, or practice, conscious realism. They embrace a view of narrative that forsakes idealism in favor of a picture of the social experience—the reality—of the time. Nonetheless, these writers sense what could be termed the mimetic fallacy. They were creating in an era in which poets were exalting the metaphor. They seem to have recognized, or intuited, that, in figurative discourse, and figuratively speaking, A=B is not the same as A=A. A metaphor is a carefully wrought approximation, the vehicle of which can, at best, only be close to the tenor. Correspondence does not mean exactness but relative equivalence. Genetic realism foregrounds similitude, while conscious realism foregrounds difference. When the picaresque authors and Cervantes move toward realism, they are mindful that re-creation is, by definition, a second-hand art, never free of mediation or of the graft of the artist. Basking in the glow of realism, Galdós appears to understand the stakes of the (oxymoronic?) realist ideal.

One of the most admirable features of *El amigo Manso* is its alternation between overtness and subtlety. The dramatic opening and the hyperbolic rhetoric—in which chickpeas receive more space than Hegel, for example—announce a writerly performance, a self-referential gesture, and a cry to the reader to be aware of the gamesmanship at work. The forty-eight chapters within the frame differentiate between the linguistic excesses of the man of ideas (and of letters) and the revelations of character through discourse. Manso's verbal histrionics permit Galdós to reveal the protagonist's strengths and weaknesses, his perspicacity on some levels and his lack of comprehension on others. Galdós communicates the scholar's feeling of superiority by having Manso play the rhetorician, adept at language and at judging his fellow men and women. The subtlety of the performance comes through Manso's divulging of more than he thinks. Galdós does what the author of *Lazarillo de Tormes* and his successors do, through a semiotic system—nominally single, effectively double—that encompasses the narrator's voice and the (implied) author's voice-over. It is in this space that the aloofness, naïveté, and false sense of security of the narrator/protagonist come to the fore, even though it could hardly be his intention to draw attention to them. The richness of the text is related to its ambiguity and to its dependence on the reader to recognize and come to terms with the ironies, the first of which is the tension between the metafictional beginning (and ending) and the realistic setting. As with the picaresque writers, Galdós places a portrayal of society within a text in the making, with point of view as a factor on each plane. The compositional process—with Lázaro, the making of a case—also becomes a means by which to represent social customs and vices. The result is a series of portraits: the self-portrait of the *pícaro* and its discursive counterpoint (counterportrait) of the author, and the narrator's vision of society and its vision of him or her. The structural pattern of *El amigo Manso* is analogous, with the artist, the work of art, the social backdrop, and the perspectival irony in play.

Máximo Manso puts his particular spin on the world around him, analyzing economics, class divisions, politics, education, and human behavior, among other topics. He is the lead character, but his story is about the events that integrate him into the social landscape, so that there is a metaphorical and metonymical force to the episodes and to the collective incidents. By entrusting the story and the storytelling to a first-person narrator, Galdós is able to deal with a series of major themes from Manso's point of view and to supplement the view through ironic recasting. The novel is a character study, which itself makes story and discourse interdependent, and it is a study of society which could be deemed a work in progress. In addition, a foundation of the novel is realism, including Zola's naturalism and its Spanish manifestations, to which Galdós attaches a metafictional codicil and thereby disturbs the narrative—and, by extension, the social—order. Forty-eight chapters are verisimilar, and two are not. The framing of realism shifts the focus and the reader response, and this could not have been lost on Galdós. He is always a conscientious artist, who uses language, irony, humor, and observation of the cataclysms and the minutiae of society to put his signature on a text. In *El amigo Manso*, he makes the creative role of the novelist more pronounced, and the allusions to *Don Quijote* in the narrative apply to elements beyond the idealistic protagonist. The fusion of history and poetry takes a special turn, as it does in Cervantes, when the impossible—here, in the existential spirals—enters the plot. Galdós is a realist, but he looks to plant art solidly within society. He moves profoundly into realism, but he initiates and concludes that movement with sabotage to his own design. This may be his homage to the early modern forebears, and conjointly saboteurs, of realism.

For Akiko Tsuchiya, "the constant play between mimesis and metafiction on the level of the text's narrative processes mirrors the protagonist's own struggle with the problems of language in the interior text," and she concludes that "[b]oth Manso and his creatures are mere signs on the page, whose apparent correspondence to a true referent is illusory" (6-7). This might imply a rejection of realism—a recognition of, or resignation to, the fact that everything is an illusion—but it may be that Galdós's message is a commentary on the art of narrative and on modes of realism. The frame of *El amigo Manso* brings the artist into the frame, as Velázquez does visually, and dazzlingly, in *Las meninas*, not necessarily to refute realism but to make clear that mimesis requires an act of mediation. When we sit in a theater and a play moves us, perhaps cathartically, we still have to have come into a building and behave as spectators, no matter how involved we may be once the lights are down. In *El amigo Manso*, Galdós sets the stage for the reader, then dims the lights until the dénouement, when he once again turns them on. The ending of the novel takes the narrator/protagonist to a higher place, and one can see here a deep structure that relates to *Niebla*, where author and character become intertwined as they face issues of mortality. Despite the academic discipline and the thoughtful nature of Máximo Manso, his dissatisfaction increases. Galdós's creation is less obsessive and less anguished than Augusto Pérez, but he enters immortality and aligns himself with an authorial persona. Unamuno intensifies existential angst, but he makes the outer world more vague. The reader knows the street address of Augusto's love object, yet the urban setting is not particularly time specific. Máximo Manso, in contrast, goes from a figuratively cloistered life to the socio-political developments of early Restoration Madrid, where character changes, *mudanzas* of various types, and narrative transitions occur. The theme of the education of the educator links the novel to Unamuno's *Amor y pedagogía*, which in turn forges a "nivolistic" path toward *Niebla*.

El amigo Manso demonstrates how realistic technique can cover the gap between reality and the written word. Máximo Manso pens his story and thus serves as the filter through which events are selected and arranged. He is the storyteller and the controller of point of view, although overwritten by an ironic but good-spirited author figure. Galdós respects the laws of verisimilitude except at the beginning and the end of Manso's story, where what some see as a classic case of disillusionment, a *desengaño*, overtakes realism. The novelist puts theory into practice by exercising realism, and then he seems to choose to negate its ties with the real world. Yet he may be writing himself into the frame for a purpose: to suggest that reality is as much fabricated as preexistent, and to alert readers of their role in the interpretive process. In *El amigo Manso*, he varies the treatment of history by allowing the narrator to critique the political system, and Spain's present in light of its past, as he scrutinizes—and asks the reader to scrutinize—the reliability and the practicality of those judgments. Manso the idealist, the quixotic philosopher, is a man of principles and a dedicated teacher, who sees instruction as all-consuming. He insists on his moral separation from his brother, but his venture into society pushes him in new directions and at times tempts him, if somewhat innocently, to answer to his own desires. One might argue that there is a different kind of history and a different kind of poetry in the novel, because the presentation of social instability, the satire, and the discourse are built around the active mind and the ingratiating distractedness of Máximo Manso. The richness of point of view enables Galdós to examine the panorama of society, the archetypes and stereotypes of the national identity, the forces of revisionism, and the conventions of literature. As Unamuno would do in *Niebla*, he devises a plot around a love triangle, supplemented by additional competition but even more by an inquiry into the aims and methods of art.

Galdós would have counted on an expectation of realism from his readership. While not disregarding that premise, he incorporates into the text a commentary on the production of the manuscript. *Lazarillo de Tormes*, in its anonymity and its divergence from romance formulas, lays claim to being a truthful account, more like autobiography than like the major fictions of the day.[31] The art, including the deconstruction of idealism and romance, lies within a strangely mimetic structure. In *Don Quijote*, Cervantes turns both romance and mimesis upside down, but his "true history" is not as far from the New World chronicles as one might imagine, and, more importantly, the *verdadera historia* of the knight errant nullifies the detachment of story from discourse and of poetry from history. *El amigo Manso* inverts the Cervantine model by taking a firm stand on the fictional status of the narrator/protagonist and progressing into the verisimilar, only to return at the end to a domain beyond narrative realism, where the author is by no means in hiding. Máximo Manso's narrative has two starting points and two endings; one set complies with the norms of realism, and the other does not. Galdós is a giant among realists, but he seems to be seeking at least a partial escape, an alternative paradigm for fiction. Peter Brooks uses the phrase "visual inspection and inventory of the world" to denote "what sometimes seems to us a misplaced faith that verbal pictures of the world are both necessary and sufficient to creating a sense of place, context, milieu that in turn explain and motivate character, their actions and reflections. To

---

[31] Cf. Rico: "La irrupción de gentecillas como los padres o los amos de Lázaro en un relato en prosa constituía una novedad absoluta y los lectores de la época, en el pronto, no podían presumir que se la habían con una ficción.... Entiendo que el autor del *Lazarillo* se propuso precisamente este objetivo: presentar la novela—cuando menos, presentarla—como si se tratara de la obra auténtica de un auténtico Lázaro de Tormes. No simplemente un relato verosímil, insisto, sino verdadero. No realista: real" (154).

understand how and what people are, and how they have become such, you need to understand their environment" (17). Without ignoring details, Galdós moves in *El amigo Manso* toward a more limited, and more ironically constructed, point of view and toward the psychological over the physical. He accommodates historical reality while hinting at—or crossing the threshold into—what could be called, in Unamuno, the environment of the mind.

The Birth of the *Nivola* and the Rebirth of the Novel: *Amor y pedagogía*

...por ahora no publica el señor Unamuno más que para lectores, no para bibliófilos...

MIGUEL DE UNAMUNO'S *AMOR y pedagogía* (1902) is an experimental novel about an experiment in child-rearing, and a prelude of sorts to *Niebla*, first published in 1920. Unamuno was a scholar, a philosopher, and a writer who cultivated a wide variety of genres. His works do not maintain strict formal or thematic boundaries. They demonstrate Unamuno's spirituality, his passions, and his obsessions, as these elements are explored and brought together in his treatises, essays, and narrative, dramatic, and poetic fictions. A common denominator of the writings is immortality, as a theological issue and as a mystery for the engaged and contemplative seeker of knowledge. Immortality is, at the same time, a function of faith and a quest that involves belief systems and special challenges, operating on universal and intimate planes. Literary recognition and fame come to be metaphors for immortality. The classic text immortalizes its writer by offering a glimpse of heaven, a glimpse of eternity. Unamuno seizes and cherishes the metaphor. The negotiations that take place within fiction acknowledge the great unknowns while never giving up on solving life's puzzles. The trials and the agonies of the search for immortality are manifest in each of the works, where one finds a complementary and equally prominent recourse: the conspicuous presence of the author himself. This particular brand of metafiction links the artistic process to creation in its broadest sense. Rather than debate the relative merits and priorities of history and poetry, Unamuno places himself in both realms.

He stands beyond the text in order to assess the world and its remaking from a distance, and he enters the fiction to guarantee that his *entes de ficción* will not overshadow him, since he will become one of them. Stated succinctly, Unamuno's metafiction is tempered with philosophy, religious doctrine, and psychology, treated as matters of life and death. It is high art, but full of wit, humor, and irony. While drawing from many precedents and categories, and emulating the art of Miguel de Cervantes, the writing has a unique flavor, as well as a unique intellectual weight.

Amor y pedagogía is Unamuno's second novel. The first, *Paz en la guerra* (1897), set in his native city of Bilbao during the second Carlist war, reflects nineteenth-century narrative realism and its interest in historical detail, the projection of a panoramic vision, and the interplay of the quotidian and the climactic. It is the author's concession to the current conventions of storytelling and, whether consciously or unconsciously, a display of his ability to write in the realist mode. *Amor y pedagogía* represents a radical modification of style, tone, and authorial intervention. Although not an *ars poetica* of the *nivola*—Unamuno's reconception of the novel—as *Niebla* would be, *Amor y pedagogía* is, in essence, the new form in practice. It is a large step away from the traditions that had developed in Spanish (and European) realism during the course of the previous century, as exemplified in the novels of Benito Pérez Galdós, Emilia Pardo Bazán, Leopoldo Alas (Clarín), and their contemporaries. These novels captured the rhythm, the discourse, and the strata of society at a moment of change. Political turmoil, economic and ideological shifts, and widening gaps between urban and rural populations transform the fabric of life, and narrative realism portrays the literal and figurative landscapes of the period. Character and setting are intricately rendered; the sense of time and place and the depiction of personality and human interactions require the novelist to observe, to analyze, to interpret, and to craft a type of mirror image of society. The exigencies of realism are distinctive, given that narrators, if not imperceptible, tend to be unobtrusive. Galdós's narrators, for example, are hardly hidden, but they fit into the narrative tapestry and encourage the reader to focus on action, dialogue, description, and message rather than on the construction and the constructor of the text. The narrative personae merge with the narrative with impressive subtlety. Correspondingly, the devices of fiction, while not concealed, do not call attention to themselves. Recurring to early modern models, some more quixotic than others, Unamuno refuses to shy away from self-referentiality.

The kinship of *Niebla* to *Don Quijote* is unmistakable. The ties between Cervantes's novel and *Amor y pedagogía* are less obvious, yet evident on a number of levels. Unamuno is assaying his now famous "viviparous" approach to narrative. The style is marked by spontaneity and randomness. Events and speeches pour out serendipitously, unpremeditatedly, as an antithesis to the programmed and preconceived works of realism, which Unamuno calls "oviparous."[1] The break from realism is stylistic, technical, and conceptual in scope. The writer wants to say something different and to say it differently. Historical data are fundamental in the narrative vision of *Paz en la guerra*, which must have been inspired, to a degree, at least, by Galdós's *episodios nacionales* and deeply inflected by Unamuno's notion of *intrahistoria*.[2] *Amor y pedagogía*, in contrast, seems calculatedly ahistorical, or, arguably, historical with respect to epistemology, psychology, and education. It might be said that sociology replaces history, but sociology here translates into a dialectics of instinct and conditioning. Sociology, as filtered through the narrative, deals with human nature, will power, and lessons in life more than with the exploration of a specifically national character or sensibility. The human psyche lies at the center of *Amor y pedagogía*. Unamuno's design, despite the claim that there is no design, allows the struggle between matter and form to define the major theses and the configuration of the text. The author makes the reader aware of external considerations of book publishing while offering internal critiques, thus giving a metafictional edge to the proceedings. Unamuno, as is customary, asserts himself by

---

[1] In "A lo que salga" (1904), Unamuno remarks, referring to viviparous writers, as opposed to their oviparious counterparts, "Hay otros, en cambio, que no se sirven de notas ni de apuntes, sino que lo llevan todo en la cabeza. Cuando conciben el propósito de escribir una novela, pongo por caso, empiezan a darle vueltas en la cabeza al argumento, lo piensan y repiensan, dormidos y despiertos, esto es, gestan. Y cuando sienten verdaderos dolores de parto, la necesidad apremiante de echar fuera lo que durante tanto tiempo les ha venido obsesionando, se sientan, toman la pluma, y paren. Es decir, que empiezan por la primera línea, y, sin volver atrás ni rehacer ya lo hecho, lo escriben todo en definitiva hasta la línea última" (1196).

[2] *Intrahistoria*, the eternal tradition or essence of a people, is a principal feature of *En torno al casticismo*, which first appeared in 1895 as separate essays and was published as a book, coincidentally, in 1902.

inserting himself into the discourse (and later, emphatically, into the story of *Niebla*). With hefty doses of irony, he relates the pedagogical undertaking of his protagonist to his own literary venture.

The author dedicates the work to the reader, thereby echoing Cervantes's summoning of the reader in the first words of the prologue to the 1605 *Quijote*. The speaker haltingly calls the narrative a novel, and then admits that he dares not classify it. If Cervantes's basic strategy is to grant the largest portion of the dialogical space to the friend, or alter ego, of the fictionalized writer, that of Unamuno's prologuist, who speaks of the author in the third person, is to disparage the text and to suggest that Unamuno may have committed an error in composing it. This offensive ploy places the reader, and potential critic, in an unusual and imbalanced position, by warning that the mixture of burlesque, implausible, and ridiculous ingredients, saved infrequently by a delicate idea or phrase, almost surely will displease its audience. The prologue condemns the author for putting his own thoughts in the mouths of his characters, who may be made to look foolish when they are expressing ideas in which he believes. It cautions that, due to misleading twists and turns, the reader may think that the narrative disparages science and pedagogy when, in fact, the author opposes only exaggerated and ill-advised uses of these disciplines. This may be attributed to Unamuno's obsession with agitating rather than entertaining the reader; he takes to unreasonable lengths his disinclination to suffer fools. The most acute defect is that the text does not make clear what the author hopes to accomplish. Can mockery and scandal be his only ends? And how should one perceive his disregard, in a double sense, of Spanish literature, and his prejudice against individual authors, including the neoclassic Francophile Moratín? The conclusion, repeated, is that the work is a lamentable blunder on Unamuno's part, and the speaker sets out to justify that opinion.

The characters, thinly drawn, are mere puppets of the author, who places them on stage while he does the talking. The reader is led to believe that Don Avito Carrascal will test a legitimate hypothesis on his son, but the alleged scientist is a poor dupe who depends too readily, and too slavishly, on books, and who trusts Don Fulgencio Entrambosmares without fully bearing in mind the eccentricities of his guide. And the less said the better about the author's skill, or lack thereof, in the delineation of Marina and other female characters. The style of the narrative is dry and sometimes careless, and the decision to write in the present tense doubtlessly will prove to be unwise. The very author who in magazines and newspapers promotes the need to reform and revolutionize the Spanish language writes in a plain and unimaginative style, with language as a means to an end, nothing more. Any lack of clarity is probably due to conceptist play that hopes to avoid the vulgar. The negative commentaries notwithstanding, this seems to be a work that is worthy of consideration, with features that would recommend it, to an extent by virtue of what the author has put in the narrative despite himself, as it were. Under the buffoonery there is a tribute to science and pedagogy. If the text appears to take a stand against intellectualism, that is because Unamuno suffers from it as few Spaniards do, and one might suspect that, hoping to correct this failing, he ends by mocking himself. But the speaker, who employs the first-person plural, decides to leave this most delicate territory. The prologue concludes with a reference to Unamuno's preoccupation with the size and shape of the book, since a bookseller in Bilbao had advocated that he aim to have all his works conform to a similar pattern. Because Don Miguel now publishes for readers and not for bibliophiles, he will defer this concern until his complete works go to press. The closing sentence invites the reader to enjoy and to learn from the narrative.

The cleverness of the prologue may reveal something more than the tricks of Unamuno's trade. Like the first *Quijote* prologue, the author has internal and external identities. Cervantes entrusts the articulation of the narrative pretext to a friend-of-the-author surrogate, who is twice-removed from the center of control. Unamuno's curious editorial "we" is a third party, detached from the author while joined at the hip, that is, fooling no one. Cervantes fabricates a friend to counsel him, to speak commandingly about the manuscript, but what he says satisfies a fictional prerequisite while opening the larger picture, which combines fiction and metafiction (and, as the reader will come to see, history). When Cervantes cedes authority, he does so ironically. His corps of narrators would seem to usurp his power over the disposition of the text, but the apparent competitors become symbols of his mastery over the material. Within the parameters of the story, as initiated in the prologue, the friend frees each of the Cervantes figures, the historical and the poetic, from criticism and blame by serving as the interpretive agent. It is he who announces the purpose of the narrative and who mounts an attack on the romances of chivalry; it is he who informs the reader (and, of course, the author) of the author's intentions. Cervantes precociously enacts the Unamunian art of *desdoblamiento* in his versions of the writer, narrator, and critic. Unamuno's prologuist is commentator and critic, but he is also, and obviously, Unamuno, the paradoxical other who never succeeds in straying from the self because he never really wishes to effect a separation. Recalling perhaps the second *Quijote* prologue, of 1615, he defends himself while professing, or pretending, to take the situation in stride. Unamuno wants to rewrite the novel, and he cannot help but show some trepidation before such an ominous task. The flaws that he signals are the indicators of his mission and of his plan to confront prospective detractors.

The most dramatic moment, from a critical stance, may be Unamuno's remarks on characterization in *Amor y pedagogía*. The representation is sketchy, the pivotal character of Don Fulgencio perplexes more than convinces, and the author cannot seem to enter the female mindset. Unamuno subtly prompts the reader to place the underlying methodology under scrutiny and to find some good in what the writer purports to be bad. The texture and the thematics of the deviation from narrative realism may baffle and even displease the reader, but Unamuno pays homage to the reader, not only in the dedication but in an implicit challenge to investigate an alternative vision. The prologue brings up the language of the text, which waivers between lucidity and haziness, as if Unamuno were attempting both to connect with and to alienate his readership. The author does not push the self-incrimination too far. He mentions the tendency toward foolishness and buffoonery, but implores the reader to penetrate the narrative and to concentrate on those factors that support an innovative formula for composition. The anecdote about the bookseller keeps the contact between author and reader in the spotlight, and the allusion to books on store and personal library shelves accentuates the metafictional flourishes that go against the realist paradigm. Unamuno constructs a frame through which his variations on novelistic themes can be judged. Whereas much of realism gestures to the senses, *Amor y pedagogía*, by a specialist in the dialogical, will emphasize the mind.

Some thirty years after publishing the 1902 edition, Unamuno writes a combined prologue and epilogue to the second edition, here in the first-person, as his historical self and as a re-reader. In the prologue-epilogue, he cites Don Fulgencio and Marina, and notes that, in this span of time, two of his children were born and two died. He refers to *Paz en la guerra* and to the *nivolas* that followed and that showcase what he terms the reality of personality. He categorizes *Cómo se hace una novela* (published in French in 1926 and in Spanish in 1927) as a tragedy not of the novelist but of the novel itself. As for *Amor y pedagogía*, he sees this early work as containing the germ, and more, of later novels. Unamuno speaks of ties between love and philosophy, and of the players that he has arranged on the stage of his imaginings. The actors include the overstated Don Fulgencio and the poet Hildebrando F. Menaguti, who deems creating poetry of a higher order than producing children, but who has no children. Unamuno maintains that feelings are more strongly conveyed in the literature of spiritualism, or idealism, than in philosophical systems or in realist novels. He reiterates his commitment to the individual reader, but realizes that fate has given him a public and publicists, and that he must turn away from pedagogy to demagogy.[3] The state (and the State) of Spain will be at the forefront of his thoughts, and when he speaks of conscience he must give space to social conscience. He ends the monodialogue with an allusion to Don Fulgencio Entrabosmares's "Apuntes para un tratado de cocotología," which is attached to the volume, and with his own observations on science (including guinea pigs), the paradox, and every novel as a kind of slow suicide. Unamuno has seen how his life has played out, how he could not let himself be lost in a world of pure ideas, and how pedagogy may be less sociology than political science.

In the prologue-epilogue, Unamano says that he began writing the

---

[3] David G. Turner sees a relation between *Amor y pedagogía* and Unamuno's essays on education, including the series "De la enseñanza superior en España" (v. 27 ff.). See also Richards, Flórez, Jongh-Rossel, Díaz Peterson, and Peset. Richards looks at the ties between paternity and education in *Amor y pedagogía* and *Abel Sánchez*. Flórez argues that "La antipedagogía unamuniana termina por ser una pedagogía vital, una apelación a la vida como suprema maestro" (201). Jongh-Rossel focuses on the Institución Libre de Enseñanza. Díaz-Peterson sees in the narratives and other writings a rejection of scholasticism—exemplified in the suicide of Apolodoro—given that "la ciencia de la escolástica ya no podía producir más que muerte, porque eso era todo lo que tenía en su esqueleto lógico" (53). Peset places Unamuno's ideas on flexibility in the educational process within the context of the writers of the Generation of '98.

series of narratives initiated by *Amor y pedagogía* as a means of stimulating a lazy reading public. He refers casually to having invented the name *nivola* for these narratives when he was in a bad mood, and he lists the later works as novels. This glibness does a disservice to the neologism, which has a point and a place in literary history. It is tempting, yet would be misleading, to call *Amor y pedagogía* a study or first draft for *Niebla*.[4] The earlier text is more disordered, more meandering, and more free-flowing, in short, more viviparous; it unquestionably provides the template for the *nivola*. *Amor y pedagogía* is about ideas, but it is also about means of communicating both concepts and a sense of style. The *nivola* combines the literary and the paraliterary. It beckons the reader to ponder form and content, and, not insignificantly, to regard Unamuno as an intellectual and as an aesthete. The conventions of realism and naturalism allow for the author to develop a distinctive signature. While one can identify features that differentiate Galdós's novels from those of Pardo Bazán, Clarín, and Juan Valera, for example, and even speak of the *personalities* of these authors and their narrators, there is no comparison between this level of mediation and that of Unamuno, who seems especially anxious to remind the reader of his presence and of his input in all areas of the narrative. Unamuno may be the ultimate puppeteer, but he has no desire to conceal the strings or to take refuge off-stage. He does nothing if not radiate personality, so that his metafictions have not only their own markings but their own intertext. The linguist and scholar of Greek, the rector of the Universidad de Salamanca, the sufferer of spiritual crises, the intrahistorian of Spain, the composer of intimate (yet public) diaries, the novelist, the playwright, the short story and travel writer, and the ardent essayist brings a special background to narrative, to the *nivola*. One may submit that, in the case of Unamuno, the background is indistinguishable from the foreground.

Don Avito Carrascal, the protagonist of *Amor y pedagogía*, has no discernible past.[5] Appropriately, as an advocate of progress, he is

---

[4] In the third chapter of *Niebla y soledad*, "La evolución de la novelística unamuniana: *Amor y pedagogía y Niebla*" (83-107), Geoffrey Ribbans surveys criticism on the concept of the *nivola* and on the two works, and looks at points of contact and contrast between them.

[5] Paul R. Olson, in *The Great Chiasmus* 53, notes the similarity between the names Carrascal and Carrasco (the *bachiller* Sansón Carrasco of the second part

dominated by the future. He is, in many respects, a servant to science. His specialization is sociological pedagogy, and his goal is to produce a genius. Everything must be thought out, and the project, like the text, (disingenuously) begins as a *tabula rasa*. In order to become a father, Avito must marry, and he decides to do so scientifically, deductively. He will seek a fitting woman for the job of bearing children, a criterion that precedes physical attraction per se. Musing over the possibilities, and depending on disciplines from anthropology to statistics, he picks the "solid" Leoncia Carbajosa as his target and embarks on a pursuit. He redacts a letter, or, more precisely, a treatise, or declaration, aimed as much at posterity (a reading public) as at the intended. The problem is that Avito, when he shows up at Leoncia's home to advance his suit, finds himself entranced, and tongue-tied, with her friend Marina del Valle. He then moves from Leoncia to Marina and from deduction to induction. He veers off course from the first stage of his proposition. On leaving the house, Avito admits to himself that the Unconscious has entered the game. That is true in more ways than one. Marina's appeal is magnetic, and it brings out in Avito an inner voice that will remain a crucial part of the dialogue (as opposed to an interior monologue). The voice is sharply and knowingly metacritical, an articulation of Avito's assessment of his behavior and his choices. Here, the confused suitor grasps that love has interfered with science, with deduction, and with procreation, for Marina will be the mother of the genius-to-be. He has fallen into induction.

The selection of Marina over Leoncia is a victory of instinct over science. Rebuffing the inner voice, Avito rationalizes that Marina will constitute the raw material and he the form—she the nature and he the art—of their son.[6] He pours himself into the letter originally intended for

---

of *Don Quijote*). Olson's section on *Amor y pedagogía* in *The Great Chiasmus* (50-65), builds upon two earlier essays, "The Novelistic Logos" and "Unamuno's Break."

[6] Olson points out that Unamuno "makes explicit the traditional dualism of form and matter identified with male and female, respectively, as found in both Plato (*Timaeus* 50c) and Aristotle (*Physics* 1.9), but the only precedent invoked in the novel… is from Molière's *Les femmes savants*" (*Great Chiasmus* 55). Roberta Johnson argues, "Like Voltaire's Dr. Pangloss, who represents the ridiculous extremes of Leibniz's philosophical optimism, Avito and Marina are respectively absurd embodiments of science and nature (tinged with religious faith). They are

Leoncia, to receive a return letter that Marina plainly has copied from a manual. He persuades himself, however, that her eyes are one of a kind, a defense against plagiarism. Avito is determined to dominate the courtship, but the heart seems to rule over the head, as the inner voice informs him. Compromise is the order of the day. Once married, Avito insists that the couple no longer belong to themselves, that they must devote themselves to their offspring, that education must commence during gestation, and that they must avoid all sentimentality. The son is born, and his training starts immediately. He is called Apolodoro, which Avito chooses for symbolic and practical reasons. The name evokes Apollo, the sun, light, and life.[7] It also means that father and son can share the same trunk and other initialed items. The voice chastises him for resorting to the pagan deity, and Avito engages in a mental polemic with the "inopportune demon," who constantly provokes him. Meanwhile, Marina has her son baptized on the sly, giving him the name of Luis, on the advice of the "deductive" Leoncia. When Marina and Avito dispute the benefits of breastfeeding versus the bottle, she says that the former is superior because it is natural, and he contends, echoing his advisor Don Fulgencio Entrambosmares, that nature is a shoddy piece of work. The domestic pair occupy their separate worlds, and each keeps a close watch on the evolution of their son, with different measuring rods, of course. And the voice keeps scolding Avito for succumbing to nature, for forgetting that love and pedagogy are diametrically opposed. Avito hangs on to the experiment, going so far as to stick pins in Apolodoro in order to study the child's reflexes and to rub his head in order to stimulate speech.

---

summaries, composites, representing the tragic dichotomy between reason and faith, the schism forged by Descartes.... Avito is a metaphor for the branch of European thought spawned by the seventeenth-century mathematician that views all aspects [of] life in terms of weights and measures. Rational idealism, the other branch equally attributable to Descartes, is embodied in Avito's friend, Fulgencio Entrambosmares. Spencer, Mill and all those who rely on materialistic, evolutionary or biological conceptions of the world... are the targets of Unamuno's satire..." (43).

[7] Gayana Jurkevich examines what she terms "inverted archetypes" in "The Sun-Hero Revisited." In *The Inverted Self: Archetypal Approaches to the Novels of Miguel de Unamuno*, she expands the base, but does not include a separate chapter on *Amor y pedagogía*.

Don Fulgencio is the compleat scientist. He disavows common sense, relegating it to the kitchen, an ironic thought from a man who will be shown to be henpecked by his wife, Doña Edelmira. He will share his "exoteric" *Libro de los aforismos o píldoras de sabiduría* with fellow mortals, but will reserve his "esoteric" *Ars magna combinatoria,* a catalog of the universe, for the ages to come. The combinatory method (scientifically, mathematically) reduces philosophy to binary, then trinary groups, ad infinitum. When asked about his faith, he says that he believes in God as long as God believes in him. Nonetheless, he seems to ascribe to the concept of the *theatrum mundi,* seeing human beings in life's tragicomedy, reacting rather than acting, through the guidance of the Prompter on a stage readied by the Set Designer. He wonders aloud if the Supreme Director has in mind the same brilliant future that Avito envisions for his son. The combination of science and determinism is an odd one. Will they be molding Apolodoro or playing their prescribed roles? Is the unfathomable a function of the unconscious? Don Fulgencio makes room for the unscripted line or ad lib (*morcilla*), a nod to free will, but he qualifies this by associating it with the Prompter, who whispers words in the subject's ear. There is a strangely, and precociously, Derridean thrust to Don Fulgencio's statements, as for example, "Nunca se empieza, todo es seguimiento" (87).[8] At the right time, Don Fulgencio will begin to instruct Apolodoro. As for now, the father must look out for his metadramatic moment. The narrator observes disapprovingly that this is the man to whom Don Avito has entrusted his son, and the inner voice is more condemning, reiterating his references to the downward spiral and calling Don Fulgencio a charlatan. Don Fulgencio, nonetheless, has the utmost self-confidence. He constantly jots down his own aphorisms for the collection.

Maternal love and paternal pedagogy reign in the household. Avito (over)reads his son's every word and movement through the lens of genius in the making, while Marina showers him with kisses. When Apolodoro speaks, it becomes clear that he relishes verbal humor, the incongruous, and the absurd. His father is alarmed, but Don Fulgencio writes it off as an exercise in independence, a wish to leave the tragicomic

---

[8] All quotations from *Amor y pedagogía* will refer to the Caballé edition, and page numbers will be indicated in parentheses.

state, to shake off verisimilitude, and advises Avito to let the child be on his own, to let him fly. Avito remains perplexed, and he plays the game of "what if?" What if Apolodoro takes after his mother? What kind of son would he have had by Leoncia? To his amazement, he learns that Marina is pregnant again. Don Fulgencio pushes for a social education, and, against his better judgment, Avito enrolls his son in school. Predictably, Avito finds the teaching methodology to be lacking and tutors the boy outside of class, beginning with linguistics but running into conundrums on the academic side. As luck would have it, Apolodoro has demons of his own, who notify him that, among other things, his father is a fool. The narrator describes Apolodoro's thought processes as a kaleidoscope whose every piece contains an enigma that must be deciphered. Avito gives his son a notebook to record his experiences and to make charts of anything that is "graphico-statisticable." On a visit to the Museum of Natural History, he is upset that the child shows little enthusiasm for knowledge. When he informs Don Fulgencio of this indifference, the master counsels him to have Apolodoro read novels and to send the boy back to school, on the condition that he be taught nothing. Avito takes his son to Dr. Herrero's laboratory, where they come across a guinea pig that intrigues Apolodoro, until he learns that the animal will die for the sake of science. He cannot stop thinking about the ill-fated guinea pig, not yet comprehending that he, too, is at the mercy of science.

A daughter is born, and named Rosa, with no opposition from the father, whose priorities lie with the male genius. The occasion gives Don Avito the chance to share his thoughts on women, via the omniscient narrator. For Avito, woman is merely a postulate, indemonstrable, vegetative. There are no feminist issues, only pedagogical issues. Women should be educated, materially and naturally, to beget men. Rosa learns to walk and to talk earlier than her brother did; Don Fulgencio ascribes this to the axiom that the more inferior the species, the sooner it reaches maturity. The two men declaim on womanhood: woman is instinctive and man is logical, woman tradition and man progress, woman memory and man understanding, woman nature and man reason. Ergo, cries Don Fulgencio, woman is born and man becomes, or makes himself. Man aspires to be superman; woman, an inert and conservative force, is the anti-superman. Following the meeting, Doña Edelmira accuses Don Fulgencio of gossiping about science and then gives him some sewing to do on the machine, promising that no one will find out about his household chores.

Time passes, and Apolodoro finally has his day with Don Fulgencio. The words of wisdom at the interview include a caution against reliance on common sense, the touchstone of the commoners. Common sense reflects the majority opinion and isolates the scientist whose break-throughs may not pass a general scrutiny. Facts only get in the way of ideas, and it is far better to be eccentric than one of the crowd. When Apolodoro says that he is studying mathematics, Don Fulgencio compares that discipline with arsenic, dangerous in large dosages. He advises the boy to study history, avowing that mathematics and history are incompatible, and he imparts other such pearls. Apolodoro speaks very little at the interview, and his father asks himself if this "sphinx" will ever come into his own. Apolodoro also meets the bohemian poet Hildebrando F. Menaguti, who urges him to read and write poetry, and who lends him books that the boy reads secretly at night.[9] Don Avito persists in explaining the need for his son to log his conception of the universe, noting that the modern genius must be a sociologist. Poetry is but a provisional, transitional art. Even so, Apolodoro gives himself to poetry, and it is his mother who guesses the reason: he is in love. Dejected, Avito, who is certain that geniuses cannot fall in love, visits Don Fulgencio. When the scholar posits that nature surpasses reason, Avito is incredulous, for it should be the other way around. Don Fulgencio blames the amorous response on fate, whose only antidote is fate itself. He delivers a disquisition on love, which he sees as moving from the

---

[9] At the beginning of chapter 9, the narrator describes Apolodoro's furtive readings of the books that Menaguti has given him: "Al llegar a ciertos pasajes el corazón le martillea, y con la boca entreabierta, respirando anheloso, tiene que suspender durante un momento la lectura. ¿Es que luego sueña? Ni él mismo lo sabe desde que le hizo leer su padre una doctísima obra acerca del sueño, sus causas y sus leyes" (117). As scholars have noted, this may be a reference to Freud's *The Interpretation of Dreams* (1899). Basing himself in part on Ricardo Gullón's *Autobiografías de Unamuno*, Olson mentions that "[a]lthough the name of Freud apparently occurs in Unamuno's correspondence as early as 1900, evidence of specific textual influence is sketchy" ("Unamuno's Break" 312). See also Olson, *Great Chiasmus* 230-31n9 and 231n11. In *Uncovering the Mind*, Alison Sinclair discusses the issue in a section entitled "Had Unamuno Read Freud?" (34-37). She believes that the lines of communication between Unamuno and Gregorio Marañón may have been one means of access to Freud.

abstract to the concrete. For the father, the circumstances are catastrophic. His familiar demon poses the question, "And what if this love becomes concrete?" That is exactly what happens. The object is Clarita, the daughter of the art instructor Don Epifanio. The bitterness of life turns to sweetness. The world seems substantial, real, to Apolodoro, not theatrical, as Don Fulgencio has told him. His mother, the dreamer, fusses over him. The demon within him asks if he has noticed how closely Clarita resembles his mother, and Marina shortly thereafter says that she has met and taken a liking to the young lady.

Love becomes laced with melancholy, as he dreams of being forever with Clarita but feels alone and unattached. Walking in the country, he encounters Federico, a cunning young man whose discourse is rife with paradoxes such as "Only the person who hates death will commit suicide." Federico toys with the lovestruck Apolodoro and left-handedly praises Don Avito's pedagogical theories. He sustains that beautiful women should be off-limits, to be looked at but not touched, yet proclaims that "we" are in love with Clarita and gloats over the competition that he has stirred up. He adds mockingly that the obligation to respect the chastity of beautiful maidens applies only to others. Apolodoro later takes refuge in his room to work on a novella that will be sentimental and poetic, with considerable measures of psychology. He approaches his next meeting with Clarita motivated by art as well as by romance. Love will help him to create literature. In the midst of his apparent ardor, he becomes increasingly analytical. Is he getting bored with Clarita? Does he find her conversation insipid? Is habit replacing passion? He knows, though, that when he sets his eyes on her, all reasoning will evaporate. When they do meet, she seems a bit standoffish. He decides to intensify his tenderness, but misfires by using "my pedagogy" as a term of affection. She asks if he will attend mass for her sake, and he agrees, but not without thinking how irrational women are. Scarcely has Apolodoro taken his leave when Clarita begins her response to a letter from Federico. She concedes that Apolodoro is good, but calls him unhappy; he is madly in love with her, yet she has the right to make her own decision. She finds Federico more desirable, and her letter will contain the ambiguities necessary to string him along. That night Apolodoro exerts himself to be extra-resolute and extra-masculine, kissing Clarita firmly on the lips, but her reaction is ambivalent. Don Epifanio tells his daughter that the choice is hers, and she determines to meet with Federico right away. Don Avito stops by Don Epifanio's studio to withdraw Apolodoro from the art classes, due to his plans for his son. Avito berates himself for his lack of character; he is pure theory, and the theories are not working, perhaps because of the maternal influence. He curses heredity, and ends up at Don Fulgencio's door. Don Fulgencio welcomes the prospect of Apolodoro's misfortune in love, for, according to him, only a failed ("dead") love bears scientific fruits. Avito feels deceived by the cavalier posture.

Apolodoro's novella has been published in a magazine and is received with absolute indifference. His father, who knew nothing of the endeavor, feels that he has lacked the will to *impose* pedagogy. As is his pattern, he begins by blaming himself and ends by blaming Marina. He does believe, however, that the novella has some merit, and he still hopes to mold Apolodoro into a success; he concedes that genius requires patience. Apolodoro himself suffers the consequences of his literary failure. The silence is deafening. His friends seem to be laughing behind his back, Menaguti praises only the allusions to him, and Clarita is colder than ever and does not mention the novella, even though she has read it. The greatest blow comes from Don Fulgencio, who, lashing out against art for art's sake, criticizes Apolodoro for overemphasizing style and for portraying his love interest through the eyes of Menaguti. Apolodoro leaves, having undergone a complete disappointment in art and life, his self-esteem totally destroyed. He ponders whether Don Fulgencio is right, that all art is worthless.

Federico pursues Clarita, and she informs Apolodoro, in a letter, that she has chosen his rival. The rejected suitor comes upon Menaguti, who advises him to kill Federico or himself. When he crosses paths with Federico, he proposes that they fight, but his opponent immediately asks if those words have come from his mouth. Federico calls him a puppet, a victim of his father's pedagogy. Apolodoro denies this, but with little basis. Distraught and offended by all those around him, he thinks about suicide and decides to visit Don Fulgencio. On his arrival, he blurts out that he wants to die. Don Fulgencio lectures him on the theme of immortality. The first example is Herostratus, credited with burning down the Temple of Diana at Ephesus, one of the seven wonders of the ancient world, for the sole purpose of gaining eternal notoriety. It was forbidden to speak his name, but the writ to that effect transforms the phenomenon into a paradox. Fulgencio bemoans the fact that he does not have children, even though his works are his offspring. Have children, he urges Apolodoro, who leaves with a frantic desire to do just that. Apolodoro thinks of Clarita, of his novella, and of the failed attempt to become a genius. He will resign from the world, but not until he deliberates further on immortality. He sees Clarita, and the flame of love is relit. He delivers a soliloquy, in which he argues eloquently that since he cannot be a genius in life, he will be one in death. He decrees that he will write a book about the need to die when love is not returned, and he will kill himself so as not to let himself die. But first he will need to make children, in order to see immortality in them, just in case. As the inner voice denounces the father, Don Avito enters to speak with his son. Apolodoro complains that pedagogy has made him unhappy, while Avito is adamant that happiness must be subordinated to science. He did not sire Apolodoro for himself, but for humanity. The culprit is love, which is anti-pedagogical and anti-scientific. Apolodoro calls this ridiculous, and his father accuses him of still being unwilling to accept the dictates of Reason. At a cemetery, Apolodoro associates love with death, with both Eros and Thanatos crying out that he should have children. And the maid Petra steps into the frame.

Avito takes Apolodoro to a doctor, who inquires as to the problem. Love, says the father. Pedagogy, says the son. The doctor cannot detect a medical problem. Apolodoro continues to agonize over his fate. He thinks of Herostratism. He thinks of resigning, but not before making children. Don Avito feels an equal letdown. He wants his son to embrace pedagogy, and his sickly daughter, spoiled by her mother, to be healthy. Rosa dies, and all grieve for her. Apolodoro explains that his tears are for his father. Apolodoro's death wish seems to grow stronger after the loss of his sister. More than anything, he wants to become immortal. He does not leave a will but a final statement. He knows that he has committed a despicable act. He bids farewell to his mother, who is mired in appearances, and to Clarita, who could have redeemed him from pedagogy but elected not to do so. Indirectly, he submits to his father that geniuses are born and not made, and that at the culmination of the experiment there remain a contemptible act by a contemptible person and a suicide. Apolodoro hangs himself, and his father discovers the body. He collapses into his wife's arms, calling her "mother" and falling into a faint. The narrator ends the narrative with the paradoxical thought that love has won a victory.

The epilogue mixes the voices of the historical Unamuno with a poetic counterpart and two corresponding associates. His "friend" Santiago Valentí Camp has brought up the issue of the book's dimensions, and the author needs to think of a way to amplify the number of pages. This leads to a digression on the constraints of publishing and on several related topics. One partial solution, used in other literary texts, is the dual ending. That is an option, but not one that Unamuno chooses.[10] The prologue alludes to another friend to whom the writer had explained the plot and major ideas. The friend was dissatisfied with the death of Apolodoro; for him, life should have won the battle, but the creator of the fiction could not bring himself to alter the dénouement, for the characters assumed lives within him and their paths have been laid out. Unamuno, or "Unamuno," notes that his appetite has been whetted by the inquiry from Valentí Camp, and that he has made an effort to look into the different characters' reactions to the death of Apolodoro. Overcome by fear, Menaguti begs a God in which he does not believe for faith. At the present, he is dying of consumption and writing a book on the death of God. Clarita is relieved that she married Federico, while he believes that Apolodoro did the right thing. Don Fulgencio shudders to think that he may have influenced the impressionable young man and plans to study suicide. The person most profoundly affected by the suicide is Petra, the maid, who suffers the misfortune of falling in love "a posteriori," when she is left alone and with child by Apolodoro. The grieving parents find consolation in each other. In a sense, they reverse roles; she ceases to live in a dream, and he is willing to pray with her. Don Avito quickly reverts to his scientific self, graciously promising to protect Petra and to raise her son according to the strictest pedagogy, with no interference from Don Fulgencio. He will raise the child alone and, having learned from his mistakes, will be able to produce a genius, one who will not be ensnared by love. He will correct the previous error by applying his pedagogy in its purest form. For whatever reason, Petra feels reassured. She will be

---

[10] David Turner looks at this passage (163-64 in the Caballé ed.) as "a clear declaration of Unamuno's belief in historical determinism, ... and the only escape from such determinism is to be found in art. He does not change the end of the novel, but this is not out of regard for determinism, but because of the way in which his characters take on a life of their own in his mind..." (37).

one of the family, and perhaps all has been for the best. Don Avito starts the regimen by offering his son's widow—as he had offered his wife—a diet of beans. Petra accedes, noting that the man does not seem well but that she will try to accommodate his whims. And that is where the plot proper ends.

Unamuno says that he leaves the story hanging, in case he wishes to write a second part, and one cannot help but hear Cervantine echoes. He returns to the concern for the size of the book, appending algebraic notations. He alludes to Lope de Vega's "Soneto de repente," a play on the theme of composition as space-filling, and to the anecdote in the prologue to the second part of *Don Quijote* on the madman from Sevilla, the message of which is that writing is never easy. What follows seems to be rambling for its own sake, as if to illustrate the points about quantitative considerations and the onus of writing. Unamuno turns to the author's duty to inspire readers, and he stresses that he hopes to inculcate in them a spark of the secret fire against logic that wells in his innermost being and that probably burns in everyone. What is comic sensibility if not an emancipation from logic, freedom from the ominous *ergo*? He speaks of a type of practical logic, but the impractical and what could be termed the ludic sense of exposition seep into the discourse, which blends allusions to *Don Quijote,* and other works, with Unamuno's personal case and with those of the characters of *Amor y pedagogía.* Unamuno links laughter with rebellion against authority and against logic, and with reader response. He takes back his cry of "¡Muera don Quijote!" as a result of a new appreciation for the imaginary knight.[11]

---

[11] Martin Nozick discusses "the myth of Don Quixote" and the progression in Unamuno's thinking on the topic (85-100). He comments on the shifts as follows: "Even in 1898, when his sensibilities were further exacerbated by the sorry defeats of Spanish forces at the hands of the foreign Colossus, he thundered: 'Don Quixote Must Die!'... The spirit of madness must be extinguished to leave room for a clear-sighted realism; the Spanish people must be cured of a desire to duplicate a glorious past under circumstances totally different; they must sweep out the tinsel of tales endlessly retold just as Don Quixote finally repudiated the romances of chivalry that had lured him to his fruitless adventures. By the next year, Unamuno had already drastically altered his view of Cervantes' creation: let Don Quixote die, he states, but only the Don Quixote dissected by professional Cervantists, for then the quixotic spirit will be free to speak to every Spanish soul and will provide the ideal for spiritual

Because he still needs to fill more pages, he visits Don Fulgencio, who prefers not to talk about Apolodoro's death but offers an early dialogue of his own on squid. Unamuno suggests that he hopes that the contents of the volume will have a unity of tone. Don Fulgencio counters with a comment as to the lack of a unity of tone in the world at large, and he cites *Quijote* anecdotes of his own. He presents Unamuno with "El calamar" and with "Notas para un tratado de cocotología" (defined as the science that deals with little birds made of paper), the latter of which is added to the volume. Unamuno concludes the epilogue with the last verse of Lope's sonnet, "Contad si son catorce, y está hecho," but the text continues with the treatise, with illustrations, though incomplete, and an appendix.[12] In the appendix, Unamuno speaks of recent correspondence with Don Fulgencio, who is continuing the study of cocotology, which now delves into sexual characteristics, among other things, of the paper birds. Unamuno keeps the appendix short for fear of launching into a tirade against *investigacionistas*, as opposed to *investigadores*. His parting words are "Tengamos la fiesta en paz, y ahoguemos en amor, en caridad, la pedagogía" (203).

Amor y pedagogía is, in a word—an ironic word—novel, more notably so when placed against the realism of the second half of the nineteenth century. It may have stronger ties to Cervantes and Sterne than to Galdós, Pardo Bazán, and Clarín, but it needs the realists and naturalists in the background in order to play with and, primarily, against them.[13] The

rejuvenation. And by 1905 Unamuno was ready to refute his earlier harsh statements completely by recognizing as the symbol *par excellence* of Spain, not the remorseful Alonso Quijano the Good, but the noble, reckless, ludicrous, and lovable benefactor of the needy: Don Quixote de la Mancha" (90).

[12] For the complete text of Lope's sonnet, see Rivers, *Renaissance and Baroque Poetry* 225.

[13] Gonzalo Navajas summarizes the Unamunian project as follows: "Para Unamuno, el mundo objetivo no es fiable. La realidad física se le presenta como una máscara engañosa que encubre la naturaleza genuina del mundo. El sujeto debe desenmascarar la realidad y penetrar el núcleo más auténtico del mundo. Su función es poner al descubierto la falacia de la objetividad y proponer una versión diferente de verdad" (*Unamuno desde la posmodernidad* 13). For a consideration of Unamuno's narrative vis-à-vis nineteenth-century realism and naturalism, see, among others, Basdekis 31-43. Ricardo Diez submits, "Después que Henri Bergson, en la última década del siglo XIX, formuló sus teorías sobre

conventions of realism are as detectable, if not as pronounced, as the conventions and counter-conventions of metafiction, and Unamuno consciously invokes tradition as he orients his narratives away from the immediate past. *Niebla* is his *arte nuevo*, his treatise on narrative contained within his maximum practice, just as *Don Quijote* is Cervantes's theory and praxis. In *Niebla*, Unamuno has found himself as a novelist, or *nivolista*. He is the master of his singular technique, and what he has found is not a voice or a style as much as a way in which to incorporate his essence into the text. Like Cervantes, he knows how to gain control by ceding control to narrators and characters, although he paints his reluctance to cede control into the picture. It could be argued that Unamuno's art, in its wide array of genres, is marked by unsuccessful efforts at decentering the subject, and, further, that the efforts are unsuccessful because they are half-hearted, at best. A pictorial correlative of *Amor y pedagogía* might be Velázquez's *Las meninas*, regularly compared with *Don Quijote*, but with the painter at work in the center. If anything, it is harder to stay focused on the plot line, fascinating though it may be, because of the authorial intrusions at the levels of story and discourse. How does Unamuno inscribe himself into the narrative threads of *Amor y pedagogía*? Let us count the ways.

Imitating the frame story of medieval and early modern literature, Unamuno is the protagonist of what can be designated as the frame story of *Amor y pedagogía*, which revolves around a book in the marketplace. There is a resonance also of the beginning of the prologue to *Lazarillo de*

---

la conciencia, el tiempo intuitivo y la insuficiencia de la inteligencia para comprender la realidad, comienzan experimentos en la novela" (39). Diez traces a path toward abstraction in Unamuno's narrative trajectory in his discussion of *Amor y pedagogía* (69-94). Ordóñez García maintains that "La forma narrativa de *Amor y pedagogía* se incardina, a mi entender, en la tradición de la llamada 'novela dramatizada', 'presentativa', u 'objetiva', que se inicia en 1889 con *Realidad*, de Benito Pérez Galdós, y que suscitó una significativa polémica entre los críticos más destacados del momento" (36). For Unamuno, according to Ordóñez García, "El lenguaje transparente y nítido, propio del Naturalismo y del positivismo, expresión del conocimiento de la ciencia positiva, no ha sido capaz de captar la realidad íntima, la verdadera realidad" (53). In *Amor y pedagogía*, "[e]l discurso lingüístico de la novela se ha convertido... en correlato o metáfora de su contenido: el problema de la conciencia de la propia personalidad..." (53-54).

Tormes, but here the concern with the size of the physical object and the implicitly adversarial, or materialist, bookseller is repeated in the epilogue. Cervantes binds storytelling to the story. So does his consummate admirer Unamuno. Similar to Velázquez, Cervantes validates the writer through symbolic representation. So does Unamuno, but less symbolically and more personally. In the *Quijote* prologue of 1605, Cervantes employs the theme of putting the book together as a means of emphasizing the trials of authorship and of introducing a new form and new contexts for narrative fiction. The rest of the novel(s) is a variation on this theme, most palpably in the chronicle of the Arab historian Cide Hamete Benengeli. Cervantes makes the reader a kind of co-protagonist with the writer, and the metafiction, self-conscious and self-referential, encompasses metatheater and metacriticism. Distancing devices are prevalent, so that the reader can notice, survey, and appreciate the recourses of the author, first-hand and in parallel patterns and imagery. The metafiction has a plot that is as rich and as dramatic as Don Quijote's sallies. Fortuitously, Cervantes's quest has a linear development with upward and downward spirals, choreographed and unexpected tensions, and literary and emotional treats for the reader, who is never kept idle. The double linearity of the narrative leads to an impeccable complementarity, which foregrounds the writer and the reader, the creator and the creation, the past and the present, history and poetry, and so forth. This becomes the template for a man hardly averse to straying from, and imposing himself upon, his model.

The speaker in the first *Quijote* prologue is a fictionalized Cervantes, who gives an advisory role to his friend. The yielding of authority, along with the comic and satirical tone, may shield Cervantes from censorship, but it also places the content at an ironic distance from reality, and from realism. By calling the reader's attention to process, Cervantes is equating the intricacies of creative writing with the act of perceiving and with the challenge of making sense of human nature, society, and the world. Not unlike the tenets of poststructuralism (and Russian Formalism's emphasis on the "laying bare of devices"), Cervantes's modus operandi includes a flaunting of seams, deferrals, and interventions because, together with his more traditional, albeit recast, chivalric plot, is an allegory of reading, writing, reception, and critique. In multiple ways, it can be said that in *Don Quijote* the book comes into its own; books occupy the center and the margins, and the margins made center, of the *Quijote.* Unamuno capitalizes on this scheme in *Amor y pedagogía* in form and especially in spirit, yet what he learns from Cervantes is transferred, or translated, to his terms. He seems to want to oust realism from the narrative center and to replace it with the *nivola*, tinged with philosophy, psychology, literary history and theory, and, indisputably, with the ego(s) of Unamuno. The prologue to *Amor y pedagogía* opens the text with a deferral of the author's voice. This voice speaks of Unamuno in the third-person, but—unidentified but unambiguous—it can only be Unamuno's. Recognizing that his best defense is a good offense, Unamuno has the prologuist malign the manuscript. If Cervantes invents a friend who seeks to define the purpose of the manuscript and to sanction the breaking of literary rules, Unamuno turns whimsical. He concocts a detractor to inform the reader of what is wrong with the text and to suggest that it never should have been published.

What are the defects of the narrative? It does not look like other novels. It seems to have been written without careful thought. It lapses into vulgarity and nonsense. It will probably cause the reader to confuse the benefits of science and pedagogy with science and pedagogy gone awry. Everything about the work lacks decorum and depth, and it is hard to believe that the author is a respected member of the academic community, or that he dislikes the title of scholar, that he has a negative attitude toward Spanish literature, and that he disrespects the reader. Given the author's penchant for language and linguistics, the discourse is flat and lackluster. Despite its "deficiencies," its *tachas*, the book merits a reading. The redeeming grace of *Amor y pedagogía* is that, when one is able to see through the surface structure, Unamuno glorifies both science and pedagogy. If he takes aim at intellectualism, he does so knowing that he is exposing himself, holding himself up to the amusement of the public. The note of pessimism segues into a recommendation, and the prologue is a preparation for a new art of writing novels. There is an air of baroque elitism to the project. For all his allegiance to the *pueblo español*, Unamuno addresses himself to the thinking person. He and his characters are name-droppers, and, furthermore, they drop esoteric and convoluted ideas, and allusions that can be subtle and remote, with barely a breath between them. Don Fulgencio Entrambosmares may be hyperbolically single-minded and self-satisfied, absurdly erudite and out of touch with practicality, but he is a distinctly Unamunian creation, which the writer of the prologue notices. The cocotological treatise may be over the top, but someone took the time to treat the topic in agonizing detail and to flavor it with sexual divagations, and we know who the uncredited collaborator was. Don Fulgencio is not the only prototypically Unamunian character. Don Avito Carrascal and the doomed Apolodoro often sound like their shared progenitor; they are men of thought rather than of action, they take themselves far too seriously, and they are so accustomed to distraction that a clear focus seems to be a blur. They are not conventional figures propelled by a conventional author.

The critique in the prologue is not only an offense-as-defense ploy but an ironic poetics. Unamuno's narrative will be character-driven, but not as manifestly as in realist novels. Those characters are material, represented dimly in *Amor y pedagogía* by Marina, for even she is but a shell of realistic portraiture. The characterization here minimizes physicality in favor of psychology and in favor of the intellect. Don Avito, Apolodoro, and Don Fulgencio are verbal and cognitive structures. These characters do not reflect the crises of urban life, the economy, or politics. Their domain is the realm of concepts, hypotheses, and theorems. The two older men lead a ludicrously emblematic variety of double lives. Avito gives himself over to science, but he goes against science in choosing a wife and the future mother of the envisaged genius. Love invades his pedagogy from the outset. Don Fulgencio seems to be lost in ruminations, but he manages to separate the contemplative from the domestic. His scholarly aspirations take him beyond the realm of mere mortals, or at least beyond the capacity of his contemporaries, yet he appears to enjoy a state of conjugal bliss, even though Doña Edelmira rules the roost. Apolodoro resists the experiment, but he is trapped within it, a veritable guinea pig (and thus the poignancy of the scene of the laboratory). His discourse of resistance contains a rhetoric that remains true to its source: his father, as monitored by the intellectual father figure, Don Fulgencio. When Apolodoro feels attracted to Clarita, his response and his courtship style bear the imprint of his education and of the mixed signals that emanate from his parents' marriage. It is easy, then, for Federico to identify his weak spots and to profit from that knowledge. Confidence is on his side. When Apolodoro grabs Clarita and kisses her passionately, she is not fully convinced. When Federico repeats this action shortly thereafter, she commits herself to him. Bad press, from the prologue itself, mars the female characters before they make an appearance. Each of the women fulfils a symbolic function: Marina as anti-scientific instinct and faith, Doña Edelmira as a combination of middle-aged siren and homebody, and Clarita as a vessel of vanity and self-interest.[14]

The misogynist pitch of the narrative—Don Avito's contention that all geniuses are male, for example, or Apolodoro's remark to Clarita that "Mi madre no es nadie en casa" (132)—highlights the irony and the studied contradictions of Unamuno's model. The author's (mediated) acknowledgment of his lack of skills in the representation of women is something more, or less, than a fact. It calls for an examination of the underlying sensibilities of the work and its slippery approach to point of view. The prologue is contentious on the subject of women and in practically every other regard, because Unamuno adheres to dialectical argumentation as a matter of course. *Amor y pedagogía* more fittingly could be titled love *versus* pedagogy, because discomfort and irreconcilability are constants in the Unamunian trajectory, the author's means of engineering dramatic conflict. In the first of the *nivolas*, science and pedagogy vie against nature and nurturing, and, whether stated directly or indirectly, against the forces of the feminine and the maternal. Marina languishes in a dream-like state, steadfastly devout and worshipping her son. Doña Edelmira is pleasant yet officious, and she exudes an inexplicable aura of sexuality that affects not only her husband but also Apolodoro. Clarita is a negotiator, who looks for the best deal for herself. Little Rosa comes into the narrative only to depart at a tender age. Her father is not interested in educating her, and her mother is incapable of protecting her against illness. Apolodoro becomes obsessed with Don Fulgencio's pronouncement that he "make" children. That is his motive, and he finds the opportunity with the gracious, robust, and inexperienced

---

[14] For a general consideration of characterization in the narratives of Unamuno, see La Rubia Prado, "Los personajes de Unamuno" (*Alegorías* 94-111). Janet Pérez stresses that Unamuno often creates female characters who are stronger than the men around them, and she points out that his defensive posture in *Amor y pedagogía* "is evinced via ridicule of women's detractors, whereby the author indirectly supports feminist tenets" ("Rereading" 61). Concentrating on the ludic elements of the novel, she adds that the author "wastes no opportunity to pillory *machista* attitudes, mercilessly subverting rationalizations of gender inequity [through] parodic exaggeration of phallocentric attitudes" (61-62).

maid Petra. Buoyed by the promise of a grandson, Don Avito is grateful to have a second chance to perfect the art, or science, of raising a genius, and Petra, willing to cater to the fancies of her former employer, becomes one of the family. Her pregnancy out of wedlock raises, rather than lowers, her socially. One cannot help but wonder what Don Avito will do to keep love from the new candidate for greatness, and, more basically perhaps, what he has learned from the previous experiment. Will he expect Petra to remain subservient to him? Has the prospective grandmother lost her faith?

The women in *Amor y pedagogía* have relatively little to say, while the men are loquacious to the extreme. Faith and domesticity spark feminine discourse, whereas the masculine counterpart is fraught with references to literature, theology, philosophy, psychology, sociology, and technology. On one end is the unadulterated man of science, Don Fulgencio Entrambosmares, and on the other the pure poet, Hildebrando F. Menaguti. In between, and arguably more absorbing for that reason, are Don Avito Carrascal, who vacillates between the know-it-all and the skeptic, and Apolodoro Carrascal del Valle, who is caught in the curious space that mediates love and pedagogy. Apolodoro is guinea pig, poet, and thinker. He has grown up with conflicting signals from his parents and with feelings that transcend science. The scientific testing tortures him, but so does love. He knows not a moment of peace, except, ironically, in the anticipation of death. His father and mentor teach him not only science but the arts of verbosity and introspection. Menaguti teaches him not only poetry but the art of suffering. With different objectives, all three prod him to express himself in writing, to share his knowledge and to bare his soul publicly. Apolodoro becomes the center of the play on intellectualism to which the prologue alludes. His blind alley stands as testament to Unamuno's configuration of the narrative, but the pedagogical and amorous failures may lead the reader (with quixotic resonance) to something beyond satire.

Amor y pedagogía does not mask its difference, its awkwardness, or its unusual agenda. When the speaker in the prologue mentions the convention of the uniform size of books, he lists as examples "Galdós, Pereda, Valera, Palacio Valdés y otros escritores de fama y éxito" (49). They are the standard, but their accomplishments suggest conformity and the mainstream or middle-of-the-road tastes of the public. Unamuno's professed lack of concern about size requirements connotes an interest in deviating from the norm, in inventing something that is solely his. Since fame and success go hand in hand with immortality, however, Unamuno is not disparaging literary distinction and critical approval as much as staking his claim to new ground. Although only in his late thirties in 1902, he wrote and acted like a curmudgeon. He was strong-willed, confrontational, animated, idiosyncratic, opinionated, and crusty. His writing often hints of frustration with people, but this does not keep him from exposing his most private thoughts. He is a professional intellectual and polemicist, a scholar, an academic administrator, a writer in numerous genres, and a family man. His research takes him far into the past, and his love of learning and of Spain pushes him to stay current. His approach to the novel demonstrates the breadth of his knowledge and the dominant traits of his personality, as well as his attention to the play of form and content. History and politics lie at the center of *Paz en la guerra*, while the new vision places characters in what might be called a universalized space. The time, while not specific, is the present, his present, when Kierkegaard, Freud, William James, and many others are updating philosophy, psychology, and ways of perceiving the world.[15] Unamuno is attracted to the paradigm shifts, but he is a man of deep spiritual convictions. He goes through a personal struggle between faith and reason that he opens to the public in his writings. In *Amor y pedagogía*, he finds a fictional cover that allows him to be himself and to speak through others, as the speaker in the prologue attests.

Unamuno chooses not to classify *Amor y pedagogía*, yet it could perhaps be labeled an interdisciplinary novel, because literature is but one of its many bases, although the most important one. In *Don Quixote*, Cervantes subsumes society and layers of epistemology within the text; it is the macrocosm, and everything else is the microcosm. The movement is dialectical, but literature is where the endeavor begins, ends, and keeps on going. Unamuno's literary vision is similar. He loads *Amor y pedagogía* with countless elements that show the scope of his hunger for wisdom, but neither fiction nor erudition is a pretext for the other, for they are part

---

[15] For an overview of Unamuno's philosophical background and thought, see Cerezo Galán. See, among other sections, "La quiebra de la 'ilusión' progresista" (257-67), "El debate razón y corazón" (412-18), and "¡Qué animal tan extraño!" (578-91).

of the same conception of narrative. Unamuno presumes a certain level of sophistication on the part of the reader. His ideal audience would seem to include readers familiar with the literary past, scholarly debates, scientific advancements, and trends in psychology. And, one might add, readers with a strong sense of irony, humor, and pathos. In chapter 14, when Apolodoro chases away a group of young boys who are taunting a man who is having an epileptic seizure, he recalls a statement by Don Fulgencio to the effect that "de lo sublime a lo ridículo no hay más que un paso, según dicen, mas deben añadir que tampoco hay más que un paso de lo ridículo a lo sublime. Lo verdaderamente grande se envuelve en lo ridículo; en lo grotesco lo verdaderamente trágico" (147). The plot-line of *Amor y pedagogía* is serious and compelling, but the tone and the style can be jarring, outlandish, indecorous, and funny.

A characteristic of realism is the psychological development of characters, seen in early form, for example, in *Celestina* or *La lozana andaluza*, and strongly associated with picaresque narrative. The picaresque protagonists, male and female, grow from childhood to adulthood, often through a process of self-fashioning on the levels of story and discourse. There is an evident psychological dimension to the exemplary novels of Cervantes and María de Zayas. Later European realism blends psychology with defined socio-historical contexts and with a rendering of individuals and societies in transition. Thus, realism, notably from the sixteenth century onward, probes sociological and psychological issues. The picaresque is a satirical mode, but the social outcasts undergo pain and suffering not always of their own making. They hold themselves up to ridicule, or are held up to ridicule, but they manage to elicit sympathy despite their less than noble behavior. The writers of picaresque fiction generally maintain a balance between distance and concern, and the symbolism of the outsider has grown over time. In *Don Quijote*, idealism is displaced both by realism and by metafiction, with the latter containing—encompassing and superseding—the former. Analogously, Unamuno in his own way contains, or restricts, realism; he borrows from the novelistic trends that precede him as he detaches himself from realism and naturalism. A summary version of the plot of *Amor y pedagogía* could fit the realistic paradigm, but the execution is another matter entirely. The setting is different, replacing specificity with vagueness, but that is nothing compared to characterization. Unamuno's *entes de ficción* inhabit a world of their own, which is to say, his world of intellectual yearning and spiritual anguish, of contrasts, of self-examination and self-doubt, and of verbal subtleties and rhetorical flashes. Still, the single most critical element of the nivolistic repertoire is the language itself, an idiolect that melds perfectly with Unamunian conceptual systems.[16]

The prologue is about Unamuno, but the author turns the introduction into a negative review of his narrative method. He places the reader in a position of judgment, of control, while exerting his own control. He implements a rhetorical strategy that juxtaposes mockery with questions of suffering. From the beginning, buffoonery coexists with suffering. Unamuno establishes a tone and a symbolic structure that mix the mimetic with the anti-mimetic to produce an ironic variation, or perhaps aberration, of realism. That is why it is not incongruous to find Don Avito Carrascal's experiment to be at once pathetic and comic, tragic and absurd. The intellectualism and blatant literariness of *Amor y pedagogía*, including Unamuno's insistent self-promotion, hardly foster a suspension of disbelief, but, like *Don Quijote*, the narrative can move the reader, despite itself. The characters are symbols, vehicles for ideas, and yet they are capable of winning empathy. Unamuno's dialogical scheme is enhanced by the brilliance of the supremely lofty and intensely creative wordplay, which never loses its sense of humor.[17] For example, when Avito (form) acts upon his attraction to Marina (matter), the narrator states, "Los labios de la pobre Materia rozan la nariz de la Forma, y ahora ésta, ansiosa de su complemento, busca con su formal boca la boca material y ambas bocas se mezclan. Y al punto se alzan la Ciencia y la Conciencia, adustas y severas, y se separan avergonzadas los futuros

---

[16] Armando F. Zubizarreta observes, "Su afán filosófico le llevaba, a veces, a empeñarse en juegos dialécticos conceptistas, 'tan españolas', aprovechando las etimologías, para buscar palabras que denominase algunos existenciales" (159).

[17] Pérez notes that "Unamuno did not allow his anti-aesthetic postures and scorn for rhetoric to preclude full utilization of rhetorical figures; his training as a classical philologist probably fomented or augmented his passionate interest in language per se, especially in issues of semantics and semiotics. Both philosophically and as a creative artist, he accorded great significance to language ..." ("Rereading" 55). Pérez uses the term *baroque* to classify Unamuno's discursive ("*conceptista*") style.

padres del genio, mientras sonríe la Pedagogía sociológica desde la región de las ideas puras" (69-70). This is a rhetoric that fits the circumstances. It is rich, exaggeratedly showy, ponderous yet energetic, and consumed by ideas.

When Avito and Marina debate the merits of nursing versus the bottle, the husband argues that the bottle is better, purer by virtue of sterilization, than the so-called natural method, and he observes, "... mira, la pedagogía misma, ¿qué es sino biberón psíquico, lactancia artificial de eso que llaman espíritu por llamarlo de algún modo?" (78-79). When Apolodoro falls in love with Clarita, he begins to comprehend eternity; as the narrator states, "El ruido de la vida empieza a convertirse en melodía; medita, comprendiéndolo ya, en aquello de los juicios sintéticos y de las formas *a priori* de Kant, sólo que el único juicio sintético *a priori*, el intenso ordenador del caos externo, es el amor" (126). In the epilogue, Unamuno cites an anecdote concerning an artillery sergeant ("que hegenializaba sin saberlo" 164), who says that to build a cannon one takes a cylindrical hole and covers it with iron. The author adds, "Tal es el procedimiento metafísico, que es, como el lector habrá adivinado, el empleado por mí para construir los personajes de mi novela. He cogido sus huecos, los he recubierto de dichos y hechos" (165). He is filling spaces around ideas and arguing that metaphysics and art are anything but mutually exclusive, and he also is offering his poetics of characterization, which operates in the same mode; characters are hollow cylinders, waiting for words and actions to give them shape. For Unamuno, the centrality of the idea is the essence of plot, character, and message. In the image of the hole, paradoxically, the center would be hollow, rather like a doughnut or a life preserver, so that the heart or soul is initially empty and given animation by the act of creation itself. The fact that there is no explicit setting and that there are no historical allusions gives *Amor y pedagogía* a sense of isolation from the real world that sets it apart from the realistic novel, which typically depends on the depiction of a concrete time and place. Simply put, in the realist novel ideas come from characters, not vice versa. One would be hard put to find in previous novels a sentence that compares with the presentation of Avito Carrascal's turmoil over the deductive versus the inductive women who have entered his life, a turmoil that he recognizes as the power of the Unconscious: "Es en [su conciencia] un terremoto; agítansele ondulantes las oscuras entrañas espirituales; el elemento plutoniano del alma amenaza destruir la secular labor de la neptuniana ciencia, tal como así lo concibe, en geológica metáfora, el mismo Carrascal, escenario trágico del combate" (65).

The reader is privy not only to the characters' linguistic gyrations, and those of the narrator, but to the inner voice—and inner demon—of Avito and Apolodoro. They are all speaking the same language, which is, in the realm of narrative discourse, a language informed by philosophy, psychology, sociology, cultural tradition, and the artistic impulse. Unamuno seems intent upon shaking foundations on several fronts. Having practiced realism in *Paz en la guerra*, he removes history from the center and replaces it with science, or, more properly perhaps, social science.[18] Like his naturalist predecessors, he cannot move toward science

---

[18] In *Unamuno y la vida como ficción*, Francisco La Rubia Prado develops a model for reading history into the narrative. He uses two variants of modernist desire as outlined by Paul de Man: "[L]os personajes deciden o 'reinventarse' a ellos mismos creándose un nuevo presente en oposición a su pasado, o inventar o crear un nuevo presente para alguien distinto de ellos mismos que representa una 'prolongación' del yo, como, por ejemplo, un hijo propio" (233). La Rubia Prado's examples are *Amor y pedagogía* and *Sombras de sueño*, published twenty-four years later, in 1926. He proposes that "[m]ientras que en *Sombras de sueño*, el rechazo de la historia y la afirmación del presente como un nuevo comienzo se concibe como algo que beneficiará al individuo por medio de la promoción de su propia espontaneidad, en *Amor y pedagogía*, la ruptura con el pasado supone no un beneficio para el individuo concreto, sino para la 'humanidad'. Apolodoro entonces se convierte claramente en un peón de los designios de su padre para realizar el 'progreso humano'" (242). Apolodoro incarnates Don Avito's break with the past, and his fall "es el resultado del olvido de la historia por parte de su padre, un olvido tan radicalmente antiviral que cualquier cosa le recuerda aquello que echa de menos en la vida: las experiencias íntimamente conectadas con lo que el texto presenta como valores tradicionales y orgánicos, a saber, el amor, la religión, y la conciencia de la muerte como experiencia existencial. Si el suicidio de Apolodoro es un rechazo de los valores de su padre, es también, e irónicamente, una caída en la acción" (242-43). La Rubia Prado continues: "Las palabras de Avito sobre la futura educación de su nieto ilustran un 'sentido cómico' dirigido a desacreditar al positivismo, y su concomitante ruptura con el pasado, que permea *Amor y pedagogía*. La actitud modernista de Avito se entiende claramente como mecanicista y contraproducente para la vida, puesto que causa la infelicidad y la muerte de Apolodoro" (245). Irony trumps irony, however: "El uso de la ironía en *Amor y pedagogía* se dirige a ridiculizar el mecanicismo con el objetivo de privilegiar la concepción del mundo organicista.

without bringing in Catholicism. His faith and his crises of faith, public and private, come into play in *Amor y pedagogía* and in most of his works. So, inevitably, do his doubts, his rationalizations, and his calibrated inconsistencies. Dialogue for Unamuno has a special meaning that links the classical with the contemporary. Profound and trivial matters are introduced with flair. Every speaker, the narrator and the voices included, is a stylist, and virtually every phrase a show of literary and cognitive gifts. Unamuno most certainly would have studied and appreciated the *conceptismo* of the Golden Age, and he places his scholarly curiosity, his theological questions, and his respect for perspectivism at the service of art, but art with substance, never art for its own sake. In *Amor y pedagogía*, he builds a linear argument around the rearing of a son by a scientist bent on creating a genius and by a religious earth mother who wants to shower him with love. Caught in the middle, Apolodoro/Luis cannot find a middle, or mediating, ground. The lessons of his father are influenced and augmented by those of Don Fulgencio Entrambosmares, whose wisdom does not conform to the practice of everyday life. Don Fulgencio's models, like his advice, are conflicting and inconsistent.[19] They trouble Don Avito and baffle Apolodoro, who nonetheless hears catch phrases such as "¡haz hijos!" The suicide demonstrates that faith has failed, but, of course, so has science. Don Avito, with a grandson on the way, will set up a new

---

Sin embargo, esta estrategia retórica es problemática porque la ironía es un tropo mecanicista, no orgánico" (245).

[19] Thomas R. Franz, in an essay on the "philosophical bases" of Don Fulgencio Entrambosmares, makes the following cautionary statement: "Before proceeding with an examination of what I believe to be the Hegelian aspects of Entrambosmares, let me say that it is at times difficult to be sure if a given reference is to Hegel or to Kant, particularly when it is a mode of expression or a life style which is being held up to ridicule. Both men lived outwardly dull lives and wrote in such a labored and conceptual prose, that the vehicle of the expression externally mocked the revolutionary tenor of their ideas" (444). Although he favors Hegel, Franz writes in the concluding paragraph, "In working out the philosophy of Fulgencio Entrambosmares, Unamuno has apparently combined ideas from a good many thinkers" (449). Bénédicte Vauthier analyzes the novel and the character of Don Fulgencio by way of the *Ars magna combinatorial.* Following Carlos Clavería and Geoffrey Ribbans, James David Earnest draws heavily on *Amor y pedagogía*, and Don Fulgencio, in his essay on ties between Unamuno and Thomas Carlyle.

experiment.

In establishing a structure for the *nivola*, Unamuno appears to follow a series of presuppositions. First, he assumes that naturalism has taken realism to its limits and that there is a place for other narrative forms. Second, a change in form assumes a change in content. Third, there is an audience for a novel of ideas, a novel of abstractions. Fourth, there is an audience for a novel of ideas in which the brilliant and controversial Unamuno positions himself as the controlling center; he is to the text what the proverbial dancer is to the dance. Fifth, recalling the miscellany of earlier times, the novel can be a synthesis of multiple elements, and art can be an instrument through which to bring new ways of thinking to readers, in a creative and "artistic" manner. Sixth, readers will be able to grasp, and will not object to, the random feel of the narrative. Seventh, readers will accept the invitation to decipher its symbolism, allegory, and mysteries. Eighth, readers will recognize and value the irony, both comic and serious, of the text. Ninth, readers will be grateful to an author who drops names, notions, and allusions, making them rise to the occasion. And tenth, readers will see the dual plan of *Amor y pedagogía* as a *Quijote*-inspired combination of poetry and poetics. Although one may tend to associate the learned, opinionated, and contemplative Unamuno with content rather than with form, *Amor y pedagogía* responds to realism and naturalism by creating a counter-style, a narrative formula that defies the norm and registers an Unamunian imprint.

The prologue contains a strange variation of the omniscient narrator. Unamuno does not try to hide the fact that he is talking about himself, that he is both subject and object, all-knowing yet critically detached. The ironic play of distance introduces the theme of metafiction and allows the author to be his first reviewer, seemingly negative but not entirely convincing. In addition to the introduction of a variety of disciplines into the narrative plan, along with the beauty, and the rarity, of the language, Unamuno explores the psyches of his two main characters by supplying them with inner (and "demonic") voices. Don Avito Carrascal and his son Apolodoro have forces within them which chastise them for their actions and warn them of dangers that await. The characters come equipped with something more than a conscience; each voice resembles an individualized Greek chorus that presages disaster, as if neither of the characters could control his course of action or his destiny. These inner dialogues are as stylized and as quirky as the characters' speech patterns, and, while they pretend to derive from the depths of consciousness, they evoke the writer as well as the character.[20] The fragmented feel of the narration—arguably, orchestrated chaos—places Unamuno with the modernists, although the latter may not be oriented to reconciling or aligning their tensions with the Catholic faith. Religion and philosophy intertwine, linked once again by the authorial persona and by the interdisciplinary nature of the text.

The plot of *Amor y pedagogía*, reduced to its basic element, focuses on education. The man of science vies with the woman of faith to educate their son, although he is the designated instructor and she must act in secret. He wants to produce a genius, and she wants her son to be safe, happy, and spiritually protected. Avito Carrascal controls the environment, from the beans that he brings into the diet of the expectant mother to the books, lessons, journals, and mentor that he provides his son. The opposite is true of his daughter, who resides in the margins of the father's plans and in the margins of the narrative. Rosa, who has no Greek name but whose name is symbolic nonetheless, is defined by her distance from science (and formal education) and by her poor health. She seems always on the verge of dying, and her physical ailments parallel the mental afflictions that torment her brother. Don Avito's contention that geniuses must be male, when viewed with Unamuno's admission, through the speaker in the prologue, that he is a failure at depicting women may sharpen the satire, but there is also a sexist inflection to the narrative. Unamuno shows Don Avito succumbing to induction when he selects Marina over Leoncia. He is a victim of feminine charm, and he lets his sexual appetite get in the way of science. Clarita, the art teacher's

---

[20] According to Michael Vande Berge, "Unamunian criticism has long recognized Unamuno's intellectual debt to William James: he is known to have read at least four of James's major works, frequently referring to and quoting from them in his articles and private letters.... [T]here can be little doubt that Unamuno's early ideas about the mind and thought processes—ideas which form an integral part of *Amor y pedagogía*—were derived at least in part from his reading of *The Principles of Psychology* [1890], the work in which James coined the term '[s]tream of consciousness'" ("An Early Application" 752). Vande Berge reiterates the connection in the preface to his translation of the novel (v-xxi). One may note the influence as profound without failing to emphasize the uniqueness of Unamuno's appropriation of the concept.

daughter, likewise distracts Apolodoro. Don Avito's program for his son does not include courtship and love, and Apolodoro's education leaves him ill-prepared for the emotional strains of amorous pursuit. Unamuno does not set forth a consistent reading of women. The women of *Amor y pedagogía* are something more, and something less, than guardians of hearth and home. Doña Edelmira, who puts Don Fulgencio in his place, manages to be dominant and surprisingly sexy at the same time, and she entices not only her husband but the young Apolodoro. Unamuno seems to represent woman as a variable in the rigidly quantitative, yet always mysterious, world of science. She looks and acts differently than man, and she is treated and educated differently. She asserts herself, in great part, by getting in the way, by disturbing the best-laid plans, and by factoring herself into the equations.

There is no question that Unamuno presents Don Avito Carrascal's methodology as extreme and often ridiculous, but the author himself is no advocate of middle-of-the-road positions. The father-son relationship, and by extension the theme of education, ultimately refers to immortality, to one's legacy.[21] The childless researcher Don Fulgencio Entrambosmares relies on his books to make him immortal. Don Avito hopes to become immortal through his son, and the training agenda is like an insurance policy, a means of preserving the family line through fame and success. Unamuno, father and writer, can count on both his children and his literary works, yet it is the world of letters to which he returns again and again as he meditates on eternity. That is probably why he reproduces himself on the page, in order to mark his candidacy for immortality in each realm. When Apolodoro comprehends that he truly loves Clarita and cannot have her, and when he is certain that he will never be a genius in life, he determines to be one in death, by committing his pitiful story to paper. This is a purely Unamunian remedy, a desperate attempt to endure beyond death. It also emulates the master's paradoxical bent by joining

---

[21] For a general consideration of the link between parenthood and immortality, see Franz, "Parenthood." Franz speaks of Unamuno's "effort to create separate fictional entities who would *objectify* his existence by serving as its reflector," and thus he "had no choice but to give them great autonomy" (654). Because their independence threatened to overpower his, he made the decision "to enter the novels as a character himself and banish the other personages to a secondary plane" (Franz, "Parenthood" 654).

the search for immortality with suicide, and by accompanying the suicide with an imminent birth, Apolodoro's honoring of Don Fulgencio's advice to have children. The introductory materials pay homage to the book and to its author, and the bookish male characters pay homage to the word. In the process, reason is honored and derided, shown to lend itself to disaster, as *la sinrazón de la razón*, one might say.

Apolodoro cannot remove the image of the guinea pig from his mind. In their first session, Don Fulgencio cautions him to beware of common sense and facts ("Huye de los hechólogos, que la hechología es el sentido común echado a perder") and to strive to make himself unclassifiable ("Extravaga, hijo,… que más vale eso que vagar a secas"), to create a system in which he will be the sine qua non (114). He throws abstruse aphorisms at him right and left, along the lines of "La escolástica es una vista y hermosa cátedra,… de admirable fábrica, pero hecha con adobes" (114). Rather than emulate the prudent or the headstrong man, counsels Don Fulgencio, the young man should think and act at the same time. The universe came into its own so that it could be explained by man. When man realizes this task, things will become ideas and ideas will become names. Silence will ensue, and reality will be transformed into a super-reality. With that, he orders Apolodoro to go away. The directions have a patent lack of direction. The student can hardly have learned a lesson, other than to doubt himself and to wonder about the pedagogical rationale of his father and tutor. A childhood memory of boys who captured a bat and nailed it by its wings to a wall comes to mind, and at this point the narrator mentions that Apolodoro has met the poet Menaguti, a priest in the sanctuary of beauty. The rewards of science are negligible. Poetry bestows the consolation of love. And for Menaguti, the only genius is poetic genius. He encourages Apolodoro to make poetry, as later Don Fulgencio will urge him to make children. Sleep is a relief for the disturbed young man, but the swarm of ideas and pseudo-ideas to which he has been exposed—not to mention the "doctísima obra acerca del sueño, sus causas y sus leyes" (117)—attacks him, interrupts his peaceful slumber, and reshapes the world in kaleidoscopic visions. His father demands that he write down his conception of the universe, but Apolodoro finds it easier, and more pleasant, to compose verses. His mother attributes the change to love, which his father believes is unbefitting a genius. To further the risk of heartbreak, love moves from the abstract to the concrete. Passion enters the scheme, and Apolodoro is subjected to the whims of Clarita and to the menacing presence of Federico.

The failure of Apolodoro's novella fuels his feelings of doubt and inferiority. Apolodoro has exposed himself to the world at large, and he senses that people are looking down on him. Menaguti offers little comfort, and Don Fulgencio insults him and art in general. Apolodoro has forsaken science for art, and now he has serious misgivings about art. He is shocked when Menaguti advises him to challenge Federico to a duel. When he puts the suggestion to the test, Federico berates him and guesses that the idea has been Menaguti's. His adversary goes further, to claim that Apolodoro is a plaything of the pedagogy of others. No denial can convince Apolodoro that the statement is false. He contemplates suicide and inwardly curses his father. Visiting Don Fulgencio, Apolodoro receives instruction on death, which can be both purposeful and beautiful, but the childless mentor stresses the need for children. Don Fulgencio states, "[N]ecesito a Dios para hacerme immortal" (145), and follows this with the comment that art derives from the thirst for immortality, yet the context is a paradoxical romanticization of death. The Unamunian thematics, with the requisite allusions to art, immortality, and the ponderous unknowns that test and help to formulate faith, emphasize another motif: the temptation toward suicide. Apolodoro has been accused of being a puppet. Suicide may seem to give him control, but even in death he acquiesces to the philosophy, or to the speculative pseudo-philosophy, of Don Fulgencio.[22] His novella will not earn him earthly glory, but he has left Petra pregnant, and, with an irony that cannot be overlooked, he has given his father another opportunity to cultivate a genius.

The presentation of the mental wanderings and perceptions of the beleaguered Apolodoro accentuates an active imagination and a troubled soul. He often sees before him shadows without substance, and he longs to stand outside himself in order to see how others view him. He plays solitaire and visualizes the figures in his life behind the cards, with Don Fulgencio as the jack of clubs. His resignation from life is well considered

---

[22] Olson calls Apolodoro's death, which he sees as motivated by heroism and curiosity, "one of Unamuno's most effective syntheses of tragedy and comedy" (*Great Chiasmus* 63).

and mindful of the future; his entire life seems to have been leading up to it. Don Avito, for his part, insists on science as the universal panacea. He tells Apolodoro that love can be moderated by nutrition and, to his son's astonishment, that he himself has gone through the ups and downs of love. Apolodoro argues for a pedagogy based on love, but Don Avito concludes that one can produce geniuses only by eliminating love from the methodology. Apolodoro's appeal for understanding—"¡Padre, no se juega así con el corazón!" (151)—falls on deaf ears. Don Avito rethinks the scientific path and decides that he should have taken more care with the mother of the genius. He vows to dedicate himself more to Rosa, but in the same thought he blames only Marina for his daughter's frailty. Apolodoro ponders his fate, feeling a bit of gratitude to Clarita for motivating him to take action against her rejection. Rosa's death pushes him to finalize his decision, but not before he seduces Petra, whom he fantasizes as Clarita, who meanwhile has announced her marriage to Federico. Apolodoro feels terrible guilt for having abused Petra and anger for the abuse committed against him, in the name of pedagogy, by his father. He prepares to hang himself, worried that he will look ridiculous hanging from the ceiling, but he goes through with the suicide, resolving, after mulling it over, that the hanging will be sublime. The epilogue elaborates upon the grief of the parents and the other members of the cast of the narrative drama, and it becomes obvious that very little has changed in the aftermath of the death.

Don Avito Carrascal's experiment is an abject failure. The men of science not only are unsuccessful in producing a genius, but the young man whom they educate is ill-equipped to cope with the demands of society. Don Avito and Don Fulgencio arrogantly defend their principles—incoherent and inconsistent though their notions may be—to the exclusion of other options. Distracted and disorganized as teachers, they place pedagogy and love in opposition. By excluding the latter from the curriculum, they subordinate maternal nurturing, affection, and tenderness, so that the instruction is both flawed and sexist. Ironically, the presumed scientists are given to conceptualization, while the lofty poet Menaguti dispenses specific remedies for love sickness and depression. Don Fulgencio does, however, plant the idea of having children, and the representatives of science and art manage to lead Apolodoro toward death. Petra's unborn child, which must be a male in order to keep hope alive in the grandfather, becomes a last chance for immortality. Given that a high-fiber diet and the exclusion of love remain fundamental desiderata of Don Avito's pedagogy, the prognosis is not good. How readers respond to, and prioritize, the psychology, the ideology, and the rhetoric of *Amor y pedagogía* depends on the relative effects of the distancing devices embedded in the narrative. If Apolodoro Carrascal is seen, quite literally, as paper-thin, he can be viewed as a function of Unamuno's message system. If he achieves a third dimension, despite the self-consciousness of the text, his story likely will become sympathetic, and tragic, as well as emblematic. Cervantes carries off this feat in *Don Quijote* by giving depth to the stick figures of traditional parody without dulling their satirical edge. Unamuno's stylistic adornments and editorializing tend to get in the way, and not necessarily unintentionally, but psychology, even when qualified as self-indulgent and self-promotional, may win out.

In *Amor y pedagogía*, Unamuno does not attempt to recreate the socio-historical backdrop that is a staple of realism. His work plays out on an empty stage, or on the stage of ideas. Don Avito Carrascal and Don Fulgencio de Entrambosmares are, in the broad sense, social scientists, but each allows philosophy—an absurdist philosophy, to be sure—to supersede psychology. Their ideas are by no means all bad, but their bits of wisdom and understanding are trapped in a rhetoric and in a rationale that obscures whatever positive benefits they may have. Don Avito never comprehends or believes in his wife; monomaniacal when it comes to the making of a genius, he is a sociologist without basic interpersonal skills. Don Fulgencio, on the other hand, constantly misses the forest for the trees. He has no sense of an audience, no awareness of the carelessness of his proclamations. He is a more successful husband than Avito because he has learned to separate domesticity from science. Having no experience as a father, he is willing to gamble on Apolodoro's upbringing, and his method is specious. If Doña Edelmira is an improbable domestic goddess who dominates the household beyond the scholar's office, Doña Marina is a shadowy presence, defined by her maternal instincts and her Catholic faith. She is part of a system of mixed messages in the upbringing of Apolodoro, as exemplified in the dual names and, by corollary, split identity of her son. Apolodoro is the product of his environment. He is conflicted, but, in his own way, rebellious. He intuits from the start that science and, more correctly, scientists are not serving him well. Yet poetry and the tutelage of a particular poet also fare poorly. Apolodoro is attached to his mother, but he sees her as belonging to another realm and as an additional victim of science. Riddled by self-doubt, guilt, and at least borderline paranoia, he feels attacked by the world. When love comes into his life, it is painful and short-lived, and when he tries to transfer his emotions to literature, success continues to elude him.

Unamuno takes the struggle between reason and faith to new levels. As an accomplished polemicist, he operates from the extreme position on each side, although he could not be called an advocate either of science or religion as they are portrayed in *Amor y pedagogía*. He allows satire to intrude upon the domains of philosophy and theology, and he complements ironic hyperbole with questions of literary practice, in general and individually, self-centeredly. The dialectics of the narrative are based largely on the perceived locus of child-rearing. Avito considers his home a laboratory, while Marina wants the home to be a sanctuary for her son. He is unwilling to compromise, and she takes refuge from the trials to which Apolodoro is submitted. There is no space for synthesis and thus no secure space for healthy development. Apolodoro is simultaneously over-programmed and left on his own. His mental and spiritual guides proliferate, but they grant him little peace or direction, and there is not a moment in which he is not floundering, whether lost in society or in his thoughts. He fears exposure, yet bares his soul. His love for Clarita is never truly personalized; he appears to prefer love in the abstract, but he transfers his passion onto Petra and then reproaches himself for doing so. He exists in a type of narrative purgatory, but always seems closer to hell than to heaven. No one in *Amor y pedagogía* can frame reality or find contentment. Avito and Marina live in two different worlds. Fulgencio and Edelmira inhabit two partial realities. Menaguti's sphere of influence extends no farther than his own reflection. Clarita and Federico are intelligent yet superficial and demeaning of Apolodoro. They probably deserve each other, but they bespeak a negative or antagonistic sensibility. Their role is adversarial; they are, ironically, forces of darkness rather than of light. Rosa is negative in another way. She is defined by illness and by her aloofness from science, from all that is depicted as masculine territory. Separated from the experiment and hovered over by her mother, she falls prey to neglect and/or nurture. Unamuno does not write women poorly, as the prologue would have it. Rather, he positions them in the margins of the text, in a manner that isolates them, symbolically, from the major action.

Amor y pedagogía is not a narrative about urban society. Its exploration of human nature has the ring of a laboratory test, with characters locked in an intellectual maze. The lead (male) characters are knowledgeable, but their erudition has no firm stakes and constantly proves itself to be incomplete and frivolous.[23] Don Avito Carrascal's quest, with Don Fulgencio Entrambosmares as his north star, is to raise a genius. The narrative focuses on the stumbling blocks and on the object of the experiment, Apolodoro, for whom no alternatives provide solace. His

---

[23] Martin Nozick offers a succinct reading of the novel's message. For Unamuno, "[r]eason is valid only if applied to abstractions, but sadly inadequate when dealing with the concrete and the unpredictable. The attempt to impose an ideological straitjacket on the mercury of life, to force instinct and impulse into preconceived molds, is a ridiculous effort which may end, as in this case, in tragedy. Thus, [*Amor y pedagogía*] is a satire of the religion of science..." (Nozick 144). David Turner comments, "One of Unamuno's favourite techniques, particularly, although not exclusively, when pouring scorn on something commonly exalted by the public, is to portray this exaltation as a religion, often with the apotheosis of the ideal or object in question" (28). Turner's précis is also worthy of note: "Beneath the superficial parody of a man with an exaggerated opinion of the domain and potentialities of science, the conflict of what is rationally true and inescapable with what is emotionally acceptable and experienced as real provides the book's theme..." (43). Gonzalo Navajas, in an essay that focuses on subjectivity and doubling in Unamuno's works, says of *Amor y pedagogía*: "La apariencia estéril y deshumanizada de la casa de Don Avito tiene un significado metonímico de toda la ciencia. Don Avito no se presenta como una aberración singular, un caso excepcional, sino como una figura representativa de la naturaleza de la ciencia.... [E]l autor... está interesado en hacer de la ciencia una forma de religión para probar la universalidad del sentimiento religioso incluso en los que dicen negarlo en nombre del espíritu científico" ("El yo" 518). In his study of *Amor y pedagogía* as a paradigm for the modern Spanish novel, Germán Gullón accentuates that "el rechazo de lo aparencial nos debe llevar a lo íntimo, al descubrimiento de lo esencial, del amor filial en este caso, y finalmente a lo contradictorio, a lo paradójico, a lo irónico" (241). Gullón notes that Don Avito Carrascal reappears in *Niebla* as "totalmente desengañado con la ciencia; de hecho, cuando lo reencontramos le está ofreciendo agua bendita a Augusto Pérez a la salida de una iglesia donde estaba rezando el rosario" (241). Gullón's starting point is the remarkable group of novels that appeared in 1902, some rooted in a glorious literary past (Galdós's *Las tormentas del 48* and *Narváez*, and Blasco Ibáñez's *Cañas y barro*) and others oriented toward future narrative creation (*Amor y pedagogía*, Valle-Inclán's *Sonata de otoño*, Baroja's *Camino de perfección*, and Azorín's *La voluntad*).

lessons, formal and informal, are certainly interdisciplinary, but the goals are too high and the educational strategies too shoddy for the ending to be happy. The discourse is lofty, elegant, contemporary, amusing, and, most of all, mystifying by design. Unamuno tosses ideas at the reader, and, while the speakers stay in character, there is an aleatory air to all aspects of the text. Because Apolodoro and pedagogy occupy a unifying center of the narrative space, the author cleverly situates readers in an analogous spot, from which they have to deal with contradictions and illogical premises. Unamuno is teaching a new way of conceiving the novel, and this involves a disorienting confusion, a chaos that comes to be associated with modernism. Linguistic and ideological complexity and shifts of tone affect word processing. If Apolodoro's suicide is the climax, the dénouement (epilogue) combines the other characters' reactions to his death with Unamuno's need to fill up space, which he does by inscribing his dilemma into the narrative and by appending the treatise on cocotology.

In the nineteenth century, a broad range of novelists exploited the richness of realism as they chronicled the history and mores of the times. Unamuno appreciates realist conventions, as illustrated in *Paz en la guerra*. Never complacent, he tries thereafter to alter the rules of novel writing and of perceiving and expressing reality. The prologue to *Amor y pedagogía* puts on display a narrator with a difference, a voice with a distinctly Unamunian inflection which assesses, and critiques, Unamuno; it establishes an ironic distance that will create special ironies and deceptive distances. Like Cervantes, Unamuno evokes reality through periphrasis, by calling attention to the devices of literature as he negotiates the currents and crosscurrents of perception. That is, he creates a fictional analogue of life experiences which ends by honoring and exceeding reality. By concentrating on the theme of immortality, he links theology, art, and procreation. He inspires a reevaluation of pedagogy in its multiple contexts and, strange as it may seem, he presents a unique glimpse into the inscrutable topic of love. He recoils from some archetypes while adhering to others, notably those that relate to the female characters, yet, even at his most conventional, Unamuno breaks molds.[24]

---

[24] In "Playing with Unamunian Paper Birds," Nancy Newton notes, "In *Amor y pedagogía* gender-role stereotypes enjoy so ironic a style that the entire

The haughtiness of the "scientists" is not without its compassion, and the women relegated to the margins are not without what might be termed an elliptical depth. The author empathizes with parents, with those in love and those whose love is unrequited, and with those intrigued and overwhelmed by ideas. Dialogue surpasses action, but the dialogue is bold, witty, and stimulating, and the narrative becomes a happening, a contest among factions in a pedagogical struggle that ably incorporates theoretical and practical issues. *Amor y pedagogía* is not a how-to book, nor is it exactly a how-not-to book, although that case could be made. It is, rather, an intellectual puzzle, an invitation to think about art, education, and life as guided by Unamuno, who renders himself, perhaps with false modesty, as more vulnerable and more fallible than Don Fulgencio.

What would be the theory of the *nivola* as conveyed in *Amor y pedagogía*? The answer would not be the same if the question were asked of *Niebla*, because that text is more explicit on the subject—Víctor Goti is an internal *nivolista*—and because the *nivola* already exists at the time of composition. Although Unamuno is writing against the grain of realism and following *Don Quijote* and other metafictional precedents, *Amor y pedagogía* has a disordered, clean-slate, and, not unexpectedly, viviparous feel to it. The author frames his narrative with references to publishers' demands, among them the need to fill a prescribed number of pages. He shows the interdependence of aesthetic and reality principles, of creation and convention, of inspiration and incertitude. The scientific experiment, the enactment of gender roles (and variations of stereotypes), the tribulations of love, the soliloquies and long-winded speeches, and Apolodoro's path toward suicide move the plot along through recourses that are both predictable and unpredictable. The discourse, however, is novel: dense, powerful, touching, invigorating, ingenious, and profoundly comic. Characters are defined by their thoughts and by their

---

question of the origin, nature, and function of cultural myths about sex is thrown open for examination and debate" (45). She refers to "Don Fulgencio's comical illustration of the construction or 'constructedness' of gender" (47) in the treatise on paper birds, and she suggests that "Unamuno challenges the reader of his fiction to think about 'being female' and 'being male' at a hermeneutic level. As signs, neither masculinity nor femininity is fixed, but we seem bent on fixing meaning on them. Gender must be acknowledged as a pivotal carrier of meaning…" (50).

verbosity. Some agonize, others pontificate. Some share their opinions and sentiments, others turn inward, but an omniscient and often judgmental narrator makes their feelings accessible to the reader. The male characters are self-absorbed, egotistical to the nth degree. For all their wordiness, the dramatis personae conspicuously talk *at* each other, and a number of messages go undeciphered, if not unheard. Despite the pathetic destiny of the man whom others attempt to mold into a genius, there is a freshness and a spiritedness to the peculiar rhetoric of the narrative, which may move and tickle the reader.

It is possible to imagine casting the basic plot of *Amor y pedagogía* in the realist mode. Realism has room for both love and pedagogy, for conducting experiments in new fields of inquiry. Emphasis on the physical setting could be intensified, and the tone would likely be somber and tragic. The father-son conflict, unrequited love, the clash between faith and science, and the pains of emerging subjectivity could be played against a recognizable backdrop of late nineteenth-century Spain. Realism does not preclude humor, but the blueprint of this plot has no innate humor. Don Fulgencio Entrambosmares could be considered a figure of comic relief, but his dismissive attitude toward his charge's well-being is by no means risible in a deep-structural context. It takes an audacious disregard for protocol to redress Apolodoro's dilemma as tragicomedy, as a cross between a crisis of subjectivity and a satirical appraisal of both outdated and newfangled pedagogy. Unamuno's metafictional and modernist inventions cover despair and desolation in such a way as to oscillate between the depths of depression and a victory of intellectualism over verisimilitude. While he does not erase sentiment from the canvas, Unamuno injects a narrative voice and a narrative stance that redirect, or disarm, their realist precedents.

Gregory L. Lucente points out that during the Italian Renaissance, *imitation* had two meanings: "first, the conscious imitation of prior artistic models, and second, the imitation of nature" (12). In *Theories of Mimesis*, Arne Melberg writes that "Aristotle insists that *mimesis* means imitation of something coming *before* the story in time[,] and this something-before is called action—*praxis*—and is given the characteristics of beginning-middle-end" (63). Melberg notes that Don Quijote's imitation of the romances of chivalry comprises a variation on the theme of reality, given that the knight errant's point of reference, and model, while real to him, is fiction. The undertaking, which depends on a reversal of time, is obviously self-defeating, and it goes against the friend's assessment of the author's aims, as stated in the 1605 prologue. Melberg uses the term "mimetic infection" (77 ff.) to address a fascinating dialectic within the narrative. Don Quijote wishes to revive the age of chivalry, the Golden Age, whereas the author proposes to do the opposite, namely, to combat this form of nostalgia, or at least its literary manifestation, by destroying chivalric romance. The knight aspires to a new story, but the author wishes to write a story that will end all such stories. Cervantes's story, then, must press toward its ending, for only with closure can it achieve its objective. There is an allegorical dimension to this internal narrative that places realism alongside truth. Neither can easily be absolute in its representation. For Melberg, "the Absolute or the Truth that was ideally posited by the work of art... can, however, never be contained in the work of art; absolute truth... is temporal..., changing, moving. The work of art may 'posit' the Absolute, but the 'Absolute' still evades naming" (81). Citing Borges's "Pierre Menard," Melberg derives a maxim from Cervantes's treatment of *imitatio*: "to make new is impossible[,] and it is impossible not to make new" (84). Imitation cannot be exact, nor is exactitude desirable. Cervantes anticipates narrative realism while resisting what would be its search for similitude, preferring to concentrate instead on difference and on distance. Aware of the artistic and epistemological arguments, Unamuno also answers the implicit questions in practice.

One might make a case for nostalgia in *Niebla*. Unamuno uses *Don Quijote* as a counterpoint to realism and naturalism, as well as a structuring agent, with Cervantes as a kindred spirit. There are unmistakable Cervantine reminiscences in *Niebla*, but emulation stands at an ironic distance from the summoned text. Unamuno strongly invites comparison, but there is no confusion about which is which or about the need to differentiate between the two. *Amor y pedagogía* is clear about the bases of its response to the realist novel, but its evocation of models is far more nuanced than that of *Niebla*. Even though his narrative decisions are being discussed in each instance, Unamuno starts *Amor y pedagogía* differently. He does not pretend to treat fiction as if it were real, as he does with Víctor Goti's prologue, and then invert the premises, as he does with Augusto Pérez's visit to Salamanca. Rather, he presupposes a divide between the creator and the creation, between Unamuno the artist and a distinctly Unamunian form of art. He appropriates Cervantes's play of praxis on two levels, by putting his theory into practice and by devoting space to the practicalities of the writing process. Unamuno devises a source of friction in the third-person references to himself in the prologue, and he continues with the contrast of intense emotions and dispassionate intellectualizing in the plot proper. Perhaps one could revise Melberg's term to call Unamuno's method "metafictional infection." Unamuno seems committed to blurring the lines between his thoughts, anxieties, and public persona and the inscription of his narrative, the discourse and contextual abstractions of which—expressed in a way that would hardly disturb the author—give him away. Although he develops the connection more fully in *Niebla*, he moves between empathy and ironic detachment, a course that helps to define structure and reader-response in *Don Quijote*. The linkage of ending the book, ending life, seeking immortality, and taking recourse to paradox is a Cervantine lesson that is not lost on Unamuno.

In *Metafiction*, Linda Waugh, echoing Mikhail Bakhtin, argues that the novel "assimilates a variety of discourses... that *always* to some extent question and relativize each other's authority," and adds, "Realism, often regarded as the classical fictional mode, paradoxically functions by suppressing this dialogue" (6). Those works labeled as metafiction tend automatically to be dialogic, because they create a fiction and offer commentary on that fiction. Thus, "[t]he two processes are held together in a formal tension which breaks down the distinctions between 'creation' and 'criticism' and merges them into the concepts of 'interpretation' and 'deconstruction'" (Waugh 6). Waugh posits that the realist tradition stems from "a firm belief in a commonly experienced, objectively existing world of history," as opposed to modernist fiction of the early twentieth century, which "responded to the initial loss of belief in such a world" (6). Just as the major works of Spanish naturalism could not break away from Catholicism, Unamuno's rendering of chaos maintains its theological—his theological—roots. As a dialoguist par excellence, Unamuno casts *his* narrative as love versus pedagogy, the first associated with religion and the second with science. He and his text seem resolutely to avoid the obvious solution: some type of compromise. Don Avito Carrascal is as much a social scientist at the conclusion as at the beginning, now that he has the promise of a grandson in tow, and Doña Marina's tragic losses have not pushed her toward science or dampened her faith. The dialogue is framed by attention to the writing process, to the book as a consumer object, and to Unamuno as an individual and as an emblematic author. Ties with realism can be identified, but these ties are challenged by the self-consciousness of the presentation. The psychological explorations are coated with discursive performances and with a narration that often appears more ironic than heartfelt.

It is to the "inner world of subjectivity and imagination" tapped by modernism to which Linda Hutcheon appeals in *Narcissistic Narrative* (25). For her, "subjective realism" shifts from the description of external reality to the inner being of characters, and from a controlled to a task-burdened reading experience. As a result, "[t]he course of literary history is being altered, and, as always, it is being altered by the texts, not the critics. In fact, this new narcissistic fiction is allowing (is forcing?) a re-evaluation of the novels of the past, thanks to its challenging of the inadequate, reified critical notion of 'realism' based on a narrow product mimesis alone" (Hutcheon 39). Hutcheon defends the narrative derived from Cervantes and Sterne, noting, "There is no *literary* reason why socialist realism should be considered more novelistic, any more mimetic, than the fantasy fictions of Borges. By claiming that there is nothing but art,... metafiction becomes more 'vital': it reflects the human imagination, instead of telling a secondhand tale about what might be real in quite another world" (47). In *Theory and the Novel*, Jeffrey J. Williams makes a similar point by attempting "to collapse the hierarchy of narrative levels, or at least to disallow its literal or referential value in grounding the narrative. In other words, the predominant trope motivating or defining narrative is not mimesis or referentiality, but narrativity or reflexivity" (9). One may approach the issue of metafiction from the opposite extreme, by focusing on naturalism, which Darío Villanueva, in *Theories of Literary Realism*, refers to as "genetic realism." The outcome should be "a faithful reproduction of this reality" (15), a concept that depends on an institutionalized interpretation of mimesis and that, of course, lends itself to deconstruction. Sensing flaws in the premises of realism and naturalism, Unamuno may find the investigation of alternate realities, as carried out in *Don Quijote* and other metafictions, appealing.

Maintaining that "the 'reality' or referential value of the story is a function of the configuration of the narrative, not the other way around" (31), Williams classifies *Tristram Shandy* as an example of the "disorderly narrative," whose "reflexive plot... inscribes its own mode, its own performative operation, while... constatively depicting that act as a normal novelistic event" (24-25). Unamuno's viviparous narrative is recognizably disorderly, but his sense of construction, or authorial interference, in my opinion, accentuates the abnormal, rather than the normal or natural, features of the discourse. The *nivola* throws curves at the reader, but with exaggerated zeal, as if the narrative aberrations were encoded in order to be noticed, to be reflected upon. This perhaps is because Unamuno is striving both for a degree of discomfort on the part of the reader and for an acknowledgment of his own eccentricities, of his desire to be visible (or perceptible) and unique. Hyperbole and unconventionality serve his ends, for his agenda is about difference as such, even though he might wish to address universal questions and the most impenetrable mysteries of life and death. Nonetheless, he fits these considerations within the parameters of fiction, and he seeks a narrative design that will accommodate his creative criteria and his personal needs. Paul Olson encapsulates the satirical depth and the conceptual diversions of *Amor y pedagogía* when he calls it "a moral tale of the tyranny of words and ideas—*logocracia* or *ideocracia* over mortal flesh and blood" (*Great Chiasmus* 53). Without mentioning deconstruction as such, he shows that the text exemplifies the deconstructive paradox: "[O]nly words and ideas—language and thought—can actually be present in the novel, and its critique of the destructive effects of ideas and words is itself an idea constituted by language" (*Great Chiasmus* 53). Yet, according to plan, the narrative belies its premises and superimposes paradox on paradox. The author and his characters are seeking immortality, not annihilation, and only words can save them.

In *Tres novelas ejemplares y un prólogo*, published in 1920, the same year as *Niebla*, Unamuno is fully in line with the theorists of metafiction. He calls the prologue a novella (and not a *nivola*) in itself. He cites Cervantes early on, in alluding to the seventeenth-century *Novelas ejemplares*. He speaks briefly but emphatically of the works that he has fashioned here, narratives that delve into human psychology, the will, and its counterpoint, *la noluntad*, something on the order of a death wish that stops short of suicide.[25] A primary message of the prologue is that reality need not

---

[25] Unamuno writes in the prologue that "¿hay quien quiere ser y quien quiere no ser, y lo mismo en hombres reales encarnados en carne y hueso que en hombres reales encarnados en ficción novelesca o nivolesca. Hay héroes del

be synonymous with realism. Conflict becomes a psychological center in which those characters who undergo internal strife—"luchadores," "agonistas"—"son reales, realísimos, y con la realidad más íntima, con la que se dan ellos mismos, en puro querer ser o en puro querer no ser, y no con la que le den los lectores" (47). Unamuno's exemplary novellas (*Dos madres, El marqués de Lumbría,* and *Nada menos que todo un hombre*) are soul-baring battles of will played out on a narrative analogue of darkened stages with limited sets. Pain and desperation reveal and unlock psyches. There is a bareness, and barrenness, to the physical landscape, and the narratives portray bottled-up emotions at war with primal urges. The three novellas exhibit Unamuno's artistry and his fondness for irony without the humor, the ostentatious erudition, and the unavoidable presence of the author. They are, as he contends, *novelas,* written in defiance of the tenets of realism and highlighting the inner life of the characters. Although composed subsequent to *Amor y pedagogía,* they are, formally and ideologically, the transitional texts between *Paz en la guerra* and the *nivola.* The tortured egos in combat with each other and within themselves underscore the precedence of the psychological over the socio-historical. This rupture from the more standard realism combines tense, emotionally-charged circumstances with a serious but stylized language, and the author comes into the scheme as he pointedly flouts conventions and seeks a linguistic correlative for the enterprise.

The model for the *nivola* goes beyond the starkness of the novellas to cast Unamuno alongside the distressed *entes de ficción* and to foreground his authorial role. In *Amor y pedagogía,* he is, like Cervantes in 1605 (or 1604), an author with a manuscript, at the mercy of publishers and publishing norms. The size and shape of the manuscript become the frames of *Amor y pedagogía,* and Don Fulgencio Entrambosmares's essay serves as an ingenious space-filler, which invites the reader alternately to dismiss it or to justify its inclusion beyond the quantitative demands. *Niebla* will become the pure and polished—the quintessential—*nivola,* but the roughness and disarray of the earlier work conform to the professed randomness of the subgenre. As in the case of Don Fermín, the "theoreti-

---

querer no ser, de la *noluntad*" (*Tres novelas* 50). Morón Arroyo clarifies in a note: "La *noluntad* es deseo de no querer, de aniquilarse. No lleva al suicidio, porque con el suicidio se quita la posibilidad de seguir deseando el no ser" (50n6).

cal anarquist" of *Niebla*, Unamuno is reflexively viviparous as a writer, and he likely succeeds in leaving the reader at loose ends and in a contemplative mood. Galdós and other novelists of realism share much of themselves through their narrators, but the story is never about the author. Within his own story line, Unamuno follows the double plot of *Don Quijote*, by tracing simultaneously the sad life and death of Apolodoro Carrascal and the making of the story. The parallel structure allows Unamuno to fashion a new type of novel and to merge theory with praxis. The Cervantine precedent is fully compatible with his obsession with doubling and, one might add, his obsession with keeping himself and his art in the center. Unamuno seizes upon Cervantes's preoccupation with the means and mechanics of representation in his own narrative methodology. *Don Quijote* registers a shift in form as it inscribes the conflict of Catholicism against Protestantism and other foes, including the new science. *Amor y pedagogía* also pairs metafiction with the encroachment of new sciences—here, social sciences—on an established order. *Don Quijote* places madness and insight side by side, accompanied by references to the writing process. *Amor y pedagogía* adheres to a similar program, alternately embracing and shunning realism, but always with its focus on a reality that is as multidimensional as the text.

In "*Amor y pedagogía* como poética unamuniana de la modernidad," Mercedes Tasende contends that Unamuno is reevaluating the role of the consumer of literature in the process of reading and writing, "como un ente activo en el acto de comunicación y en la actualización del texto," in a reciprocal process—or "mutuo monodiálogo"—in which "[e]l autor escribe para un lector imaginado por él, y a su vez, el lector lee la obra como producto de una entidad llamada autor" (79). Caught between competing strains of modernism, Unamuno, "who was horrified by the term, appears as one of the most typically modernist spirits in the Hispanic world," according to Matei Calinescu in *Faces of Modernity* (75).[26]

---

[26] Manuel Durán places the narratives of members of the Generation of '98 within European experiments in modernism. He states, "En efecto, el gran tema de Unamuno es la realidad íntima—por 'concepto' entiende Unamuno a veces una visión íntima, inminente, que se proyecta desde el interior hacia fuera y, al proyectarse, modifica o aniquila la realidad circundante pero una realidad íntima 'químicamente pura', condensada alrededor de un problema central, único. Idea y emoción quedan fundidas—y así opera la intimidad de un ser vivo—pero se

The fact that modernism as a category is full of contradictions, real and apparent, may be the sign of a fit with Unamuno. Citing Georg Lukács, Astradur Eysteinsson, in *The Concept of Modernism*, argues that "by showing the individual as being 'thrown into existence,' modernism basically negates outward reality, and equates man's inwardness with an abstract subjectivity" (26). As a consequence, modernist aesthetics covers two terrains: "On the one hand,… by directing its attention so predominantly toward individual or subjective experience, [modernism] elevates the ego in proportion to a diminishing awareness of objective or coherent outside reality…. On the other hand, modernism is often held to draw its legitimacy primarily from writing based on highly antisubjectivist or impersonal poetics" (Eysteinsson 27). When one looks at the headings of Eysteinsson's chapter on "The Making of Modernist Paradigms" — which include "Complementing History," "Aesthetics of Subversion," "Crisis of the Subject," "Modernism and Its Discontents," and "Discontent as Negation" — these subdivisions would seem to apply to Unamuno's protocols, precisely because they play to his dialectical order, or disorder.

In an examination of subjectivity and textuality in *Amor y pedagogía*, including prologues, epilogues, and an esoteric treatise, Marilyn D. Rugg believes that "[i]n addition to this erosion through excess of traditional narrative structure, there lies an implicit disdain for the literature that has so strong an impact on Apolodoro's life; the disparity between literature and life as Apolodoro experiences them underscores the inherent falseness and artificiality of the texts he reads" (355). For Rugg, Unamuno is not necessarily searching for a "truer" representation of reality but, instead, his narratives — his *nivolas* — radically question "that reality and… the possibility of conveying that reality through fiction" (355). Rugg compares Apolodoro's "longing to step outside of himself and observe himself as an Other, thereby guaranteeing his selfhood," to Unamuno's critique of his work in the prologue, in which he turns "an 'objective' and disapproving eye on himself," thus simultaneously affirming "his individuated being and… inserting an authorial self into the text" (356). This is the beginning of the narrative. At the end, and framing the doubling, is what Rugg characterizes as the "contested authorship of the

---

trata de una sola idea, una sola emoción, lo cual permite, claro está, condiciones ideales de experimentación 'in vitro'" (23).

'Apuntes para un tratado de cocotología'" (360). Not only is Unamuno the self-serving writer and polemicist, but he is the champion of the *pueblo* and its *intrahistoria*. He shares the center of his narratives and of plays such as *El otro*, which are ultimately about him and about something else. He discovers, in the complex structure of *Don Quijote*, Cervantes's ability to fuse proximity, or empathy, and distance. In *Amor y pedagogía*, Unamuno operates on an extravagantly intellectual plane, and he brings his trials as a writer and public figure into the text, yet he also would seem to demand that the reader respect Apolodoro Carrascal and other characters as one would respect, and feel for, fellow or sister human beings. Subjectivity and various forms of mediation, together with randomness and chaos, frequently studied or calculated, contribute to the modernist paradigm, but it is what T. S. Eliot designates as "the individual talent" (in "Tradition and the Individual Talent") that distinguishes one writer from another, especially in the case of an iconoclast such as Unamuno. The same can be said of literary creations.

Relying on Lukács's model, Lucente notes that "characters are free to represent both the concrete moment within the fictional world and the broader historical concerns of the ongoing struggles that define their class, thereby mediating the rival claims of the particular and the universal" (13). He signals Lukác's emphasis on "the inherent temporality of narrative, in combination with the infinite play between character and narrator consciousness," which allows the realist text to develop and critique "its own ideological underpinnings in one multilayered operation" (Lucente 13). In *Don Quijote*, Cervantes, whether wittingly or intuitively, blends exposition and criticism, and he offsets his own centrality with narrative substitutes. In Part 1 and especially in Part 2, he disturbs the centrality of his protagonist in similar fashion, by offering a show of competition that relates as much, or more, to reading as to chivalry. The prologue to *Amor y pedagogía* joins a break from nineteenth-century realism with a critique of the author himself. It is not merely the form of the novel, nor its inscription of ideology, but the issue of history that Unamuno undertakes to modify. History becomes the history of ideas, or ideas in time, and Unamuno alternately embraces and revises the past as he confronts, cautiously but with undeniable zeal, the promise of the present and future. He is often caught between faith and love for his country, which direct him toward powerful precedents, and the achievements of the present, which force him to reflect, respond, and initiate dialogue. His creative spirit and the productive negativism that marks his writing, as well as his public persona, find a superb outlet in the angst-laden *Amor y pedagogía*. The "concrete moment" here is a moment in intellectual history. Unamuno the writer can face the anxiety of influence while understanding the existentialist struggle of the protagonist, and he can duplicate and reduplicate the conflict between established systems of thought and rapidly changing socio-cultural, economic, scientific, and, of course, poetic, conventions. He is very much of this world, yet is always mindful of eternity.

Surveying the phenomenon of modernism, Michael Levenson asserts that "the aim could never be simply to set the imagination free; it was rather first of all to challenge an unfreedom, the oppressions of journalism, of genteel audiences, of timid readers, and political and religious orthodoxies. So much of the story that [those who would be deemed modernists] told themselves was a tale of tyranny and resistance" (2). Levenson cites among general preoccupations "the recurrent act of fragmenting unities…, the use of mythic paradigms, the refusal of norms of beauty, [and] the willingness to make radical linguistic experimentation" (3). Turbulence in the streets and on the field of battle is matched by turbulence in texts, and, according to Michael Bell, "well before the turn of the century science itself was losing some of its epistemological self-evidence and privileged status" (11). Bell also notes a central paradox of modernism: acknowledgment that "the most sophisticated achievement of the present is a return to, or new appreciation of, the archaic" (20), together with a revamping, and problematizing, of mythologies. It is as if Cervantes produced his art with a sense of modernism, and as if Unamuno were obeying the rules of an earlier age as he helped to inspire and to make a new one. The quest for immortality, itself a variation on numerous Cervantine or quixotic themes, dominates *Amor y pedagogía*, which incorporates science and technology into its ideological base. Holding onto a past—comprised of a conflictive history and an idealized intrahistory—Unamuno inserts himself into contemporary philosophical, scientific, and literary debates. His dissatisfaction with narrative realism becomes motive and motif, a new form for new content.

In an essay on the modernist novel, David Trotter states, "Whatever is described in the most innovative fiction of the period is described in relation to, and only in relation to, a perceiving mind. [Henry] James's later novels—*The Wings of the Dove* (1902), *The Ambassadors* (1903), *The*

Golden Bowl (1904)—create centers of consciousness through which the apprehension of events is filtered" (71). *Amor y pedagogía*, published during the same period, explores the minds of its characters and its author. The incipient *nivola* gives Unamuno the chance to hone his skills as a writer, thinker, and performance artist. His special contribution to modernism may be a revision of the deep structure of narrative, to set forth a competition between author, narrator, and character. Within the randomness—hardly random, in the final analysis—of the storytelling process, Unamuno devises ways to bring depth and abstraction to the narrative structure, while placing himself in the center as professional writer, public figure, philosopher, arbiter of scientific discoveries, and purveyor of language. One can almost imagine Don Miguel admonishing those who would apply principles of Freudian psychoanalysis to literary characters, advising them to seek the subconscious of the author in the text. As he bares Apolodoro's soul, and Don Avito's, Unamuno is baring his own. In his hands, metafiction acquires a determinedly profound contour without relinquishing playfulness or a dialectical treatment of mimesis. Unamuno's eclecticism serves his art, by accentuating the key function of linguistic invention in contexts that align his creative writing to broader issues and to his thought patterns in general. Pedro Calderón de la Barca, for example, could take a theological matter, or debate, and transform it into a work of dramatic intensity and rhetorical beauty. Cervantes could transform a satirical send-up of chivalry into a narrative whose intricacies engage readers four hundred years after its publication. Unamuno takes advantage of these and other models to reconstruct the novel at the beginning of the twentieth century, when the notion of the modern was being examined and modified. *Amor y pedagogía* marks a new page in his trajectory and in that of modernism.

The fascinating elaboration of the viviparous novel may leave the reader with what may be termed, rather unpoetically, an oxymoronic aftertaste.[27] Its lauded spontaneity comes after a period of gestation, of

---

[27] Paul Olson and Thomas Mermall have emphasized the figure of chiasmus in the thought and writing of Unamuno. See Olson, "Sobre las estructuras" and *The Great Chiasmus* esp. 1-11, and Mermall, "Chiasmus." Olson notes, "The contemplative, synoptic vision of the creative imagination permits the simultaneous presence in poetic space of all things desired by the visionary, even if conjoined in oxymoron, paradox, and chiasmus" (*The Great Chiasmus* 9).

mental reflection. It is, then, both spontaneous and thought-out, and the development of the narrative deviates from the norm because certain elements that formerly had made their way into the text through an evolving process become, in a manner, predetermined. In a passage that reflects the mode and myth of Unamunian creation, Manuel Durán comments, "Sabido es hasta qué punto Unamuno desprecia la novela realista. El mundo exterior es, hasta cierto punto, una impostura; hay que 'creer para crear'. Unamuno empieza por creer en la mayor parte de sus personajes[y] procede luego a crearlos" (23). The narrative innovations are mediated by literary theory and practice, philosophy, science, and gamesmanship. Unamuno gives new meaning to the idea of deliberation. The phrase "a lo que salga" does not refer to unpremeditated, impulsive behavior but to its opposite, where contemplation precedes writing to the fullest degree. Unamuno places cogitation (and, as a corollary, one would suppose, memory) as the most important item in the writer's repository. Throughout *Amor y pedagogía*, he focuses on reception by asking the reader to note, understand, and accept his methodology, but his promotion, which includes self-promotion, always crosses the line into irony. Unamuno is writing with a sense of difference, but he brings poetic license into philosophy, just as he brings philosophy into fiction. The narrative text becomes a bouncing-off place in which the author can multitask: he can ruminate about the challenges that face him, he can appeal to the public, and he can test a style and an ideology.

Unamuno's outline for the *nivola*, and more specifically the structure of *Amor y pedagogía*, derives from a reaction against realism and naturalism. His response to earlier narrative forms takes him in the direction of a loosely-defined modernism. An air of free-spiritedness, fragmentation, and resourceful disorder pervades the text, which admits large doses of tragedy, ingenuity, and metafiction. The Unamunian persona—or, more accurately, personae—must be credited, above all else, as the symbolic and subjective writer, as the inventor of anguished souls (and exploiter of his own), and as a narrator and deep thinker who obviously has a way with words. Love and pedagogy, independently and interdependently, give focus to the narrative, which could be categorized as a satirical tragedy or tragic satire.[28] In chapter 13 of *Niebla*, after

---

[28] Víctor Goti notes in the prologue to *Niebla*, "Don Miguel tiene la

Eugenia Domingo del Arco has chastised him for having paid off her creditors, as if he were trying to buy her affection, Augusto Pérez wanders aimlessly for a while and then enters a church, where he spots Don Avito Carrascal. Don Avito says that, following the suicide of his son, he has concluded that "no hay pedagogía que valga" and that he has taken refuge in "ese hogar de todas las ilusiones y todos los desengaños" (*Niebla* 173). When Augusto asks if he is a believer, Don Avito responds, "No sé si creo o no creo; sé que rezo.... Y ahora pienso que a la humanidad maldita falta que le hacen los genios" (*Niebla* 174). He mentions that he has joined his wife in the shared grief and that, never having known his mother, he has gained a mother figure. He also advises Augusto to pursue the woman who loves him, rather than the woman whom he loves, for it is easier for a person to learn to love than to convince another to love. Love outlasts pedagogy, but that lesson here is imparted in a spiritual setting, which eerily recasts hope, alternately, as hopelessness or as the last ray of hope. In the text of *Amor y pedagogía* and beyond, Unamuno reads the story (and life) as uncontrollably sad, but not without its moments of comic relief, in which discourse—a festive discourse, one might submit—becomes a formidable rival.

Point of view is a crucial factor in the development of the novel, and within the developing novel, and it is, one could contend, Unamuno's specialty, understood as something that he executes well and something that he executes in a unique way. He decides to make the prologue mainly about himself, through a deferral that resembles the first *Quijote* prologue. He stamps " Unamuno" onto the subconscious of the reader and tells the tale of Don Avito Carrascal and Apolodoro in a distinctly Unamunian style. The story of the misguided father and the ill-fated son is narrated with an excitement about ideas and about life not only as theater but as science, as laboratory. Unamuno is bound to theology and to classical philosophy, but he is energized by science and always ready for conflict and debate, and there is a Hegelian rhythm to *Amor y pedagogía*. A glory of *Don Quijote* is the process through which Cervantes

---

preocupación del bufo trágico, y me ha dicho más de una vez que no quisiera morirse sin haber escrito una bufonada trágica o una tragedia bufa, pero no en que lo bufo o grotesco y lo trágico estén mezclados o yuxtapuestos, sino fundidos y confundidos en uno" (101).

makes himself—as creator and as an artist seeking recognition—the ironic center of the text. Unamuno emulates Cervantes, but he ignores the subtle grace of his predecessor, preferring instead to underscore his centrality. His love of ideas crosses with his love of words, of arranging words, of flaunting words and bewildering with words. He rewrites the novel and redefines tragicomedy as he demonstrates that language itself can be uplifting, that it can grant a paradoxical consolation to life's woes. For Unamuno, language is friend and foe of feeling. Discourse is a force to be reckoned with, and he is its enforcer.

The minutiae of daily existence subsist, for Unamuno, alongside the larger, more profound issues that preoccupy us and that get lost among quotidian "realities." Narrrative realism and naturalism capture the details and, with them, the thematic landscape. Unamuno builds narratives such as *Amor y pedagogía* around ideas, and for the details he substitutes more ideas and a self-consciously rhetorical foundation. His characters are his thoughts, and vice versa, and therefore his ideology and his doubts take center stage. That he is an artistic philosopher or a philosophical artist—and a scientific philosopher or a philosophical scientist—would seem to be the ultimate oxymoron, but that is not the case. Unamuno breaks the mold, "naturalizes" antitheses, and, as he says, fuses and confuses contradictory elements into one. He may be part of a community of modernists, but his conventional course of action is to work alone, or to work with a supporting cast that consists of shadows or duplications of himself. His revision of the novel projects not only an anti-model but an inimitable model. Almost a century before it becomes fashionable to do so, Unamuno suggests that fictional discourse is one discourse among many. He accomplishes this goal without sacrificing the joy of art and without relinquishing the literariness that permits poetry to stand apart from history, or that encases history in poetry. To call *Amor y pedagogía* a trendsetting narrative is perhaps to overstate its impact, because *Niebla* covers similar ground in glossier packaging, and with brilliant links to *Don Quijote*. Still, the earlier work is *nada menos que toda una nivola* and arguably the more acute deviation from the realist intertext. Off-putting and heart-rending, *Amor y pedagogía* elevates ironic distance to an art form. Its pedagogy is strange but loving. Like Cervantes and Velázquez, Unamuno exalts the artist and the consumer of art, armed as he is with the freshness and the challenges that the new century provides him. He is over-confident and perplexed, driven to articulate his sentiments and driven by uncertainty. His "historical moment" is abstract, but no less precise or perceptive than that of the realists.

Paralleling Cervantes, Unamuno approaches realism indirectly. Paralleling Spanish naturalism, Unamuno's modernism is inflected by theology, in addition to his *vital* doubts. That he found a soul mate in the tormented Kierkegaard—John Updike refers to "the great Dane's short and not entirely unhappy life" (71)—is not surprising. *Amor y pedagogía* is an updating of the reason-faith dichotomy and a scientific rewriting of the concept of nurturing. The failure of Don Avito Carrascal's project is symbolic, but not transparent. Don Avito becomes closer to his wife and makes her into a mother figure (as did Unamuno following the death of a son),[29] and he shows up in church in *Niebla*. Unamuno seems to be demonstrating that science cannot function in isolation. One has to learn to draw on science in viable ways. The old systems are not enough, but new practice has to insert itself into established, albeit changing, orders. The same is true of the author's task, and here this relates most obviously to the norms of narrative. The individual writer cannot break away from

---

[29] Unamuno married Concepción Lizárraga in 1891. Martin Nozick observes, "Contrary to a Kierkegaard or a Kafka who felt that marriage meant defection from a higher way of life, Unamuno looked upon his Concha as a serene, healthy, warm spirit in a world of stupidity, selfishness, and routine, a mate who would exercise a civilizing influence on his unsociability and would provide a refuge from the nonsense all around him and refreshment from the arduous tasks that lay ahead. Although his wife remained always in the background, Unamuno's references to her provide ample testimony of her indispensable role in his life. Indeed, his greatest homage was to call her 'Concha, my habit'" (23). José Rubia Barcia points out that in January of 1896 Unamuno's "son Raimundo Jenaro was born and a short time later an attack of what was probably meningitis left the child permanently afflicted with hydrocephaly, from which he died in 1902 after a prolonged agony. About the time when Unamuno found out how bad his son's condition was, his second important spiritual crisis took place. He broke down one night, and the following day left his home and went to spend a few days in a Dominican convent to try to recover his childhood faith and pray to God for help in his sorrow. He even went to see a priest friend of his, looking for religious consolation and advice in the faraway town of Alcalá de Henares" (8). He also notes, "The depth and spontaneity of his sorrow cannot be denied, but the duration and permanent consequences of the crisis were quite another matter. How can one explain the fact that Unamuno was able to keep a diary of all his emotions and thoughts during those nightmarish days?" (8-9).

the past, nor dismiss the intertext, whether emulating or reacting against it. Unamuno the scholar, philosopher, and essayist finds a special outlet in fiction. Poetic license gives him the opportunity to combine ideology and aesthetics. He explores the issues that inform his other writings and personalizes his crises and agonies, through his characters and through his own appearances in the texts. He is a gifted poet, but it is his prose—powerful, learned, ironic, and with a distinctive brand of humor—that perhaps best defines him as a novelist, as a *nivolista*. *Amor y pedagogía*, his first attempt at sustained metafiction, references a rich literary past while marking, and opening, a significant space at a crucial time for the interplay of life and art. Love and pedagogy are misfocused, and the narrative, in turn, operates on a principle of indirection. Apolodoro's life and death resemble Don Quijote's as the base of the linear argument, shadowed—arguably overshadowed—by a self-consciousness that begs the question of stability. Unamuno may have been thinking of Velázquez as well as Cervantes, as he stands behind, and in, his metafiction.

Quixotic Inscription:
Niebla and the Theory of the Novel

Lo vivo es lo que yo allí descubro, pusiéralo o no Cervantes,
lo que yo allí pongo y sobrepongo y sotopongo, y lo que
ponemos allí todos. Quise allí rastrear nuestra filosofía.
Del sentimiento trágico de la vida

ONE OF THE MAJOR achievements—among many, of course—of *Don
Quijote* is Cervantes's ability to write a narrative that both endorses and
eschews realism. Like its picaresque predecessors, including *Lazarillo de
Tormes* and *Guzmán de Alfarache, Don Quijote* offers an antidote to the lofty
idealism of sentimental, pastoral, and chivalric romance. While presenting
the underside of society and the darker side of humanity, the anonymous
author of *Lazarillo* and Mateo Alemán create distinctive voices and
distinctive psyches for their narrator/protagonists. In the self-consciousness and self-fashioning of the eponymous characters, they anticipate
Cervantes's achievement in the realm of metafiction. At the satirical end
of *Don Quijote*, the reader seems to be invited to laugh at the anachronistic
knight errant and at his literature-induced madness, which leads to
ludicrous situations and battles of the will. The knight is paired with an
illiterate and incongruous squire, whose idiolect, native wisdom, and
reluctance to enter the fray amuse and entertain. At the other extreme lies
the empathy factor, a breach of the ironic distance between Don Quijote
and the reader. Miguel de Unamuno, obsessed with Cervantes and *Don
Quijote*, also attempts to break away from the narrative mold, in this case,
and ironically, from realism and naturalism. The structure of *Niebla* can
be seen as a type of *ars poetica*—Unamuno's theory of the novel—and as
an homage to, and an updating of, *Don Quijote*. Both Cervantes and

Unamuno underscore approaches to reality, and both distance themselves from purely mimetic goals in order to accentuate the role and the operating principles of literature. I do not believe that *Niebla* is primarily a philosophical novel, and it is certainly not an anti-novel, but rather—emulating its predecessor—an example of theory in praxis, a commentary on the art of making art and, not coincidentally, a commentary on life.

The prologue to Part 1 of *Don Quijote* teases and illuminates the reader, who will hardly be idle. Cervantes fictionalizes himself and supplies an alter ego in the form of the friend, whose exposition and advice stand twice-removed from the historical author. The friend speaks of the author's crusade against the romances of chivalry, and he addresses the writing of the prologue, which introduces questions of precedents, authority, and literary protocol. He deals with the nearly complete manuscript and with books in general. While Don Quijote's enterprise will point backward, Cervantes's will point forward, to a world impacted by the printing press, the New World, the new science, and challenges on the theological front. Stated succinctly, the friend admonishes the author to replace the paradigms of the past and to work confidently within his own parameters. Taking to heart the Horatian dictum of blending entertainment with instruction, Cervantes manages to be serious and playful at the same time. He is breaking away from something more than the books of chivalry. He is advocating fresh ways of perceiving the written word and the world, and in a humorous manner he is advocating multiperspectivism and depth of thinking. Literature can be a tool, a buffer, and a microcosm (or, in the hands of Cervantes and Unamuno, a macrocosm). Cervantes intuits that verisimilitude is not synonymous with objectivity and that the interpretation of reality is dependent on the mediating force of the writer and on the response of the individual reader. *Don Quijote* demystifies, to a large degree, the separability of history and poetry. It stresses what could be termed the worldliness of literature, as well as the act of producing a text. It thus implies that every writing and reading instance is a redefinition of sorts, a figurative treatise on the mutability of reality.

Víctor Goti, character and prologuist of *Niebla*, alludes to Hamlet, who famously contemplates suicide, as does Unamuno's protagonist Augusto Pérez. Both figures are consumed by divagations, and both dramatize abstract thinking. But it is not Hamlet nor his Iberian counterpart Segismundo of Calderón's *La vida es sueño* but Don Quijote who most attracts Unamuno. Don Quijote is an *ente de ficción* driven by books and by the fantasies that they inspire. His contact with the so-called real world comes, then, with a layering of fiction, and Cervantes devises a fascinating dialectics of the observable and the imaginary. *Don Quijote* becomes an allegory of the intersection of fiction and nonfiction, played as a series of shifts. Books enter the *hidalgo's* reality and transform him into a knight errant, an anachronism that sallies forth into his contemporary society, and books are an ever-increasing presence in that society. In Part 2 of *Don Quijote,* Part 1 and the Avellaneda sequel simultaneously represent the internal accumulation of literary allusions—a high point of self-consciousness and self-referentiality—and a recognition of the significance of the book, not only in general but in the specific cases of Cide Hamete Benengeli's chronicle, Cervantes's narrative, and the spurious continuation. Books appear at inns, in printing establishments, and in dreams; they show up on the road in unnamed places and also in the grand city of Barcelona. Don Quijote is pushed aside as his narrative incarnation—a specter of a specter—becomes a center of attention and a guide for readers such as Sansón Carrasco and the duke and duchess, who engage in their own metafictions. The book is on the outside, subsequently returns to the inside, and moves outward again. The pseudonymous Avellaneda wages war on Cervantes, and his invasion helps to sustain the disappearing borders between the literary domain and historical reality and between Miguel de Cervantes and his fictionalized other.

Building on the self-fashioning of the picaresque, Cervantes in *Don Quijote* takes the extraordinary step of recording the adventures of an out-of-date knight errant along with the details of the composition proper. The construction of the text mirrors our contemplation of the world, our configuration of reality. Correspondingly, Cervantes glorifies the writer and acknowledges the crucial role of the reader, as Velázquez was to do some thirty years later with the painter and the observer in *Las meninas.* What is key in this process, I would submit, is that Cervantes is able to have it both ways. *Don Quijote* is profoundly about art and life, and it is humorous, satirical, and bewildering. It gives us process and product, cause and effect, floating signifiers, and abundant surprises. Within the narrative continuum, Don Quijote practices chivalry, and his encounters on the road make the reader more aware of literature and its conventions and of the relativity of reality and truth. By combining fiction and metafiction, Cervantes links creation with self-reflection, and theory with praxis. He involves the reader on multiple, and seemingly contradictory, levels. He bears Aristotle in mind and foreshadows Brecht by detaching readers from the narrative circumstances *and* drawing them into the emotional ups and downs of the protagonists. Don Quijote would appear to be the epitome of the overtly literary character, a shadow figure with negligible ties to reality and lacking a psyche. If anything, he seems to retrogress from the real as he immerses himself in fictions within fictions. But very early on, we start to care about him, as if he were a person, as if we suspended disbelief. The sensation is much the same as that of the picaresque reader, who, despite an authorial emphasis on distancing techniques, may feel sympathy for Lazarillo, Guzmán, Pablos, Justina, and their brothers and sisters in delinquency. Even the elitist and staunchly hierarchical Francisco de Quevedo, whose *pícaro* is a verifiable criminal, grants Pablos a soul. Whether advertently or inadvertently, and through a type of double determinism (social protocol and authorial intervention), Quevedo shows the suffering and humiliation that contribute to Pablos's character formation and aid in explaining his decisions. We see that Pablos is scarcely in control of his fate, although the text may seem to suggest otherwise, and that may strike a chord of compassion or understanding.

Don Quijote satirizes the romances of chivalry and comments on a wide variety of literary forms and models. It delves into such topics as historiography, truth, madness, point of view, and the literary canon. Its guiding trope is, without a doubt, irony, but irony with a rationale, with a philosophical thrust. P. E. Russell has argued that Cervantes takes comedy quite seriously, and that it is a fundamental aspect of *Don Quijote*. The paragons of the baroque, among them Góngora, Quevedo, and Gracián, endeavor to embellish and complicate their works in order to test and overwhelm the reading public and to reserve accessibility to the chosen few. The complexity of *Don Quijote* resides not in rejecting readers but in catering to a range of expectations and intellectual capacities. In a strategy that has ties with Lope de Vega's formula for the Comedia in the *Arte nuevo*, retouched with baroque flourishes by Calderón, Cervantes mixes popular culture with high culture. *Don Quijote* can please the general public and the most discriminating reader because it caters to a broad array of literary appetites. It treats the big issues subtly and not so subtly, using reading and writing as frames. If one thinks of the metaphorical structure—the metaphors within metaphors and the dynamics of the transitory and the eternal—of Calderón's *La vida es sueño*, it may be possible to discern a similar design in *Don Quijote*. Focusing on earthly perception, Cervantes provides variations on the theme of making history (the all-purpose Spanish *historia*), from Don Quijote to Cide Hamete Benengeli to the countless narrators, storytellers, and metadramatists in the text. As Sansón Carrasco notes in Part 2, chapter 3, readers have diverse responses to the narrative. As with *Guzmán de Alfarache, Don Quijote* perhaps could be classified as a miscellany, but its organization of events—its *dispositio*—does not have the random or meandering feel of Alemán's work. Don Quijote's chivalric enterprise and Guzmán's professed conversion are thematic centers, but the execution is more dissimilar than similar.

The narrative flow of *Don Quijote* can be captured in the dual linear progression and in the image of strata or concentric circles. The experience of the adventures is an analogue of the construction of the text (Cide Hamete's chronicle, Cervantes's books, the interpolated tales, and so forth). The narratives are embedded in a vehicle propelled by Cervantes the writer and Alonso Quijano the reader. Cervantes ingeniously seems to relinquish control to a corps of narrators, but he maintains authority by flaunting the literary armature, by extending the action to the wings, by revealing the props and the secrets of his craft. The friend who communicates with the writer in the 1605 prologue is the first of many authorial alter egos, and the historical Cervantes slips into the scrutiny of the library (1,6), the introduction to the reading of *El curioso impertinente* (1,32), the captive's tale (1,40), and the battle against Avellaneda in Part 2. Guzmán de Alfarache is a brilliant creation, as richly textured a character as one is likely to find before the beginning of the seventeenth century. This is due, to an extent, to his unchecked loquaciousness. His tribulations impel him to talk, to opine, to editorialize. He is angry and resentful, and he wants to justify his newly acquired faith, but certainly not in isolation. Alemán's plan seems to be to unify the narrative through the interplay of transgression and repentance, which some (myself included) see as supremely ironic. The conversion can and has been deconstructed. The problem is not the tension between wrongdoing and righteousness but the confusion between Guzmán and Alemán. The decision to identify and berate the author of the false sequel to the *Guzmán* and to demonstrate the superiority of the legitimate protagonist causes Alemán to go off track, to cede control of the plot and of point of view in an effort to prepare a counterattack. Although indignant at the literary theft, Cervantes puts Avellaneda in his place without disrupting the narrative order, or, it could be said, by disrupting it to his benefit.

Don Quijote and Sancho Panza initially are one-dimensional characters, but they develop during the course of the narrative. Despite his reduced mental capacity, Don Quijote learns from the tests that he faces. While the publication of the chronicle energizes others, he seems passive until the Avellaneda tome gives him a new direction, a revived combative spirit. Sancho is untested and a bit green when he sets out as squire, but he becomes accustomed to the habits of his master and to the tricks of the trade, as it were. In Part 2, he "enchants" Dulcinea and orients Don Quijote—and the plot line—toward the disenchantment motif that occupies much of the text. Having observed the knight and those with whom he has come into contact, Sancho manages to maintain a balance between chivalric illusion and social norm. Blessed with common sense, he sharpens his practical skills as he witnesses and often participates in the trials of the knight errant. Don Quijote and Sancho Panza may not share the emotional intensity of the *pícaros*, but they are evolving characters, consistent in their inconsistency, which seems entirely appropriate for this particular narrative. They inhabit a text dictated by mutability, and although they are different from us, they affect us intellectually and emotionally. Cervantes does not lose his concentration, but instead takes advantage of the Avellaneda intrusion to animate and laud his protagonist and, alas, to kill him off, somewhat ambiguously, in order to portray a moment of dis-illusionment (*desengaño*) or to ward off further continuations. We may have the impression that it is Alonso Quijano who dies and Don Quijote who enters immortality.

Cervantes's break from idealism in *Don Quijote* places the narrative, along with the Italian *novella*, *Celestina*, and the picaresque into the category of an emerging realism, but it is a brand of realism that needs to be qualified. In each of the parallel plot strands—the exploits of the knight errant and the recording of those exploits—literature impinges on a reality already marked by flights of fantasy. *Don Quijote* illustrates daily existence in specified and unspecified locales in Spain, yet the sites form the backdrop to the geography of chivalric romance, to words on the pages of books and to imprints on the mind. Cervantes seems to comprehend and to incorporate what would come to be known as narrative realism into the text, while prioritizing the process of textual production. Metafiction is conspicuously self-centered, but it is far more than "laying bare the devices" —as Russian Formalism would call it—for its own sake (see, e.g., Shklovsky). Cervantes associates textuality—book-making—with notions of perception and with the arrangement of thoughts in written documents. He opens with a manuscript in need of a prologue and with a dialogue on nothing less than the nature and laws of literature, and literature positioned against philosophy, theology, science, and politics, at that. Comedy in *Don Quijote* keeps subversion in check, as it does more obviously in the daring indictment of blood purity in the dramatic interlude "El retablo de las maravillas." The prologue to Part 1 announces its uniqueness and its deviation from current literary practice. It articulates a satirical intention, but goes well beyond satire to probe the status of the author and the bases of authority at a decisive juncture in history. Cervantes brings epistemology into the artistic sphere, and *Don Quijote*, indirectly and paradoxically, is able to summon reality and its aesthetic antithesis precisely by seeking alternatives to mimesis.

One could defend the thesis that Cervantes maps a design for Part 1 of *Don Quijote* in the prologue and the first chapter, for they contain his (mediated, or deferred) thoughts on changes in the status quo—changes that shape the narrative formally and conceptually—and his introduction of the principal allegories that occupy the text. Don Quijote's preparation for the first sally and his envisioning of a chronicle that will celebrate his victories, like the unfinished manuscript of the prologue, convey the flavor of a work in progress. From the outset, the knight must contend with the gap between his grasp of the world around him and that of those less chivalrically inclined and, *con perdón*, less mad. Cervantes puts an ironic cast on the incongruity by having characters, from the innkeeper and the demi-maidens of chapter 3 onward, partake of Don Quijote's illusions. Alonso Quijano reinvents himself, but he needs the complicity of his fellow (and sister) citizens, much as Cervantes the author needs a readership, a public disposed to enter his private territory and to acknowledge his mindset. Don Quijote's encounters on the road force him to repeat the explanation of his mission and to verbalize his visions. Through the narrators, Cervantes matches this with a report on the fact-gathering for the chronicle, which culminates in the serendipitous discovery of Cide Hamete Benengeli's manuscript in chapter 9 and the opening of many intriguing cans of worms in the areas of story and discourse. The manifestations of Don Quijote's madness permit the reader to reflect on departures from the accepted standards and to judge society from the margins. This may be a legacy of the picaresque, and it is also where Cervantes situates himself as a social and literary critic. Don Quijote is a fiction within a fiction. So is Cide Hamete's "true history," and so are the intercalated narratives. Nonetheless, fictions only come into their own when bracketed by a facet of reality. The psychological and the physical are interdependent, and Cervantes takes pains to inscribe the ongoing conflicts and mergers between the two as a constant in the text.

Cervantes seems to borrow from *Guzmán de Alfarache*—or to arrive at on his own—the motif of the "atalaya de la vida humana" as monitored from the vantage point of the outsider. Alemán's work possesses a kind of (pseudo)autobiographical unity in the narrative and commentary of Guzmán, which results in something on the order of an early modern stream of consciousness. Neither this bond nor the conversion pretext is fully convincing, because Alemán jeopardizes the constancy and the continuity by failing to differentiate his motives from the *pícaro*'s. He cannot separate the implied author from the man who wishes to air his personal grievances and to protect his authorial rights. Alemán recreates the theft through a robbery in the narrative, and that is superb, but he does not sustain the focus. He is obsessed with the affront and, ultimately, becomes distracted. Beyond the prologue to Part 2 of *Don Quijote*, Cervantes keeps his emotions in check, and even in the prologue he goes to his comic and rhetorical arsenal to defend himself against Avellaneda. Wronged, irate, and offended as he will have been when the false sequel is published, he adjusts the narrative as a writer, by undermining his adversary within the context of the plot. Opportunely, the spurious continuation spurs Cervantes and Don Quijote to action. The former must rethink the trip to Zaragoza and conceive an alternate plan. The latter must leave aside the specter of his bookish other—Cide Hamete's creation—to fight a new and more dangerous rival. Cervantes makes his argument, but at Don Quijote's expense, given that he condemns the knight to be dead and buried when the text reaches closure. He surveys the environment, literary and otherwise, from a distance that Alemán only partially attains. Each contest is intriguing, but one is more respectful of the fictional agenda. Both writers are victims of sequels, which induce them to revise their respective dénouements, and which induce them and their protagonists to safeguard their reputations.

Following the lead of *Lazarillo de Tormes,* Alemán and Cervantes make visible their authorial strings. The picaresque relies on a ventriloquism effect, whereas *Don Quijote* makes a sport of what Michel Foucault centuries later would denominate the *author function* by doubling and redoubling the narratological entities ("What Is an Author?"). Cervantes activates the tasks of reading and writing, and makes the reader and the writer, in various guises, co-protagonists. Echoing a title of E. C. Riley, Cervantes's theory of the novel consists of a depiction and critique of society through periphrasis. The mediation is accomplished through literature or, more exactly, through literariness. Headed by chivalric romance, the genres and subgenres of the day fit comfortably into the narrative, as do the tales and interpolations, but it is the attention to the inner workings of the books that we are consuming—the translation of Cide Hamete's chronicle, Part 1, and Part 2—that is truly unique. Not only is there a dual plot based on knightly deeds and the composition of the book(s), but each of the components is informed by the causal, and reciprocal, relation of reading and writing. Don Quijote and Cide Hamete Benengeli initially may strike us as ludicrous, but satire quickly is subsumed by a comic vision of enormous intensity and breadth. Cervantes displays his mastery of the old and his commitment to the new through the art of contextualization, through an ability to glorify and to reorient *la razón de la sinrazón.* He polemicizes—and on occasion reifies—what we have termed the "big issues," as he evokes laughter and much more. He yields the word to significant others, but he never hides, or only pretends to hide. He is the chief narrative agent, if not as exuberant an interloper in his own works as Miguel de Unamuno.

To study the Cervantine intertext in Unamuno, one may point to the following milestones: the publication of *Amor y pedagogía* in 1902, of the *Vida de don Quijote y Sancho* in 1905 (the *Quijote* tercentenary), of *Niebla* in 1914, and of the prologue to the *Tres novelas ejemplares* in 1920. *Amor y pedagogía* signals a break from narrative realism, *La vida* is an exhaustive—and distinctly Unamunian—reading of the *Quijote,* and the prologue to the exemplary novellas is a justification of the move away from realism and naturalism. *Niebla* may be considered a synthesis of Unamuno's narrative practice, which also contains a theory of the *nivola,* the word that the writer, and linguist, coined to distinguish his form and objectives from those of the realists. It is possible to look at the structure of *Niebla* from several angles, including as a response to realism, that is, as a metafictional alternative to conventional realism. What stands out from the beginning is the role of the romances of chivalry with respect to *Don Quijote*, as contrasted with the role of *Don Quijote* with respect to *Niebla*, in essence, two extremes of the anxiety of influence (see Bloom): the parodic and the reverential. Unamuno, however, is no Pierre Menard. He idolizes and employs Cervantes, while forging his own literary inscription. He is cognizant, as is Borges's narrator, of the fact that—to use the words of the personified Comedia in Cervantes's *El rufián dichoso*—"Los tiempos mudan las cosas" (II, 1229; 178). *Niebla* becomes Unamuno's *Quijote* and, for all "practical" purposes, his theory of the novel.[1]

Don Quijote may be a truly funny book, but it is also a speculative narrative. Satire, intuition, and common sense have a place in the scheme of events, but Cervantes uses art—its creation, reception, and critique—as a means by which to ponder the act of representation in its most comprehensive scope. Readers, narrators, and critics abound, and the motif of getting the story right is a constant in the text. As in the *comedia nueva*, there is something for everyone in *Don Quijote*, and that includes a comic vision aimed at the intelligentsia, those privileged by rank and education, as well as at a popular audience. The theme of art as intimately related to life allows for humor and for an investigation of both the mechanics of artistic production and underlying meanings. Risibility hardly precludes depth. Cervantes amuses the reader as he extends the boundaries of fiction and aesthetics, and it must be recalled that his *historia* encompasses story and history, the imaginative and the real. His

---

[1] For studies of ties between Cervantes and Unamuno, see, among others, King, Baskekis (45-58), Galbis, Gunn, and Friedman ("Guerrillas"). Armando F. Zubizarreta takes the comparison beyond the realm of literature: "Unamuno se halla en la más auténtica tradición española de Cervantes, en la literatura cervantina, en cuanto ésta implica una vida que vivifica su arte. En este sentido, la vida concreta de Unamuno... es un quijotesco hacer salir de las casillas y, en suma, es una *imitatio* del Quijote, que quizá rebasa, en la práctica, al hombre Cervantes que no fuera comprometido y redimido plenamente por su arte" (288). Cesáreo Bandera has a chapter entitled "El quijotismo de Unamuno y la envidia de Caín" in *La humilde historia* (179-204).

route to reality is calculatedly off-putting, invasive as well as circumlocu-tory, because he seems to want reading to be an all-consuming, mind-altering process, one that promotes a consciousness of the material world and of the burdens and responsibilities of authorship. Readers share in the rewards of this effort, and also in the burden, extending from the written word to the world at large, seen as coming together and confusing. Cervantes creates a definite—paradoxically definitive and variable—place for the reader, in which comprehension involves looking inward and outward by turns. As author, he playfully and unsuccessfully (by intention) hides within the fiction without eliding his historical self. Like the Velázquez of *Las meninas,* he is, at once, symbolic and egre-giously, *en el buen sentido de la palabra,* self-centered, artist and social being. *Don Quijote* and *Niebla* are, for me, first and foremost intellectual novels.[2] They toy with readers while insisting that books stimulate thinking, and that ruminations on literature are virtually synonymous with the most incisive searches for answers to the mysteries of the life and the people around us.

The *Vida de don Quijote y Sancho* might be called an explication of Cervantes's novel, while *Niebla* might be an homage to *Don Quijote,* deferential and stridently derivative yet by no means a copy of the original. If Cervantes can be compared to Velázquez, Unamuno can be compared to Picasso, who does everything but paint his own face into his reworking of *Las meninas.* (That was left to the British artist Richard Hamilton, whose variation features Picasso behind the easel.) Without Velázquez, there would be no Picasso *meninas,* but the style, the personal energy, and the signature belong to the later artist, who collaborates with his precursor while staking his own claim. The association with Velázquez serves as tribute and stepping stone. Picasso locates himself alongside the master as he figuratively draws himself into the picture. His method relies, interestingly, on a dual form of abstraction. Picasso competes with classical representation, but he honors the self-referential-ity and the artistic integrity of Velázquez. Analogously, Unamuno competes with nineteenth-century realism as he foregrounds the metafictional aspects of Cervantes's novel. A forerunner of European

---

[2] Concerning *Niebla,* Geoffrey Ribbans remarks, "...creo que importa recalcar que es una obra intelectual, casi puramente intelectual" (*Niebla* 139).

realism, *Don Quijote* contains, defends, and counters verisimilitude. The move away from idealism takes several directions. Cervantes's heirs are Fielding and Defoe, but also Sterne. Unamuno is writing as realism reaches its culmination in naturalism, and he finds inspiration in the anti-mimetic and self-reflexive patterns of the *Quijote*. His characters, settings, and dialogue need the context of conventional realism—and readers accustomed to these conventions—in order fully to express the spirit of rebellion, of difference. Don Quijote is real for Unamuno, but in a Cervantine—and, later, Unamunian—way. That is, the bottom line for Unamuno is the signified, the metaphysical. His characters put thoughts before actions. They intellectualize, philosophize, and often fail to distinguish between mental exercises and feelings. We get to know them through their minds, and the physical world becomes a type of supplement.

Unamuno's preoccupations in *Niebla* revolve around the life of the mind, the creative process, and the artist himself. Like Shakespeare in *Hamlet*, Unamuno makes indecision dramatic, active. What could be deemed the materialism of the realist novel lies in the margins, and when it enters the text, it is accompanied by discomfort; it seems to be out of place. In *Don Quijote*, Cervantes represents the world by re-presenting it, by forcing the reader to factor in the seams of literary construction. Reality becomes a series of alternate realities, or fictions of perception and perspective. Cervantes deconstructs the myth of objective history (as opposed to subjective poetry). He poeticizes history while historicizing poetry, by bringing books into the mainstream. He shows that the play of art in life and of life in art is never-ending, and he documents that point by providing a model for future writers. The landscape of *Don Quijote* rotates between the authentic and the counterfeit, and between the lucid and the vague, and the text belongs to social and literary history. Unamuno takes pains to redress the trappings of realism and to mark a space for his innovations. He clearly has discovered a soulmate in Cervantes, as one who wishes to record the artistic experience in the practice of fiction and who approaches reality unconventionally. In each case, the burdens of authorship, of tradition, and of epistemology become internalized, as narrative becomes metanarrative. Unamuno's protagonist is obsessed with ideas, and the tensions of *Niebla* have to do with the conflicts of perception and ways of judging reality, with the travails and triumphs of writing always in the frame. Detaching himself from the immediate past, Unamuno reverts to the distant past, to the origins of the modern novel. He seeks a separation from the norm, and he finds an ironically distinctive voice and structural plan by exploiting the legacy of Cervantes and by dwelling on his own idiosyncrasies. *Amor y pedagogía* is his trial run at the *nivola*. With *Niebla* comes the extra magic of the Cervantine graft.

Having scrutinized the novel and added a personal and critical gloss in the *Vida de don Quijote y Sancho*, Unamuno appropriates *Don Quijote* again as an adoring reader, but also as a writer caught—fortuitously, some might say—between imitation and innovation. In the *Vida*, he finds a conduit for his private philosophical and socio-historical musings, although it may be noted that Unamuno's private thoughts—his excursus, reflections, and *monodiálogos*—frequently become soul-baringly public. As in *En torno al casticismo*, of 1895, the subject of the *Vida* is Spain: its institutions, national character, and religion (see Ugarte and the Navarro introduction to *Vida*). As the author admits, Don Quijote is a catalyst for thought, and this gives Unamuno, known for his willingness to debate both sides of an argument, ample interpretive and analytical flexibility. Like the German Romantics, he turns Don Quijote into a symbol that he can mold to fit into his reading of the essence of his own time and place (see Close, *Romantic Approach* esp. 136-59). Unamuno may be seen to practice early versions of structuralism and cultural studies, respectively, as he situates Don Quijote within the deep structure of Spanish identity and as he uses history to contemplate and configure literature, and vice versa. The *Vida* is not so much literary criticism as a meeting point of social philosophy, intellectual history, and the imagination (Cervantes's and Unamuno's).[3] The central images of Spain and Don Quijote cannot be separated from their Unamunian inflection. The same is true of *Niebla*, in which every nod to Cervantes is further mediated by the commanding presence of the writer.

Niebla is at once more subtle and more broadly constructed than *Amor y pedagogía*.[4] It would be misleading, and unfair, to call *Amor y pedagogía*

---

[3] In *Unamuno y la vida como ficción*, Francisco La Rubia Prado reads *La vida de don Quijote y Sancho* as a response to Plato's *Republic*. See pp. 116-64.

[4] Roberta Johnson notes, "*Niebla* was for Unamuno a continuation of *Amor y pedagogía*, but one, he believed, that was more artistically successful," "más

a study for *Niebla*, but it offers a blueprint that the writer sharpens, refines, and unifies, and a base for this unity is *Don Quijote*. The predominant voice in the prologue to Part 1 of *Don Quijote* is that of the friend of the authorial figure. The prologue is about Cervantes and his unpublished manuscript, and the ironic circumlocution provides a sublime combination of literary play and ironic distance. The distance is ironic, not because the reader needs distance to grasp the irony but because, ironically, the distance between the subject and the object of the discourse is illusory. As he replicates—or originates, depending on one's perspective—the plot design, Víctor Goti cannot break away from comparison, from ready-made analogues. He is at the service of his creator. He comments on the literary success of Unamuno and the role of the public as arbiter of value and taste. He catalogs Don Miguel's extravagances and personal manias, of the theoretical, theological, political, philosophical, and orthographical varieties. He isolates a triad of elements at the core of Unamuno's thought: religion, Spain, and Cervantes. For Unamuno, each is exalted, and each is productively problematic. In its allusion to an ambiguous death, the end of the prologue resembles the end of the second *Quijote* prologue. Goti rules Augusto Pérez's death a suicide, but Unamuno, in the post-prologue, disagrees. The mystery defines a linear movement that both helps to shape the novel and to prepare for the narrative surprises that follow. As he experiments with form, Unamuno tests the reader's expectations and proceeds with a strong commitment to difference. As in *Amor y pedagogía*, the personality and the quirks of the author unmistakably appear from the beginning. *Niebla* could be subtitled "cómo se hace una novela unamuniana," because the writer as a man, as a public persona, and as a creative artist makes a show of presiding over the narrative events.

Evoking history and truth, Cervantes opens *Don Quijote* by inviting the reader to notice point of view. The episode of Marcela and Grisótomo (1, 11-14) is an analogue on that theme. The deceased suitor, through his poetic lament, and his associates describe a cruel and disdainful woman, while Marcela's defense shifts the tone and the culpability. Her side of the story opposes the verbal portrait that precedes her entrance and expands the interpretive options. Unamuno sets *Niebla* in motion with a

---

novela y más entretenida, creo," she quotes him as saying (*Crossfire* 93).

riddle and two proposed answers. As in the second part of *Don Quijote*, the text reveals the death of the protagonist, and the question of how the demise will be executed frames the argument. Unamuno initiates a series of dialogues in which everything and everyone, including himself several times over, are fair game. He continues to assume that his readership is interested in the literary and the historical, or extraliterary, Unamuno: his personality, his pronouncements, his fighting spirit, his trials, his confrontation with tradition, and his search for fame and glory. *Niebla* is metafictional and metacritical. It exposes its devices and its author's concerns. It "speaks" to the reader by acknowledging its constructedness, its artificiality, its nominal separation from the real. Unamuno clearly wants to meet narrative realism head-on, but not necessarily to cut himself off from reality. His generic novelty, the *nivola*, can only exist as a variation of the *novela*, to which it is bound even as it seeks to force a separation. The experimental nature of *Niebla* permits the reader to negotiate the merging of artistic self-consciousness, showmanship, and a sense of history. As the prologue and post-prologue attest, Unamuno is an unusual guide, but his peculiarities are orchestrated to give randomness a wittingly artful edge.

The first gesture of *Niebla* is especially eloquent. Augusto Pérez stands in the doorway of his house, with his right palm turned downward and his eyes facing the heavens. This is not a spiritual moment, but a test to see if it is raining. There is a slight drizzle, which disturbs him not because he has no umbrella, but because he will have to convert an aesthetic object into a utilitarian one. He is consumed by concepts, yet his life is directionless, more so since the death of his beloved mother. His vigor comes from the mind, not the body. Poised to follow the first dog that comes within his purview, he catches sight of an attractive woman, whom he pursues to her home. Augusto finds out from the superinten-dent's wife that the young lady is Eugenia Domingo del Arco, an orphan who lives with her aunt and uncle and who gives piano lessons. The situation starts his mind working, but his preoccupation with her name (the illogic of Domingo instead of Dominga) would seem to supersede his passion and his courtship strategies. Unamuno is working against type here, converting the standard man of action into an introspective character, quite literally lost in thought. His method flies in the face of norms for plotting and characterization. Augusto believes that he is driven by love, but he is more a pawn of the imagination than of destiny.

When he casts his fate to chance at the beginning of the first chapter, he recognizes this free will as a type of control, but he will have Unamuno to do battle with on that point, and the author is always in the picture. The character is a rare breed of passive aggressive, while his creator is actively pulling strings and laboring to inscribe himself into the story and into literary history. Augusto is a loner, financially comfortable but with no life beyond a dull routine. He relates his thoughts to the mysteries of psychology, and he distinguishes between the image that occupies his solitary mind and the flesh-and-blood Eugenia, significantly "the other." He has sallied forth, or has lain in wait, to experience what providence has in store for him, and he credits the encounter with Eugenia as that response.

Augusto Pérez has his own theory of *intrahistoria*. He concentrates on the small incidents that surround the greatest joys and sorrows, and that end by defining people's lives. From this "mist" has surged Eugenia to give him a purpose: "¿No salió la América a buscar a Colón? No ha venido Eugenia a buscarme a mí?" (115).[5] Augusto writes Eugenia a letter, in which he expresses his love. He pardons himself for sentimentalism, but confesses, "Yo vivo en perpetua lírica infinitesimal" (116). He is so consumed in thought, which he often confuses with feeling, that he passes Eugenia on the street without noticing her, for, as the narrator explains, "La niebla espiritual era demasiado densa" (117). He discovers that Eugenia has another pretender, and the idea of conflict animates him; if life is a battleground, he is willing to arm himself in order to win his lady. His tactics will be based, of course, on the force of will, on the force of the mind, on theoretical referents. The intellectualization of action—which is to say, inaction—will be a challenge for Unamuno as well as for Augusto Pérez. When something similar happens in Part 2 of *Don Quijote*, the despicable Avellaneda sequel becomes a boon by inciting the knight and his creator to defend themselves. Unamuno must devise means by which to move his plot and his protagonist along.

Unamuno brings Víctor Goti into the text proper in chapter 3, when Augusto joins him for a game of chess.[6] Víctor recognizes that his friend

---

[5] All quotations from *Niebla* will refer to the Valdés edition (Cátedra), and page numbers will be indicated in parentheses.

[6] In "Unamuno's Anecdotal Digressions," Gayana Jurkevich discusses the

is in love with love; he knows of Eugenia and accepts the news in a rather patronizing manner. Like Sancho Panza, Víctor Goti is a dialogue partner, and he brings cynicism and wit to the proceedings. He is smart and a smart aleck, and he is also a novelist, a *nivolista*. Unamuno gives the writer within the narrative the opportunity to discuss the theory of the *nivola*, to spur and annoy Augusto, and thus to complement the author and the main character. What could have been a treatise on form is now a part of literature, with Unamuno comfortably ensconced in a foreground that presents itself as background. If not a paragon of practicality, Víctor is nonetheless a foil figure to Augusto, who is always distracted, always in the clouds. A Don Diego de Miranda with attitude, Víctor Goti has a family and a level of satisfaction that Augusto Pérez does not achieve. As in the case of Don Quijote, a type of normalcy, albeit ironic and ripe for deconstruction, hangs over the protagonist. Augusto's life is out of kilter, and he is ill equipped to deal with human nature, that is, with the self-serving nature of humanity. Love for Augusto is the contemplation of love. He considers it better to fall in love before knowing the object of his affection. And correspondingly, he passes Eugenia on the street without spotting her. He thinks of his mother's advice to get married. The fact that Eugenia plays the piano attracts him, perhaps because it is a non-utilitarian pastime, part of a determination to savor the agreeable boredom ("un dulce aburrimiento" 127) of life. By searching for a bride, he honors Doña Soledad's wishes and he inaugurates a quest. Víctor will be on hand to critique the process.

Augusto Pérez's highlighting of the minutiae of quotidian life offers a surprising variant of the structure of narrative realism, which often is seen as the representation of everyday life, with an emphasis on details, interaction among characters, and individual and group psychology. Augusto speaks of details, but here they are mental distractions that tend to conceal the so-called reality of this fictional realm, an undisclosed Spanish urban setting presumably in the early twentieth century. The

game of chess and the "allusion to men as chess pieces moved about the board of life by an authority superior to their own" (13). In broader terms, she submits that "the novel's structural arrangement follows the same patterns at all its narrative levels, each bound to the other by an intricate network of game-playing, *burlas*, and metaphysical deceptions" (12). See also Blanco Aguinaga, who examines Augusto Pérez as a plaything of fate from all sides.

young man is cared for by a devoted couple, Liduvina and Domingo, whose service frees him to lose himself in thought. They have the onus of substituting for the absent mother, who guided Augusto through his studies and who, in her widowhood, lived only for him. In his solitude, Augusto is aware that if she were still alive, she would have solutions for his problems. At the end of chapter 5, he comes across Orfeo, the dog who will become the confidant of his soliloquies. In the following chapter, he rescues the canary owned by Eugenia's aunt Doña Ermelinda and gains entry into her home, where he meets Don Fermín, mystical anarchist and devotee of Esperanto. When Eugenia learns of the visit, she is less than thrilled that her aunt is an advocate of Augusto, and she tells her uncle that she is also an anarchist, although not mystical. Augusto, meanwhile, feels that he has crossed a decisive threshold, and he continues to ponder the source of his love. He wonders aloud to Orfeo, "¿De dónde ha brotado Eugenia? ¿Es ella una creación mía o soy creación suya yo?" (139). A notable feature of Augusto's discourse in chapter 7 is the Cartesian rewriting, "*Amo, ergo sum*" (141), but the words that contextualize the statement are far more striking. He presents a view of eternity as a return to the past, in which the innermost part of history becomes a counterhistory, a subterranean river that is restored to its source. According to this speech, it is love, not religion, that moves his soul. The allusion to the splendor of Eugenia's eyes recalls the conventions of amorous poetry, yet not unconditionally, for Augusto compares the glow to the splendor of his mother's tears.

When Augusto meets with Eugenia at the home of her uncle and aunt, she is aloof and disinterested. She identifies him as "el del canario" (144), and she refutes his description of her as a lover of the arts, assuring him that, for her, music is merely a means to an end. He is not disillusioned, however, because he admires in her a drive and a spiritedness that he lacks. As Liduvina serves him his dinner that evening, she discerns a change in her master, a change wrought by love. That love is one-sided, for Eugenia is attached to Mauricio, who considers—and, unfortunately, not incorrectly—that, to some women, disrespect can be a form of ingratiation. He does not hide the fact that he is both lazy and immoral. When he suggests that Eugenia take advantage of her new suitor's prosperity, she reacts with indignation, but she is not as insulted as she would have him believe. In Mauricio, a rogue and a materialist, Unamuno creates the antithesis of the cerebral, refined, idealistic, and guileless Augusto. The dialogue between Eugenia and Mauricio foreshadows their duping of the naïve protagonist. Augusto's assertion that his new object in life "es conquistar a esta muchacha o que ella me conquiste" (153) has a sadly ironic resonance. From his mental meanderings on love, on the theme of the other, and on additional topics comes his "heroic resolution" to pay off the mortgage that Eugenia's late parents have left her, whether he can win her love or not. He wants to rescue her and to astound her with his magnanimity. At this point, Víctor Goti catches up with him. After hearing more about his friend's feelings for Eugenia, Víctor concludes that Augusto has been in love in the abstract and that Eugenia has concretized those latent emotions; his love is "de cabeza" (157). When Augusto protests, Víctor says that since he is pushing the issue, it must be stated that Augusto himself is nothing more than a pure idea, "un ente de ficción" (157). The discussion recurs to the topic of love, but when Augusto returns home and to Orfeo, he questions his sentiments and his being. He is committed to proving that he is equal to his fellow man.

Unamuno unites philosophy and fiction-making. His characters analyze love from a number of perspectives. As with Cervantes and Don Quijote, he invents an *ente de ficción*, literary to the extreme, that is nevertheless capable of producing reader empathy. When Augusto Pérez visits Eugenia in chapter 11, his anxiety is palpable. He is trembling, but he speaks words of passion that do not move Eugenia, who reminds him that such words come from books and not from real desire. Amid this crisis of love and being, Augusto pledges to Doña Ermelinda and Don Fermín that he is willing to sacrifice his own happiness for the sake of their niece. He speaks of himself in the third-person as he announces that he will do anything in order to comply with his "heroic determination." It is at this juncture that Unamuno introduces the laundry girl Rosario, to contrast with the ethereal and unattainable Eugenia. Augusto needs the humble girl's physicality to corroborate his own. Rosario is tangible and sensitive. She takes pity on Augusto, who asks if she would be capable of loving him. He is so self-absorbed that he does not recognize the error of his ways, and Liduvina must remind him that his indecorous behavior would seem to prove that he is madly in love with Eugenia. Even in the dialogue with Rosario, Augusto cannot shake the introspection that mediates his course of action; he requests, "… no digas nada, déjame hablar solo, conmigo mismo" (167). His self-confidence suffers greatly when Eugenia comes to his home to chastise him for paying off her debt. She accuses him of wanting to buy her love and to play the martyr. Augusto, in a "mist of confusion," takes refuge in a church, where he runs into Don Avito Carrascal, of *Amor y pedagogía*, who cautions him that experience is one's only teacher, that there is no pedagogical method that works. Don Avito advises Augusto to get married. When Augusto inquires, "Deductively or inductively?," Don Avito replies, after alluding to his personal tragedy, "Intuitively," and with a woman who loves him, even though he may not love her. Augusto thinks immediately of Rosario. He decides to clear his head by engaging in a game of chess with Víctor Goti.

Víctor, it turns out, has his own mind-body dilemma. After many years of marriage, his wife has become pregnant, and Víctor is none too happy with the prospect of losing the comfortable status quo of his wedded life. When Víctor raises the question of a future wedding and parenthood, Augusto focuses on the role of the wife as a figurative mother of the husband. The ironically named Doña Soledad is a continual factor in his deliberations, a presence so strong that she could be called an Unamunian tribute to Freud. Augusto becomes so engrossed in the circumstances of his friends that he momentarily forgets Eugenia's ire and Rosario's calming influence. When his thoughts shift once more to the two women, he finds it difficult to maintain the categories of the mental and the physical. He tells Orfeo that, while Eugenia has a magnificent body—a divine body—her body is her soul, and he avers that the tears that he shed when embracing Rosario stemmed not from his body but from his soul. His self-analysis goes in a different direction: "A mí me sobra el cuerpo, Orfeo, me sobra el cuerpo porque me falta alma" (182). Eugenia, for her part, has no use for heroism. She informs her aunt that she is not interested in good men, but in bona fide men, who are by nature vulgar and brutish. The others, including Augusto Pérez, are less than real men. Eugenia is not averse to supporting a man; she argues that if a man believes that he can buy her, she believes that she can buy a man. She makes it clear, though, that she is not for sale. Augusto comes by to talk with her, but she has left to be with Mauricio. When they are together, she pretends to dislike the crassness that she has just praised to her aunt. Addressing Eugenia's doubts about his seriousness regarding a job and marriage, Mauricio is principled enough—or egotistical enough—to say that he has little interest in earning a livelihood, yet he would not want to be supported by his wife. He submits that Augusto Pérez may help them to resolve both problems, if Eugenia were to agree to marry her luckless suitor. The comment causes her to become ill; she rushes away from him and locks herself in her room.

The crucial chapter 17 begins with Víctor Goti's story about the marriage of convenience of the noble but impoverished Don Eloíno Rodríguez de Alburquerque to the humble but well-to-do landlady Doña Sinfo, a marriage that fails because the ailing Don Eloíno does not die by the expected date. This intercalated tale will follow the model of Cervantes and will go into the novel that Víctor is writing.[7] Augusto wants to know more about the venture, and Víctor describes the evolving manuscript: it will be written spontaneously, proceeding as life proceeds. It will center on nothing in particular, and there will be a considerable emphasis on dialogue, although those who speak may say very little. Details are out, while conversation is in. And, amazingly, the author is out, to a degree: "Y sobre todo que parezca que el autor no dice las cosas por sí, no nos molesta con su personalidad, con su yo satánico. Aunque, por supuesto, todo lo que digan mis personajes lo digo yo..." (200). Augusto argues that this is true up to a point, "... que empezarás creyendo que los llevas tú, de tu mano, y es fácil que acabes convenciéndote que son ellos los que te llevan. Es muy frecuente que un autor acabe por ser juguete de sus ficciones" (200). Víctor Goti is granted the authorial space in which to define the parameters of the *nivola,* and to point out that if there is no dialogue partner one may produce a dog, but it is Augusto Pérez—seemingly out of control at this moment in the narrative—who brings up the question of upstart characters that may elude the clutches of their creators. The dialogue with Víctor is a rehearsal of sorts for his confrontation with Unamuno. Unamuno mixes literary theory with existential debate in a way that seems to be more and more natural, despite its conscious flight from realism.

Suffering from Eugenia's rejection, Augusto finds comfort—and control—in the arms of Rosario. He speaks of taking a trip and asks if she will accompany him, and she says, here as elsewhere, "Como usted

---

[7] For commentary on the intercalated narratives in *Niebla,* see Morón Arroyo (*Hacia el sistema* 73-79), Olson (*Unamuno* 68-75 and *Chiasmus* 77-87), Sepúlveda, and Guerrero. See also Palomo.

quiera..." (204). He realizes that he has been lying to her and to himself, "representando a solas mi comedia, hecho actor y espectador a la vez" (205), and he soliloquizes, in the presence of Orfeo, on the relation between love and jealousy. If in chapter 18 Augusto Pérez seems defeated by the circumstances in which he has placed himself, or in which fate has placed him, in chapter 19 he is noticeably different. His dialogue with Doña Ermelinda is a superb complement to the conversation with Víctor Goti two chapters earlier. Doña Ermelinda appears at Augusto's home to inform him that her niece regrets having offended him and that Eugenia now is willing to accept the generous gift, provided that there are no strings attached; she esteems Augusto but has no interest in marrying him, for she does not love him. Doña Ermelinda expresses herself tactfully, but Augusto is offended, and angered, that Eugenia would think that he had ulterior motives. Augusto's assertive response reveals a certain vitality. He notes that now he is the one, not the other. He questions the neutrality of Doña Ermelinda's position. It is Eugenia who may have ulterior motives, who may be trying to reel him in. He declares that he will not be trifled with: "... no soy un piano en que se puede tocar a todo antojo, que no soy un hombre de hoy te dejo y luego te tomo, que no soy sustituto ni vicenovio, que no soy plato de segunda mesa" (210). Doña Ermelinda is insulted, as well as surprised by his aggressive attitude, and Augusto adamantly affirms that he accepts Eugenia's apology and that he will continue to consider her a friend, but only a friend. When Doña Ermelinda asks if he will visit her home, Augusto mentions that he is preparing to leave on an extended trip.[8] Hearing her aunt's report of the visit, Eugenia concludes that there is another woman in the picture, and she determines that she must "reconquer" Augusto. For his part, Augusto feels that, thanks to Eugenia, he indeed has character, a personality. She has awakened his amorous faculties, but, that having been done, he no longer needs her, for there are plenty of women from which to choose, including Rosario, "la inocencia maliciosa,... esta nueva edición de la eterna Eva" (211).

Unamuno keeps Augusto in character, so to speak, while using the impetus of Eugenia's professed change of heart and Doña Ermelinda's

---

[8] Thomas Franz looks at the implications of the planned trip in "Los misteriosos planes de viajar en *Niebla*" (*Niebla inexplorada* 77-96).

visit to push him forward. It is important to note that Augusto's boldness is directed to the aunt, not to Eugenia, and that his stance can never be separated from his philosophizing tendencies. Eugenia has taught him how to love "generically," how to appreciate women en bloc and to realize that there are many fish in the sea. He will not be played with, especially by a woman, he avows, most ironically. "¡Yo soy yo!," he cries. "¡Mi alma será pequeña, pero es mía!" (211). Although the statements suggest an increasing awareness of his physicality, Augusto Pérez is the contemplative character par excellence, for whom thinking is the most strenuous form of exercise. Here, he exhibits a false sense of security. He believes that he is several steps ahead of Eugenia, but he is flattering himself, as both the aunt and the niece discern. He feels that now no one can mock him, but, of course, he is grossly mistaken. Eugenia comes to his home and immediately disarms him. She employs her feminine wiles to the fullest. Although he understands that she is "diabolical" and that "la fatalidad eres tú" (216), he is under her spell. Eugenia suggests that his payment of the mortgage has sullied her image and thereby linked their destinies. She is pulling the strings, and Rosario, who is delivering the laundry, tells Augusto that Eugenia is deceiving him. He is confused by his feelings, and, once he is alone, he finds himself bereft of confidence: "Entre una y otra me van a volver loco de atar… Yo ya no soy yo…" (216). Liduvina attempts to distract Augusto, and Domingo waxes philosophical, noting that "nadie es el que es, sino el que le hacen los demás" (221). By all accounts, reality seems to be a conceptual phenomenon.

Chapter 21 centers on the intercalated tale of Don Antonio, a man with two wives and paradoxically successful marriages. This is followed, in chapter 22, by the account of Víctor Goti's reaction to paternity. Initially dismayed at his wife's pregnancy, he is ecstatic over the birth of his son. The delivery and its aftermath have taken their toll on his wife, but she seems more beautiful to him than ever. This leads to the story of the master of pyrotechnics who, when blinded, continues to praise the beauty of his wife, who was burned in the accident that cost him his vision. When the discussion turns to Augusto, Víctor advises him to devote himself to philosophy (a profession for bachelors), as Liduvina has advised him to devote himself to politics. At the end of the chapter, Augusto gives alms to a beggar whom he calls a philosopher. Nothing can shake the protagonist of his desire for women. He cannot choose between Eugenia and Rosario, nor can he cease to be enamored of all women, to the point at which he must avoid the robust Liduvina. He seeks the counsel of the scholar Antolín S. Paparrigópulos, the ultimate pedant, to guide him in his quest to master feminine psychology. Don Antolín submits that the first question is whether women have souls and then insists that a scientific study must have a minimum of three subjects, for dualities cannot reach closure. The result is the addition of Liduvina, as representative of the stomach, to correspond with Eugenia as symbolic of the head and Rosario of the heart. Certain that she will reject him, he will court Eugenia as a means of testing her, yet he cannot rule out completely the possibility that she will accept his proposal. When he is with Rosario, he showers her with kisses, noting that he is losing his scientific objectivity as the experiment begins. She is aware that he has failed to differentiate between her and Eugenia. He, meanwhile, must refrain from attacking Liduvina out of lust, and he runs out of the house. On the street, he tries to convince himself that he is not mad. The world as laboratory is pushing him through its maze.

Augusto pays a visit to Víctor at his home, in order to partake in his friend's happiness at fatherhood and, "in passing," to consult on "the state of his spirit." He has the occasion to peruse a section of Víctor's *nivola*, which he finds pornographic in spots. Víctor responds, "Lo que hay aquí son crudezas, pero no pornografía. Alguna vez algún desnudo... pero nunca un desvestido... Lo que hay es realismo..." (249). The writer admits to a degree of cynicism and to a penchant for "los chistes lúgubres, las gracias funerarias," but he qualifies the crudeness as "pedagogical" (250). For him, laughter is a preparation for tragedy. When Augusto expresses displeasure at the "bufonadas crudas," Víctor replies that he writes for his own enjoyment, but that he also hopes that his writings can place a doubly solitary person like Augusto—solitary in body and soul—on the road to recovery. He urges Augusto to marry, for only through matrimony can one conduct an experiment in feminine psychology; single men deal with metaphysics, not psychology. Augusto must worry not only about marriage but about which of the women in his life would best suit him. Calling him "pequeño Hamlet," Víctor sees the doubt as a positive force: "¿Dudas?, luego piensas; ¿piensas?, luego eres" (252). Víctor ends the dialogue by stressing that he himself has doubts, before and after the fact, when it comes to composing his *nivola*, but he places his trust in the imagination. At the end of chapter 25, Unamuno intervenes to wink at his characters and to attempt to tower above them as "el Dios de estos dos pobres diablos nivolescos" (252). This is yet another instance of prolepsis, a sign of things to come in the debate of chapter 31. Unamuno belittles his creations as a means of marking their inferiority to the one who has fabricated them, but he has planted the seeds of a counterargument by indicating that characters can reach beyond the aims and insights of their authors.

Bound to complete his experiment, Augusto makes his way to Eugenia's house. From the start, it is she who is definitively in charge. With a tremendous effort, he asks for her hand in marriage. She brings up Rosario. He begs her to forget Rosario. He suffers profoundly, realizing that he is the guinea pig in this experiment, even after she accepts the proposal. Thus begins a "new life" for Augusto, spent in great part in his fiancée's home "studying not psychology but aesthetics," as the opening of chapter 27 puts it. At his own home, a new woman brings the laundry. As Eugenia plays the piano, Augusto writes a poem, in which he describes her as spirit and himself as form. She critiques the verses, objecting to such phrases as "según dicen." He works the word *nivolesco* into the conversation, and she warns that there will be no room in their marriage for his in-jokes with Víctor and no room for dogs (and, by extension, for monologues). Eugenia sets Augusto up for her cruel deception. She says that Mauricio has continued to prey on her, but that he has promised to leave her alone if Augusto can find him a position in another place. In the beautifully conceived chapter 28, Augusto comes face to face with Mauricio, who shows up unannounced at his home, supposedly to thank him for arranging a job but really to torment him to the maximum. Mauricio cagily says that he may take with him a young woman who has likewise been rejected, and that woman turns out to be Rosario. Unable to control himself, Augusto pushes Mauricio onto the sofa, and Mauricio chides him, "Mírese usted ahora, don Augusto, en mis pupilas y verá qué chiquitito se ve," and, in fact, "El pobre Augusto creyó derretirse" (262). Augusto cannot determine whether this has been a dream or a real event. He informs the trusty Orfeo of his concerns, including the imminent arrival of one who has no tolerance for dogs.

Augusto would prefer a modest ceremony, but Eugenia plans a more elaborate wedding. He feels pangs of jealousy when he thinks of Rosario and Mauricio, and he is described as "pensive." Naturally, he is taken aback when he receives Eugenia's letter with an explanation of the plot to dupe him, and a postscript that adds insult to injury by stating that

Rosario will not be accompanying the couple, should he wish to take advantage of that situation. Even Don Fermín, the theoretical anarchist, is shocked by his niece's boldness. Walking on the street, Augusto becomes calm, and this calmness leads him to doubt his own existence: "Si yo fuese hombre como los demás—se decía—, con corazón; si fuese siquiera un hombre, si existiese en verdad, ¿cómo podía haber recibido esto con la relativa tranquilidad con que lo recibo?" (269). At home, Orfeo greets him, and he finds comfort in knowing that his canine friend will remain at his side. But his heart finally bursts, his emotions pouring out, and sadness and bitterness overtake him. Augusto tells Liduvina that "she has killed me," and he locks himself in his room, where he thinks of his mother and dissolves into tears. When Víctor finds Augusto hiding from the world, his words are arguably more provocative than consoling. Their dialogue in chapter 30 sets up the meeting with Unamuno in the decisive chapter 31. Víctor suggests that his friend, the scientist turned guinea pig, experiment on himself. Augusto takes this to mean suicide, but Víctor is noncommittal; his cry of "Devórate" is open to interpretation. Hamlet and Descartes are prominent presences in the dialogue, and when Augusto mentions *"Cogito, ergo sum,"* Víctor counters that "Descartes no ha sido más que un ente ficticio, una invención de la Historia, pues… ¡ni existió… ni pensó" (276).[9] Augusto has been betrayed and ridiculed. He feels that he can go on no longer, and he makes the journey to Salamanca to inform Don Miguel de Unamuno that he has decided to kill himself.

Unamuno the persona enters the frame of *Niebla* from the prologue onward. There may be an ironic and jocular presentation, but the author immediately stakes a space for himself as a blend of the driven writer and the public figure. In the aside in chapter 25, he, in effect, lords himself over his creations, and by asserting his authority, in the double sense, he opens the door for the dramatic confrontation with Augusto Pérez, in which he will be fighting for his position while choreographing both sides of the battle. The very phrasing of "ocurriósele consultarlo conmigo, con

---

[9] Stephen G. H. Roberts finds that "Víctor Goti mezcla ideas shakesperianas, cartesianas y unamunianas para explorar la naturaleza de la duda. Víctor parece estar citando *Del sentimiento trágico de la vida* al subrayar el papel vivificador de la duda tanto en la fe como en los procesos cognitivos, y le ofrece a Augusto la posibilidad de convertir su condición hamletiana en una nueva forma de vida más positiva y creadora" (104). See also 109-10.

el autor de este relato" (277) conveys the play of power. Unamuno is the acknowledged author, but the maker of the decision is, as the verb choice deftly discloses, not clear-cut. Augusto enters Unamuno's study "como un fantasma, miró a un retrato mío al óleo que allí preside a los libros de mi librería" (277). Unamuno takes pains to differentiate the *hombre de carne y hueso* from the *ente de ficción*, but, evoking Sor Juana Inés de la Cruz, Velázquez, and Cervantes, among others, he places artists within (and alongside of) works of art and works of art in the world at large. Unamuno is in the fiction, and Augusto Pérez is in Salamanca. Augusto is a reader of Unamuno. He compliments the writer and then recounts his life and misfortunes. Unamuno goes several steps beyond his predecessors. He not only erases borders, but he offers direct discourse between the creator and the creation. He precedes the existential debate with an establishing shot that aprioristically helps to negate his standpoint in the argument. That viewpoint is, of course, that Augusto cannot commit suicide because he is not a living, breathing man, but a figment of the author's imagination, a literary character. This is, of course, where Augusto stages his oft-cited counterattack: "No sea, mi querido don Miguel..., que sea usted y no yo el ente de ficción.... No sea que usted no pase de ser un pretexto para que mi historia llegue al mundo" (279). When Unamuno begins to fight back, Augusto uses a phrase that others have employed when they think that he has overreacted: "No se exalte usted..." (279).

The most disarming of Augusto's rhetorical strategies is to quote Unamuno against himself: "Vamos a cuentas: ¿no ha sido usted el que no una, sino varias veces, ha dicho que Don Quijote y Sancho son no ya tan reales, sino más reales que Cervantes?" (279). And he maintains that Don Avito Carrascal and Don Fulgencio Entrambosmares would agree with him. When his opponent persists, Augusto covers both sides by adding that "[h]asta los llamados entes de ficción tienen su lógica interna" (280). He goes further, to note that fictional entities have been known to kill those who claim to have brought them into (fictional) being. With that comment, Unamuno reaches the limit of his patience: "Y para castigar tu osadía y esas doctrinas disolventes, extravagantes, anárquicas, con que te me has venido, resuelvo y fallo que te mueras. En cuanto llegues a tu casa te morirás" (283). Now Augusto wants to live, but Unamuno says that it is too late. He responds to Augusto's cries of "¡por Dios!" with "No hay Dios que valga. ¡Te morirás!" (283, 284). Distraught, Augusto can only contend that "también usted se morirá, también usted, y se volverá a la nada de que salió" (284). Unamuno calls Augusto's desperation, along with his attempt to bring his inventor into the equation, a "supremo esfuerzo de pasión de vida, de ansia de inmortalidad" (285); needless to say, the commentary is not without its own irony. As he departs with his head held low, Augusto Pérez seems to be doubting his own existence. Unamuno, who sheds a "furtive tear," ostensibly for the *ente de ficción*, may also be having some doubts. Whatever the case, he plants Augusto on firm rhetorical ground. The analogy with Cervantes and Don Quijote could hardly be more on target. Literary survival is as close as one can get to immortality in this life. The death sentence has been pronounced, but it is carried out in a strikingly ambiguous manner.

Augusto Pérez suffers over the troubles that he has had to endure and even more over the thought that his existence has been only a dream, and the dream of another, at that, or so his creator (in his role as omniscient narrator) informs the reader.[10] On his return, he stuns Liduvina, who observes that he seems more dead than alive, like something from the other world, and he replies that he is headed in that direction. He is, after all, only a fictional entity, like a character in a novel. She orders him to dine and go to bed, and she reminds him that tomorrow is another day. He reflects, "Pienso, luego soy," but then inverts the Cartesian dictum to "Soy, luego pienso" (287). All of a sudden, a voracious appetite seizes him, and he begs Liduvina for more and more food. At the same time, he reasons that if he is not alive, he cannot die; thus, he is immortal. And he keeps eating, shouting triumphantly, "*Edo, ergo sum*" (288). He writes a note to Unamuno—"Se salió con la suya. He muerto" (290)—and asks that it be sent on his death. He makes Domingo help him get undressed, for

---

[10] On the dream motif in *Niebla*, see Weber and Batchelor. R. Batchelor believes that Unamuno's answer to the question of whether life is a dream is that "it seems to be a dream or even a mist ('niebla') which causes us to see through a glass darkly. The smothering process of nothingness merging all impressions into the same pedestrian level of indifference and boredom creates in Augusto the sense of the phantom existence, of the two-dimensional, cardboard figure. His character is completely flat, deprived of all psychological relief. It is as though he were not living but dreaming. Thus, the transitional moments between sleep and wakefulness in Augusto's life are particularly indicative of Unamuno's ambiguous act which creates a kind of no man's land" (210).

he wants to end his life as naked as when he was born, and to have his servant recite prayers in his ear. When Domingo tells him that the things he is saying are "cosas de libros," Augusto answers, "¿Y quién no es cosa de libros?" (291). He wonders if Domingo knows Miguel de Unamuno, and Domingo replies that he is "un señor un poco raro que se dedica a decir verdades que no hacen al caso" (291). Augusto notes, "Pues también Unamuno es cosa de libros... Todos lo somos" (291). He goes to bed and dies. The doctor rules it a heart attack, Domingo blames indigestion, and Liduvina believes that it was "un suicidio y nada más que un suicidio. ¡Se salió con la suya!" (293). All three versions imply the protagonist's agency or ironically natural causes, but they cannot remove Unamuno from the picture. As he thinks about death, Augusto thinks about Unamuno. Domingo shows that Unamuno is a public figure, an iconoclast known to his fellow men and women and to *entes de ficción.*

When Unamuno (the *ente de ficción*) receives a telegram notifying him of Augusto's death, he questions the validity of his decision to kill the character. He considers bringing him to life again and to allow him to commit suicide, as Augusto had planned. He dozes off, and Augusto appears to him in a dream. Augusto says that he is there to bid Unamuno farewell for eternity and to order him to write the *nivola* of his adventures. The author says that the work has been done, and Augusto adds that the idea of bringing him back to life so that he may kill himself is not only absurd, but impossible. Can one bring Don Quijote back to life? he asks. Reiterating the thrust of his argument in chapter 31, Augusto says, "... mi querido don Miguel,... no vaya a ser que no pase usted de un pretexto para que mi historia, y otras historias como la mía[,] corran por el mundo" (296). It is Augusto who explains the limits of dreams to Unamuno, who then dreams that he is dying and awakens with a heavy heart. The last chapter—significantly numbered 33—unites intertextuality and Christian symbolism, not to mention Freud. The multilayered central metaphor of Calderón's *La vida es sueño,* where earthly existence, the world as stage, and contemplation of the afterlife coalesce, seems to hang in the background. The theme of resurrection stands boldly in the foreground. In the dream, Augusto Pérez is omniscient, able to read Unamuno's thoughts about bringing him back to life. Augusto is, in a sense, at rest. Unamuno seems to become increasingly irresolute and increasingly skeptical, but he has mapped a winning strategy. If Augusto Pérez is right, Unamuno profits. This is not so much the consequence of irony as of premeditation, of the viviparous showing its oviparous lines.[11] *Niebla* is a quixotic narrative, but its concentricity and its revolving metaphors call to mind the sublime construction of *La vida es sueño*, in which borders are generated, expunged, and rebuilt with equal ease. Unamuno reduplicates himself and multiplies his options. Unlike Cervantes and Velázquez, with whom he has so much in common, he resists placing himself in the margins.

The narrative ends with an epilogue in the form of a funeral oration delivered by Orfeo, which often has evoked Cervantes's *Coloquio de los perros*. The narrator observes that, typically in novels, the reader finds out the fate of all the characters and perhaps their reactions to the hero's death. That will not be the case here, but there is one exception. Orfeo will deliver a eulogy. He remarks that Augusto Pérez led a dog's life, that he was the victim of the malice and ruthlessness of others. In a scene that he replicates with Blasillo in *San Manuel Bueno, mártir*, Unamuno has Orfeo die of grief at the side of his master. The highest emotional level and the deepest feelings in the narrative come from a dog, and Unamuno is not

---

[11] It is generally conceded that *Niebla* is an "oviparous" text posing as "viviparous." See Ribbans ("Structure"), Vento, Pérez, and Jurkevich ("Unamuno's Gestational Fallacy"). The recognition that the *nivola* is less than spontaneous has not freed it from listings of perceived defects. Calling *Niebla* a "highly organized work," Ribbans sees its "faults" as "not of organization as such, but of a certain failure on the part of the author to curb his inveterate tendency to reiteration and overinsistence" (405). Essentially agreeing with this position, Batchelor writes, "the conspicuous weakness in *Niebla* and all the other *nivolas* for that matter may be attributed to their repetitive nature, as well as to what appears to be their excessively intellectual content.... [I]t is arguable that Unamuno's idealism is too exclusive, dry and cerebral to produce a vigourous and fertile texture in his *nivola*.... *Niebla* is totally deprived of the abundance of feeling, surge of energy and even awareness of society that we normally associate with Romantic thinkers, and Unamuno is assuredly a writer of Romantic temperament" (311). Ciriaco Morón Arroyo offers the following judgment: "*Niebla* es el primer experimento. El deseo de ser denso le hace superponer problemas y situaciones; de esa manera, el resultado es desordenado y la obra fracasa en todos los sentidos como intento de obra artística. La perfección se lograría suprimiendo elementos secundarios y concentrándose en uno presentado con claridad y proporción. Así surgen *Abel Sánchez*, *La tía tula*, *Tres novelas ejemplares*, etc." (*Hacia el sistema* 84). The earliest version of this commentary (2003) dates from 1966.

only paying homage to Cervantes's canine colloquy, itself an ironic refurbishing of the picaresque, but to the play of metafiction and realism in *Don Quijote*.[12] There is no mention in *Niebla*, as in *Amor y pedagogía*, of filling spaces. Every event seems to have its place and its function, although paradox and ambiguity may be at the heart of things. Like the methodical Antolín S. Paparrigópulos, Unamuno seems to measure the elements of his experience to formulate something on the order of a science of the absurd, with ties to reality and with glaring impossibilities. The *nivola* within the *nivola* framed by literary tradition and Cervantine lessons in perspectivism becomes a vehicle for Unamuno's creation, critique, and personal ideology. Augusto Pérez worries about not having a personality. Unamuno displays a surfeit of personality, which could be translated as egotism, as he seeks a variety of audiences. His aim may be not so much to please as to reframe the novel, to defy expectations, to stir controversy, to define a niche in the annals of performance art, and, last but hardly least, to confront immortality in literature and in life, which become inseparable.

Fittingly, there are multiple ways of approaching the calculatedly unstable center of *Niebla*. One would be through the poetics of the *nivola*

---

[12] Alexander A. Parker's study of *Niebla* accentuates the role of Orfeo as a reader and marker of human emotions and behavior. After stating that there was "no abnormality" in Unamuno's life, Parker finds that "there is an abnormality in the relations between men and women in his novels, revealing an underlying repulsion or... an unease, a dissatisfaction with the scheme of things. His men are generally weak, often abjectly humiliated by the women who alone are masterful and who... are praying mantises who devour their mates" (137-38). Parker places *Niebla* in this context because, for him, "its central theme is the sadness of the human condition which makes the brotherhood of men impossible on earth, since truth and innocence cannot coexist in love with sexual passion" (138). Cf. Close: "In Unamuno's philosophy, one mounts the ladder of faith not only by the rung of *congoja* (anguish), but also, like Augusto Pérez in *Niebla*, by the rung of love. Love is the root of all willed heroic action and its original form is that between man and woman or mother and child. For this reason, the knight's attitude to Aldonza Lorenzo, as Unamuno interprets it, becomes an important part of his psychological pre-history. It is transformed from the tepid and superficial acquaintance that Don Quixote evokes in conversation with Sancho in Part I, Chapter 25, into a poignantly sentimental passion, modestly unconfessed for twelve long years. Blocked, this passion sublimated itself into the higher love for Dulcinea" (*Romantic Approach* 151).

as a reaction to literary realism and naturalism. Víctor Goti's writing of a *nivola* within the narrative and his elaboration of its form and general premises, with obvious parallels to Unamuno's text, emphasizes the broad range of metafiction and introduces the concept of what might be termed creative concentricity. Víctor's work is a reflection of and a blueprint for Unamuno's *nivola*, but it is, of course, penned by Unamuno and contained within the larger text. Víctor is the mechanism through which Unamuno presents theory in praxis, with ingenuity and distance. Víctor Goti is the character as author, and Unamuno is the author as character. The implied competition between them mirrors the ideological combat between Unamuno and Augusto Pérez. The ironic ventriloquism is a diversion in the double sense: part of the entertainment value of the work of art and part of the fragmented ego of Miguel de Unamuno. Víctor Goti is the author of the prologue, the topic of which is Unamuno. The prologue to Part 1 of *Don Quijote* places the manuscript, a novel response to romance, in the center, with the creator positioned comfortably just off-center. The theme is the development of a strategy to complete the task of writing the book, so that it may be published. The prologue to *Niebla* seems to do the opposite, by eliding the book for the moment in order to isolate its creator. The theme, in this case, is Unamuno himself, as much the public figure and professional polemicist as the novelist, likely because he prefers to overlook the dividing lines between the two. Thus, Víctor writes the prologue, characterizes and comments on Unamuno, and casts the narrative as a mystery, with his judgment in competition with Don Miguel's. The story being created is new, more by virtue of its style than its content per se. Pedro Salinas notes that the Renaissance artist is more in love with the idea of nature than with the objects in nature.[13] Unamuno is more captivated by the idea of reality than by mimesis.

Metafiction is, one might say, sweet and useful. The reader accepts the move away from traditional representation to a commentary on the art of composition and on the problems of representation. There is no

---

[13] Pedro Salinas notes, "The Renaissance poet of nature sees nature through a complicated set of reflections. Between real nature and his mind the wonderful and subtle lenses of ideas are interposed. They cannot be satisfied with the trees but only with the idea of the trees" (*Reality* 80).

willing suspension of disbelief, but rather a shared contract between the producer and the consumer of the art object concerning the creative, and interpretive, act. Profound inquiries about the universe and humanity cross with preoccupations about expression, reception, analysis, and success. Because the artist refuses to hide behind the figurative (or literal) curtain, the reader enters the frame as a participant in the unfolding events. If Cervantes attains an enviable balance between the author and the reader, Unamuno tends to favor the author, that is, to favor himself and his alter ego Víctor Goti, but he certainly realizes that a reciprocal relationship is necessary and therefore that his conventions must be understood and appreciated. The model consistently bears his imprint, but it is a model that strives for a unique disbursement of ideas and means to incorporate, among other things, age-old theological and existential questions and advancements in the science of psychology into narrative as an abstract art. *Niebla* uses the challenge of writing as a means of access to the interstices of fact and fiction. The unconventional detective story is also an unconventional love story and a controlled experiment, with interpolations, a most sensitive talking dog, an internal narrative, and a debate between the protagonist and the author. The most evident frames—from the prologue and post-prologue to the epilogue—are death and the intervention of Unamuno, who not coincidentally is obsessed with death, the dialectics of philosophy and theology, and eternity. Immortality may be the most conclusive center of *Niebla*.

Their many points of contact notwithstanding, the formal differences between *Amor y pedagogía* and *Niebla* are worthy of note. The plot of *Amor y pedagogía* revolves around Don Avito Carrascal's experiment in raising his son, which constitutes, in this case, producing a genius. Love manifests itself in parental devotion, however misguided, and in Apolodoro's unrequited love for Clarita. Unamuno encodes himself as the author, dealing with the demands of writing and with art as a commercial venture. Don Fulgencio Entrambosmares is a writer within the narrative, but he more resembles Don Antolín S. Paparrigópulos than Víctor Goti (or Unamuno), and his closing essay is more a space-filler than a correlative of Víctor's *nivola*. The duality of the title *Amor y pedagogía* repeats itself in the dual protagonists, Don Avito and Apolodoro, the actor and the acted upon. Unamuno produces a variation on the theme of nature and nurture, and he brings modern science and technology to bear on a classical concept of tragedy. Although Don Avito appears in a church in *Niebla*, Apolodoro's suicide is not discussed in terms of Catholic doctrine. Always a man of ideas, Unamuno writes a cautionary tale about good science (and pedagogy) and bad. Don Avito's experiment coincides with a narrative experiment, a response to realism and naturalism. One might claim that Unamuno replaces action with thought, which will mean a shift in characterization and an increased emphasis on dialogue. It will also mean a revised role for the narrator and a discourse that targets, precisely, an audience willing to forsake the norms of narrative realism and to enter the territory of abstraction, intellectual play, and modernity according to Unamuno. There is an aleatory feel to *Amor y pedagogía*, to correspond to the notion of the viviparous narrative. This tragedy in a new key thrives on disorder and on an intellectual connection with the reader. *Niebla* takes its lead from the earlier text as it continues to reorient both the process and the consumer.

Niebla is plotted randomly only in a limited sense. At the beginning, Augusto Pérez allows fate to determine his course of action, but, coincidences aside, he takes matters into his own hands by pursuing Eugenia, organizing a psychological experiment, and planning a suicide. Unamuno seems to be in control from the start, and in the crucial instances in which that control appears to slip, the ceding of power is as manipulated as the God-like stance of Unamuno. Philosophy, theology, morality, and psychology are central to the narrative. Although class consciousness,[14] economics, and the rights of women enter the scheme, the social sciences do not carry the weight that they bear in eighteenth- and nineteenth-century narrative realism. Eugenia Domingo del Arco is, in her manner, a feminist and a femme fatale. She is not unwilling to support a husband, nor is she unwilling to use her wiles in order to deceive a suitor. It may seem to be incongruous that this piano teacher who hates music is the supreme woman in Augusto Pérez's mind, but he recognizes that she is a catalyst, an agent that awakens him to the realm of the senses, and he is grateful to her for that. She gives him the chance to be noble and, more simply and more importantly perhaps, she makes him feel alive. Augusto never finds it feasible, however, to view life in concrete terms. Eugenia is a mental vision more than a flesh-and-blood woman, even when they are together, and when they are apart, she is a

---

[14] See Franz, "El discurso de clases en Niebla" in *Niebla inexplorada* 49-75.

pure abstraction, a generic ideal. For much of Part 2 of *Don Quijote*, the protagonist is considerably more passive than in Part 1, because his literary other—the hero of the published book—usurps his space and because characters who have read the book act on their own. The unauthorized sequel pushes him back into action, since he must defend his good name and confirm his superiority. Eugenia motivates Augusto Pérez in much the same way, by stirring him to assert himself.

Augusto's search for humanity provides an ironic foil for the project of the *nivola*, which puts forth the *ente de ficción* as a standard bearer for a new kind of narrative. In *Don Quijote*, Cervantes deconstructs the history/poetry dichotomy and, as a corollary, a faith in the distinction between objectivity and subjectivity. Using history as the focal point for his assay of fiction, he makes historiography an open, flexible, and frameless discipline. The printing press has changed the world, and it has appeared providentially with other discoveries, mechanical and theoretical. The new modes of thinking and the new forms of inquiry set in motion a reexamination of *idées fixes*, at times amusingly and at times subversively. The friend's advice in the prologue to Part 1 encapsulates the spirit of upheaval and the demystification of the past. The fact that Cervantes chooses to effect this revisionist endeavor under the guise of—or in brilliant combination with—humor makes it more palatable, more subtle, and more daring. Despite the presence of several ecclesiastical figures and the Christian death of Alonso Quijano, the events of *Don Quijote* have a secular rhythm. With its underlying interest in immortality, *Niebla* may more closely resemble *La vida es sueño* in this respect, but Unamuno owes to Cervantes a paradigm for marking new literary paths by uniting poetics, perspective, and ideology. Unamuno places his narrative in the present, as defined by ideas rather than by the specifics of time and place, as if consciously resisting the tenets of realism. Like Cervantes, he breaks the rules of verisimilitude as he explores thought processes and as he inserts the author into the text.

In *Don Quijote* and *Niebla*, metafiction is seen as compatible with realism, a realism that differs according to the periods in which the works were conceived. Metafiction may connote a sense of playfulness, while the concepts of mimesis and verisimilitude may point, in contrast, to a seriousness of purpose. The laying bare of devices and the concealing of devices become two means of approaching reality. Both the representational and the anti-representational modes, the latter more likely to be flavored with irony and humor, include expositions on society, on the world, on human nature, in short, on reality. Cervantes and Unamuno look backward for inspiration and for a driving force, a center for literary creation, and they look forward to instituting new models. For Cervantes, the product is an anti-romance; for Unamuno, it is, in its way, a type of anti-realism and anti-naturalism. In Part 2 of *Don Quijote*, Cervantes becomes his own intertext. He is also at the base of Unamuno's intertext, but so is Unamuno himself. The result, in each case, is the propagation of ironic metafiction and bidirectional intertextuality. The criticism of *Don Quijote* has taken on a life of its own, dividing scholars into schools and informing readings of the text. A notable example would be what Anthony Close has called "the Romantic approach to *Don Quixote*," a demonstration of the impact of the German Romantics' (re)interpretation of the novel on two hundred years of reading and criticism.[15] One may consider commentaries on *Niebla* (and on the novel in general), principally with regard to the question of realism, in order to see how critics have addressed the structure and the openness of the narrative, and how they have—as reader-response theory might state it—filled in gaps and placed themselves in the text.[16] Just as *Don Quijote* becomes a different text after the growth of realism in the eighteenth and nineteenth centuries (and after twentieth-century developments in narrative), *Niebla* is transformed through the lens of postmodernism, or postmodernisms.

In the prologue to the *Tres novelas ejemplares* and elsewhere, Unamuno underscores the fact that realism need not correspond directly to reality, that is, that the approach to reality can be circuitous. He states, "Una cosa es que todos mis personajes novelescos, que todos los agonistas que he creado los haya sacado de mi alma, de mi realidad íntima—que es todo un pueblo—, y otra cosa es que sean yo mismo" (*Tres novelas* 55). The concepts of mimesis and verisimilitude are fundamental in this context, because they are at the base of Unamuno's divergence from the conventions of narrative realism in which the nineteenth-century novel is grounded. In *The Narrative of Realism and Myth*, Gregory L. Lucente

---

[15] See *Romantic Approach*, esp. 136-59, for Close's consideration of Unamuno. Antonio Vilanova discusses Unamuno, Víctor Goti, and "el nuevo género del *bufo trágico*" (189) in light of Romanticism and its aftermath.

[16] See, for example, Iser 163-79 ("Asymmetry between Text and Reader").

notes that "mimesis may be construed as the faithful reflection of the world's surface, and verisimilitude as the narrative's obedience to deeply ingrained cultural models for character motivation and plotting" (1), yet at the same time he recognizes that realism is bound to rhetoric as much as to epistemology and morality. Lucente makes the point that Plato acknowledged a dialectical aspect of imitation, in which artistic copying, however accurate, may be unable to recreate value. Thus, "[t]he first full-blown critique of mimesis in the West was… profoundly negative, and in precisely those terms that the continuing dialogue on realism has not yet succeeded in discarding, or fully clarifying" (Lucente 3). Aristotle was less interested in the idealistic past than in poetry as "an inquiry into the progressive refinement of existing models. What *is* remains constantly open to comparison with what *should be*. Description and prescription balance each other, and both appear essential to poetry's creation and critical assessment" (Lucente 3). According to Lucente, Aristotle's setting up of a distinction between history and poetry isolates the question of aesthetic unity, "the factitiousness of art, which pleases not because it is true to the disordered surface of human existence, but because it selects and arranges privileged elements to satisfy the given instincts of harmony and rhythm and the artistic criterion of wholeness" (4). In sum, "[d]enied the possibility of the exact representation of worldly life, Aristotelian poetry… resorts to a 'superior' form of realistic effect, substituting the aesthetic truth of conventionalized unity for Plato's realm of transcendent forms" (Lucente 4). Ironically, but justly, history can mediate the distinction.

Lucente contrasts the historiography of Herodotus, who "intends to record everything of note that he has seen, heard of, or read, regardless of his belief in his sources' veracity," with that of Thucydides, for whom "'scientific accuracy' meant the exclusion of all material irrelevant to the inquiry's central thesis" (5). Platonic mimesis moves toward Aristotelian verisimilitude, wherein historical truth is linked to unity, to a planned arrangement of the materials. The randomness of Herodotus's model is replaced by a concern for internal unity, and unity implies interpretation and mediation. One may view these dichotomies historically, and they clearly play a role in commentaries on realism in the novel. Early nineteenth-century realism places the narrating subject, rather than literary precedent and the outside world, at the core of artistic invention. With Gustave Flaubert and the *style indirect libre*, "the readily indentifiable position of the narrator began to disappear, creating the sustained impression of a multicentered text that worked from the inside against the apparent priorities of its own characters" (Lucente 15). Flaubert combined objectivity with irony, which, for Lucente, disrupts the contact with the world. The elimination of conscious irony allows Émile Zola to pursue a program of naturalism dependent on objective observation and scientific determinism. Although naturalism sanctions the seemingly random accumulation of data to study humanity in specific social settings, Zola qualifies the ends of objectivity. Still, the method develops means to approximate reality, and "[t]ruth [is]conceived of as residing in the immediate perception of the world" (Lucente 20).[17] The variations on the theme of history and the range of options within realism and naturalism can aid in approaching Unamuno's narrative through questions of genre.

In *Don Quijote*, Cervantes makes poetry into history, or vice versa. The clash of the objective and the subjective negates mutual exclusion. Because irony is inscribed into the text from the opening words, history may seem to be part of a satirical game, but it does not appear likely that Cervantes is ridiculing history as much as challenging the objectivity and unmediated quality of historiography. The same applies, more emphatically, to truth, in a victory of the relative over the absolute. *Don Quijote* is analogical and metonymical, and all the more effective because its excursions into the spheres of theory, abstract thought, and human nature, broadly defined, are tempered with humor. Chapters 1 through 8 of the 1605 *Quijote*, and, arguably, much more of the two parts, could be said to pay homage to Herodotus, as described by Lucente: "The result... is a collection of moral anecdotes... and *faits divers*, many of which make fine short stories, but none of which is ordered in accordance with an overriding organic unity" (5). There is, nonetheless, at least a nominal attempt to clear the imperfections of Part 1 in Part 2, and with the goal of greater unity comes an affirmation—or partial affirmation—of the guiding principles of Thucydides. In light of the later development

---

[17] The opening chapter of Lucente's book offers a comprehensive view of mimesis and verisimilitude. His reading of Zola through Compte (along with Vico and Hegel) is enlightening. See esp. 16-21. I cannot do justice here to the richness of the first chapter and to the readings of individual authors.

of narrative, it is useful to consider Cervantes's decision to divide the narrative duties, while incorporating an author figure, and a team of surrogate authors and narrators into the text. Unity is both a given (the chivalric quest, reading put into practice, the pre-announced death) and a cause for frustration (the supplementary material and changes in direction, literal and figurative). Cervantes seems to be experimenting as he moves forward, with a general diagram that permits him a great deal of flexibility. The unexpected appearance of the Avellaneda sequel causes him, along with his protagonist, to take alternate routes.

Don Quijote refuses to believe that he is creating fictions, or to comprehend that he is a character within a fiction. The very fact that fictional characters engage in discussions of history calls attention to the crossing of boundaries. Like Shakespeare in *Hamlet*, Cervantes uses metatheater to establish levels of fiction, which, to a degree, makes some characters more "real" than others, as if to imply that poetry cannot be dissociated from history. In the discussion in I, 32, the innkeeper Juan Palomeque debates the merits of the romances of chivalry versus historical books. He finds the former far more compelling than the latter, and he argues that the Royal Council would not have approved the romances if they had contained lies. The priest Pero Pérez attempts to explain that the parameters of fiction allow for fabrication, more as invention than falsehood, but Palomeque insists that chivalric romance is yesterday's history. The statement baffles Sancho Panza, who believes that he and his master are living chivalry in the present, but it shows Cervantes's nuanced vision of the relation between history and poetry. The dispute also serves as an introduction to *El curioso impertinente* and the captive's tale, both of which fall clearly into one category (poetry and history, respectively), but by no means eliminate the other. *El curioso impertinente* ends with a reference to Gonzalo Fernández de Córdoba, used by the priest to exemplify historical narrative, and the captive's tale is, in part, a fictionalization of Cervantes's captivity in Algiers. The modes of delivery—the reading aloud of a manuscript and the oral performance—stress the distinctions and the points of contact between writing and speech.

Unamuno brings the cross of history and poetry into *Niebla* by abstracting the first and reformatting the second.[18] Don Miguel de Unamuno and the city of Salamanca take Augusto Pérez into an identifiable reality as the narrative situates them in the fiction. History here is not so much a moment in time as a state of mind. There are temporal coordinates, but they summon scientific advancements, fin de siècle polemics, social issues, and literary history. Following the lead of Cervantes, Unamuno blurs the line between reality and fiction, but his method bespeaks a different age and a different personal sensibility. He sees the development from the regional novel to the spectrum of realism and naturalism. The narratives of Galdós alone encompass the thesis novel, a range of realistic novels, naturalism, and a late recourse to what has been called idealism (in *Misericordia*, for example); *El amigo Manso* offers evidence of his metafictional impulse. Unamuno's creative power—his anxiety of influence—demands a move away from these models to new forms of fiction, but both the intertext and the measure of metafiction remain firmly in the mix that produces *Niebla* and the other narratives. The *nivola* seems to shy away from data and details. It cannot be called a socio-cultural document with a plot and solid characterization, as can many a realist novel. The structure is dissimilar because its canvas and its palette, to use art imagery, are dissimilar. The Cervantine paradox of reality without realism pervades the design of the *nivola*, and *Niebla* seems constantly to look for rules to break. Gregory Lucente maintains that "[t]he direct visual experience of the material world plays a large part in Zola's characteristic metaphor of the human environment as a scientific laboratory. The artist thus presents himself as an objective observer/reporter rather than as a subjective creator" (20). *Amor y pedagogía* and

---

[18] Cf. Longhurst on Unamuno's concept of the novel: "La novela no es comparable con el libro de historia porque no tiene ningún referente externo. En esto apreciamos claramente la actitud antipositivista y antinaturalista de Unamuno. La novela comienza siendo la manifestación de una conciencia, y esta conciencia se revela en el acto de la escritura.... Al verter su conciencia el artista se descubre a sí mismo, se ve objetivado en las páginas de su libro, en su espejo, aunque aquí observamos cómo Unamuno utiliza un vocablo tradicional con una acepción bien distinta.... Esa conciencia del mundo no tiene un sentido previo sino que adquiere sentido mediante el acto de lectura. El lector es depositario de las convenciones de la lectura; pero el escritor crea nuevas convenciones de leer" (150).

Niebla include laboratory experiments, but their science is psychology, and the experimentation ends in failure. Unamuno the social scientist is every bit the subjective creator, and it is authorial subjectivity that dominates the *nivola*.

Lazarillo de Tormes establishes a paradigm for the novel in progress: the narrative form that it helps to bring into being and the narrative purportedly written by Lázaro de Tormes. The anonymity of the text allows Lázaro to operate under the rubric of author, narrator, and protagonist. One cannot help but be struck by the defensive posture of the speaker and the judicial-like process that his response to Vuestra Merced would seem to evoke. The story and the making of the story are equally significant and interdependent, and the levels of irony and satire involve the reader in a process that is imaginative, judgmental, and collaborative. In *Don Quijote*, Cervantes expands on this pattern by multiplying the narrators and the points of view. By making the process of composition more prominent and more problematic, he amplifies the role and the responsibilities of the reader. Unamuno casts himself alongside Augusto Pérez as the protagonist of *Niebla* and thereby fuses history with poetry. The prologue is not about the writing of a prologue but about Unamuno's character and the oddities of his personality. The connection to the narrative proper is his assessment of Augusto's death. By entrusting the prologue to Víctor Goti, Unamuno begins with the intersection of the historical author and his fictional alter ego. Each is a *nivolista*, each has a stake in the interpretation of Augusto Pérez's death, and each has a theory concerning the enigmatic death of the protagonist. The prologue deals with the real Unamuno, while exaggerating its fictional status. Víctor Goti speaks of the skepticism of Hamlet, in a discourse that has ties with Don Quijote's commentary on the madness of Amadís de Gaula (I, 25), as he considers the fate of Augusto and the quirks of Don Miguel. Unamuno draws no dividing lines between the prologue (and post-prologue) and the rest of the text. They are bound by fiction and by its unyielding, if precarious, grip on reality. The correlation of Víctor Goti the writer with Unamuno the author does not emerge in medias res; it is the first narrative thread, the first discursive event.

Niebla depends on a curious shattering of expectations that turns into expected differences. Unamuno is doing to realism something on the order of what Cervantes does to chivalric romance and idealistic narrative in general. There is little subtlety in the pronouncement of the "friend" in the prologue to Part 1 of *Don Quijote* that the objective of the book (or, at that point, manuscript) is to destroy the ill-founded machinery of the vile tomes. The reader may recognize not only the deferred statement of purpose—attributed to the alter ego of the author's alter ego—but the fact that the text veers considerably from its announced intention. (*Lazarillo de Tormes*, likewise, is more, and less, than the explanation of the "case.") Unamuno seems to have taken into account the complex and ironic rhetoric of the first *Quijote* prologue, with its division of labor and call for a break from the past, and also the personalization or subjectivity of the second prologue, in which the speaker becomes the real Cervantes. The 1615 prologue announces the death of the knight errant, so that the author may comply with the exigencies of his own honor and reputation; he wants to eliminate the possibility of further continuations. The novel ends, however, with the disillusionment, remorse, and Christian death, preceded by ominous signs, of Alonso Quijano el Bueno. Unamuno's prologue and post-prologue proclaim the death of Augusto Pérez in two registers, one that would have Unamuno kill off the *ente de ficción* over whom he has control, and another that would rule the death a suicide caused by overeating. The duality in both narratives prohibits, or certainly complicates, closure. At the heart of the *Quijote* and *Niebla* prologues is a synthesis, notably awkward, of poetics and pragmatics. The author is an artist and a citizen, a style setter and a subject of public taste. He must seek and satisfy constituents, and he must be true to himself. His presence in the narrative makes that dilemma known and enduring.

In *Amor y pedagogía*, Unamuno seems preoccupied with the demands of publishers regarding the length of a manuscript, as if content and concept were secondary matters. He casts himself not only as a public figure but as an aesthete vexed by mundane details that may compromise his creative energy. In *Niebla*, the self-portrait is of a confident writer and intellectual, whose eccentricities may bother some but who thrives on polemics. Much of his confidence derives, paradoxically, from having publicized his insecurities and crises. Thinkers are, by nature, *agonistas*, and suffering is, at the same time, a factor of the human condition and a means by which to acquire knowledge (and self-knowledge).[19] One might

---

[19] For Roberta Johnson, "*Niebla* is a novel about the acquisition of knowledge. In fact, knowing is ubiquitous and absurd; everyone knows everyone else

submit that, pun intended, he lords his position over the fictional creatures that he claims to have invented, but he also places himself on their level, or raises them to his. The playfulness of *Niebla* is counterbalanced on every front by philosophical-theological subtexts, themselves informed by advances in the science of psychology. Unamuno wants to transfer his world view to the novel. Although he can be part of a collaborative effort in the move from realism and naturalism, he is obviously proud of his unique vision and of his reputation as an independent thinker. It is not by chance that Unamuno is the ultimate subject of many of his works, and some might argue that he makes himself the universal signified. He is, nonetheless, attuned to the tradition from which he is deviating. He alludes to the realist novel with some frequency, and *Paz en la guerra* shows him at a major point of transition.[20] The background of his first novel is a well-defined time and place; the historical, or ideological, moment inspires the action and affects the storytelling. The later style mixes a vagueness of locale—a subordination of the temporal and the geographic—with a conceptual sharpness.

Unamuno's *nivola* has been associated with literary modernism, so that the deep-seated individualism of the author must be weighed against his participation in the modernist agenda and its multiple manifestations.

(Eugenia's aunt knew Augusto's mother; Liduvina knows Eugenia; Mauricio knows Rosario), except for Augusto, who does not know any of them.... [K]nowledge was a topic Unamuno intended to take up in his philosophical treatise 'Filosofía lógica,' but he was unable to develop it at that time. Unamuno returned to epistemology in *Del sentimiento trágico de la vida*, and *Niebla* essentially embodies in a complex dialogic manner the ideas he tendered on the subject in that essay" (*Crossfire* 96).

[20] Nicholas Round believes that *Paz en la guerra* "is turned decisively away from realism of causal processes because an account of the world in terms of dialectical processes seemed to Unamuno to be inherently more truthful" (113). He continues, "Yet it cannot... fairly be seen as a work of philosophic abstraction in some grandly Hegelian manner. It is too substantial a fiction for that. It exists, rather, in the middle ground—the place where abstract thought and concrete experience meet: its personality, its pursuit of identity, its quest for solidarity. We might speak, perhaps, of the novel's 'dialectical humanism'.... *Paz en la guerra*... moves beyond the genre altogether, in that it has a self-referring aspect, characteristic of post-realist fictions. At the same time, its roots within realism are deep and sustaining" (115-16).

Discussions of modernism are, of course, inflected and redirected by postmodernism, in much the same way that the development of the novel from the eighteenth century onward intrudes, if productively, on considerations of *Don Quijote*. The ongoing dialogue on modernism is useful, even when general descriptions fail to serve a given author or text. In *The Idea of Modernity*, Matei Calinescu analyzes the relation between modernity and secularism in order to demonstrate that "the death of God" may be applied too hastily. Taking his lead from Octavio Paz, Calinescu argues that "the separation between modernity and Christianity… turns out to be an illusion if we think that a large number of the most prominent authors whom we label as 'modern' either are incomprehensible outside the Judeo-Christian tradition (which they continue to represent, no matter how deviantly), or practice a passionate atheism about whose religious inspiration and motives there is little doubt" (62). He concludes that "modernity, even if it attempted to do so, did not succeed in suppressing man's religious need and imagination, and… it may even have intensified them in the guise of an untold flourishing of heterodoxies—in religion proper, in morals, in social and political thinking, and in aesthetics" (63). Analogous to the Spanish writers who embraced naturalism and integrated its tenets with Catholic doctrine, Unamuno questions theology from the perspective of a man desperate to cling to his faith. The tide of skepticism in an industrial and scientific age, the political tensions within his country, and the intense search for answers to life's mysteries distress and invigorate him. He is never *menos que todo un católico*, but—as a writer of fiction and as a philosopher, often united—he relates best to other tormented souls.

William D. Melaney refers to "the modernist assault on the classical equation, which positioned the artist as a detached spectator vis-à-vis the scene encountered" and to "the emergence of a new literature that ceased to employ cultural signs as representations of a long-standing equilibrium" between art and the world (5).[21] These are aspects of modernism

---

[21] Cf. Foucault: "*Don Quixote* is the first modern work of literature, because in it we see the cruel reason of identities and differences make endless sport of signs and similitudes; because in it language breaks off its old kinship with things and enters into that lonely sovereignty from which it will reappear, in its separated state, only as literature; because it marks the point where resemblance enters an age which is, from the point of view of resemblance, one of madness

that fit Unamuno's modus operandi: the glaring centrality of the author, the construction of the art object as a substitute for action (or as a form of action), the search for new varieties of signifiers, the fragmented picture of the universe, and so forth. Focusing on modernism and what he calls the crisis in aesthetics, Melaney proposes that "the new art might derive from the ontological stance that originated in seventeenth-century rationalism. The philosophy of Descartes is a... tribute to the clarification of method that adopts the *ego cogito* as the only legitimate basis for scientific thought. Descartes... provides basic clues concerning the importance of *the subject* as a modern category" (3). The Cartesian underpinnings of *Niebla*, which lead to Augusto Pérez's cry of "*Edo, ergo sum*" as he reaches the end of the line and to Orfeo's ontological meditations in the funeral oration, acknowledge, first, the writer's debt to a system of thought and, second, a transposition based on his own yearnings and quest for knowledge.[22] Unamuno gains momentum through the guideposts of the past, while he manages to move forward—toward poststructuralism—through staged contests between similitude and difference. The combatants come from institutions and from a self-consciously amorphous other; they cover literary history, social practice, religious dogma, and the individual will. Unamuno battles

---

and imagination" (*Order* 48-49).

[22] For a discussion of the influence of Descartes on Unamuno, see Livingstone 103 ff. and Johnson, *Crossfire* 94 ff. Roberta Johnson believes that "[u]nlike his methodology in *Amor y pedagogía*, in which opposing character pairs carry the satirical message, Unamuno abandoned Hegelian dialectics altogether in *Niebla* to offer a more complicated design in which the Cartesian rationalist Augusto (whose namesake St. Augustine, like Descartes, had faith in the individual soul's knowledge of God) encounters a number of alternatives" (97). See 102-04 for Johnson's discussion of the influence of Kierkegaard on *Niebla*; see also Webber, Stern 29-45, and Nozick esp. 49-52 and 147-49. In an essay entitled "Hunger and Desire: The Origins of Knowledge in *Niebla*," incorporated into ch. 5 of *Crossfire*, Johnson demonstrates Unamuno's awareness of *Orígenes del conocimiento: El hambre*, by his friend the "Catalan biologist-philosopher Ramón Turró.... As the title of his book indicates, Turró posits the origins of knowledge in the trophic system. In stating that we know the world exists because we ingest it in the form of food, he achieves the enviable feat of centering the origins of knowledge within the individual while simultaneously confirming the existence of the physical, material world" ("Hunger and Desire" 93).

and internalizes forces from the outside, and he competes against himself. He sets forth a new literary form that, like *Don Quijote*, maneuvers time and space in extraordinary ways.

There is a political dimension to modernism, including a reaction to capitalism. The ideology of *Niebla* may be more existential and aesthetic than political, but Unamuno's public stand on many issues was strong enough to bring about his exile in 1924. In *The Concept of Modernism*, Astradur Eysteinsson notes the contradictions inherent in Georg Lukács's approach to modernism, while contending that "his contradictions are illuminating. They illustrate how the historical conception of a modernist paradigm can (and has tended to) vacillate between mimetic notions of a modern 'chaos' reflected in one way or another by modernist works and an understanding of modernism as a chaotic subversion of the communicative and semiotic norms of society" (24). When he uses Franz Kafka as an example, Lukács "claims that modernists reduce social reality to nightmare and portray it as an angst-ridden, absurd world, thus depriving us of any sense of perspective," whereas Lukács himself believes that "literature must have a clear social-human concept of the 'normal,' and this is precisely what modernism denounces" (Eysteinsson 25). Citing another "insightful paradox" of Lukács, Eysteinsson writes, "While he finds modernism to have severed the essential ties between subjective experience and objective reality, he still sees in its portrayal of the human character an *aggressive* social (that is *antisocial*) attitude, which he and several other critics have judged to betoken a crisis of humanism" (29). The terms in this and many commentaries on modernism justify Eysteinsson's concern with the contradictory nature of the label and the enterprise that it describes. One could certainly defend the position that Unamuno depicts himself in a manner that could be categorized as antisocial, but, not surprisingly, the description would have to be qualified in light of both the creation of a public persona and the contradictions that form his principal rhetorical tool.

Unamuno's devotion to Spain—more than anything, to its pervasive essence, its *intrahistoria*—is attached to his writing in general. *Niebla* is more manifestly a response to a literary genre, which he could modify according to his own standards and in line with his agenda. If the point of departure is an alternative to narrative realism, the text also treats love, class, social custom, academic scholarship, and, through the concept of theoretical anarchy, politics. Moreover, the central question in *Niebla* is

the central question in the Unamunian corpus: immortality, as synthe-
sized in theology, philosophy, and literature. The markers of difference,
then, relate as much, or more, to the execution than to the themes
themselves. Unamuno does not pay homage to Calderón in the way that
he does to Cervantes, but he finds earthly metaphors (and metonyms) for
eternity. Like *La vida es sueño*, for example, *Niebla* explores multiple points
of view and aligns the *theatrum mundi* with higher orders. It is Cervantes,
however, who flouts the division of history and poetry and who
reconceives reality by placing it at the service of art. He rejects narrative
idealism, but he compromises incipient realism by framing it in
metafiction. Unamuno similarly sees creative invention as a composite
of art and life and as a highly intellectual pursuit. His means of
demystifying objective reality joins aesthetics and spirituality. If he can
live on as an artist, he can hope to extend the analogy, or the metaphor,
to a higher plane. Writing himself into the text, he necessarily appends
what José Ortega y Gasset denominates his "circunstancias" to the
construct. In analyzing modernism through a critique of Patricia Waugh's
Metafiction, Eysteinsson states, "The issue of self-consciousness is pivotal,
since... it relates to the very possibility of becoming aware of the social
process of operating communication and generating meaning" (112).
Niebla reflects Unamuno's self and circumstances, which refer to Spain
in the early twentieth century, as well.

In *Mapping Literary Modernism*, Ricardo J. Quinones submits that
"[t]he Renaissance discovery of time carried with it a complex of values
that could be called historical. More faith came to be placed in those
earthly things that promised continuity: the polis, marriage, family,
children, and fame. These were redemptive counters, significant
achievements in man's need to rescue himself from nothingness" (30).
Alluding to Shakespeare's Henry IV and James Joyce's Stephen Dedalus,
he writes, "When we come to the first stirrings of Modernism, it is clear
that something has happened to this code. History, once redemptive in
its processes for Hal, has for Stephen Dedalus become nightmarish" (30-
31). This period in Spanish history encourages Unamuno to reevaluate
the past. When this critical revisionism is coupled with his inclination—anticipating poststructuralism—to invert the priorities in traditional
dichotomies, Unamuno favors the small events that collectively comprise
the Spanish nation and its people. His view is more nostalgic, even
idealistic, than nightmarish, and his personal philosophy and self-

confidence allow for a selective and flexible vision of history that wavers between a hard-line assessment of problems and a romanticized reconstruction of earlier times, that is, between realism and a kind of neo-idealism. History, for (and in) Unamuno, is always, in a sense, relegated to the margins, because chronology and progression cannot vie with an eternal transcendence of time. *Don Quijote* presents history as incomplete, in a perpetual state of rediscovery. Ironically, Don Quijote, grounded on earth, becomes immortal, while Alonso Quijano el Bueno, the good Christian, merely disappears from the picture. Calderón's Segismundo, in contrast, sacrifices pleasure in this life for heavenly rewards. Unamuno takes no chances. He seeks heaven on earth as a step toward—and confirmation of—the glory to come.

Niebla may be, then, an allegory of Unamuno's desire to validate—and, ironically, to rationalize—his faith. The literary and critical frame places attention on poetics. The mystery of Augusto Pérez's death is a diversionary tactic, and doubly so, but death is a unifying element at every level, literal and figurative, of the story. The matter of the protagonist's fate has an impact on each of these levels. Unamuno may argue against Augusto, but his own destiny and the limits of free will stand in the balance. As metafiction, *Niebla* foregrounds issues of authority and control from the vantage points of the writer and the character, but the structure is rarely self-contained. Rather, it seems to beg for symbolic transferal, through a type of spiritual overlap that becomes a given in Unamuno's writing. *Niebla* has a three-dimensional design, based on the interaction of literature, society, and theology. This structural depth appears to be far removed from a tenet of modernism. Peter Nicholls, in *Modernisms: A Literary Guide*, notes that for a writer such as Charles Baudelaire, who "had only contempt for the culture of his day, it was... crucial that art be in no sense 'useful'. Théophile Gautier, one of his mentors and an early proponent of the 'art for art's sake' doctrine, had already provided the essential formulation in the preface to his novel *Mademoiselle de Maupin* (1835)" (8-9). The opening passages of *Niebla*, featuring Augusto Pérez's pronouncements on umbrellas and oranges, seem to echo Gautier's harsher, if poetically inspired, commentary: "Nothing beautiful is indispensable to life.... Nothing is really beautiful unless it is useless; everything useful is ugly, for it expresses a need, and the needs of man are ignoble and disgusting, like his poor weak nature. The most useful place in a house is the lavatory" (qtd. in Nicholl 9).

Augusto is both an exemplar and a send-up of exaggerated artfulness, a fictional entity who may enjoy the luxury of pure abstraction denied to his creator. The chapter of *Modernisms* quoted here is titled "Ironies of the Modern," and one of the ironies—which Unamuno seems to recognize—is that art cannot exist in a vacuum.

The place of language in this broad (and ironic) system is a complex topic, but modernism differentiates here, as in other contexts, between the imaginative and the purely functional. Michael Bell, in an essay on "The Metaphysics of Modernism," writes, "The pervasive concern with the construction of meaning helps explain the emphasis in all the modernist arts on the nature of their own medium, and in the case of . literature this means, as well as literary genres and forms, language itself. Furthermore, by the early teens of the century, there had occurred what has come to be known as the linguistic 'turn'[23]: rather than describing or reflecting the world, language was now seen to form it" (16). The statement relates to modernism as a whole, but naturally its manifestations vary according to genre and to individual styles and priorities. Unamuno heightens the complexity by devising a plan based on analogical and hierarchical relations. As a God-like figure, he creates a world unto itself, whose inhabitants are subject to his decisions and whims.[24] As an allegorist, he is reliant on a preexisting edifice, where he is subject to the decisions and whims of another, more powerful creator. He is caught in a conceptual trap, which he seems to take as a positive sign. The making of the *nivola* offers a new word for a novel undertaking. Characters are preoccupied with language. Augusto Pérez, for example, is baffled by the lack of coordination between the name Eugenia and the

---

[23] Paul Olson uses the term as a point of departure for his study of *Amor y pedagogía.*

[24] Jaime Alazraki comments, "Puesto que la existencia de Dios es indemostrable a través de ningún razonamiento, buscará Unamuno, en cambio, vivir el problema, vivirlo con una intensidad desacostumbrada, sentirlo y hacérnoslo sentir hasta colocarnos frente a la muerte y reducir al absurdo la posibilidad de la nada" (247). He observes that "la creación del binomio autor-personaje de ficción le permite a Unamuno reproducir aquel otro primer binomio—Dios-hombre—y mostrar en aquél lo que no hubiera podido hacer en éste. La incógnita insoluble en el binomio Dios-hombre se resuelve en el binomio autor-personaje de ficción" (248).

surname Domingo, Don Fermín is a devotee of Esperanto, and, as Víctor Goti mentions in the prologue, Unamuno is peevish about orthography and punctuation, fixated on generic labels, and inclined toward an "adusto y áspero humorismo confusionista" (102). Moreover, Augusto and Don Miguel take refuge in *monodiálogos* and mental flights of fancy that cast them into worlds of their own.

There is an obvious poeticism, or literariness, to *Niebla*, but the disciplines from which Unamuno borrows ideas and lexicons—philosophy, the sciences, and religion, to name but three—help to give shape and a special idiolect to his narrative. Although Augusto Pérez has a background, a family history, his appearance at the doorway of his house and the initiation of a fresh and purposeful adventure marks a rebirth of sorts. Like Don Quijote, who reimagines the events on his journey as mediated by chivalry, Augusto turns quotidian reality into intellectual exercises in which the abstract overshadows the concrete. He is in his own world, the master of his imagination, even if a pawn of other characters (including Eugenia and Mauricio) and of Unamuno, if the reader is to trust the author's fictionalized counterpart. Whether Augusto establishes the parameters or whether they are established for him, the result is a unique, and uniquely literary, universe. Augusto's thoughts and interventions in the dialogue form the discursive center of *Niebla*. He projects his image of the world onto the text. Although he is immersed in thought and oblivious to much of what is happening around him, he can be self-critical; he knows that he is the guinea pig of his psychological experiment, that the women involved are monitoring him. Víctor Goti the writer is weaving a story that resembles that of his friend, and it is he who first hints of self-destruction, although he will later argue against the death as a suicide. The ambiguity of the demise of the protagonist duplicates the indecisiveness and inner turmoil of Augusto Pérez, itself a mirror of Unamuno's existential anguish. In this regard, the debate in chapter 31 epitomizes the Unamunian mindset, in which every theory has an opposing theory and every argument a counterargument, and in which fiction and reality know no boundaries.

The self-consciousness of *Niebla* and Unamuno harkens back to picaresque narrative and *Don Quijote* and forward to postmodernism. It falls within the broad and varied modernist project, but, like Federico García Lorca, Unamuno is more influential than imitated. Cervantes and Velázquez depict the artist in the work, and at work, as a means of exalting the creative enterprise. Accentuating the burden of production, the art object features the performer, the performance, and tradition (books and paintings). Fiction and reality meet and occupy each other's space. The early modern artists are symbolic, as emblems and as metonyms; they represent the producer of art, and they fashion a place for the consumer. Unamuno personalizes the role of the creator. On either end of the continuum, whether from history to fiction or vice versa, he evokes himself. There is a microcosm (the work of art), but its relation to the macrocosm (the world at large, including the spiritual realm) is not so much a move upward as a process of equalization, or rendering of equivalence. Writing becomes an intricate and arduous game, because behind the comic façade the stakes are high. Beyond the act of egotism — the insistence on Unamuno as puppeteer and actor — there lies life's greatest mystery, with eternal bliss, damnation, and nothingness as the options. Cervantes asks readers to think about history and historiography, fictional genres, forms of discourse, social institutions, and perspective. Unamuno asks them to reflect on literature and mortality. His faith is an anchor in a world in which anchors are in short supply and will become practically nonexistent.

Niebla mixes poetics with metaphysics, science, and theology. In the prologue, Víctor Goti remarks that Augusto Pérez "llegó hasta a dudar de su propia existencia," and he adds that "estoy por lo menos firmemente persuadido de que carezco de eso que los psicólogos llaman libre albedrío, aunque para mi consuelo creo también que tampoco goza don Miguel de él" (97). That Víctor situates Unamuno with the fictional entities is noteworthy. That he situates free will with psychology is also noteworthy, a sign of the blending of associative fields. Víctor Goti and Augusto Pérez stand, ironically, between Hamlet and Miguel de Unamuno, somehow more real than Shakespeare's character and less real than the author, on one level, and equally "real," on another. The *nivola* form and the shared, or contested, authorship call to mind the act of creation, not from a void but from a rich and diverse intertext that is literary, socio-political, philosophical, and theological. Augusto Pérez may be an *ente de ficción*, but his fears and insecurities are moving, and that could be because they were inscribed by a master of the art of self-reflection and angst. By removing his protagonist from the real world — but not entirely — Unamuno can maneuver his own entry into the realm of fiction, without straying from his office in Salamanca. Uncertainty becomes the essence of both; it is a character builder, in more than one sense, and it is the basis of the dual quest: for the comfort of a recognizable identity for Augusto and for the prospect of eternal life for Unamuno. For the latter, the lack of proof is excruciating and inspirational, a defining agent in itself. The recent prize-winning play *Doubt*, by John Patrick Shanley, opens with a priest delivering a sermon in which he speaks of crises of faith and declares, "Doubt can be a bond as powerful and sustaining as certainty" (6). This would seem to be Unamuno's message, and motivation, as well, given that when he obscures the distinctions between life and art he converts questions of faith into aesthetic objects.[25] Writing provides a means of communication with his readership and with himself, an intimacy made public and made to conform with—or, more often, to break—the rules of art.

The fusion of reality and fiction within *Niebla* corresponds to Unamuno's bringing together of literary form (the objectives and recourses of the novel) and existential concerns, notably his own.[26] Víctor Goti is the author's alter ego, spokesman for the theory of the *nivola*, and the protagonist's dialogue partner. Augusto Pérez is a guinea pig not only in the psychological experiment that turns him from subject to object, but in the experiment in which Unamuno explores and attempts to glimpse a higher order. Unamuno seems aware of the double plot, and double bind, for on one plane he is the God of the work, in charge of Augusto's fate, and on another Augusto is his stand-in, and, like him, a pawn in a scheme beyond his control. The balance between the seriousness and humor,[27] and between the metafiction and metaphysics, of the text is

---

[25] Eva Núñez emphasizes the element of uncertainty in "Criatura y creador en *Niebla*." She concludes that Unamuno works toward leaving the text open, caught in the nebulous region of doubt.

[26] For Morón Arroyo, "*Niebla* trata el problema más radical de la persona humana: ser o no ser, estructurada conforme a los elementos de la filosofía clásica, anterior al *existencialismo*. Estos elementos eran esencia *(quod est)*, existencia *(esse)*, hombre *(ens)*" (*Hacia el sistema* 85).

[27] On humor in *Niebla*, see Franz ("El sentido de humor"). Franz argues, "El efecto total de este abundante sentimiento humorístico en *Niebla* es el de señalar el abyecto castigo a los esfuerzos racionales del hombre por encontrar significación a su vida, esfuerzos e intentos que son invariablemente cómicos dada la absurda discrepancia existente entre la medida o magnitud de la empresa y la debilidad o anemia de los recursos del hombre" (7).

nothing short of sublime. Unamuno knows the classics, he is obsessed with *Don Quijote,* and he is attuned to the aims of realism. In *Amor y pedagogía* and *Niebla,* he hits upon a means of addressing the literary climate of his time and of offering a model of his own. Cervantes shows him the value of metanarrative, which coincides with his own tendency to write himself into the frame of his fictions (and, of course, his nonfiction). *Niebla* may be a rare form of entertainment, but it is profoundly entertaining, constantly pointing inward and outward, in a lesson learned from Cervantes. Its richness can best be observed, appropriately, from an ironic distance.

In the introduction to *The Birth of Modernism,* Leon Surette suggests that modernism "presented itself as the end of historical writing. It would be difficult to find any modernist flatly expressing such a claim, but the claim is implicit in the... modernist principle of the autonomy of the work of art, which has been deployed within literary scholarship to liberate the work of art from the tyranny of authorial intention and hence from the cult of personality" (3). The statement may serve to show that Unamuno walks a modernist tightrope in the matter of history. With respect to the "cult of personality," he seeks no liberation whatsoever. For John Macklin, "*Niebla* occupies a place among those Modernist novels which reject stable systems of thought, discard reason and embrace indeterminacy, construct complex imaginary worlds competing for supremacy, enter into dialogue both with themselves and with the whole system of literature which is available for appropriation, rivalry and parody, and exploit the openness and novel-ty which provide the dynamics of the genre" (189). Literary history and the history of thought prevail. Demetrios Basdekis sees *Niebla* as a "decisive farewell to nineteenth-century aesthetics,... a definitive answer to the mechanical 'professionalism' which had infected European realism during the closing decade of the nineteenth century. As an answer to the biological and environmental determinism which frequently dictated the personalities created by the realism in vogue, Unamuno... created personalities who were independent of their milieu as well as of their author" (57-58). Perhaps the operative term here should be *interdependence* rather than *independence,* for Augusto Pérez and Miguel de Unamuno seem to be in each other's pocket. The generic deviations, and innovations, and the plot of *Niebla* depend on the intersection of reality and fiction, process and product, aesthetics and idea, and, certainly, creator and creation. Augusto may wish to free himself from Unamuno, but, no matter how tempting and clever the notion may appear, the author's vision would appear to preclude that option.

In *Unamuno's Webs of Fatality*, David Turner contends that "[t]he ultimate truth is that the Author-God controls Augusto and has him at his mercy.... Unamuno tries to evade this conclusion by searching for an element of substantial reality in his fictional characters, and, by extension, in himself, especially by making Víctor and Augusto argue with their Creator, but this is a trick applicable only to fiction and not to life" (59). Turner sees the chance events from which Augusto derives his self-awareness as "governed by the Author-God who... indirectly controls the character's formation," but only indirectly, because, "while the Author-God can kill him at will, the methods by which he can do so seem to be limited. Here is an element of autonomy for the individual, slender indeed, but nevertheless real, just as the possibility of living on in the Author's mind is real. The same possibilities exist for Unamuno if his world is in the same relationship to God as Augusto's is to him" (61). Unamuno clearly seems to recognize and play with the analogy, both for similitude and difference, but his concern may be less with the character staying on his mind than with guaranteeing him an identity beyond death. This forms part of the paradoxes of *Niebla*. Unamuno counts on Augusto Pérez to keep his memory alive after death, as Don Quijote has kept Cervantes alive, and God counts on adherents to maintain the faith, to acknowledge the existence of a supreme deity. As Gabriel Berns describes it, "Unamuno must depend on his readers for his total being, and Augusto Pérez, his antagonist that day in Salamanca, is among this group. As such, he is a possible creator of his Creator and not merely a puppet at the mercy of his puppeteer" (29).[28] In *Uncovering the Mind*, Alison Sinclair points to the importance in chapter 31 of Augusto's

---

[28] In "*Niebla* and the Varieties of Religious Experience," Thomas Franz argues the case from a somewhat different angle: "If everyone in life, as in this novel, both fictionalizes everyone else and is a character in everyone else's fiction, then existence can be prolonged indefinitely and even death can be made into life in countless readers' interiorizations of the ongoing 'novel.' In this novel God is continually created by all men who need him, and they in turn see their lives in a more bearable state once they believe that He is creating the means to overcome death" (103-04).

presence in the study in Salamanca, where he speaks with the author and observes the portrait that is hung over Unamuno's books. Augusto challenges Unamuno's defense of his superiority and "literally *takes back his personality,*" seeking "to threaten Unamuno himself, and to turn the tables upon him and to suggest that he, Unamuno, may be the adjunct, not the principal, in the drama." Whatever the outcome of the debate, "Augusto cannot help being pivotal in provoking that conflict-ridden, irresoluble situation in which Unamuno is told that he has an identity *not because he has created something, but because he cannot destroy it*" (Sinclair, *Uncovering* 121). But, of course, the result is the same, because Unamuno wants and needs Augusto Pérez to create him.

Francisco La Rubia Prado views the lead character's demise as a victory, since "la experiencia de Augusto Pérez lo lleva no sólo a la construcción de su propia subjetividad, sino también a su acto final de voluntad, de no querer ser, que es el suicidio, acto que reafirma la autenticidad de haber llegado a ser quien realmente es" (*Alegorías* 198).[29] Although he stresses the ambiguity of *Niebla* by focusing on the calculated struggle between organicist and mechanistic principles, La Rubia Prado may not give sufficient weight to the dual nature of the ending. Augusto leaves Salamanca resigned to die, but wanting to live, and his death is not universally ruled a suicide. Gayana Jurkevich places the question of authority and the inconclusiveness of the ending in a different frame: "By 'reinventing' the novel, Unamuno... gains the artistic freedom to manipulate the customary reader/author relationship. At the same time that Unamuno uses the reader's willing suspension of disbelief to lull him into accepting Augusto's viability as a self-determining entity, he ends the 'novel' by violating the very literary convention he had initially espoused," thus assaulting "the reader's ontological complacency" (*Elusive Self* 82-83). Jurkevich captures the generic shift and the dialectics of *Niebla*, but, in light of the overt ironies of the narrative, it is hard to imagine a reader convinced by the proposition of Augusto Pérez's autonomy.[30] Substituting the work itself for the protagonist, Gonzalo

---

[29] La Rubia Prado expands upon the ideas presented here in "Deconstrucción."

[30] Cf. Juan Villegas, who affirms that "la estructura de *Niebla* tiene como elemento organizador a la ruta que el protagonista tantea y vive en su esfuerzo

Navajas sees writing as an extension, or what poststructuralism would call a supplement, of Unamuno's subjectivity. Something is gained and something is lost, since "la obra tiende a independizarse y separarse del autor, de modo que las partes del yo del autor que han quedado extendidas en el texto se pierden en el espacio incontrolable de lo otro" (Navajas 77).[31] The text becomes, figuratively, a son that a father has sired and educated, only to lose control over him, and for Navajas, the "paternofilial" metaphor serves to concretize "esta ambivalencia irresoluta" (77).

Pedro Cerezo Galán inquires whether the symbolic mist refers to nothingness or transcendence, and, alluding to Orfeo's funeral oration, he describes the openness of *Niebla* in this way: "Lo extraño del hombre es su naturaleza ambigua, intermedia entre el ser y el no-ser, y entre la realidad y la ficción. Extraño por el carácter de su tiempo ambiguo, que es tanto sueño inconsistente como ensoñación creadora. Extraño, sobre

---

por arrancar de la niebla y sobrevolar las nubes en busca del sol autentificador" (584); and Pedro Ribas, who notes, "Ambos, autor y lector, saben que el texto es un juego, una ficción, pero ésta, justamente por ser creación de un mundo imaginario, ofrece vías abiertas a la utopía" (77). Rosendo Díaz-Peterson studies *Niebla* and other narratives as Unamuno's confrontation with scholasticism; for him, "Augusto Pérez constituye en la novela el vehículo de la lucha entre lo abstracto y lo concreto, la necesidad y el azar, lo que personifica el enfrentamiento de la escolástica con las disciplinas nacientes" (66).

[31] See Zavala: "[L]o que se pone en juego a partir de *Niebla* es una redefinición del yo en cuanto sujeto sociabilizado: el *otro*.... La lección definitiva es que no existe comunicación sin el otro; que es imposible concluir el diálogo infinito, o concluir los relatos; abandona, por así decirlo, el libro convencional 'redondo', a favor de lo incompleto, digresivo, sin prueba ni conclusión, que se interrumpe, recoge y reproduce las contradicciones" ("Unamuno" 43). For another formulation of alterity, see Franz: "*Niebla*... constitutes a grand artifice elaborated to convince us (and, doubtless, to convince Unamuno as well via the reflection of his imagined reader's novelistically inscribed conviction) that the universe is an infinity of potentialities which become actualized only when a consciousness of them is produced. Thus visualized, man can both become aware of his own potentiality clusters and recognize those of others. But since he perceives himself as a unit of an 'other,' the process of acquiring existence is aways social. We feel ourselves existing when others react to us in some way, when we react to others, or when we step back—as in laughter—and react to different parts of ourselves" ("*Niebla*: Infinite Authors" 9).

todo, por la doblez de su palabra, en el quicio de la verdad y la ocultación.... El enigma es su elemento, su condición de posibilidad" (591). Cerezo Galán accentuates the verbal edifice of *Niebla*, and this suggests its ties with modernism. Language has been a means of access for critics. Taking his lead from a passage in *Del sentimiento trágico de la vida*, Allen Lacy writes, "Reason renders faith transmissible and faith makes reason available for living—yet faith is not transmissible nor reason vital. Unless they are seen as statements about *language*, and recommendations for its use, they are only slightly removed from seeming nonsense" (225).[32] In *Beyond the Fictional Mode*, Robert C. Spires submits that "[t]he textual strategy behind the theme of fiction versus reality in the case of *Niebla* involves foregrounding the fascinating capacity of language to give birth to itself, to create illusion in the very act of destroying illusion" (44). While Spires speaks of an inventive victory, Alison Sinclair believes that *Niebla* is informed by a distrust of the signifying capacity of language: "One of the most striking consistencies in Unamuno's writings is his emphasis on the need for inconsistency, for flexibility of response, for individuality and quirkiness as opposed to lucidly organised and sterile systems" ("Definition" 188). It follows, then, that language, as a system, "is at odds with the shifting and elusive nature

---

[32] Roberta Johnson posits that *"Niebla*'s composition is inextricably intertwined with that of *Del sentimiento trágico de la vida*, which began as early as 1899.... It was to draw on sociology and ethics to treat the unknowable finality of the universe and the concept of the deity, ending with the doctrine of the happy uncertainty that allows us to live" ("Hunger and Desire" 93). Iris Zavala also sees the two texts as complementary: "[S]on el modo expreso de un sistema. Van dirigidos contra la concepción racionalista, anti-dramática, anti-trágica del ser humano. El anti-conformismo y la lucha contra la falsa conciencia de un yo organizado y unitario que se despliega en el tiempo... atraviesa la obra de Unamuno con el hilo de la dialogización" (*"Niebla*: La lógica" 92). See also Franz, who cites *Del sentimiento trágico*: "Unamuno's language of fiction becomes the great mediator between man and the great unknown which surrounds him, and... it is through the diffusing, confusing function of such language that the unknown becomes relatable to our considered feelings about ourselves. A novel without closure, where everyone is a changing fiction of everyone else, is the creation of a great 'mist' where our many-mirrored worlds miraculously may coalesce and agree, proclaiming in unison the realizable immortality we all—according to Unamuno—seek from within" (*"Niebla*: Infinite Authors" 10).

of life itself, [and] it is hardly surprising that he should at times have had such a declared lack of faith in the validity of words *per se*, or in groups" ("Definition" 188). In his psychological experiment and elsewhere, Augusto Pérez discovers that "language, which is the tool he wants to use to carry out his explorations, while appearing to epitomize rationality (and therefore, wrongly thinks Augusto, truth) in fact impedes him at every turn" ("Definition" 199). Similarly, Paul R. Olson states, "Even more serious a caveat than the irony of tone... is the novel's implicit and explicit denunciation of the radical antinomy of thought and objective being, the intrinsic inability of thought to hold and of language to impart the truth" ("Unamuno's *Niebla*" 672).[33]

Mary Lee Bretz takes Mikhail Bakhtin's concept of "authoritative discourse" as a starting point for her analysis of language in *Niebla*. Bakhtin employs the term to express the predominant ideology, or dogma, and the socio-cultural norms of a given place and time. The novel opens the field to dialogue, as writers fight to challenge the single voice of authoritative discourse. Bretz maintains that the early chapters show Augusto Pérez trapped by the discursive structure: "The composite picture reveals an overly protected only son whose life has been organized for him by his mother and the other authority figures with which he has come into contact: the church, the educational system, the literary establishment, and the Spanish bourgeoisie. Augusto has no identity of his own, and consequently he has no authentic voice, no personalized language" (230). Bretz notices that Augusto speaks of himself "as if he were another person" (230). Analogous to Don Quijote's dependence on the discourse of chivalry, Augusto's speech is inflected by Romantic and post-Romantic poets, among other influences. It is language that affects the protagonist's perceived inauthenticity and inability to act, and "his subsequent evolution toward authenticity is

---

[33] Ch. 2 of Olson's *Great Chiasmus* and his critical guide offer masterful commentaries on the design and ideology of Niebla. Note, among a multitude of other elements, the discussion of the symmetrical or chiastic structure of the novel and Unamuno's concept of *contrahistoria*, related to the Nietzschean idea of the Eternal Return (*Great Chiasmus* 77 ff. and 95 ff., respectively). I am most grateful to have had the opportunity to participate in a seminar on Unamuno taught by Professor Olson during my first semester of graduate studies at Johns Hopkins University in the fall of 1970.

effected primarily through dialogue with others and the gradual shedding of others' languages" (Bretz 233). Interestingly, after his first meeting with Eugenia, Augusto is speechless, and this signals a transition toward the development of his own voice. Bretz contrasts the theoretical discourse that gives an impetus to his pursuit of women with the dissolution of confidence when he must interact directly with Eugenia or Rosario, and she demonstrates how Bakhtin's categories come into play in the famous debate, in which "Augusto both echoes and refutes Unamuno, ridicules and paraphrases him. Augusto's linguistic autonomy is verified when he mocks Unamuno's speech pattern" (237).[34] The progression of discourse runs parallel to the character's search for autonomy and is enhanced by the metalinguistic commentaries, such as the dialogues on the *nivola* form. The tracing of Augusto Pérez's discursive shifts helps to clarify the movement of *Niebla*, from a number of perspectives.[35] Language functions as analogue and allegory. As Augusto attempts to break away from Unamuno, Unamuno attempts to break away from nineteenth-century realism. Neither effort is perfectly successful, largely because that would run counter to the message of interdependence—or, stated more combatively, of irreconcilable differences—that characterizes the enterprise. Linguistic autonomy is an illusion, but, as with other types of autonomy, one worth fighting for.

In *The Great Chiasmus*, Olson underscores the meaningful tensions of

---

[34] In "Reinterpretación de *Niebla*: El carácter de la comunicación literaria," Germán Gullón analyzes the text from the perspective of speech-act theory. His primary example is the intercalated story of the *fogueteiro*. María del Carmen Grillo reads *Niebla* through Gérard Genette's concept of *transtextuality*. Influenced by poststructuralism, Rose Marie Marcone argues that "*Niebla* distinguishes between 'ideas about the thing' and 'the thing itself.' They are exclusive. Augusto fails to understand this point. The world of ideas and perceptions is the only realm he can accept, and this factor is the cause of his anguish" (12). Chantal Pestrinaux also focuses on "la inadecuación entre lenguaje y pensamiento" (98). Basing her comments in part on Paul Ilie's "Language and Cognition in Unamuno," Marsha S. Collins ("Orfeo") looks at Unamuno's treatment of the distance between thought and expression and the poet's ability to reach a type of synthesis. A central focus of her in-depth study is Orfeo's funeral oration.

[35] In contrast to Bretz, Anne Marie Queraas argues for the static, unchanging quality of Augusto Pérez's discourse.

Niebla—between desire for limits and limitlessness, between individuality and totality, for example—within Unamuno's antithetically structured patterns of thought. What appears at first to be primarily a problem of narrative form has existential dimensions: "For although this exemplary *nivola* demonstrates that linguistic creations… can be given symmetrical structures that create the aesthetic but illusory *effects* of coherence, closure, and reversibility, it must ultimately be realized, as the life and death of Augusto Pérez make clear, that to live with this fiction is to live in the inauthenticity of existential bad faith" (98). For Olson, "when Augusto tells Unamuno to abandon the thought of reviving him, it is because he has come to realize that the basic reality of existence in time is its irreversible openness toward the future, in which time is not cyclical, and the dead—whatever be their fate—are not reborn to life in this world" (*Great Chiasmus* 98). In this universe, Augusto can appear, in a dream, to announce he cannot be revived.[36] Olson concludes, "*Niebla* demonstrates that the idea of the ontological primacy of language and thought—which Unamuno himself seems to assert—is a snare that tempts the intellectual and all who intellectualize, and the work also poignantly expresses the alienation produced by believing that the realm of language, thought, and mind is of an order of being radically distinct from that of physical reality"; what makes Augusto Pérez a creature of language is that "he exists in and by it, and within the immense nebula of potential forms…, he… is only an evanescent shape in the mist" (*Great Chiasmus* 98-99). As a purely fictional entity, Augusto Pérez is composed of words, not flesh and blood, and he confuses his identity on the pages of fiction with reality, but he is in good company, namely, the company of Don Miguel de Unamuno. Olson's reading invites an inquiry into questions of discourse and authenticity in *Niebla*.

Unamuno's discursive practice in *Niebla* is marked by a deferral of voice. The prologue by Víctor Goti, a prologue more oriented toward Unamuno than toward Augusto Pérez, initiates a model that the narrative will sustain: Unamuno is doing the talking, or the writing. The fictional conventions include the ironic ventriloquism through which the text

---

[36] See "Una entrevista con Augusto Pérez" (1915), as well as "Pirandello y yo" (1923) and "Historia de *Niebla*" (1935), reprinted in the Valdés edition of *Niebla* 73-93.

conveys its messages. Víctor is the intermediary between the historical author and the *ente de ficción*. He is, of course, a literary character, but his position in the prologue breaks with custom and gives him an authority that is both ironically validated and negated, not just by the rejoinder (the post-prologue by Unamuno) but by the obviously artificial presentation of the prologue itself. Unamuno composes Víctor Goti's opposition to his determination concerning the death of Augusto Pérez, only to discredit the suicide theory. Although the "real" author may have the last word in the introductory materials, Unamuno gives Víctor Goti a degree of control that is rarely granted to a fictional personage. That is justified, perhaps, by Víctor's role as *nivolista* and apologist for the new narrative form. By becoming an interlocutor with his creation, Unamuno elevates Víctor or reduces himself, depending on one's perspective. As in the first *Quijote* prologue, in which the friend speaks for and with a fictionalized Cervantes, the writer delegates authority in such a way that the reader understands perfectly from whom the words derive. Naturally, every text has an author—even those that are anonymous—but the incorporation of the author as character and the act of composition into the plot is daring, amusing, and illustrative. On the most basic level, the writer is foregrounding the creative process and allowing the reader to comprehend the burdens involved in that process.

Metafiction instantly engages readers and forces them into the frame, much as Velázquez does to the spectators in *Las meninas*, who now have dual identities within and beyond the work of art. The Velázquez of the painting is a symbol of the artist, not only on the canvas but in the royal court, and he is alleging that he is worthy of the company by virtue of his talent and the dignity of his profession; he is immortalizing the regal subjects, the fruits of the artist's labor, and himself. His art is representational, but its self-referentiality adds another dimension, and that is why the motif of observation—from the Infanta and her retinue to the mirror to the figure in the open doorway to the viewing public—is a critical aspect of the painting. The convergence of the discrete domains of reality and art eliminate the external audience, which now operates within the imaginary space, that is, within the broader, synthetic picture. Cervantes and Unamuno work along the same lines, the former from an ironic distance and the latter from an ironic center. Unamuno as the God of the work functions metaphorically, suggesting an autonomy that he wishes for but knows that he does not possess. In this regard, a whimsical rhetoric fits the situation, which is more about vulnerability than omni-potence. The intratextual Unamuno debates Víctor Goti and Augusto Pérez, yet he relies on them to articulate his existential and aesthetic doubts. They may push him from the pedestal of absolute authority, but they are at his service, and he is aware of the richness and of the ironies contained in these propositions. When the nivolistic characters leave the territory of realism, they may be said to lose their grasp on reality, for they enter the (fixedly) transitional zone of metafiction, where they interact with others of their kind and with the likes of Miguel de Unamuno. His role is also redefined, because he is not satisfied with being author, director, and stage manager, but he must become an actor, as well. He not only addresses his subjects, but he transforms himself into one of them. The dialectics of discourse builds a foundation for reflection, which in turn generates commentary and metacommentary.

When he speaks of Unamuno in the prologue, Víctor Goti sounds like Unamuno. He is direct, confrontational, and witty. He knows how to make a point with style, and he seeks the rhetorical and psychological edge. When he describes the conventions of the *nivola*, he shows the confidence and audacity—some would say arrogance—of the master, and the new genre demonstrates a meeting of the minds. Unamuno seems less concerned, however, with sharing the narrative duties than with allegorizing the onus of authorship and the break from tradition. Literature is an art worth cultivating in order to satisfy the creative instinct, but it is also a means by which to conquer the world, to win a glory that is short of eternity, but that may be the tenor of a divine metaphor. As he was thinking and writing about the tragic sense of life, Unamuno had the chance to shift genres and to combine philosophy, theology, and art. In *Las meninas*, there is one painter, along with works of art and a group of observers. The painter is made to fit into a scene that imitates reality, but that figure does not fashion the piece. In *Don Quijote*, there is the author, along with a historian, a score of narrators, and books and readers in a variety of forms. The real Cervantes is wise enough to know that there is safety in distance and that a fictional Cervantes, with a team of surrogates, can argue more forthrightly during inquisitorial times. His outer bounds seem to be history and historiography, but the content may apply to higher authorities. Velázquez can be said to paint art into reality and to paint reality into art, as he recognizes but minimizes the difference. Cervantes employs the motifs of reading and writing to treat, among other topics, perspective, perception, truth, and control. He evokes reality through art—art unconcealed, art foregrounded—and emphasizes their reciprocal relation. Unamuno's preoccupations go beyond both realism and reality. His thoughts are on the afterlife, and literary success is a key to his approach.

Augusto Pérez, Víctor Goti, and the other characters of *Niebla* are unique creations, designed as an antidote to their counterparts in realist narrative and as functions within Unamuno's systems, literary and ideological. Unamuno has Augusto claim to be in charge of his destiny, by having his protagonist "elect" to kill himself after the deception that has deflated his ego, just as he has Víctor claim to be the inventor of the *nivola* form. The dialogues between the characters and the author reflect the strangeness of the encounters, wrought by the literariness and the magic of fiction. In a paradox that hardly seems casual, the search for authenticity is a factor in the content but not in the form of *Niebla*. Unamuno anguishes over the inner self, and he takes the narrative away from the realistic depiction of a socio-historical present that typifies the nineteenth-century novel. The principal analogue places Augusto and Víctor in an internal realm, where Augusto tries to forge an identity and Víctor to craft a new genre. Love is the impetus for Augusto, but thinking subordinates feeling. He is in love with the concept of love, and the specific love object is, at first, almost irrelevant. Although the "heroic action" of paying the mortgage, the ominous presence of a rival suitor, and the physicality of Rosario make the protagonist more attuned to the world around him, thought prevails as he conducts the psychological experiment. No longer the aimless gentleman at the doorway of chapter 1, Augusto Pérez has a goal in life, however misdirected and ingenuous his approach. The earnestness is more formidable than the execution, because Augusto is ill-equipped to exist in a world of malice and deceit. Even when he spends time with Eugenia during their engagement, he finds little comfort in her attitude; if they marry, he will be forced to get rid of Orfeo, for example. Love, if more theoretical than practical, is his first stimulus. The death wish is his second, and it is the source of his greatest energy, as manifested in the debate with Unamuno.

Niebla opens with a prologue in which Unamuno writes about Unamuno in the "voice" of Víctor Goti. The verbal self-portrait has an odd sense of alterity, because the rules of the game are being exposed. The mysterious death of Augusto Pérez is a staged mystery. The dispute initiated in the prologues is an element of the plot continuum and a pretext for a variation of Unamuno's *monodiálogos*. The author is, in every sense, a character. He is a public personality who shares his private life and his feelings with the audience, and he is a supremely self-conscious writer. By giving Víctor Goti the task, or honor, of composing the prologue, he flaunts a deviation from the norms of realism and verisimilitude. Víctor is a symbol and a competitor of the author, and he is also a collaborator and a link to Augusto Pérez. The *nivola* and his newborn son exemplify art and life, respectively. Like Unamuno, as described by Olson, Víctor favors a rhetoric of antithesis, and there is little distinction between his voice and Unamuno as quoted in the prologue, and his presentation of the poetics of the *nivola* exhibits the feistiness and the buoyancy of his creator. Augusto first appears as a milquetoast, a cipher. His magnificent commentary on the beauty of non-utilitarian objects beautifully captures his essence, that is to say, his non-essence.[37] Even the background information about his childhood and youth makes him seem unformed and excessively dependent on his mother, whose passing has left him without grounding. The vision of Eugenia awakens something in him, and he grows during the course of the narrative, yet his development is stunted by his propensity for reflection. He sacrifices the concrete for the abstract, and he is constantly out of touch with his surroundings. Within the story—and as a recourse on Unamuno's part—Eugenia keeps Augusto alive; she fosters his ambition, and she motivates his actions. Through his contact with her, he learns rudimentary assertiveness skills.

Eugenia is incensed by Augusto's grand gesture, and her anger hurts his pride. He tests his attitude with Doña Ermelinda before proceeding, more meekly, to face her niece. In general, he is tongue-tied with Eugenia, and with Víctor Goti he regularly is reduced to playing the straight man. Víctor is always the dominant figure, whether the dialogue refers to analyzing Augusto's behavior, offering his opinion, recounting his response to paternity, or describing the *nivola*. Augusto is a nervous, reticent speaker, and he often stands to the margins of discourse. This is significant because the awkwardness of his communicative style contrasts with the eloquence of his thoughts, for, though his mind may wander, he

---

[37] Cifo González initiates a study of symbolism in *Niebla* by looking at the rain and the umbrella of the opening sequence.

expresses his inner struggle with sophistication. The slow start gives more power to Augusto's role in the debate with Unamuno, the culmination of his speech acts. Here, he holds his own and may even better his opponent, but he does this by citing the author. Finally, Unamuno's aggressiveness and sense of superiority seem to knock the wind out of Augusto, who keeps fighting to the end. Unamuno gives him the will to live, but now the creator of the fiction must prove himself. The contest moves from *querer no ser* to *querer ser*, but the question of will shifts from Augusto to Unamuno. Ironically, in the end it does not matter how Augusto Pérez dies, or that he dies, because the book makes him immortal. And it makes Unamuno immortal. Don Quijote and Augusto Pérez stem from words on a page. The knight is Alonso Quijano's invention, and Alonso Quijano is Cervantes's invention, each representing a distinct level of fiction, with the Cervantes of the two prologues—one more fictional than the other—adding other layers. Augusto Pérez, the product of Unamuno's imagination, lives on the pages of *Niebla*, but his literariness shows through, and this sets him apart from the characters in realist novels. Unamuno's literariness shows through, as well, to set him apart from realism and from those authors who would dare not appear in their novels. It is not Augusto's discourse, as much as his abstractness, that makes him indispensable.

In the first part of his conversation in chapter 31, Augusto shows an awareness of Unamuno's works—literary and "more or less" philosophical—which he praises. When he proceeds to summarize his vicissitudes, Unamuno catches him off-guard by saying that this exposition is unnecessary, that he already knows everything about Augusto, and he offers several intimate details to prove the point. Augusto reacts in horror to the God-like presence of the author, *his* author. In the ensuing polemic, Augusto's strategy is to underplay—and undercut—Unamuno's authority over him, and his emphasis on the internal logic of fictional characters sounds, in this context, much like free will. Unamuno has entered into a fascinating area, which includes the sacred and the profane, the connotations of which vary according to the rubric. Unamuno operates under the premise that they are by no means equals. Augusto must convince him that they are subject to the same laws of art, which make them equally vulnerable. Moreover, Unamuno is an *ente de ficción*, and no more proof is needed than the dialogue itself. If Unamuno is indeed a type of deity before his creation, Augusto professes to have little faith.

Because he has read Unamuno, he knows the paradoxical form of argumentation in which the writer engages, and he uses that method to his benefit. When Augusto cites Unamuno to Unamuno, he would seem to have arrived at the apex of his assertiveness. Having lacked confidence in the past, he becomes a fighter, an advocate for himself. And yet that pang of recognition—of terror—in the first stage of the debate must stay with him (and probably with the reader): Unamuno is always a few steps ahead of him. Not only is Augusto a verbal construct, but he now faces an author bent on his destruction. This is theater of the absurd, but it is a parable, as well. Unamuno is as radically committed to demonstrating the significance of point of view as Cervantes, but here the implications are stronger, and more unsettling.

From the beginning of the narrative, Augusto Pérez desires to experience life, to be part of humanity, to have a purpose. He knows that his mind is active, even hyperactive, but that is not enough. He seems to be challenging the Cartesian principle. Thought needs a supplement, which he hopes to find in love (*"Amo, ergo sum"*), and, when that fails, in eating (*"Edo, ergo sum"*). The problem is that Augusto Pérez is not a human being and that Unamuno exposes his fictional identity at every opportunity. Augusto is an instrument of his author's being, and it is a consummately ironic touch that he becomes a sacrificial victim of Unamuno's existential quandries, which the writer seems implicitly to want to resolve through the dictum *"Scribo, ergo sum."* Unamuno fills the narrative space with the story of a character who longs to find direction, to fulfill his potential, to live. The prospect of love and the motif of a quest push Augusto and the narrative forward. The deception perpetrated by Eugenia and Mauricio leads Augusto to despair and then to consider suicide. This prompts the visit to Unamuno, who manages to control the discourse, especially (and ironically) when Augusto is most persuasive. The contest between reality and fiction is more viably a rumination on human legacies and on the unknowable beyond. The rejection of realist style comes with a shift in goals and in focus. Society, a determined historical moment, and a literary rendering that befits them yield to metaphysical questions and to a format commensurate with the task, and to an author who insists that the reader knows from where his characters' discourse emanates. Although Rosario is moved by Augusto, she and Mauricio seem to belong in the material world of narrative realism. The protagonist and his friend the *nivolista* bear the Unamunian imprint; they live in his world, and their words—and, to be sure, those of the narrator—are clearly his.

Don Quijote confuses literature and history in order to force a reexamination of each, and, it may be supposed, to suggest connections that previously had been overlooked. Cervantes sees the intertext as a source of inspiration for new directions in fiction and an increased consciousness of the audience. Unamuno approaches the writing of fiction with a special seriousness and with a combative spirit. His attitude toward realism is not satirical but wary. He wants to change and outdo custom, and the innovative form will house a unique content. Augusto Pérez's dependence on abstractions is an extension of Unamuno's philosophical obsessions, and, with Víctor Goti's outline for the *nivola*, the lost-in-the-clouds frame of mind dominates the trajectory of *Niebla*. The result is a comic, or tragicomic, narrative, which is at the same time a reaction to realism and a reflection of *Del sentimiento trágico de la vida*. Augusto Pérez is a remarkable misfit, who starts with only a modicum of vigor and ends by standing up to his maker. Because his imagination never tires, he makes active pursuits of contemplation and, emulating Hamlet, indecision. Unamuno takes a chance here by placing the burden of the narrative squarely on his own shoulders. If the reader loses interest in the author—as internal and external player—the text will have only marginal redeeming value, for Augusto Pérez, Víctor Goti, and company have, at best, half-lives in the *nivola*. They are truly Unamunian subjects.

Niebla is, then, self-referential on multiple levels. Art, for Unamuno, is a means to an end and a field worthy of pursuing in its own right. Accordingly, literature is a channel and an escape, a way of broaching and redressing his most profound fears. Realism, for him, is time-bound and shallow, consumed with details of the present and overlooking the matters of greatest interest. He does not want to write a bad novel, that is, to be *accused* of writing a bad novel, but rather to be judged by criteria that will take into account his particular methodology. That would explain the invention of the *nivola*, a new structure for a poetics of change. Unamuno is trying to alter the narrative panorama, and it must strike him that his position resembles that of Cervantes, who associates radical transformations with a tribute to precedent. The concept of intertextuality presupposes the borrowing, refurbishing, and dismissal of texts and traditions. The exceptional artist—and Cervantes definitely belongs in that category—can surpass predecessors by turning reverence into advancement and by turning what begins as imitation into distinctiveness. Unamuno may compete with Galdós and his brethren, but he sees Cervantes as an aesthetic—and, it would seem, spiritual—guide. *Don Quijote* is not merely a book, but a rite of entry into literary composition and into the Spanish sensibility. To call *Niebla* a rewriting of *Don Quijote* is not an exaggeration, for, despite their differences, they are cut from the same cloth, and they explore the unlimited possibilities of writing.

Unamuno clearly recognizes the importance of the *Quijote* prologues, especially the first, in which the alter ego of the fictionalized Cervantes offers directions on the fabrication of prologues and a commentary on the aims of the author. There is little doubt that the prologue is meant to sanction and to showcase a new way of writing, a new flexibility for the creator of fiction, and increased responsibility for the reader, addressed tongue-in-cheek as "desocupado." The prologue to *Niebla* expands this base. The prologuist is Víctor Goti, fictional entity and friend to both Unamuno and Augusto Pérez. In the opening paragraph, Goti refers to a skepticism worthy of Hamlet on the part of Augusto Pérez, but he unites the contemplative aspect of the story with the mystery of Augusto's death. Like the prologue of the 1615 *Quijote*, Goti's prologue announces the demise of the protagonist, and he lets the reader know that there are conflicting interpretations of the death, thus setting into motion a debate between author and character, a foreshadowing of the climactic meeting of Augusto and Don Miguel in chapter 31. The intertextual ties to Cervantes do not cloud a brilliant strategy of self-promotion by Unamuno, who has Goti discuss his mentor's character, intellect, accomplishments, biases, and eccentricities, including his passion for inverting terms and arguments. And Unamuno ices the cake by giving himself the final word in an ingenious post-prologue, in which, evoking Cervantes, he stakes a claim to the truth. The Cervantes of the first *Quijote* prologue is a fictional character drawn from reality. The Cervantes of the second prologue is, above all, a victim of the Avellaneda sequel, a man entrenched in history. The Unamuno of the *Niebla* prologue(s) interacts—naturally, if not seamlessly—with the fictional being whose discourse he invents and refutes. He seems to demand of his readers not so much a suspension of disbelief as a belief in the power of the word, in the authority of fiction, and in Cervantes's crusade for the interdependence of life and art.

Alonso Quijano is an *hidalgo* trapped in a routine but given direction by the romances of chivalry. He may be more than a bit off-balance, but he is determined to venture forth in search of fame. As *Niebla* opens, Augusto Pérez is likewise immobile, until he vows to follow the next dog that crosses his path. Even as he galvanizes his forces, he stands at some distance from the typical man of action. He follows an attractive woman, Eugenia Domingo del Arco, instead of a dog, but he is lost in his thoughts, in love with love, as his urbane and adept Aldonza Lorenzo becomes more and more his Dulcinea del Toboso. Just as the first chapter of the *Quijote* serves as a microcosm of the narrative as a whole—fiction, metafiction, and "true history"—the first chapter of *Niebla* depicts Augusto Pérez as a new brand of leading man, defined by mental digressions and, accordingly, described vaguely, in a manner entirely at odds with realism and naturalism. He seems devoid of physicality, and the setting lacks specificity. Augusto is as absorbed in affairs of the psyche—in his quest for his lady's approval—as Don Quijote in his knightly pursuits. Analogously, the aspiring writer Víctor Goti is to Augusto Pérez as the Arab historian Cide Hamete Benengeli is to Don Quijote. Cide Hamete and the narrators within the text remind the reader of a work in progress, as does Goti's *nivola*, whose plot is eerily and engagingly reminiscent of Unamuno's. The *nivola* form belongs jointly to the author and his protégé, and, through Goti's account of his artistic project, the narrative contains an internal poetics, an image of itself. Unamuno, the supreme auto-polemicist, finds a dialogue partner for Augusto Pérez—his Sancho Panza—in the dog Orfeo, who speaks only at the end, out of respect, perhaps, for *El coloquio de los perros.*

In addition to a number of intercalated stories—probably not coincidental—Unamuno borrows from the *Quijote* what can be called the double death of the protagonist (see, among other studies, those of Lo Re and Friedman, "Executing"). In the prologue to Part 2, Cervantes discloses that he will kill off Don Quijote in order to prevent further sequels. In chapter 74, he supplies Don Quijote with a moment of dis-illusionment that leads to a denunciation of his mad wanderings and of the books of chivalry. Does Cervantes smoothly transfer his personal exigencies—avenging the wrongs committed against him by Avellane-da— to the plot proper, or do his anger and desperation lead to an abrupt ending that seems more tacked on than fully coherent, in unison with what precedes it? The Unamuno of the *Vida de don Quijote y Sancho* has no trouble adjusting the dénouement to his analysis of the novel, because he needs death to complete his representation of Don Quijote as a Christ figure. Immortality remains at the center of *Niebla*, but the frame and the tone are different. In the *Vida*, the symbolic and spiritual nature of Don Quijote supersedes not only chivalry and early modern Spanish society but also the metafictional impetus that drives Cervantes's narrative. In *Niebla*, on the other hand, metafiction is the agent through which Unamuno approximates immortality. The literary classic furnishes the author with an earthly correlative of eternal life, and the battle for supremacy between Augusto Pérez and Miguel de Unamuno is a critical factor in the evocation of a higher order. Unamuno is wise and wily here, and, after all, he is writing both parts of the dialogue. He knows that he must lose the debate, so that he can win immortality. The decisive moment in the exchange would seem to be Augusto Pérez's citing of Unamuno's argument that Don Quijote invented Cervantes. Augusto uses his opponent's point of view to his advantage, yet the rationale that Augusto Pérez invents Unamuno is to Unamuno's advantage, as well. The author finds a way to cohabit the historical and the fictional planes, to coexist on the inside and on the outside, to cover all his bases, one might say. Augusto Pérez dies, but lives through the text. Whether that death be a suicide or a homicide committed by Unamuno, the message relates to living, to survival, to enduring beyond death.

   Niebla juxtaposes the real and the ideal through Augusto Pérez's psychological experiment, which brings him abject failure in amorous matters. Unamuno's distracted and theoretical lover is, in a word, quixotic, preferring the mental image to the flesh-and-blood woman. More than once, he walks past Eugenia in the street, engrossed in his thoughts of her. His discomfort with the laundry-girl Rosario is telling, and almost palpable. There is no connection, no fit, between them; she seems too corporeal for him. The experiment parallels the play of realism and idealism in the narrative. If Cervantes reacts against literary idealism by moving toward realism—realism tempered by metafiction, to be sure—Unamuno reacts, ironically, against the realist novel by devising an alternate form, the *nivola*, which also contains large doses of metafiction. Like Cervantes, he savors what Russian Formalism calls *literariness*. He wants technique to be noticed and to figure into the depiction of reality. In chapter 17 of *Niebla*, Víctor Goti categorizes the *nivola* that he is writing as marked by a feeling of spontaneity (*vivípara*), studied though it may be, stemming from no preconceived plan, and having intercalated stories, a great deal of dialogue—with characters who are verbose, "aunque no digan nada" (a pre-Seinfeldian moment)—and who come into their own little by little (199). Regarding the participation of the author in the proceedings, Goti notes that authors should not bother readers with their personalities, while appreciating both the source of discourse and the tendency of characters to become the playthings of their fictions. And thus we have the setup—in the double sense—for the debate.

In the *Vida de don Quijote y Sancho*, Unamuno comes close to worshipping Don Quijote. In *Niebla*, it is Cervantes whom he holds in reverence and who guides him as a novelist and as a purveyor of process. Cervantes may be listed among the founders of realism, but he is equally a forerunner of modernism and its flight from the mimetic, and therein would have lain *Don Quijote's* appeal to Unamuno. The *Vida* is Unamuno's paean to the moral fiber of Spain, to the innermost recesses of the Spanish soul, which traditionally has been located off-center. Don Quijote "incarnates" the essence of the country and its people, their creative and combative spirit. *Niebla* reiterates, and intertwines, two of Unamuno's preferred themes: immortality and the production of art. Cervantes the writer, *Don Quijote* the book, the search for novelty, and public and critical endorsement—without which Don Quijote could never have invented Cervantes—coalesce in the nivolesque universe, where the farther one goes into self-reflection, the closer one may study reality and the spaces beyond reality. *Niebla* is a comic, and Cervantine, exploration of immortality, and a text that Unamuno will rewrite in a radically somber mode in *San Manuel Bueno, mártir*, published in 1933. *Niebla* is powerful and moving, but it does not appear to strive for emotional weight per se. The reader may be drawn to ideas rather than attached sentimentally to the characters. The indirect approach to reality applies also to affective questions. Logically, new writing implies a new kind of reading, one that, in this case, would be driven by intellectual and psychological involvement, distanced from, but by no means devoid of, feeling. It is not the mystery of Augusto Pérez's death but the conversion of death and the narrative into emblems of immortality which "transcends" the mundane frame of this story about nothing. In the *Vida, Don Quijote* serves as the medium for Unamuno's philosophy of Spanish culture. Although Unamuno is an exceptional close reader of the text, he tends more toward reader-response, in which interpretation by association vies compellingly with formal analysis. In *Niebla*, anchored by the

Quijote, the making of the novel negotiates literature both metaphorically and metonymically, as an analogue of creation, in its multiple contexts, and as an intimation of immortality.

Rose Marie Marcone judges that *Niebla* "is a commentary on the limits of art. Art remains inferior to life because it cannot capture the transitory quality of existence nor can it ascribe to it a specific truth. All it can do is relate a secondary and subjective experience. At best, art is an ordered fiction, a point of view, and an interpretation" (14). This is a valid argument, one that should be defended by quoting from the text. My own view is diametrically opposite, for several reasons, all of which seem to allude in some way to Cervantes and *Don Quijote. Niebla* does "capture the transitory quality of existence," whereby the characters—author included—know that life is predictably unpredictable and threateningly finite, and, as would follow, that all truth is relative. This does not render art inferior to life; rather, it serves as a reflection of reality and of humanity's striving to seek answers and to seek continuity. The knowing disorder of *Niebla* suggests Unamuno's disinclination to gloss over the pieces of life's puzzle that do not fit easily into the frame, but his literary analogue shows a faith that, despite crises and low points, remains, if not always firm, decisive. Neither language nor the recourses of fiction can achieve plenitude, but they can add a special dimension—complementary, supplementary— to the perception of the world. Pedro Salinas's formulation of "the poetic insufficiency of reality" to describe the artistic premises of Góngora is relevant in this context. Salinas maintains, "Telling and describing what one sees is not poetry. What must be done to convert it into poetry? Raise it, intensify its characteristics to an extreme degree, elevate it above its natural forms and extract from the latter all their esthetic content by means of the imagination and fantasy. Reality must be transformed, transmuted into another kind of poetic reality, material, sonorous, plastic, but not idealized; the artist must operate on it with the magic power of word, metaphor, image" (139-40). Góngora and other baroque writers make literature the macrocosm; nature, not art, has limits. Cervantes and, later, Unamuno transform the microcosm-macrocosm dichotomy into a dialectical struggle with no clear winner, but with a victory for both art and life.

The prologue to the exemplary novellas appears six years after the publication of *Niebla.* Unamuno teasingly labels the prologue "también una novela… y no una *nivola*" (45). He claims to offer in the novellas examples of life and reality, but reality with a difference, reality that does not equate with realism, and that replaces the will, *voluntad*, with the neologism *noluntad*, a defining attribute of the Unamunian protagonist. Aligning recreation with re-creation, he grants the reader a major role in the final inquiry into the text. And, not surprisingly, he illustrates the point by recurring to Cervantes. He realizes that there are those who believe that the Don Quijote and Sancho Panza of the *Vida* are not those of Cervantes: "Lo cual es muy cierto. Porque ni Don Quijote ni Sancho son de Cervantes ni míos, sino que son de todos los que los crean y re-crean. O mejor, son de sí mismos, y nosotros cuando los contemplamos y creamos, somos de ellos" (57). Cervantes and Don Quijote—his Don Quijote, and his Cervantes, for that matter—motivate Unamuno and encourage him to experiment as a writer and thinker. The gallant, if over-zealous, knight errant lends himself to Unamuno's meditations on faith, on literary composition, on national identity, and on the here-and-now as a taste of eternity. While they are centuries—and miles—apart, there is a kinship between Don Quijote's illusions and delusions and Unamu-no's crises of faith. For the invention of the *nivola*, Unamuno needs realism against which to play his innovations. He takes recourse to philosophy and psychology to further the endeavor, and he turns to the master literary alchemist—the man who transforms baser fiction into gold—as his tutor and exemplar. Like Cervantes, he anticipates future theoretical discourse: on modernism and postmodernism, reader-response, mimetic and anti-mimetic representation, and so forth. He even precedes Salvador de Madariaga's famous thesis concerning the "quijotización" of Sancho Panza and "sanchificación" of Don Quijote, in a statement from the prologue to the *novelas ejemplares*, to the effect that "Don Quijote era sanchopancesco y Sancho Panza era donquijotesco, como creo haber probado en mi *Vida de Don Quijote y Sancho*" (57).[38] Unamuno comes into his own—paradoxically—through the lessons and the poetic license that Cervantes affords him. In the palimpsest that is the Unamunian novel (or *nivola*), double-dipping is permitted: Unamuno is conspicuous by his presence, yet *Don Quijote* is never far from the surface.

---

[38] For Madariaga's formulation, see esp. 137-56.

Works Cited

Abel, Lionel. *Metatheatre: A New View of Dramatic Form*. New York: Hill and Wang, 1963.

Alas, Leopoldo, "Clarín." *Galdós, novelista*. Ed. Adolfo Sotelo Vázquez. Barcelona: PPU, 1991.

Alazraki, Jaime. "Motivación e invención en *Niebla*." *Romanic Review* 58.4 (1987): 241-53.

Alemán, Mateo. *Guzmán de Alfarache*. Ed. José María Micó. 2 vols. Madrid: Cátedra, 1998.

Archer, Robert. "The Fictional Context of *Lazarillo de Tormes*." *Modern Language Review* 80.2 (1985): 340-50.

Asún, Raquel. "Máximo Manso y Benito Pérez Galdós en defensa de la novela." *Homenaje al Profesor Antonio Vilanova*. Ed. Adolfo Sotelo Vázquez and Marta Cristina Carbonell. 2 vols. Barcelona: U de Barcelona, 1989, 2: 41-57.

Avellaneda, Alonso Fernández de [pseud.]. *El ingenioso hidalgo don Quijote de la Mancha, que contiene su tercera salida y es la quinta parte de sus aventuras.* Ed. Fernando García Salinero. Madrid: Castalia, 1987.

Ayala, Francisco. *La novela: Galdós y Unamuno*. Barcelona: Seix Barral, 1974.

Bakhtin, Mikhail. *The Dialogic Imagination: Four Essays*. Ed. Michael Holquist. Austin: U of Texas P, 1981.

Bandera, Cesáreo. *"Monda y desnuda": La humilde historia de don Quijote. Reflexones sobre el origen de la novela moderna*. Navarra, Madrid, Frankfurt am Main: Universidad de Navarra, Iberoamericana, Vervuert, 2005

Basdekis, Demetrios. *Unamuno and the Novel*. Estudios de Hispanófila, 31. Chapel Hill: Department of Romance Languages, University of North Carolina, 1974.

Batchelor, R. "Form and Content in Unamuno's *Niebla*." *Forum for Modern Language Studies* 8.3 (1972): 197-214.

Bell, Michael. "The Metaphysics of Modernism." Levenson ed. 9-32.

Berkowitz, H. Chonon. *Pérez Galdós: Spanish Liberal Crusader*. Madison: U of Wisconsin P, 1948.

———. "Unamuno's Relations with Galdós." *Hispanic Review* 8.4 (1940): 321-38.

Berns, Gabriel. "Another Look through Unamuno's *Niebla*: Augusto Pérez, 'Agonista-lector.'" *Romance Notes* 11.1 (1969): 26-29.

Blanco Aguinaga, Carlos. "Cervantes y la picaresca: Notas sobre dos tipos de realismo." *Revista de Filología Hispánica* 11 (1957): 313-42.

———. *La historia y el texto literario: Tres novelas de Galdós*. Madrid: Nuestra Cultura, 1978.

———. "Unamuno's *Niebla*: Existence and the Game of Fiction." *MLN* 79.2 (1964): 188-205.

Blanquat, Josette. "Le Naturalisme espagnol en 1882: *El amigo Manso*." *Bulletin Hispanique* 64 bis (1962): 318-35.

Bleiberg, Germán, and E. Inman Fox, eds. *Spanish Thought and Letters in the Twentieth Century*. Nashville: Vanderbilt UP, 1966.

Bloom, Harold. *The Anxiety of Influence: A Theory of Poetry*. 2nd ed. New York and Oxford: Oxford UP, 1997.

Bly, Peter A. *Galdós's Novel of the Historical Imagination: A Study of the Contemporary Novels*. Liverpool: Francis Cairns, 1983.

Booth, Wayne C. *The Rhetoric of Fiction*. Chicago: U. of Chicago P, 1961.

Borges, Jorge Luis. "Pierre Menard, autor del *Quijote*." *Prosas completas*. 2 vols. Barcelona: Bruguera, 1980. 1: 425-33.

Boudreau, H. L. "Máximo Manso: The *Molde* and the *Hechura*." *Anales Galdosianos* 12 (1977): 64-70.

Bretz, Mary Lee. "Voices of Authority and Linguistic Autonomy in *Niebla*." *Studies in Twentieth Century Literature* 11 (1986-87): 229-38.

Brooks, Peter. *Realist Vision*. New Haven and London: Yale UP, 2005.

Calderón de la Barca, Pedro. *La vida es sueño*. Ed. José M. Ruano de la Haza. Madrid: Castalia, 1994.

Calinescu, Matei. *Faces of Modernity: Avant-garde, Decadence, Kitsch*. Bloomington and London: Indiana UP, 1977.

Casa, Frank P. "In Defense of Lázaro de Tormes." *Crítica Hispánica* 19 (1997): 87-98.

Casalduero, Joaquín. *Vida y obra de Galdós (1843-1920)*. Madrid: Gredos, 1951.

Castillo, Debra A. "The Problematics of Teaching in *El amigo Manso*." *Revista de Estudios Hispánicos* 19.2 (1985): 37-55.

Castillo Solórzano, Alonso de. *La niña de los embustes, Teresa de Manzanares. La garduña de Sevilla y anzuelo de bolsas*. Madrid: Aguilar, 1980.

Cerezo Galán, Pedro. *Las máscaras de lo trágico: Filosofía y tragedia en Miguel de Unamuno*. Madrid: Trotta, 1996.

Cervantes, Miguel de. *El coloquio de los perros. Novelas ejemplares*. Ed. Harry Sieber. 2 vols. Madrid: Cátedra, 2000. 2: 297-359.

———. *Don Quijote de la Mancha*. Ed. del Instituto Cervantes, dir. Francisco Rico. 2 vols. Barcelona, Crítica, 1998.

———. *El ingenioso hidalgo don Quijote de la Mancha*. Ed. Tom Lathrop. Newark, DE: Juan de la Cuesta, 2002.

———. "El retablo de las maravillas." *Entremeses.* Ed. Nicholas Spadaccini. Madrid: Cátedra, 1990. 215-36.

———. *El rufián dichoso. Pedro de Urdemalas.* Ed. Jenaro Talens and Nicholas Spadaccini. Madrid: Cátedra, 1986.

Chaguaceda Toledano, Ana, ed. *Miguel de Unamuno: Estudios sobre su obra, I.* Salamanca: Ediciones Universidad de Salamanca, 2003.

Chatman, Seymour. *Coming to Terms: The Rhetoric of Narrative in Fiction and Film.* Ithaca and London: Cornell UP, 1990.

———. *Story and Discourse: Narrative Structure in Fiction and Film.* Ithaca and London: Cornell UP, 1978.

Cifo González, Manuel. "Literatura y vida: algunas consideraciones acerca del simbolismo en *Niebla.*" Chaguaceda Toledano 61-80.

Close, Anthony. *Cervantes and the Comic Mind of His Age.* Oxford: Oxford UP, 2000.

———. *The Romantic Approach to* Don Quixote. Cambridge: Cambridge UP, 1977.

Cohn, Dorrit. *The Distinction of Fiction.* Baltimore and London: Johns Hopkins UP, 1999.

Collins, Marsha S. "*El Humorismo*, Romantic Irony, and the Carnivalesque World of Galdós's *El amigo Manso.*" *Romantic Review* 88.4 (1997): 607-28.

———. "Orfeo and the Cratyline Conspiracy in Unamuno's *Niebla.*" *Bulletin of Spanish Studies* 79 (2002): 285-306.

Correa, Gustavo. "Pérez Galdós y la tradición calderoniana." *Cuadernos Hispanoamericanos* 250-52 (1970-1971): 221-41.

———. *Realidad, ficción y símbolo en las novelas de Pérez Galdós: Ensayo de estética realista.* Bogotá: Instituto Caro y Cuervo, 1967.

Cruz, Anne J. *Discourses of Poverty: Social Reform and the Picaresque Novel in Early Modern Spain.* Toronto: U of Toronto P, 1999.

Currie, Mark. *Postmodern Narrative Theory.* New York: St. Martin's, 1998.

Davies, G. A. "Galdós' *El amigo Manso*: An Experiment in Didactic Method." *Bulletin of Hispanic Studies* 39.1 (1962): 16-30.

Davis, Lennard J. *Resisting Novels: Ideology and Fiction.* New York and London: Methuen, 1987.

del Río, Ángel. "Notas sobre el tema de América en Galdós." *Nueva Revista de Filología Hispánica* 15 (1961): 279-96.

Delicado, Francisco. *La lozana andaluza.* Ed. Bruno M. Damiani. Madrid: Castalia, 1969.

Díaz-Peterson, Rosendo. *Las novelas de Unamuno.* Potomac, MD: Scripta Humanistica, 1987.

Diez, Ricardo. *El desarrollo estético de la novela de Unamuno.*" Madrid: Playor, 1976.

Durán, Manuel. "Picaresque Elements in Cervantes's Works." Maiorino 226-47.

———. "La técnica de la novela y la generación del 98." *Revista Hispánica Moderna*

23 (1957): 16-27.

Earnest, James David. "The Influence of Thomas Carlyle on the Early Novels of Miguel de Unamuno." *Kentucky Philological Association Bulletin* 11 (1984): 25-35.

Eisenberg, Daniel. *A Study of* Don Quixote. Newark, DE: Juan de la Cuesta, 1989

El Saffar, Ruth S. *Novel to Romance: A Study of Cervantes's* Novelas ejemplares. Baltimore and London: Johns Hopkins UP, 1974.

Engler, Kay. *The Structure of Realism: The* Novelas contemporáneas *of Benito Pérez Galdós*. Chapel Hill: U of North Carolina Studies in the Romance Languages and Literatures, 1977.

Eliot, T. S. *The Sacred Wood: Essays on Poetry and Criticism*. London: Methuen, 1920.

Eoff, Sherman H. *The Novels of Pérez Galdós: The Concept of Life as Dynamic Process*. Saint Louis: Washington U Studies, 1954.

Eysteinsson, Astradur. *The Concept of Modernism*. Ithaca and London: Cornell UP, 1990.

Flórez, Ramiro. "Sistema de pensamiento y razón educativa en Unamuno." *Cuadernos Hispanoamericanos* 440-41 (1987): 187-204.

Foucault, Michel. *The Order of Things: An Archaeology of the Human Sciences*. New York: Vintage Books, 1973.

———. "What Is an Author?" *Textual Strategies*. Ed. Josué V. Harari. Ithaca: Cornell UP, 1979. 141-60.

Franz, Thomas R. "*El amigo Manso, Niebla,* and *Oblomov*: Three Related Incarnations of the 'Superfluous Man.'" *Anales Galdosianos* 29-30 (1994-1995): 63-73.

———. "*Niebla* and the Varieties of Religious Experience." *La CHISPA '85: Selected Proceedings*. Ed. Gilbert Paolini. New Orleans: Tulane U, 1985. 103-13.

———. Niebla *inexplorada: midiendo intersticios en el maravilloso texto de Unamuno*. Newark, DE: Juan de la Cuesta, 2003.

———. "*Niebla*: Infinite Authors / Infinite Fictions." Occasional Papers in Language, Literature, and Linguistics. Series A. Ames: Iowa SU, 1987. 1-12.

———. "Parenthood, Authorship, and Immortality in Unamuno's Narratives." *Hispania* 63.4 (1980): 647-57.

———. "The Philosophical Bases of Fulgencio Entrambosmares in Unamuno's *Amor y pedagogía*." *Hispania* 60.3 (1977): 443-51.

———. "El sentido de humor y adquisición de autoconciencia en *Niebla*." *Cuadernos de la Cátedra Miguel de Unamuno* 23. Salamanca: U de Salamanca, 1973. 5-25.

Friedman, Edward H. *The Antiheroine's Voice: Narrative Discourse and Transformations of the Picaresque*. Columbia: U of Missouri P, 1987.

———. "Coming to Terms with Lázaro's Prosperity: Framing Success in *Lazarillo de Tormes*." *Crítica Hispánica* 19 (1997): 41-56.

———. "'Cómo se hace un autor': *Lazarillo de Tormes* and the Rigors of Anonymity." *Studies in Honor of Donald W. Bleznick*. Ed. Delia V. Galván et al. Newark, DE: Juan de la Cuesta, 1995. 33-48.

———. "Executing the Will: The End of the Road in *Don Quixote*." *Indiana Journal of Hispanic Literatures* 5 (1994): 105-25.

———. "The Fortunes of Irony: A Metacritical Reading of *Lazarillo de Tormes*." *Essays in Literature* 15.2 (1988): 285-93.

———. "Guerrillas in the Mist: Inscription and Mediation in Unamuno's *Niebla*." *Romance Languages Annual* 4 (1993): 442-45.

———. "*Guzmán de Alfarache, Don Quijote*, and the Subject of the Novel." *Cervantes for the 21st Century / Cervantes para el siglo XXI: Studies in Honor of Edward Dudley*. Ed. Francisco La Rubia Prado. Newark, DE: Juan de la Cuesta, 2000. 61-78.

———. "Novel Groupings: The Order of Things." *Rocky Mountain Review* 37 (1983): 237-61.

———. "Trials of Discourse: Narrative Space in Quevedo's *Buscón*." Maiorino 183-225.

Galbis, Ignacio R. M. "De técnicas narrativas e influencias cervantinas en *Niebla* de Unamuno." *Cuadernos Americanos* 221.6 (1978): 197-204.

García Gascón, Eugenio. "La doble vida escatológica y terrenal de Máximo Manso: Un metaevangelio de Benito Pérez Galdós." *Letras Peninsulares* 12.2 (1999): 201-16

Gebauer, Gunter, and Christoph Wulf. *Mimesis: Culture—Art—Society*. Trans. Don Reneau. Berkeley: U of California P, 1995.

Genette, Gérard. *Narrative Discourse Revisited*. Trans. Jane E. Lewin. Ithaca: Cornell UP, 1988.

Gillespie, Gerald. "Reality and Fiction in the Novels of Galdós." *Anales Galdosianos* 1 (1966): 11-30. Reprinted in Labanyi 77-102.

Gilman, Stephen. *Galdós and the Art of the European Novel: 1867-1887*. Princeton: Princeton UP, 1981.

Gómez Martínez, José Luis. "Galdós y el krausismo español." *Nueva Revista de Estudios Hispánicos* 32.1 (1983): 55-79.

Gómez Molleda, Dolores, ed. *Actas del Congreso Internacional Cincuentenario de Unamuno* (1986). Salamanca: U de Salamanca, 1989.

Grillo, María del Carmen. "*Niebla*, de Miguel de Unamuno: Metanovela y relaciones textuales." *Alba de América: Revista Literaria* 16.30-31 (1998): 133-47.

Guerrero, Vladimir. "Diéresis y realidad en *Niebla*." *Revue Romane* 36.2 (2001): 255-64.

Gullón, Germán. "Un paradigma para la novela española moderna: *Amor y pedagogía*, de Miguel de Unamuno." *MLN* 105.2 (1990): 226-43.

———. "Reinterpretación de *Niebla*: El carácter de la comunicación literaria." *Nueva Revista de Filología Hispánica* 35.1 (1987): 293-98.

Gullón, Ricardo. "*El amigo Manso,* nivola galdosiana." *Técnicas de Galdós.* Madrid: Taurus, 1980. 57-102.

———. *Galdós, novelista moderno.* Madrid: Gredos, 1966.

Gunn, James Dayton. "The Creation of the Self: The Influence of *Don Quixote* on Unamuno's *Niebla.*" *Romance Notes* 21.1 (1980): 54-57.

Harvey, Elizabeth D. *Ventriloquized Voices: Feminist Theory and English Renaissance Texts.* London and New York: Routledge, 1995.

Higuero, Francisco Javier. "Tensiones dialécticas del narrador-personaje en *El amigo Manso* de Galdós." *Hispanic Journal* 16.2 (1995): 387-98.

Hoddie, James H. "Hegel in Galdós' *El amigo Manso.*" *Revista de Estudios Hispánicos* 23 (1996): 52-72.

Hutcheon, Linda. *Narcissistic Narrative: The Metafictional Paradox.* New York and London: Methuen, 1984.

Iffland, James. "Pablos's Voice: His Master's? A Freudian Approach to Wit in *El Buscón.*" *Romanisches Forschungen* 91 (1979): 215-43.

Ilie, Paul. "Language and Cognition in Unamuno." *Revista Canadiense de Estudios Hispánicos* 11.2 (1987): 289-314.

Iser, Wolfgang. *The Act of Reading: A Theory of Aesthetic Response.* Baltimore and London: Johns Hopkins UP, 1978.

Jagoe, Catherine. *Ambiguous Angels: Gender in the Novels of Galdós.* Berkeley: U of California P, 1994.

Johnson, Carroll B. "Defining the Picaresque: Authority and the Subject in *Guzmán de Alfarache.*" Maiorino 159-82.

Johnson, Roberta. *Crossfire: Philosophy and the Novel in Spain, 1900-1934.* Lexington: UP of Kentucky, 1993.

———. *Gender and Nation in the Spanish Modernist Novel.* Nashville: Vanderbilt UP, 2003.

———. "Hunger and Desire: The Origins of Knowledge in *Niebla.*" *Selected Proceedings of the* Singularidad y trascendencia *Conference.* Ed. Nora de Marval-McNair. Boulder, CO: Society of Spanish and Spanish-American Studies, 1990. 93-98.

Jongh-Rossel, Elena de. "La Institución Libre de Enseñanza, el joven Unamuno y la pedagogía." *Hispania* 69.4 (1986): 830-36.

Jurkevich, Gayana. *The Elusive Self: Archetypal Approaches to the Novels of Miguel de Unamuno.* Columbia and London: U of Missouri P, 1991.

———. "The Sun-Hero Revisited: Inverted Archetypes in Unamuno's *Amor y pedagogía.*" *MLN* 102.2 (1987): 292-306.

———. "Unamuno's Anecdotal Digressions: Practical Joking and Narrative Structure in *Niebla.*" *Revista Hispánica Moderna,* nueva época, 45.1 (1992): 3-14.

———. "Unamuno's Gestational Fallacy: *Niebla* and '*Escribir a lo que salga.*' *Anales de la Literatura Española Contemporánea / Annals of Contemporary Spanish*

Literature 15.1-3 (1990): 65-81.

Kafalenos, Emma, guest ed. Special Issue: *Contemporary Narratology. Narrative* 9.2 (2001).

Kartchner, Eric J. "Playing Doubles: Another Look at Alemán's Vengeance on Martí." *Cincinnati Romance Review* 16 (1997): 16-23.

King, Willard F. "Unamuno, Cervantes y *Niebla.*" *Revista de Occidente* 5, 2ª época, no. 47 (1967): 219-31.

Kronik, John W. "*El amigo Manso* and the Game of Fictive Autonomy." *Anales Galdosianos* 12 (1977): 71-94.

———. "*Our Friend Manso* and the Game of Fictive Autonomy." Labanyi 157-80.

———. "La reseña de Clarín sobre *El amigo Manso.*" *Anales Galdosianos* 15 (1980): 63-71.

Labanyi, Jo. *Galdós.* London and New York: Longman, 1993.

Labanyi, Jo, ed. "Unamuno and the Aesthetic of the Novel." *Hispania* 24.4 (1941): 442-50.

Lacy, Allen. *Miguel de Unamuno: The Rhetoric of Existence.* The Hague and Paris, Mouton, 1967.

Lanser, Susan Sniader. *The Narrative Act: Point of View in Prose Fiction.* Princeton: Princeton UP, 1981.

La Rubia Prado, Francisco. *Alegorías de la voluntad: Pensamiento orgánico, retórica y deconstrucción en la obra de Miguel de Unamuno.* Madrid: Libertarias/ Prodhufi, 1996.

———. "Deconstrucción: *Niebla* de Miguel de Unamuno: ironía y deconstrucción." *El hispanismo en los Estados Unidos: Discursos críticos, prácticas textuales.* Ed. José M. del Pino and Francisco La Rubia Prado. Madrid: Visor, 1999. 111-32.

———. *Unamuno y la vida como ficción.* Madrid: Gredos, 1999.

Lazarillo de Tormes. Ed. Francisco Rico. Madrid: Cátedra, 1987.

Lazarillo de Tormes. Ed. Robert L. Fiore. Asheville, NC: Pegasus P, 2000.

Levenson, Michael. Introduction. Levenson ed. 1-8.

Levenson, Michael, ed. *The Cambridge Companion to Modernism.* Cambridge: Cambridge UP, 1999.

Lida, Denah. "Sobre el 'krausismo' de Galdós." *Anales Galdosianos* 2 (1967): 1-27.

Livingstone, Leon. "Interior Duplication and the Problem of Form in the Modern Spanish Novel." *PMLA* 73.4 (1958): 393-406.

———. "The Novel as Self-Creation." Rubia Barcia and Zeitlin 92-115.

Lo Re, A. G. "The Three Deaths of Don Quixote: Comments in Favor of the Romantic Critical Approach." *Cervantes* 9.2 (1989): 21-41.

Longhurst, Carlos Alex. "Teoría de la novela en Unamuno. De *Niebla* a *Don Sandalio.* Chaguaceda Toledano 139-51.

López de Úbeda, Francisco. *La pícara Justina.* Ed. Bruno Mario Damiani. Madrid:

José Porrúa Turanzas, 1982.

López Morillas, Juan. *El krausismo español: Perfil de una aventura intelectual*. Mexico City: Fondo de Cultura Económica, 1956.

Lucente, Gregory L. *The Narrative of Realism and Myth: Verga, Lawrence, Faulkner, Pavese*. Baltimore and London: Johns Hopkins UP, 1979.

Luján de Sayavedra, Mateo. *Segunda parte de la vida del pícaro Guzmán de Alfarache*. Intro. A. Valbuena Prat. Madrid: Aguilar, 1980.

Macklin, John. "Competing Voices: Unamuno's *Niebla* and the Discourse of Modernism." *After Cervantes: A Celebration of 75 Years of Iberian Studies at Leeds*. Leeds: Trinity and All Saints, 1993. 167-93.

Madariaga, Salvador. *Don Quijote: An Introductory Essay in Psychology*. Rev. ed. London: Oxford UP, 1961.

Maiorino, Giancarlo, ed. *The Picaresque: Tradition and Displacement*. Hispanic Issues 12. Minneapolis and London: U of Minnesota P, 1996.

Marcone, Rose Marie. "The Role of Augusto Pérez: A Study of *Niebla*." *Confluencia* 5.1 (1989): 11-15.

Mariscal, George. *Contrary Subjects: Quevedo, Cervantes, and Seventeenth-Century Spanish Culture*. Ithaca and London: Cornell UP, 1991.

McGovern, Timothy. *Galdós Beyond Realism: Reading and the Creation of Magical Worlds*. Newark, DE: Juan de la Cuesta, 2004.

McGrady, Donald. *Mateo Alemán*. New York: Twayne, 1968.

Melaney, William D. *After Ontology: Literary Theory and Modernist Poetics*. Albany: State U of New York P, 2001.

Melberg, Arne. *Theories of Mimesis*. Cambridge: Cambridge UP, 1995.

Mermall, Thomas. "The Chiasmus: Unamuno's Master Trope." *PMLA* 105.2 (1990): 245-55.

Montesinos, José F. *Galdós*. 3 vols. Madrid: Castalia, 1968.

Morón Arroyo, Ciriaco. *Hacia el sistema de Unamuno: Estudios sobre su pensamiento y creación literaria*. Palencia: Cálamo, 2003.

———. "*Niebla* en la evolución temática de Unamuno." *MLN* 81.2 (1966): 143-58.

Navajas, Gonzalo. *Unamuno desde la posmodernidad: Antinomia y síntesis ontológica*. 2nd ed. Barcelona: PPU, 1992.

———. "El yo, el lector-otro y la duplicidad en Unamuno." *Hispania* 71.3 (1988): 512-22.

Newton, Nancy A. "*El amigo Manso* and the Relativity of Reality." *Revista de Estudios Hispánicos* 7 (1973): 113-25.

———. "Playing with Unamunian Paper Birds." *Self-Conscious Art: A Tribute to John W. Kronik*. Ed. Susan L. Fischer. Lewisburg: Bucknell UP, 1996. 42-53.

Nicholls, Peter. *Modernisms: A Literary Guide*. Basingstoke, Hampshire, and London: Macmillan, 1995.

Nimetz, Michael. *Humor in Galdós: A Study of the* Novelas contemporáneas. New

Haven and London: Yale UP, 1968.

Nozick, Martin. *Miguel de Unamuno.* New York: Twayne, 1971.

Nünning, Ansgar. "Reconceptualizing the Theory and Generic Scope of Unreliable Narration." *Reconceptualizing Trends in Narratological Research.* Ed. John Pier. GRAAT (Publication des Groupes de Recherches Anglo-Américaines de l'Université François Rabelais de Tours) 21 (1999): 63-84.

Núñez, Eva. "Criatura y creador en *Niebla* de Unamuno." *Explicación de Textos Literarios* 28.1-2 (1999-2000): 133-44.

Olson, Greta. "Reconsidering Unreliability: Fallible and Untrustworthy Narrators." *Narrative* 11.1 (2003): 93-109.

Olson, Paul R. *The Great Chiasmus: Word and Flesh in the Novels of Unamuno.* West Lafayette: Purdue UP, 2003.

———. "The Novelistic Logos in Unamuno's *Amor y pedagogía.*" *MLN* 84.2 (1969): 248-68.

———. "Sobre las estructuras quiásticas en el pensamiento unamuniano (interpretación de un juego de palabras)." *Homenaje a Juan López-Morillas.* Ed. José Amor y Vásquez and A. David Kossoff. Madrid: Castalia, 1982. 359-68.

———. *Unamuno*: Niebla. Critical Guides to Spanish Texts. London: Grant and Cutler, 1984.

———. "Unamuno's Break with the Nineteenth Century: Invention of the *Nivola* and the Linguistic Turn." *MLN* 102.2 (1987): 307-15.

———. "Unamuno's *Niebla*: The Question of the Novel." *The Georgia Review* 29.3 (1975): 652-72.

O'Neill, Patrick. *Fictions of Discourse: Reading Narrative Theory.* Toronto: U of Toronto P, 1994.

Ordóñez García, David. "La mimesis artística en *Amor y pedagogía* (1902)." *Letras de Deusto* No. 84 [Vol. 29] (1999): 35-55.

Palomo, María del Pilar. "La estructura orgánica de *Niebla*: nueva aproximación." *Volumen homenaje a Miguel de Unamuno.* Ed. Dolores Gómez Molleda. Salamanca: Casa-Museo Unamuno. 1986. 457-73.

Parker, Alexander A. "On the Interpretation of *Niebla.*" Rubia Barcia and Zeitlin 116-38.

Parr, James A. Don Quixote: *An Anatomy of Subversive Discourse.* Newark, DE: Juan de la Cuesta, 1988.

———. Don Quixote, *Don Juan, and Related Subjects.* Selinsgrove: Susquehanna UP, 2004.

Pattison, Walter T. "El amigo Manso and el amigo Galdós." *Anales Galdosianos* 2 (1967): 135-53.

———. *Benito Pérez Galdós.* Boston: Twayne, 1975.

Peñuel, Arnold M. "Some Aesthetic Implications of Galdós' *El amigo Manso.*" *Anales Galdosianos* 9 (1974): 145-48.

Pérez, Janet. "Rereading *Amor y pedagogía*: Unamuno as Baroque Stylist, Comic Satirist and Anti-*machista*." *Letras Peninsulares* 9.1 (1996): 49-66.

———. "Rhetorical Integration in Unamuno's *Niebla*." *Revista Canadiense de Estudios Hispánicos* 8.1 (1983): 49-73.

Peset, Mariano. "Miguel de Unamuno escribe acerca de amor y pedagogía." *Cuadernos Hispanoamericanos* 326-27 (1977): 450-60.

Pestrinaux, Chantal. "*Niebla*: ¿Una 'nivola' lógica o una lógica 'nivolesca'?" *Miguel de Unamuno (1864-1936)*. Ed. Jack Schmidely. Rouen: U de Rouen, 1985. 85-106.

Pérez Galdós, Benito. *El amigo Manso*. Ed. Francisco Caudet. Madrid: Cátedra, 2001.

Price, R. M. "The Five *Padrotes* in Pérez Galdós' *El amigo Manso*." *Philological Quarterly* 48.2 (1969): 234-46.

Queraas, Anne Marie. "El tema de la literatura en *Niebla*: Augusto Pérez ¿pseudo-agonista?" Gómez Molleda 561-67.

Quevedo, Francisco de. *La vida del Buscón llamado Don Pablos*. Ed. Francisco Lázaro Carreter. Prólogo y notas de Juan Alcina Franch. Barcelona: Juventud, 1968.

———. Ed. Domingo Ynduráin. Madrid: Cátedra, 1998.

Quinones, Ricardo J. *Mapping Literary Modernism: Time and Development*. Princeton: Princeton UP, 1985.

Reed, Walter L. *An Exemplary History of the Novel: The Quixotic versus the Picaresque*. Chicago and London: U of Chicago P, 1981.

Rey Poveda, Juan J. del. "Galdós, Clarín y *El amigo Manso*." *Espéculo: Revista de Estudios Literarios* 19 (November 2001–February 2002): 1-8.

Ribas, Pedro. *Para leer a Unamuno*. Madrid: Alianza, 2002.

Ribbans, Geoffrey. *History and Fiction in Galdós's Narratives*. Oxford: Clarendon P, 1993.

———. *Niebla y soledad: Aspectos de Unamuno y Machado*. Madrid: Gredos, 1971.

———. "The Structure of Unamuno's *Niebla*." Bleiberg and Fox 395-406.

Richards, Katharine C. "Unamuno y la paternidad espiritual." *Hispanófila* 83 (1985): 53-60.

Rico, Francisco. *Problemas del* Lazarillo. Madrid: Cátedra, 1988.

Ridley, Alison J. "Mateo Alemán's Literary Exorcism: Ousting the Apocryphal Imposters from Part Two of *Guzmán de Alfarache*." *Hispanic Journal* 16.2 (1995): 377-86.

Riley, E. C. *Cervantes's Theory of the Novel*. Oxford: Clarendon P, 1962.

Rimmon-Kenan, Shlomith. *Narrative Fiction: Contemporary Poetics*. London and New York: Methuen, 1983.

Rivers, Elias L. *Quixotic Scriptures: Essays on the Textuality of Hispanic Literature*. Bloomington: Indiana UP, 1983.

Rivers, Elias L., ed. *Renaissance and Baroque Poetry of Spain*. Prospect Heights, IL:

Waveland P, 1988.

Roberts, Stephen G. H. "Oyéndose casualmente a sí mismo: de Hamlet a Augusto Pérez." Chaguaceda Toledano 95-112.

Rodgers, Eamonn. "Galdós ¿escritor disolvente?: Aspectos de su pensamiento político." *A Sesquicentennial Tribute to Galdós 1843-1993.* Ed. Linda M. Willem. Newark, DE: Juan de la Cuesta, 1993. 269-82.

——. "Realismo y mito en *El amigo Manso.*" *Cuadernos Hispanoamericanos* 250-52 (1958): 430-44.

Rojas, Fernando de. *La Celestina.* Ed. Dorothy S. Severin. Madrid: Cátedra, 1987.

Round, Nicholas G. "'Without a City Wall': *Paz en la Guerra* and the End of Realism." *Rereading Unamuno.* Ed. Nicholas G. Round. Glasgow: U of Glasgow, Department of Hispanic Studies, 1989. 101-20.

Rubia Barcia, José. "Unamuno the Man." *Unamuno: Creator and Creation.* Ed. José Rubia Barcia and M. A. Zeitlin. Berkeley and Los Angeles: U of California P, 1967. 4-25.

Rubia Barcia, José, and M. A. Zeitlin, eds. *Unamuno: Creator and Creation.* Berkeley and Los Angeles: U of California P, 1967.

Rugg, Marilyn D. "Self and Text in Unamuno's *Amor y pedagogía.*" *Anales de la Literatura Española Contemporánea / Annals of Contemporary Spanish Literature* 17.3 (1992): 347-64.

Russell, P. E. "*Don Quixote* as a Funny Book." *Modern Language Review* 64 (1969): 312-26.

Russell, Robert H. "*El amigo Manso*: Galdós with a Mirror." *MLN* 78 (1963): 161-68.

Rutherford, John. "Story, Character, Setting, and Narrative Mode in Galdós's *El amigo Manso.*" *Style and Structure in Literature: Essays in the New Stylistics.* Ed. Roger Fowler. Ithaca: Cornell UP, 1975. 177-212.

Salas Barbadillo, Jerónimo de. *La hija de Celestina. El sagaz Estacio, marido examinado.* Madrid: Aguilar, 1980.

Salinas, Pedro. *Reality and the Poet in Spanish Poetry.* Trans. Edith Fishtine Helman. Baltimore: Johns Hopkins P, 1966.

——. *Seguro azar.* Madrid: Revista de Occidente, 1929.

Sepúlveda, Emma. "Reducción y expansión: Las novelas intercaladas en *Niebla.*" *Crítica Hispánica* 7.2 (1985): 133-40.

Shanley, John Patrick. *Doubt: A Parable.* New York: Theatre Communications Group, 2005.

Shen, Dan. "Defense and Challenge: Reflections on the Relation between Story and Discourse." *Narrative* 10.3 (2002): 222-43.

——. "Narrative, Reality, and Narrator as Construct: Reflections on Genette's 'Narrating.'" Kafalenos 123-29.

Shipley, George A. "The Critic as Witness for the Prosecution: Making the Case against Lázaro de Tormes." *PMLA* 97 (1982): 179-94.

Shklovsky, Victor. "Art as Technique." *Russian Formalist Criticism: Four Essays.* Trans. and intro. Lee T. Lemon and Marion J. Reis. Lincoln and London: U of Nebraska P, 1965. 3-24.

Shoemaker, William H. *The Novelistic Art of Galdós.* 2 vols. Valencia: Albatros/Hispanófila, 1980.

Sieber, Harry. *Language and Society in* La vida de Lazarillo de Tormes. Baltimore and London: Johns Hopkins UP, 1978.

Sinclair, Alison. "Definition as the Enemy of Self-Definition: A Commentary on the Role of Language in Unamuno's *Niebla." Words of Power: Essays in Honour of Alison Fairlie.* Ed. Dorothy Gabe Coleman and Gillian Jondorf. Glasgow: U of Glasgow, 1987. 187-225.

———. *Uncovering the Mind: Unamuno, the Unknown and the Vicissitudes of Self.* Manchester and New York: Manchester UP, 2001.

Sinnigen, John H. *Sexo y política: Lecturas galdosianas.* Madrid: Ediciones de la Torre, 1996.

Spires, Robert C. *Beyond the Metafictional Mode: Directions in the Modern Spanish Novel.* UP of Kentucky, 1984.

Stern, Alfred. "Unamuno: Pioneer of Existentialism." Rubia Barcia and Zeitlin 26-47.

Sternberg, Meir. "How Narrativity Makes a Difference." Kafalenos 115-22.

Surette, Leon. *The Birth of Modernism: Ezra Pound, T. S. Eliot, W. B. Yeats, and the Occult.* Montreal and Kingston: McGill-Queen's UP, 1993.

Tarr, Courtney F. "Literary and Artistic Unity in the *Lazarillo de Tormes." PMLA* 42.2 (1927): 404-21.

Tasende, Mercedes. "*Amor y pedagogía* como poética unamuniana de la modernidad." *Letras Peninsulares* 9.1 (1996): 67-84.

ter Horst, Robert. *The Fortunes of the Novel: A Study in the Transposition of a Genre.* New York: Peter Lang, 2003.

Thompson, Currie K. "Galdós's *El amigo Manso* and the Engendering of Knowledge." *Revista de Estudios Hispánicos* 28.1 (1994): 43-64.

Trotter, David. "The Modernist Novel." Levenson ed. 70-99.

Tsuchiya, Akiko. *Images of the Sign: Semiotic Consciousness in the Novels of Benito Pérez Galdós.* Columbia and London: U of Missouri P, 1990.

Turner, David G. *Unamuno's Webs of Fatality.* London: Tamesis, 1974.

Turner, Harriet S. "The Control of Confusion and Clarity in *El amigo Manso." Anales Galdosianos* 15 (1980): 45-61.

Ugarte, Francisco. "Unamuno y el Quijotismo." *Modern Language Journal* 35.1 (1951): 18-23.

Unamuno, Miguel de. "A lo que salga." *Obras completas,* I. Madrid: Escelicer, 1966. 1194-204.

———. *Amor y pedagogía*. Ed. Ana Caballé. Madrid: Espasa-Calpe, 1992.

———. *Amor y pedagogía (Love and Pedagogy)*. Trans. Michael Vande Berg. New York: Peter Lang, 1996.

———. *Del sentimiento trágico de la vida*. Madrid: Espasa-Calpe, 1976.

———. *En torno al casticismo*. Madrid: Espasa-Calpe, 1961.

———. *Niebla*. Ed. Mario J. Valdés. Madrid: Cátedra, 2000.

———. *San Manuel Bueno, mártir y tres historias más*. Madrid: Espasa-Calpe, 1969.

———. *Tres novelas ejemplares y un prólogo*. Ed. Ciriaco Morón Arroyo. Madrid: Espasa-Calpe, 1999.

———. *Vida de don Quijote y Sancho*. Ed. Alberto Navarro. Madrid: Cátedra, 2000.

Updike, John. "Incommensurability: A New Biography of Kierkegaard." *The New Yorker*, March 28, 2005: 71-76.

Urey, Diane. Galdós and the Irony of Language. Cambridge: Cambridge UP, 1982.

Vande Berg, Michael. "Unamuno's *Amor y pedagogía*: An Early Application of James's 'Stream of Consciousness.'" *Hispania* 70.4 (1987): 752-58.

Vauthier, Bénédicte. "Ejercicio(s) de estilo(s) en *Amor y pedagogía* de Miguel de Unamuno: el *Ars magna combinatoria* del gran mixtificador unamuniano." Chaguaceda Toledano 113-22.

Vega, Lope de. *El arte nuevo de hacer comedias en este tiempo*. Ed. Juana de José Prades. Madrid: Consejo Superior de Investigaciones Científicas, 1971.

Vento, Arnold C. "*Niebla*: Laberinto intencionado a través de la estructura." *Cuadernos Hispanoamericanos* 203 (1966): 427-34.

Vilanova, Antonio. "La teoría nivolesca del *bufo trágico*." Gómez Molleda 189-216.

Villanueva, Darío. *Theories of Literary Realism*. Trans. Mihai I. Spariosu and Santiago García-Castañón. Albany: SUNY P, 1997.

Villegas, Juan. "*Niebla*: Una ruta para autentificar la existencia." Bleiberg and Fox 573-84.

Waugh, Patricia. *Metafiction: The Theory and Practice of Self-Conscious Fiction*. New York and London: Routledge, 1984.

Webber, Ruth House. "Kierkegaard and the Elaboration of Unamuno's *Niebla*." *Hispanic Review* 32 (1964): 118-34.

Weber, Frances W. "Unamuno's *Niebla*: From Novel to Dream." *PMLA* 88.2 (1973): 209-18.

Weinstein, Arnold. *Fictions of the Self: 1550-1800*. Princeton: Princeton UP, 1981.

White, Hayden. "The Historical Text as Literary Artifact." *Tropics of Discourse*. Baltimore: Johns Hopkins UP, 1978. 81-100.

Willem, Linda M. *Galdós's Segunda Manera: Rhetorical Strategies and Affective Response*. Chapel Hill: North Carolina Studies in the Romance Languages and Literatures, 1998.

Williams, Jeffrey J. *Theory and the Novel: Narrative Reflexivity in the British Tradition*.

Cambridge: Cambridge UP, 1998.

Williamson, Edwin. "The Conflict between Author and Protagonist in Quevedo's *Buscón.*" *Journal of Hispanic Philology* 2 (1977): 45-60.

Willis, Raymond S. "Lazarillo and the Pardoner: The Artistic Necessity of the Fifth *Tractado.*" *Hispanic Review* 27 (1959): 267-79.

Yacobi, Tamar. "Fictional Reliability as a Communicative Problem." *Poetics Today* 2.2 (1981): 113-26.

———. "Narrative Structure and Fictional Mediation." *Poetics Today* 8.2 (1987): 335-72.

———. "Package-Deals in Fictional Narrative: The Case of the Narrator's (Un)Reliability." Kafalenos 223-29.

Zavala, Iris M. "*Niebla*: la lógica del sueño." *La Torre.* Nueva época. 1.1 (1987): 69-92.

———. "Unamuno: *Niebla*, el sueño y la crisis del sujeto." *Estelas, laberintos, nuevas sendas.* Coord. Ángel G. Loureiro. Barcelona: Antropos, 1988. 35-50.

Zubizarreta, Armando F. *Unamuno en su nivola.* Madrid: Taurus, 1960.

Index

Printed in the United States
53161LVS00005B/103-150

9 781588 710918